SMOKE OVER THE PRAIRIE

It is ground into dust now like Mobeetie and
Tascosa, swallowed up by the grass and desert
along with split ox-shoes, shaggy buffalo trails,
and the crude cap-and-ball rifle. And how can I
say it so that you who were not there may see it
as I did, rolling, surging, fermenting under the
brazen territorial sun, that vanished rude empire
of which my father was a baron, a land as feudal
as old England, larger than the British Isles, with
lords and freemen, savages and peons, most of
them on horseback, all here in America a little
more than half a century ago, and yet in another
world and another age that was just then—although
we didn't know it—drawing to a violent close?

from "Smoke Over the Prairie" by Conrad Richter

SOUTHWEST FICTION

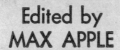

Edited by
MAX APPLE

SOUTHWEST FICTION

A Bantam Book / January 1981

COPYRIGHT NOTICES AND ACKNOWLEDGMENTS
The copyright notices listed below and on page v
constitute an extension of this copyright page.

The editor would like to thank Lee Goerner and Barbara Rader for their suggestions and assistance.

Contents

Introduction

The Southwest is a territory of great open spaces. A hundred years ago a rider on horseback could travel its vast distances in almost total loneliness. Today, in an automobile a driver can still experience the loneliness of Route 66 after leaving Oklahoma City. If anything takes him from the expressway to any of the local highways, say around Abilene or San Angelo, Texas, he can still know the strange openness of this landscape, a sense of the desolate that is apparent to all who have come to conquer and then to inhabit these territories.

There are great cities in the modern Southwest, Houston, Dallas, Albuquerque, Phoenix, Tulsa. . . . But these cities seem accidental, mere diversions from the hostile and seductive emptiness that surrounds them. Much of the area is still underpopulated, still dominated by sun and wind, still hostile to the necessities of civility. While the writers of more settled areas explore the nuances of manners, in the Southwest it sometimes seems that geography is destiny.

The reality of the plains and the desert reminds us that the central episode in American history, the settling of the frontier, is still happening in the Southwest of the 1980s. The frontier, officially closed since about 1890, is nevertheless a constant presence. Almost one hundred years after the settling of the frontier, Texas and Arizona are growing as never before. The population shift from the Northeast to the Southwest is a well-defined pattern. It is not a dramatic flight—the new Southwesterners are not the starving "Okies" of the 1930s but, like their predecessors in American history, they seek the open territories because the frontier is not a line of demarcation but a condition of hopefulness. A hundred years ago the cattle drive and then the railroad brought new life and activity to the Southwest; today it may be oil or real estate, but these are merely the modern versions of what the West has always offered, cheaper land and a chance for new work.

The open space, the great distances between places, the hostility of nature, and the native Indian and Spanish populations—these are the primary characteristics of the Southwest. Yet the cowboy is so dominant in the popular imagination that he has overshadowed every other aspect of the area. The cowboy on his horse somewhere in Texas, a herd of longhorns in the deep background, a criminal gang rampaging in town, a lonely schoolmarm staying at the boardinghouse, these are the types we associate with the Southwest. Other regions in America seem far less burdened with their historical images, but in the Southwest, where settling the frontier is the vocation, playing cowboy continues to be the number one hobby.

Of course, the cowboy whom we know best is the movie Westerner, the ultimate American as he is incarnated by Tom Mix or Randolph Scott or John Wayne. But in his purest form he is the nameless masked man disappearing on the horizon. He is the "lone" ranger because there is all that space for him to be alone in. In San Francisco or Manhattan he would be a comic character, but a mile out of Lubbock, San Antonio, or Tucson he and Tonto could ride for days, making camp in the comfort of waste places, smelling out evil, and taking good care of their horses.

The cowboy of the past is still in the saddle in a particular kind of fiction. The cowboy story is a historical set piece recreating or even creating the conditions of about 1870 on the frontier. In Louis L'Amour's work the old West lives on. The men are strong and violent, and vengeance is a dominant theme. Cavagan in "The Strong Shall Live" struggles through the desert with superhuman strength so that he might live to take vengeance on the man who threw him into a pit in the wilderness. In such an extreme setting behavior is merely survival; man is not distinguished from animals by his intelligence. In fact, the intelligent man is he who understands most about the animals. Cavagan notices a red spotted toad.

* * *

Long ago he had learned that the red spotted toad always lived within the vicinity of water and never got far from it.

This habit of observing nature saves Cavagan's life. It is the only kind of wisdom that is useful. Human life in these tales of the old West is indeed "nasty, brutish and short," and yet these frontier myths have a kind of dignity beyond their stereotyped characters and simple narrative style. The cowboy is our splendid barbarian. He appears as the historical embodiment of all those forces that crushed the Indian and Mexican civilizations. Whether as sheriff or outlaw, he performs the same cultural function; he brings in his wake the modern bourgeois world. Yet the cowboy will never live comfortably in that safe world of which he is the harbinger. He moves on to the next encounter with nature or justice. Business and civilization come after him—the wagon train, the shop, and the schoolmarm—but he stays on the periphery of society. By definition an outsider, he is like the bully of childhood, that monster who will grow up to be perfectly, almost disappointingly, ordinary.

The professional Western writers have maintained almost intact the tales of the old West, but the serious realistic writers of the modern Southwest have set themselves in opposition to this two-dimensional embodiment of the past. As early as 1925 *The Wind* punctured the romance of the open range by showing us that a decent, civilized woman could not survive there.

Larry McMurtry's modern cowboy is deliberately pedestrian, merely another sort of blue-collar worker. He drives a pickup, plays football, engages in the complicated rites of small-town life. He is far from the necessity of survival in the desert, farther still from the sweat and grandeur of the long cattle drive. Yet in the chapter from *Terms of Endearment* we see a kind of vulgar grandiosity in McMurtry's contemporary Texan.

Royce Dunlap spends his days "lying in bed with a cold can of beer balanced on his stomach." When he decides to defend his "honor" as a husband, he drives his pickup through the wall of the J-Bar Korral during the Friday night "East-Tex Hoedown." The J-Bar Korral is filled with customers divided into three groups:

> . . . those who came to drink, those who came to dance, and those who hoped to accomplish a little of both. Brylcreem and Vitalis gleamed on the heads of those

men who bothered to take their Stetsons off, and the women's hair was mostly upward coiffed, as if God had dressed it himself by standing over them with a comb in one omnipotent hand and a powerful vacuum cleaner in the other.

Royce tears up the honky tonk almost as fully as the trail riders of legend "freed" Dodge City, but his action is full of comic pathos. The J-Bar Korral is not Dodge City; the East-Tex Hoedown is not the open range. Royce is merely a bully, a comic creation driving through the walls of a world too much for him to imagine. The cowboy is left with a few primitive gestures. He fights, he drinks, he leaves town. Sparseness of language is his trademark.

The narrator of Carolyn Osborne's "My Brother is a Cowboy" says to her brother,

"You're the last of a vanishing breed, the tail end of the roundup of the longhorn steers, the last great auk alive, a prairie rooster without a hen!"

"Sister, there ain't no substitute for beef on the hoof."

The sister in this story is thwarted from pursuing a career as a nightclub singer by her family's conservative values. She is frustrated by the laconic, indifferent life of the contemporary cowboy as it is lived by her brother and his friends. She understands that his life is not authentic, merely a posture, but when she confronts him with his own obsolescence, "he gets out real quick" before she can "go on about helicopters substituting for horses and feed lots replacing the open range."

The cowboy, shrouded by the romanticism of his image, can turn his back on the question of his own authenticity; the Indian, his partner in the drama of the Southwest, cannot pretend that everything is still as it was. The helicopters and feed lots have not put the cowboy out of business; his pickup is more useful than a horse ever was. But the Indian had an investment in the open range that was far more profound. The Indian spent centuries in the life that the cowboy practiced for a few generations.

The Indian is essentially out of business. He is the tragic loser in American history, and more devasting than the loss of his land has been the loss of his "Indianness." The sense of this loss is evident in each of the selections that is either written by an Indian or concerned with Indian life.

In *The Bronc People*, William Eastlake's two Indians, "My Prayer" and "President Taft," watch a gunfight between a white man and a black man. The gunfight is over water rights. It takes place in about 1950. While the Indians watch the battle they are as detached as television news reporters.

"Do you think it's right of us to do this?" the taller Indian said.

"Why not?"

"Watching?"

"Why not?"

"It's none of our business."

"Why not?"

"You're doing awfully well with the why not's."

"I don't think it will matter at all. I know it will not matter at all. It will come out the way it's going to come out whether we watch or not. It would not have made any difference whether anyone was watching when the whites drove us out."

"We're still here."

"I don't think we are. We're not Indians any longer."

In Eastlake's clever rhetoric you can almost pass over the pathos of not being "Indians" any longer; you cannot pass over it in Leslie Silko's "Lullaby." In this story the Indian woman, Ayah, is the only one in her family who remains an Indian. Her son Jimmie is killed in the war; her other children are taken from her when they contact tuberculosis, and they return only as uncomfortable visitors. Her husband is transformed from the independence of Indian life to the petty servitude of day labor. Even the English language betrays her. But Ayah remains an Indian. She covers her old, sick husband with a blanket and sings to him the song her grandmother sang.

> We are together always
> We are together always
> There never was a time
> when this
> was not so.

There are no villains in this story. Ayah's Indian world has vanished as if its disappearance were part of nature's plan. The lament in her grandmother's song "we are together always" suggests the powerful sense of tribal love and responsibility that permeates the Indian culture. It is evident too in Scott Momaday's Kiowa myth. In it, a lovely young woman mates with the sun, but even such splendor does not distract her from her people.

> The woman grew lonely. She thought about her people, and she wondered how they were getting on. One day she had a quarrel with the sun and the sun went away.

These Indian stories present with quiet clarity the sense of loss that is as understated as the cowboy is overstated. The cowboy and the Indian of popular culture: these two form the dialectic of the Southwest. Neither really exists any longer. The cowboy has left behind an inflated legend, the Indian a muted tragedy. Whenever that tragedy alights in literature, its touch is wondrous. It infuses John Graves's "The Last Running." In this story Starlight, an old Comanche, comes to Texan Tom Bird's ranch to kill a buffalo. Starlight is a survivor, an old raider and warrior who remembers the days of the Civil War, a time when it had been good to be a Comanche.

> In those days, Starlight said, Comanches held Texans to be another breed of white men, and even after they were told that peace had smiled again among whites, they did not consider this to apply to that race which had swarmed over the best of their grass and timber.

Starlight is no sweet old man. He has been a raider and a killer and he has experienced the white man's revenge. Yet as he and Tom Bird face each other, using words and patience as their only weapons, the Indian and the white man are infused with the wonder of the hunt, the pride of this singular act, the ritual they are reenacting. The buffalo reminds the old men of their youth. The white man says to his nephew:

* * *

"Damn you, boy, damn you for not ever getting to know anything worth knowing. Damn me, too. We had a world once."

The nostalgia for the world Tom Bird and Starlight once had is a lament for the old ways, a lament that characterizes any changing society. The Southwest may now be changing more rapidly and more profoundly than other areas of the country, but for the past two generations it has been a part of the country alien to its young. The small towns, the farms, and the ranches may be good breeding grounds for ambition, but fruition has usually taken place elsewhere. In Allen Wier's "Things About to Disappear" the narrator, as he leaves, recites to himself the melodious names of the Texas hill country places he is leaving, "names like Dripping Springs, Round Mountain, Marble Falls, Spicewood, Calf Creek, Air. . . . San Saba, Cherry Spring, Mountain Home, Morris Ranch, Stonewall, Blanco."

The narrator, driving away after his father's death, carries in his wallet a word his father has recalled from his own childhood, *crickadee*. The son writes the word on a scrap of paper and puts it in his wallet. There, in the darkness of money and the smell of leather, that word powers the story, feeds the nostalgia. Words are what we pass on. Crickadee, a personal link of love between the young man and his father, becomes an emblem of all those places the young man is leaving.

I drove on across the lovely little Angelina River, through New Summerfield, away from the people who had given me my past and into whatever life I could find in the dark distances ahead, listening for Crickadees and loving so many things that were about to disappear.

This elegiac strain is common to much of the fiction of our area. The homogenizing culture is transforming the Southwest, is modifying the country just as the railroad did. This may be the last generation of the cowboy's modern offspring, the "redneck." Just as he fades into obscurity, a century after his ancestor, he, too, is beginning to be romanticized; his music, his language, even his surly image are coming to seem genuine and charming.

The language of the Southwest tends to be flat but full of folksy surprises. It comes closest to musical splendor in the East Texas prose of William Goyen. In "Ghost and Flesh,

Water and Dirt," the widow of "Pore Raymon Emmons" tells her tale of a bleak and sorrowful life. The story is grim but the language sings.

> I wish I'd melt—and run down the drains. Wish I uz rain fallin on the dirt of certain graves I know and seepin down into the dirt . . . wish I uz dirt.

The story is told in repetitious rhythms and cadences that are peculiar to the area. There is a touch of the Southern in this rhythm but the Southwest is, on the whole, remarkably separate from the literary territory of the South. The South has the Civil War and slavery as its unique heritage; the Southwestern motif is distinctly Spanish. The Indian occupies the tragic center of Southwestern history and fiction, but it is the Spanish culture that marks the area with its particular regionalism. Spanish words are a part of Southwestern language; Mexican food is almost as pervasive as pizza and hamburgers. "Remember the Alamo" is still the ringing phrase of the Southwest, and school children in Texas celebrate the victory over Mexico on San Jacinto Day, but the Mexican culture has not been destroyed. The Indian was obliterated; the Chicano merely went underground.

The two Chicano selections, Durango Mendoza's "The Woman in the Green House" and the excerpts from Rudolfo Anaya's *Bless Me, Ultima,* concentrate on the effect of barrio life on children. In Anaya's chapter, there is a rich interplay between the boy pretending he is taking confession from his playmates and the awesome seriousness of genuine confession.

In Durango Mendoza's story, the three children of the woman in the green house suffer the fate of the fatherless and the ignored. Their mother has gone to the hospital to give birth once more. Their stepfather denies them.

> "Those ain't my kids," he told her and went on into the other room. . . .
> The little boy began to whimper.

Mendoza's story ends in a state of despair. There is none of the naiveté of Ralph Ellison's *Invisible Man,* who thinks the white businessmen are listening to him as he recites his graduation speech after a bloody "battle royal." It is as if the Chicanos have taken the advice of Invisible Man's grandfather, "overcome em with yeses, undermine em with grins, agree em to death and destruction."

The realities of the land and its inhabitants obviously color the fiction of any area, but there is also a literary style that thrives on exaggeration. The exaggerations of the Texan comprise a distinct body of folk material, but nowhere has exaggeration been more artfully cultivated than in contemporary fiction.

In Donald Barthelme's "I Bought a Little City" the narrator casually buys Galveston, Texas. The act pleases him enough to inspire verse.

> Got a little city
> Ain't it pretty

He redesigns his city, shoots 6,000 dogs and falls in love with Sam Hong's wife.

> So I ate the Col. Sanders Kentucky Fried Chicken, extra crispy, and sold Galveston, Texas, back to the interests. I took a bath on that deal there's no denying it, but I learned something—don't play God.

Barthelme's narrator keeps his exaggeration a solid deadpan. From Galveston he migrates only to a Houston suburb.

> What happened was that I took the other half of my fortune and went to Galena Park, Texas, and lived inconspicuously there, and when they asked me to run for the school board I said, "No, I don't have any children."

But in Charles Portis' *The Dog of the South*, "Speed" has lost much more than a little city. His wife has run off and actually taken his Ford Torino. Speed is left with only a Buick Special, leaking oil, in which to pursue the illicit couple to Honduras. Along his comic route in search of his car he learns that "John Selmer Dix, M.A." is the world's greatest writer.

> "They say Shakespeare was the greatest writer who ever lived."
> "Dix puts William Shakespeare in the shithouse."
> "I've never heard of him; where is he from?"
> "He was from all over; he's dead now. He's buried in

Ardmore, Oklahoma. He got his mail in Ft. Worth, Texas. . . . He did his clearest thinking while moving. He did all his best work on a bus."

In *The Dog of the South* it is a comic chase that propels Speed through the Southwest and Mexico. Whether the chase involves a car, a horse, a wife, or a fortune, the quest itself often substitutes in Southwestern literature for the close observation of manners that is characteristic of a more settled society. The chase through the open territories is a solid ingredient of the cowboy stories because the uninhabited land is a good place to run to, a haven for the criminal. In "Billie Loses Her Job" Robert Henson uses the deadpan, exaggerated narrative style to tell the story of John Dillinger's true love. In her own voice Billie recounts what it was like to be the Indian girl whom John Dillinger wanted to marry.

. . . outside it was still hard times for women, Indians, and ex-cons. How'd you like to be all three?

Billie joins Dillinger's father as a sideshow attraction. "We were getting near the Oklahoma line . . . heading into real Dillinger country." As the survivors of John Dillinger try to make some money out of his fame, they connect him to the romantic past of the cowboy. Young Dillinger "liked to read wild West stories, especially about Jesse James. He admired Jesse for fighting railroads and the money boys back East. Jesse was the one that inspired Johnny to respect women."

Jerome Charyn's "El Coco" is even more exaggerated than John Dillinger. The innocent narrator of *The Catfish Man* stumbles into the world of "El Coco."

The cape dropped under his nose. He eyes fell on me. He was a killer, all right. . . .
El Coco held the pockets of my shirt and shook them hard. "Pig, why did you come here?"
"Green sauce," I said. "Enchiladas. . . . We wanted Mexican food."

Jerome has discovered a violent heart in Little John Woods. He is the outsider looking for enchiladas and green sauce; a generation ago it was the outsider looking for land; before that, oil and cotton and cattle. But more fundamental than the search for material wealth has been the constant difficulty of seeking the ways to recognize love and honor in a society that has not been organized long enough to give many clues.

Newness stands out in the Southwest. The cities are barely unwrapped from their expressways, and some inhabitants have not even learned to eat Mexican and wear cowboy boots. But they will. The superficial will point to the central, the Spanish heart and the frontier soul of the area. In such ways do manners aspire to the universal.

Fiction, by its very nature, is universal. Neither culture nor language is an ultimate barrier, and time, which mocks so much human effort, barely scars the story. The imagination is securely settled in the timeless, but the body lives in times and places. When those times and places are fictionally created, they are never obscure; they are rooted in truths beyond history, yet they occasionally illumine the historical. A good example is William Brammer's Austin, Texas, in *The Gay Place*—obscure in the 1950s, not so obscure when Lyndon Johnson was in the White House.

Fictional "truths" are always obscure, insignificant, personal, local; they are "truths" made of words and memories. Invisible Man's graduation speech, Allen Wier's crickadee: these make up the substance of literature.

The whole is always too much to see. C. W. Smith's young musician agog with the mystique of jazz does not notice that his magical blacks are, by day, the dishwashers and shineboys of his town. The story tells us what he does not see. There are no boundaries to regionalism; when you see the Southwest you are seeing everything. The local language and customs, the small matters that separate us, these things, properly noticed, become the bond that unites us.

MAX APPLE

SOUTHWEST FICTION

EDWARD ABBEY

The Brave Cowboy

Jackson!
    Yay!
    Has you seen my ole gray mule?
    That I has not.
    Has somebody here seen my gray mule? Six feet high and
bucks like a fool; likes gingerbread cookies and pampas grass,
has a notch in his ear and a star up his ass. Now if you done
seen my ole gray mule, I'm tellin you straght don't be a
damn fool; but show me where he is and sure as I'm alive,
you'll get a pot of honey from the ole beehive.
    Greene, ain't you never gonna pipe down?
    Never!
    You better.
    Never!
    Timothy, you got the makins?
    I got a half sack Bull Durham and not a single goddamn
paper.
    I got paper.
    It's a deal, son. Save that light, Hoskins, we got two hot
babies comin up. Steady boy and watch her roll, save that tobacco while I get the coal.
    Thanks, Timothy.
    How long you in for, boy?
    Thirty days flat.
    Vaggin, pimpin, or hustlin?

1

Went through a red light with my eyes shut. Judge called it reckless driving.

Mighty reckless drivin. Now tell me the truth, boy.

I lifted a knife at Monkey Ward's.

Ah hah. You tried to. Good knife?

Seven ninety-five plus tax.

Good, good, son. You shrewd like a chicken.

Butt, Timothy?

Butt me no butts. Already spoken for. Hoskins gets it. Rev'rend Hoskins on his Flyin Machine, waitin for Peter to open the door, got hog drunk and hit the floor.

Lay off it, Greene.

Never!

I'm tellin you.

Never!

Paul Bondi smiled as he listened, his hands clasped under his head, his body stretched out at full length on his steel bunk. A gray Navy blanket, a pad and a steel bunk for tonight. He lay watching the stripes of sunlight on the steel ceiling, listening to the others but thinking his own thoughts:

These fellows have something, he thought, have something which I lack. The vital impulse, along with their lice and bad-smelling itches and wino-red eyeballs. They—

Someone flushed a toilet; the powerful gasping explosion of water sent a wave of reverberations through the steel walls over the cement floor; the entire plumbing system strained and vibrated with the detonating ferocity of a heavy machine gun. Bondi could feel as well as hear the clangor and clamor of outraged steel; the vibrations passed in sine curves through his skull, vertebrae and the bones of his legs.

That plumbing, he thought—like a siege, jazzy and vigorous. Suction strong enough to drown a man. Why? Must be a reason. A reason for everything in the county jail. County jail is a thoroughly rational institution, is it not? What could ever take its place?

Crazy, man!

Crazy is right. See that ole cat there, steppin on his tongue, belly bulgin with beans—?

Fuller'n a tick—

That's right, fuller'n a tick. Ole Hoskins, thass who; ole black-balled sonsabitch. Hoskins!

Ho?

Les hear tell about the man what ate electric eels to give the girls a charge.

Go long, man. You divin for Hell, talk like dat.

Rev'rend Hoskins is now gonna say a prayer for us all, poor sorry sinners like we is.

My butt, Timothy?

Take it and keep it, friend, or pass it on, as you please.

Thanks, Timothy. You can have my oatmeal in the morning.

Keep it, friend, I beg you.

Character or depravity, what does it matter? Under the aspect of eternity, so to speak? Now you're talking like an old balding philosopher, tovarish. Watch that stuff. Keep it screened out. Serenity is for the gods—not becoming in a mortal. Better to be partisan and passionate on this earth; be plenty objective enough when dead.

Again the explosion of a flushing toilet and the barrage of anguish from the pipes; through bone and marrow the vibrations jittered, grinding down delicacy, grace, tact, the arts of sense and human concord. Forty men locked, barred and sealed in a cage of steel and cement. Forty bellies semibloated with gas, intestines packed with the residue of half-digested pinto beans. Long conversations lost in the shuddering roar and rattle of plumbing.

Sic transit gloria mundi, he thought.

Think we'll get a break tomorrow?

Quién sabe, cuate?

Well we should. They got men sleepin on the floor downstairs. Hate to think what she'll be like come Saturday night.

Who said Saturday night is the lonesomest night?

They got worse jails. Ever been in the one at Juarez?

Ho, Jackson! Gimme light, man, light.

Oh I'm walkin to the river, gonna jump in, I can't float and I can't swim, but I'm an easy man . . . to drown. Cause my baby done leave me, yes my baby done leave me down. So I'm walkin to the river, gonna jump in and drown. And drown. And drown.

Flush that noise! Pass it on to Texas!

Go fly a kite on the moon, you slew-balled old fart.

Chinga madre! Eh, cabrón!

You shut up, Greene.

Never!

I said shut up.

Never!

Who got a match?

I ain't got a match. Ain't nobody got a match. What you want a match for, man?

Gimme a match before I spit in your eye.

Sure, sure. Don't get mad.

Don't get mad, he says. Don't get mad, the man says.

When they gonna let me outa here? Why don't the Judge gimme a break? I ain't no bad boy; just a happy little wino.

You'll get a break all right—right over that thick dumb empty halfbreed skull of yours.

Ah, chinga tu . . .

Greene?

Never!

Where's that little book I give you?

Ain't here, man. All gone, man. I give it to that smooth cat in Cell Number Three. Now that's for a fact, man.

Well I want it back.

Kiss it goodby, friend. Give it a wave, *cuate*. Don't cry.

Goddamnit, Greene.

Never!

Greene—

Never!

Now defiance is all very well (said Bondi to himself: the last thread of sunlight had vanished from the steel ceiling) and very sweet, an ideal tonic for the delectation of the soul. Pure naked sheer defiance—defiance for the sake of defiance—sweet and precious as liberty itself. The act of liberty. Timothy Greene and his perpetual thundering Never. But is there a blind edge to it? Should be tempered, no doubt, with good manners. Also, it might be enslaving. Always defiant, a man would be mad, would have destroyed his power of choice. And the power of choice—that is what I am here for.

What are you in here for, Rev'rend, anyway?

Me, son? My body's here but the spirit's free as a bluebird.

Okay, then why is your body here?

Well now, the Judge he calls it assault. I done hit a man and he falls down. Didn't hit him hard but he falls down like a log. Maybe he wasn't standin very good.

Why'd you hit him, Rev'rend?

Well now, you see it was like this: this here fella and me was workin together in this barbershop. He was barber, I was

porter and shoeshinin man. One day we have a argument
about who left the soap where. A argument.

Hoskins, you ain't got sense enough to pour piss out of a
boot.

What happened then, Rev'rend?

Well now, we's havin this here argument about who left
the soap where when the boss walks in. The boss. Manager.

What soap, Rev'rend?

This soap what we use for washin up our hands and so on.
In the crapper. Both of us usin the same piece of soap. I dis-
remember what kind of soap it was, exactly. White, that's all,
and not very big. Kinda little.

What happens when the boss walks in, Rev'rend?

Well damned if he doesn't tell me to get my hat and coat
and get out. Just like that. Don't even wanta know what we
arguin about. Well I tell him about the soap and he just gets
mad. Like that. Just gets mad.

. . What'd you do then, Rev'rend?

Nothin. I get my hat and coat only I ain't got no coat and
starts to leave and then ole boss he thinks I ain't leavin fast
enough so he tries to gimme a kick. Don't that beat all? Tries
to kick me cause I ain't movin fast enough to suit him. Man
musta been crazy.

Is that when you got mad, Rev'rend?

Oh I don't get mad. I never get mad. I'll punish a man,
maybe, but I never gets mad. It ain't right for a man to get
mad. A man ain't no dog, even if he smell like one. That's
the way I feels about it. Yessir. Never get mad.

Well, why'd you hit him, Rev'rend?

Oh I didn't hit him. I hit t'other fella.

The other fella? Which fella?

The barber. The fella I hit. No sir, I don't get mad never.
It ain't right. No sir.

Well, which one did you hit, Rev'rend, the barber or the
boss?

Well now, the boss he was a barber too. Yes, he barbered
there just like t'other fella. Only he owned it too. Owned ever
bit of it. Yessir. Only he don't own me. No sir.

You got me kinda mixed up, Rev'rend.

Yessir, thass just the way I felt: kinda mixed up. I weren't
mad, no sir, but I hit him and he falls down. Didn't hit him
hard but he falls down anyway. Like a dead log. Falls right
down.

You kill him, Rev'rend?

No sir, I don't think so. He's all right. Leastways he look all right when he come to court. Not a mark on him, except on his left eye. No sir. He looked fine. I shoulda hit him harder.

Well, Rev'rend, I still can't figure which man you hit.

Well now, I don't remember too good myself but I sure hit one of them. Yessir. Knocked him right down. Right down on the floor. Now I weren't mad but I hit him. Not hard but he falls down. Down like a log. Thass the way it was.

I wish I'd seen that fight, Rev'rend.

Well now, it was really somethin. Sure was.

An aquatic implosion and the rattle of strangled pipes: the steel bars hummed, the steel walls vibrated, the resonance flashed through the recumbent bones of forty living men. Again, from a different cell, another roar of water: again the plumbing shook and groaned and whistled with the intensity and lunacy of impending disaster.

While Bondi wrangled with himself: Oh, that dreary old paradox? The libertine-anarchist choosing himself into prison? That? A little simple conviction would help here. My emotions become ideas, my ideas emotions. But here I lie, a victim of both. Should be home milking the goddamned goat. Minding my own business.

He watched a breath of moisture evaporate from the steel barrier three feet above his face. He sniffed and rubbed his eyes.

Agua!

The word passed with telegraphic speed from one end of the cellblock to the other. *Agua!* Water! Douse your lights, hide your smokes, your weapons, hide your words and thoughts.

Agua, agua, agua!

The five cells occupied about half of the block. They were divided by a narrow corridor from the single rectangular steel cage called the bullpen, where the prisoners spent their daylight hours and ate their meals. The corridor had one entrance, or exit, a steel door heavy and ponderous as the gate of a bank vault, which permitted passage from the cellblock to an adjoining anteroom and the rest of the building. This door was now being opened, screeching on its bearingless hinges, rumbling and grinding and scraping on the cement floor.

The forty men in their five cells became silent, cautious. The door stopped, fully open, and a man came in, stooping under the lintel. A huge man, shambling like a trained bear, and wearing the khaki uniform and leather harness of a Bernal County deputy. His holster was empty; in his left hand he held a billyclub. Slowly he lumbered down the corridor, stopping for a minute or more in front of each cell, carefully inspecting each man within, then moving on.

No one would look at him; all eyes were turned to the floor under the pressure of his red stare. Only when he had passed to the next cell did some of the men dare to glance at one another with shamed and half-frightened faces.

No one spoke a word; no one whispered. The only sound was the shuffling tread of the huge man in the uniform; when he stopped to examine the inmates of a cell the silence became complete.

He came, this bear, this dark enormous man, to the cell in which Bondi lay. He stared balefully at the seven prisoners crouching on their bunks, studying each one in turn, and then raised his eyes to Bondi. And Bondi, who had never seen him before, stared back.

He saw two red eyes, small and intent and without depth, as if made of tin, sunk deep in a welter of corrugations and protected by an overhang of bone and leather and ragged black brows. He saw these two eyes, dangerous and animal and implacable with power and hatred, and could see nothing else. And as he looked and waited he became aware of the challenge passing and growing between them, of the silent instinctive struggle for recognition and submission. Bondi felt the chill of fear on the skin of his neck, at his fingertips, and a deadly dryness in his mouth; he turned his head, looked away and though instantly conscious of shame, even of anger, could not compel himself to return that man's unblinking gaze. Could not, though he hated himself for his cowardice. Instead he lay still and silent on his bunk, watching the black forearm of Timothy Green braced rigidly against the opposite wall. And until the guard moved away, for a full five minutes he lay fixed and tense in the same position looking at the same object, waiting with a burning face and cold queasy stomach for the enemy to release him from the implied violence of that stare.

Gutierrez the guard tramped the length of the corridor, huge and silent and malevolent, crouched to pass through the doorway and was gone. After him the massive door swung slowly shut, dull gray iron grinding in friction, harsh and cold in its finality.

An instant of silence and then the men remembered their humanity, became unrigid and looked at each other and talked, grinned and laughed uneasily, relit cigarettes and talked.

He's after somebody.

Now that ain't no lie. The Bear is a-lookin for somebody. Somebody is in bad trouble.

He's in for it.

That ain't no lie. He's gonna get it. Yessir.

Glad it ain't me. Brother!

You said it, chum. You done said it.

Bondi sat quiet on his bunk, saying nothing aloud, busy at disemboweling his own soul, examining with an attempt at a sterilized logic the soft glistening blue-veined innards of his spirit. While darkness gathered within and around him and the bad air of the cell settled heavily under its own weight of smoke, sweat, human vapors. The sun was gone—its light was gone. Through the filthy frosted glass of the window beyond the grid of bars he could see the muted glow of evening neon, the swing of automobile lights, the yellow rectangles of lighted windows, all the multiple refractions of the great American night.

And then from far below, from somewhere deep in the heart of the labyrinthine jailhouse, came the sound of a man's voice—singing. As if from far away, muffled by barriers of steel and brick and cement, the thin dim sound of a man singing, a wild drunken singing with the quality of an Indian's wail and the wind's intoxication, the music that a wolf might make if it could sing like a man.

I'm dreaming, thought Bondi, sitting up suddenly, hearing that old and remembered song, that familiar voice, I'm dreaming like a kid on the night before Christmas, like an angel the day before Easter. He sat upright on his steel bed, listening tensely, straining his senses to hear and to feel. I'm dreaming, I'm dreaming, I'm dreaming, he thought.

The sound of a man singing.

RUDOLFO ANAYA

Bless Me, Ultima

Dieciocho

Ash Wednesday. There is no other day like Ash Wednesday. The proud and the meek, the arrogant and the humble are all made equal on Ash Wednesday. The healthy and the sick, the assured and the sick in spirit, all make their way to church in the gray morning or in the dusty afternoon. They line up silently, eyes downcast, bony fingers counting the beads of the rosary, lips mumbling prayers. All are repentant; all are preparing themselves for the shock of the laying of the ashes on the forehead and the priest's agonizing words, "Thou art dust, and to dust thou shalt return."

The anointment is done, and the priest moves on; only the dull feeling of helplessness remains. The body is not important. It is made of dust; it is made of ashes. It is food for the worms. The winds and the waters dissolve it and scatter it to the four corners of the earth. In the end, what we care most for lasts only a brief lifetime, then there is eternity. Time forever. Millions of worlds are born, evolve, and pass away into nebulous, unmeasured skies; and there is still eternity. Time always. The body becomes dust and trees and exploding fire, it becomes gaseous and disappears, and still there is eternity. Silent, unopposed, brooding, forever . . .

But the soul survives. The soul lives on forever. It is the soul that must be saved, because the soul endures. And so when the burden of being nothing lifts from one's thoughts

9

the idea of the immortality of the soul is like a light in a blinding storm. Dear God! the spirit cries out, my soul will live forever!

And so we hurried to catechism! The trying forty days of Lent lay ahead of us, then the shining goal, Easter Sunday and first holy communion! Very little else mattered in my life. School work was dull and uninspiring compared to the mysteries of religion. Each new question, each new catechism chapter, each new story seemed to open up a thousand facets concerning the salvation of my soul. I saw very little of Ultima, or even of my mother and father. I was concerned with myself. I knew that eternity lasted forever, and a soul because of one mistake could spend that eternity in hell.

The knowledge of this was frightful. I had many dreams in which I saw myself or different people burning in the fires of hell. One person especially continually haunted my nightmares. It was Florence. Inevitably it was he whom I saw burning in the roaring inferno of eternal damnation.

But why? I questioned the hissing fires, Florence knows all the answers!

But he does not accept, the flames lisped back.

"Florence," I begged him that afternoon, "try to answer."

He smiled. "And lie to myself," he answered.

"Don't lie! Just answer!" I shouted with impatience.

"You mean, when the priest asks where is God, I am to say God is everywhere: He is the worms that await the summer heat to eat Narciso, He shares the bed with Tenorio and his evil daughters—"

"Oh, God!" I cried in despair.

Samuel came up and touched me on the shoulder. "Perhaps things would not be so difficult if he believed in the golden carp," he said softly.

"Does Florence know?" I asked.

"This summer he shall know," Samuel answered wisely.

"What's that all about?" Ernie asked.

"Nothing," I said.

"Come on!" Abel shouted, "bell's ringing—"

It was Friday and we ran to attend the ritual of the Stations of the Cross. The weather was beginning to warm up but the winds still blew, and the whistling of the wind and the mournful cou-rouing of the pigeons and the burning incense made the agony of Christ's journey very sad. Father Byrnes stood at the first station and prayed to the *bulto* on the wall that showed Christ being sentenced by Pilate. Two highschool altar boys accompanied the priest, one to hold the lighted candle and the other to hold the incense burner. The hushed journeyers with Christ answered the priest's prayer. Then there was an interlude of silence while the priest and his attendants moved to the second station, Christ receiving the cross.

Horse sat by me. He was carving his initials into the back of the seat in front of us. Horse never prayed all of the stations, he waited until the priest came near, then he prayed the one he happened to be sitting by. I looked at the wall and saw that today he had picked to sit by the third fall of Christ.

The priest genuflected and prayed at the first fall of Christ. The incense was thick and sweet. Sometimes it made me sick inside and I felt faint. Next Friday would be Good Friday. Lent had gone by fast. There would be no stations on Good Friday, and maybe no catechism. By then we would be ready for confession Saturday and then the receiving of the sacrament on the most holy of days, Easter Sunday.

"What's Immmm-ack-que-let Con-sep-shion?" Abel asked. And Father Byrnes moved to the station where Christ meets his mother. I tried to concentrate. I felt sympathy for the Virgin.

"Immaculate Conception," Lloyd whispered.

"Yeah?"

"The Virgin Mary—"

"But what does it mean?"

"Having babies without—"

"What?"

I tried to shut my ears, I tried to hear the priest, but he was moving away, moving to where Simon helped Christ carry the cross. Dear Lord, I will help.

"I don't know—" Everybody giggled.

"Shhh!" Agnes scowled at us. The girls always prayed with bowed heads throughout the stations.

"A man and a woman, it takes a man and a woman," Florence nodded.

But the Virgin! I panicked, the Virgin Mary was the mother of God! The priest had said she was a mother through a miracle.

The priest finished the station where Veronica wiped the bloodied face of Christ, and he moved to Christ's second fall. The face of Christ was imprinted on the cloth. Besides the

Virgin's blue robe, it was the holiest cloth on earth. The cross was heavy, and when He fell the soldiers whipped Him and struck Him with clubs. The people laughed. His agony began to fill the church and the women moaned their prayers, but the kids would not listen.

"The test is Saturday morning—"

Horse left his carving and looked up. The word "test" made him nervous.

"I, I, I'll pass," he nodded. Bones growled.

"Everybody will pass," I said, trying to be reassuring.

"Florence doesn't believe!" Rita hissed behind us.

"Shhhh! The priest is turning." Father Byrnes was at the back of the church, the seventh station. Now he would come down this side of the aisle for the remaining seven. Christ was speaking to the women.

Maybe that's why they prayed so hard, Christ spoke to them.

In the bell tower the pigeons cou-rouing made a mournful sound.

The priest was by us now. I could smell the incense trapped in his frock, like the fragrance of Ultima's herbs was part of her clothes. I bowed my head. The burning incense was sweet and suffocating; the glowing candle was hypnotizing. Horse had looked at it too long. When the priest moved on Horse leaned on me. His face was white.

"*A la chingada,*" he whispered, "*voy a tirar tripas—*"

The priest was at the station of the Crucifixion. The hammer blows were falling on the nails that ripped through the flesh. I could almost hear the murmuring of the crowd as they craned their necks to see. But today I could not feel the agony.

"Tony—" Horse was leaning on me and gagging.

I struggled under his weight. People turned to watch me carrying the limp Horse up the aisle. Florence left his seat to help me and together we dragged Horse outside. He threw up on the steps of the church.

"He watched the candle too long," Florence said.

"Yes," I answered.

Horse smiled weakly. He wiped the hot puke from his lips and said, "*Ah la veca,* I'm going to try that again next Friday—"

We managed to get through the final week of catechism lessons. The depression that comes with fasting and strict penance deepened as Lent drew to its completion. On Good Friday there was no school. I went to church with my mother and Ultima. All of the saints' statues in the church were covered with purple sheaths. The church was packed with women in black, each one stoically suffering the three hours of the Crucifixion with the tortured Christ. Outside the wind blew and cut off the light of the sun with its dust, and the pigeons cried mournfully in the tower. Inside the prayers were like muffled cries against a storm which seemed to engulf the world. There seemed to be no one to turn to for solace. And when the dying Christ cried, "My God, my God, why hast Thou forsaken me?" the piercing words seemed to drive through to my heart and make me feel alone and lost in a dying universe.

Good Friday was forlorn, heavy and dreary with the death of God's son and the accompanying sense of utter hopelessness.

But on Saturday morning our spirits lifted. We had been through the agony and now the ecstasy of Easter was just ahead. Then too we had our first confession to look forward to in the afternoon. In the morning my mother took me to town and bought me a white shirt and dark pants and jacket. It was the first suit I ever owned, and I smiled when I saw myself in the store mirror. I even got new shoes. Everything was new, as it should be for the first communion.

My mother was excited. When we returned from town she would not allow me to go anywhere or do anything. Every five minutes she glanced at the clock. She did not want me to be late for confession.

"It's time!" she finally called, and with a kiss she sent me scampering down the goat path, to the bridge where I raced the Vitamin Kid and lost, then waited to walk to church with Samuel.

"You ready?" I asked. He only smiled. At the church all the kids were gathered around the steps, waiting for the priest to call us.

"Did you pass?" everyone asked. "What did the priest ask you?" He had given each one of us a quiz, asking us to answer questions on the catechism lesson or to recite prayers.

"He asked me how many persons in one God?" Bones howled.

"Wha'daya say?"

"Four! Four! Four!" Bones cried. Then he shook his head vigorously. "Or five! I don't know."

"And you passed?" Lloyd said contemptuously.

"I got my suit, don't I?" Bones growled. He would fight anyone who said he didn't pass.

"Okay, okay, you passed," Lloyd said to avoid a fight.

"Whad' did he ask you, Tony?"

"I had to recite the Apostles' Creed and tell what each part meant, and I had to explain where we get original sin—"

"¡Oh sí!" "¡Ah la veca!" "¡¡Chingada!"

"Bullshit!" Horse spit out the grass he had been chewing.

"Tony could do it," Florence defended me, "if he wanted to."

"Yeah, Tony knows more about religion and stuff like that than anyone—"

"Tony's gonna be a priest!"

"Hey, let's practice going to confession and make Tony the priest!" Ernie shouted.

"Yeahhhhh!" Horse reared up. Bones snarled and grabbed my pants leg in his teeth.

"Tony be the priest! Tony be the priest!" they began to chant.

"No, no," I begged, but they surrounded me. Ernie took off his sweater and draped it around me. "His priest's dress!" he shouted, and the others followed. They took off their jackets and sweaters and tied them around my waist and neck. I looked in vain for help but there was none.

"Tony is the priest, Tony is the priest, yah-yah-yah-ya-ya!" they sang and danced around me. I grew dizzy. The weight of the jackets on me was heavy and suffocating.

"All right!" I cried to appease them, "I shall be your priest!" I looked at Samuel. He had turned away.

"Yea-aaaaaaaye!" A great shout went up. Even the girls drew closer to watch.

"Hail to our priest!" Lloyd said judiciously.

"Do it right!" Agnes shouted.

"Yeah! Me first! Do it like for reals!" Horse shouted and threw himself at my feet.

"Everybody quiet!" Ernie held up his hands. They all drew around the kneeling Horse and myself, and the wall provided the enclosure but not the privacy of the confessional.

"Bless me, father—" Horse said, but as he concentrated to make the sign of the cross he forgot his lines. "Bless me, father—" he repeated desperately.

"You have sinned," I said. It was very quiet in the enclosure.

"Yes," he said. I remembered hearing the confession of the dying Narciso.

"It's not right to hear another person's confession," I said, glancing at the expectant faces around me.

"Go on!" Ernie hissed and hit me on the back. Blows fell on my head and shoulders. "Go on!" they cried. They really wanted to hear Horse's confession.

"It's only a game!" Rita whispered.

"How long has it been since your last confession?" I asked Horse.

"Always," he blurted out, "since I was born!"

"What are your sins?" I asked. I felt hot and uncomfortable under the weight of the jackets.

"Tell him only your worst one," Rita coaxed the Horse. "Yeah!" all the rest agreed.

The Horse was very quiet, thinking. He had grabbed one of my hands and he clutched it tightly, as if some holy power was going to pass through it and absolve him of his sins. His eyes rolled wildly, then he smiled and opened his mouth. His breath fouled the air.

"I know! I know!" he said excitedly, "one day when Miss Violet let me go to the bathroom I made a hole in the wall! With a nail! Then I could see into the girls' bathroom! I waited a long time. Then one of the girls came and sat down, and I could see everything! Her ass! Everything! I could even hear the pee!" he cried out.

"Horse, you're dirty!" June exclaimed. Then the girls looked shyly at each other and giggled.

"You have sinned," I said to Horse. Horse freed my hand and began rubbing at the front of his pants.

"There's more!" he cried, "I saw a teacher!"

"No!"

"Yes! Yes!" He rubbed harder.

"Who?" one of the girls asked.

"Mrs. Harrington!" Everyone laughed. Mrs. Harrington weighed about two hundred pounds. "It was biggggggggg—!" he exploded and fell trembling on the ground.

"Give him a penance!" the girls chanted and pointed accusing fingers at the pale Horse. "You are dirty, Horse," they cried, and he whimpered and accepted their accusations.

"For your penance say a rosary to the Virgin," I said

weakly. I didn't feel good. The weight of the jackets was making me sweat, and the revelation of Horse's confession and the way the kids were acting were making me sick. I wondered how the priest could shoulder the burden of all the sins he heard.

. . . The weight of the sins will sink the town into the lake of the golden carp. . . .

I looked for Samuel. He was not joining in the game. Florence was calmly accepting the sacrilegious game we were playing, but then it didn't matter to him, he didn't believe.

"Me next! Me next!" Bones shouted. He let go of my leg and knelt in front of me. "I got a better sin than Horse! Bless me, father! Bless me, father! Bless me, father!" he repeated. He kept making the sign of the cross over and over. "I got a sin! I got to confess! I saw a high-school boy and a girl fucking in the grass by the Blue Lake!" He smiled proudly and looked around.

"Ah, I see them every night under the railroad bridge," the Vitamin Kid scoffed.

"What do you mean?" I asked Bones.

"Naked! Jumping up and down!" he exclaimed.

"You lie, Bones!" Horse shouted. He didn't want his own sin bettered.

"No I don't!" Bones argued. "I don't lie, father, I don't lie!" he pleaded.

"Who was it?" Rita asked.

"It was Larry Saiz, and that dumb *gabacha* whose father owns the Texaco station—please father, it's my sin! I saw it! I confess!" He squeezed my hand very hard.

"Okay, Bones, okay," I nodded my head, "it's your sin."

"Give me a penance!" he growled.

"A rosary to the Virgin," I said to be rid of him.

"Like Horse?" he shouted.

"Yes."

"But my sin was bigger!" he snarled and leaped for my throat. "Whagggggghhh—" he threw me down and would have strangled me if the others hadn't pulled him away.

"Another rosary for daring to touch the priest!" I shouted in self-defense and pointed an accusing finger at him. That made him happy and he settled down.

"Florence next!" Abel cried.

"Nah, Florence ain't goin' make it anyway," Lloyd argued.

"That's enough practice," I said and started to take off the cumbersome costume, but they wouldn't let me.

"Abel's right," Ernie said emphatically, "Florence needs the practice! He didn't make it because he didn't practice!"

"He didn't make it because he doesn't believe!" Agnes taunted.

"Why doesn't he believe?" June asked.

"Let's find out!" "Make him tell!" "¡Chingada!"

They grabbed tall Florence before he could bolt away and made him kneel in front of me.

"No!" I protested.

"Confess him!" they chanted. They held him with his arms pinned behind his back. I looked down at him and tried to let him know we might as well go along with the game. It would be easier that way.

"What are your sins?" I asked.

"I don't have any," Florence said softly.

"You do, you bastard!" Ernie shouted and pulled Florence's head back.

"You have sins," Abel agreed.

"Everybody has sins!" Agnes shouted. She helped Ernie twist Florence's head back. Florence tried to struggle but he was pinned by Horse and Bones and Abel. I tried to pull their hands away from him to relieve the pain I saw in his face, but the trappings of the priest's costume entangled me and so I could do very little.

"Tell me one sin," I pleaded with Florence. His face was very close to mine now, and when he shook his head to tell me again that he didn't have sins I saw a frightening truth in his eyes. He was telling the truth! He did not believe that he had ever sinned against God! "Oh my God!" I heard myself gasp.

"Confess your sins or you'll go to hell!" Rita cried out. She grabbed his blond hair and helped Ernie and Agnes twist his head.

"Confess! Confess!" they cried. Then with one powerful heave and a groan Florence shook off his tormentors. He was long and sinewy, but because of his mild manner we had always underestimated his strength. Now the girls and Ernie and even Horse fell off him like flies.

"I have not sinned!" he shouted, looking me square in the eyes, challenging me, the priest. His voice was like Ultima's when she had challenged Tenorio, or Narciso's when he had tried to save Lupito.

"It is God who has sinned against me!" his voice thundered, and we fell back in horror at the blasphemy he uttered.

"Florence," I heard June whimper, "don't say that—"

Florence grinned. "Why? Because it is the truth?" he questioned. "Because you refuse to see the truth, or to accept me because I do not believe in your lies! I say God has sinned against me because He took my father and mother from me when I most needed them, and He made my sisters whores— He punished all of us without just cause. Tony," his look pierced me, "He took Narciso! And why? What harm did Narciso ever do—"

"We shouldn't listen to him," Agnes had the courage to interrupt Florence, "we'll have to confess what we heard and the priest will be mad."

"The priest was right in not passing Florence, because he doesn't believe!" Rita added.

"He shouldn't even be here if he is not going to believe in the laws we learn," Lloyd said.

"Give him a penance! Make him ask for forgiveness for those terrible things he said about God!" Agnes insisted. They were gathering behind me now, I could feel their presence and their hot, bitter breath. They wanted me to be their leader; they wanted me to punish Florence.

"Make his penance hard," Rita leered.

"Make him kneel and we'll all beat him," Ernie suggested.

"Yeah, beat him!" Bones said wildly.

"Stone him!"

"Beat him!"

"Kill him!"

They circled around me and advanced on Florence, their eyes flashing with the thought of the punishment they would impose on the non-believer. It was then that the fear left me, and I knew what I had to do. I spun around and held out my hands to stop them.

"No!" I shouted, "there will be no punishment, there will be no penance! His sins are forgiven!" I turned and made the sign of the cross. "Go in peace, my son," I said to Florence.

"No!" they shouted, "don't let him go free!"

"Make him do penance! That's the law!"

"Punish him for not believing in God!"

"I am the priest!" I shouted back, "and I have absolved

him of his sins!" I was facing the angry kids and I could see that their hunger for vengeance was directed at me, but I didn't care, I felt relieved. I had stood my ground for what I felt to be right and I was not afraid. I thought that perhaps it was this kind of strength that allowed Florence to say he did not believe in God.

"You are a bad priest, Tony!" Agnes lashed out at me.

"We do not want you for our priest!" Rita followed.

"Punish the priest!" they shouted and they engulfed me like a wave. They were upon me, clawing, kicking, tearing off the jackets, defrocking me. I fought back but it was useless. They were too many. They spread me out and held me pinned down to the hard ground. They had torn my shirt off so the sharp pebbles and stickers cut into my back.

"Give him the Indian torture!" someone shouted.

"Yeah, the Indian torture!" they chanted.

They held my arms while Horse jumped on my stomach and methodically began to pound with his fist on my chest. He used his sharp knuckles and aimed each blow directly at my breastbone. I kicked and wiggled and struggled to get free from the incessant beating, but they held me tight and I could not throw them off.

"No! No!" I shouted, but the raining blows continued. The blows of the knuckles coming down again and again on my breastbone were unbearable, but Horse knew no pity, and there was no pity on the faces of the others.

"God!" I cried, "God!" But the jarring blows continued to fall. I jerked my head from side to side and tried to kick or bite, but I could not get loose. Finally I bit my lips so I wouldn't cry, but my eyes filled with tears anyway. They were laughing and pointing down at the red welt that raised on my chest where the Horse was pounding.

"Serves him right," I heard, "he let the sinner go—"

Then, after what seemed an eternity of torture, they let me go. The priest was calling from the church steps, so they ran off to confession. I slowly picked myself up and rubbed the bruises on my chest. Florence handed me my shirt and jacket.

"You should have given me a penance," he said.

"You don't have to do any penance," I answered. I wiped my eyes and shook my head. Everything in me seemed loose and disconnected.

"Are you going to confession?" he asked.

"Yes," I answered and finished buttoning my shirt.

"You could never be their priest," he said.

I looked at the open door of the church. There was a calm in the wind and the bright sunlight made everything stark and harsh. The last of the kids went into the church and the doors closed.

"No," I nodded. "Are you going to confession?" I asked him.

"No," he muttered. "Like I said, I only wanted to be with you guys—I cannot eat God," he added.

"I have to," I whispered. I ran up the steps and entered the dark, musky church. I genuflected at the font of holy water, wet my fingertips, and made the sign of the cross. The lines were already formed on either side of the confessional, and the kids were behaving and quiet. Each one stood with bowed head, preparing himself to confess all of his sins to Father Byrnes. I walked quietly around the back pew and went to the end of one line. I made the sign of the cross again and began to say my prayers. As each kid finished his confession the line shuffled forward. I closed my eyes and tried not to be distracted by anything around me. I thought hard of all the sins I had ever committed, and I said as many prayers as I could remember. I begged God forgiveness for my sins over and over. After a long wait, Agnes, who had been in front of me, came out of the confessional. She held the curtain as I stepped in, then she let it drop and all was dark. I knelt on the rough board and leaned against the small window. I prayed. I could hear whisperings from the confessional on the other side. My eyes grew accustomed to the gloom and I saw a small crucifix nailed to the side of the window. I kissed the feet of the hanging Jesus. The confessional smelled of old wood. I thought of the million sins that had been revealed in this small, dark space.

Then abruptly my thoughts were scattered. The small wooden door of the window slid open in front of me, and in the dark I could make out the head of Father Byrnes. His eyes were closed, his head bowed forward. He mumbled something in Latin then put his hand on his forehead and waited.

I made the sign of the cross and said, "Forgive me, Father, for I have sinned," and I made my first confession to him.

MAX APPLE

My Real Estate

I

I have always believed in property. Though a tenant now, I have prospects. In fact, Joanne Williams, my realtor, thinks I have the greatest prospects in the world. She has always dropped in on me now and then, but these days she comes up almost every time she leaves her seat for popcorn or a Coke. She brings her refreshment with her and she refreshes me. She has done so right from the start, ever since I first realized that I really wanted to own my own home.

She picked me up outside my apartment house. She gave me her card. We shook hands. She looked me over.

"You want a bungalow," she said, "two bedrooms, one and a half baths, central air, hardwood floors. You don't need the headache of a lawn."

In her big Oldsmobile we cruised the expressways. Short skirts were the style then. Joanne drove in bursts of speed. She was learning conversational Spanish from a Berlitz eight-track recording that played as we headed toward the fringes of the inner city, where she said there were "buys."

"*Hágame usted el favor de . . .*" said the tape.

"There are a lot of Spanish speakers entering the market," said Joanne. A small card on her dashboard, the type that usually says "Clergy," proclaimed *Se Habla Español*. "Once you show someone a house," she said, "it's a moral obligation. You take them in your car, buy them lunch, introduce

21

them to some homes in their price range. It's as if you've been naked together." She had long thin legs, all shin until they disappeared only a few inches below where her panty hose turned darker. When the tape ended, she asked if I was a wounded veteran and then if I had ever been in the army at all. She was sorry.

"With a VA loan you could float into a house. Conventional will be tougher. Still, you've got thirty years to cushion one or two percent." She shrugged her small shoulders, asked me about how much I earned.

I declined to say. Her skirt edged higher. I never knew what a VA loan meant. When I saw the VA signs around the housing developments, I thought that the whole thing was exclusively for veterans, that there were lots of crutches and wheelchair ramps and VFW halls in there. She laughed when I told her this.

"There is a lot to know in real estate." She was twenty-eight, she said, and divorced from a man who had liked furnished apartments. My efficiency in the beams is also furnished, but with great luxury. Simmons' Hide-A-Bed, chrome-and-glass coffee table, Baker easy chair, Drexel maple bed and dresser. There is a hunting tapestry on my living-room wall. My bathroom fixtures are gold leaf and the tub has a tiny whirlpool. When she wants nothing else, Joanne sometimes comes up just to soak her toes in the hot bubbles.

When she was the salesperson and I the client, she told me I was her first bachelor. "I know your type," she said. "When I went to singles' bars, you were all I ever met. You think apartments are where you'll meet people, you believe the managers who show you game rooms and swimming pools. Listen to how people talk. In apartments they don't have 'neighbors'; they say, 'He lives in my complex.' If you want to meet people, you buy a house."

Joanne refused to believe that I wanted a house for reasons other than neighbors and schools. "So what if you have no wife and children," she said, "why not be near kids that are well educated, less likely to soap your windows on Halloween and put sugar in your gas tank."

I told her the simple truth. "I want a house because my people have owned land and houses in Texas for four generations. We lived here with the Mexicans and the Indians. I'm the first Spenser who hasn't owned a tiny piece of Texas."

"You still can live with Mexicans and Indians," she told

me, "in the fifth Ward. But if you go there, you'll go without me."

She drove extravagantly and used no seat belts. I slid toward her on all the turns. She used the horn but not while listening to the tape. "In the suburbs," Joanne said, "I can put you into a two bedroom plus den and patio for eighteen five. I can get you all-electric kitchens and even sprinkler systems for a lot less than you'll pay for an old frame bungalow close in." But no matter what she said, she couldn't convince me to look at Sharpstown and Green Acres and Cascade Shores. They sounded like Hong Kong and Katmandu. I grew up in Houston and never knew about these far-away places until I started noticing some of the addresses printed on the checks we took in at the store. Sometimes it was a long-distance call to trace down a local bad check.

"My great-grandfather fought at the Alamo," I told her. "He was one of those who left when Santa Anna gave them a last chance. My grandad owned a farm near where the Astrodome is now." This was the first time the Dome entered our conversation. Joanne was unimpressed and it didn't seem very important to me either. The Dome was just another big building, the colonel who owned it, just another big businessman, and my grandad just another old memory, dead fifteen years.

In my case she was wrong about the suburbs, but Joanne did have an instinct for a client's needs. She was flexible. The one thing she could not do was pretend to like a house. If she didn't like the place, she got out fast, sometimes without leaving her card. She held her nose all the way to the car and refused to answer questions about the place. "Go back without me," she said, "go alone or take a lawyer or an interior decorator." Even when she liked a house, she made the home owners open their drapes. "I want to see everything in the bright light," she said. She came into a house like an actress to center stage. Buyers and sellers moved close to the walls. She sized places up as she walked through in long strides. She noticed inaccuracies in thermostats and recommended plasterers and electricians as she passed needed repairs. Whenever there was a child, she chased him down to pat his head. On our first day we spent three hours together. At four thirty, she told me there was a Mexican couple, thus the tape. At seven there was an Open House in Sharpstown. I should call her in the morning.

The next day, Sunday, she was at my door at eight A.M.

She had a tennis dress so white that it literally blinded me as the sun reflected from it into my dark apartment.

"Sorry to wake you," she said, "but I was in the neighborhood and I need to use a phone, please." While I showered she made what seemed like dozens of calls. She had played tennis from six to eight. "Sunday is my big day. I have three listings in Montrose and one in Bel Air. With good weather we'll close something today." She joined me for what was her second breakfast. I knew that as she ate she was itemizing my establishment and judging my taste. She was doing even more than I thought. We finished breakfast at eight forty-five. "I don't have to be in Bel Air until ten fifteen," she said, and took off her tennis dress.

Joanne's style was intact, flawless, efficient. She was done in time to have a quick shower herself and give me a brief rundown on mortgage rates.

Later in the week, as she led me from house to house, I learned more personal information, facts from the life of Joanne Williams. She rattled them off as briskly as the square footage of a room. Born in Chicago, moved to Houston at fourteen, married high-school sweetheart; at twenty-five, childless, living in a furnished apartment where Chuck still resided only a few complexes east of me; left Chuck and job as legal secretary; became cocktail waitress. There amid "ups that would make your head swim," she met Vince, her sales manager. "What the hell," Vince asked her, "is a girl with your personality doing as a waitress? You should be out on the street." He opened his Multiple Listings book and started to show her some pictures. "There's a five-bedroom rancher than can bring you a four-thousand-dollar commission." Vince told her to think of herself as an obstetrician. A house on the market was like a pregnant woman. She had to go, she would burst if nobody helped. You wanted to make it fast, painless, smooth.

She worked days for Vince, nights as a waitress. "At the end of the month I sold that five-bedroom rancher that Vince had randomly picked out of the book." "It was no accident," he said, "it was your career. I showed you the picture of it." She sold close to a million dollars in each of her first two years. This year she wanted to go over.

"The kind of house you want is chickenfeed," she told me, "but I've got the time for it. And who knows, you might one day have a rich friend who'll use me to buy a mansion in Green Meadows."

Because I was in the eighteen-to-twenty-two-thousand range with conventional mortgage, mediocre credit, and less than ten percent down, Joanne could not give me her best hours. I drew dinner times and late nights usually, but this made it convenient for us to eat and occasionally sleep together. She did not have to mix business and pleasure, any more than she had to hurry. Speed and pleasure and business all combined in her like the price and sales tax. The only noise she made was a small grinding of the teeth like a nervous signature on a deed. We rarely kissed and used only the most explicit embraces.

And Joanne did not pressure me to buy a house. As I wavered and mused upon closing costs and repair bills and termites and cockroaches, she just paid less and less attention to me. Finally, in spite of mutual fondness, we never saw each other at all. I kept up with her, though, by her signs around the city. She married Vince, but because his Italian name was so long they both used hers. Williams and Williams signs, bright orange with a green border, sprang up throughout various better neighborhoods. Whenever I saw the signs, I knew that there Joanne had once opened drapes and frightened owners. She and Vince made a good team. He ran the office and took care of all the paperwork. This left her free to sell. Judging by the frequency of her signs, I guessed she now sold many millions in a year and had forgotten me as a truly bad investment of her time.

I underestimated her loyalty and her memory. Months after our last encounter I met her in the express lane at Krogers. It was around supper time and she was buying three Hershey bars.

"With all the money you must earn now," I asked, "can't you take time out for a regular dinner?"

"Sweetheart," Joanne told me, "you never did understand real estate." She bought me a Hershey bar too. I left my less-than-purchases in the cart and followed her to a long white Cadillac. "Deductible," she said, "might as well." She made a U-turn and parked across the street among a group of vans belonging to plumbers who had gone home for the evening. She checked the clock on the panel. "I should be in River Oaks in thirty minutes to show five bedrooms, but they'll wait a few minutes if they have to."

They didn't have to. In the backseat of the Cadillac Joanne was her old self. I looked up and saw wrenches and plungers hanging from the ceilings of the plumbers' vans. "I haven't forgotten you, Jack," she said. "Every time I see a two bedroom one bath in the medical-center area I mean to give you a call."

"Congratulations," I said, "on your marriage [I had read about it in the financial pages, they took out a quarter-page ad] and your own business."

"Yes," she said, "it's wonderful. If interest stays down we might even go into our own development."

II

When I next saw her, it was at my own apartment complex. I was on the balcony looking out at the tennis courts below me. Joanne saw me, halted her doubles match, and invited me to bring them all some Cokes after the set.

Vince was as tall as Joanne but so thickset that she seemed to tower above him. He played the net and she took the long ones that he couldn't reach. She wore a tennis dress exactly like the one I remembered. Joanne introduced me to my landlords, Ben and Vera Bloom.

"I'm glad to have a tenant like you," Ben Bloom said. "You know the kind of people that usually rent these, twenty-two-year-olds that like to drink beer and screw and write on the walls. They never dump their garbage, but every time they see a roach they run to call the manager. You can't satisfy people like them. No matter what you do they move out. They break leases. Who's going to take a traveling salesman to court?"

Vince treated me like an old friend, claimed that he recognized my name as a former client of their old company. When he and Joanne went into the business for themselves, most of the old company came along with them. "We closed the deal for the land you're standing on," Vince said, "so you might say we did a little bit to help you find a place." He seemed to feel guilty that their company had not matched me with a house. "It's his own fault," Joanne said, "he had chances; by the time he decides someone else has put in a bid."

"Oh, one of those," Vince said. Still he invited me to join

them that night at the ball game. The Astros were playing the Cubs. "I've never been to the Dome," I admitted.

"It's a separate world," Ben Bloom said. He wiped the perspiration from his eyes and took off his tennis glove. "People like me put up these developments and tract houses and zoned subdivisions, but not the Colonel. The Colonel left us to fuck around with the small stuff. He went for the pie in the sky."

"And he made it," Vera said; "he puts us on the map more than the moon did. Nobody even remembers the moon any more, but just mention Houston at a convention and they all ask about the Dome."

They were going to a party celebrating the fifth anniversary of the stadium. Joanne asked me to meet them at the Colonel's penthouse.

That night, watched by ushers and security guards, I entered the penthouse in the beams. I felt underdressed in my corduroy trousers and sports shirt. Joanne, I noticed, was wearing a black dress with a cut-out back, but Vince was as casually dressed as I. They made me feel very comfortable in the Colonel's living room. The Blooms were there and many other couples. The tuxedoed ushers carried trays full of martinis and Tom Collinses.

"It's a nickel-beer night in the grandstand," Vince said. "No matter how much you drink you won't be able to keep up with the slobs down there. You couldn't get me to nickel-beer night. They piss down all the corridors leading to the men's rooms."

Joanne took me by the elbow and introduced me to some guests. She was relaxed and elegant. I had never seen her in company before, only in business and in bed. She was not even wearing a watch.

"What can I do," she told me when I asked, "I'm here for the evening just like the baseball players. When there's nothing to do, I play ball. That's something else you don't know about real estate."

If I could have looked out from this Dome toward the east, I would have seen my grandfather's former seventy-five acres only a city block away. There are gas stations and motels on the property now and the roller coaster of an amusement park. My grandfather died broke in the Christian Brothers Home for the Aged. He sold his land right before World War II to buy a liquor store. My dad ran the store.

While I was thinking what might have been if Grandad had held onto the land instead of going into the liquor business, the Colonel rolled in, a big gray-bearded man in an expensive-looking wheelchair. An Astros blanket lay across his knees. A nurse in white and an usher in her gown stood on each side of the chair. Ben Bloom proposed a toast. "To the head of the Dome," he said, "to the man who made it all possible." We clinked our glasses. The Colonel could neither drink nor hold the glass.

"A bad stroke," Joanne whispered to me, "during the first football season. He's never even felt the AstroTurf, poor man." She smiled and went over to pat the Colonel on the shoulder. He seemed to understand everything but could barely speak.

As the nurse wheeled him through the guests, it came my turn to meet the great man. The room seemed more crowded, Joanne was nowhere in sight.

"Jack Spenser, sir," I said, not really knowing how to explain my presence, "my grandfather once owned seventy-five acres on Old Spanish Trail. I'd like to buy myself a house in this area."

I could not be sure if he had even heard me. The nurse pushed with some effort his polished chair over the thick carpeting. The room was quite full now, of people with drinks and loud voices. Nobody was watching the TV or cared about the game itself hundreds of feet below.

"Lyndon Johnson used to stay in this suite," I heard someone say, "and get drunk on his ass for the whole weekend. He'd send the Secret Service out to the ranch so everyone would think he was there worrying about Vietnam. It would have taken a pretty shrewd assassin to look for him way up at the top of the Dome."

The splendor of the Astrodome was not the baseball I knew. My dad and I used to go to Texas league games at Haynes Stadium for Saturday-night doubleheaders. We packed a lunch and a lot of mosquito repellent and sat out in the bleachers for twenty-five cents each. My hero was a black first baseman named Eleazer Brown who never made it to the big leagues. He was six feet eight and for a while did play with the Globetrotters. When my dad closed the liquor store after the eighth robbery and his second bullet wound, the police brought him to a lineup to identify one of the holdup men. It was a cinch. Dad knew the big torso of Eleazer

Brown even when Eleazer was slouched over and in dark glasses. "It was a sad day for me," Dad said, "fingering that coon who could hit the ball five hundred feet. That's him, I told the cops, and you know, in spite of everything, I almost went up and asked that black bastard for his autograph." At least Brown hadn't shot at Dad; it was his friend who did that, an average-sized numbers runner from Dallas.

The roof of the Dome was so high, I had read, that you could put the Shamrock Hotel into it. I tried to imagine the biggest thing I could, the Goodyear blimp, dwarfed against the ceiling. As a store manager I was entitled to one ride a year in the blimp. When I first met Joanne, I had taken her as my guest. She pointed out landmarks to the children of other managers. When we landed, she ran toward her car. "It made me nervous," she said, "it reminded me of a mobile home."

"I've been looking for you," Joanne said. "The Colonel wants to see you. He never asks for anybody."

"Why does he want me?"

"Who knows," Joanne said, "but it's a great honor. Vince and Ben thought you went down to the game. Go ahead, he's in the other room with his nurse." I knocked at the door.

The Colonel and his nurse awaited me in a smaller sitting room. I was surprised that he smoked a pipe. The nurse held it for him between puffs. As I waited for the Colonel to begin, the nurse played with the pipe stem. With a small knife she shaved the dark tobacco and repacked the bowl. She caressed the stem. It took the Colonel a long time to say anything. He had to get his mouth in the right position. I could see how difficult it was for him. When he did begin, the words came out loud and uneven, like a child writing on a blackboard.

"Your grandpa," he got out, "was a dumbass son of a bitch." He puffed on the pipe and then the nurse repacked it. I waited for the second sentence.

"He could have had a piece of the world . . . wanted a liquor store instead." As the Colonel, between puffs and silences, got out his story I learned that he had bought most of the Dome land from Grandad and had offered my ancestor a part of what, at that time, was going to be a housing development. Just as I hesitated with Joanne over my would-be bungalow, so Gramps had hemmed and hawed with the

Colonel and finally taken his money instead for the liquor-store enterprise.

"We grew up together on the Buffalo Bayou," the Colonel said. "He sold booze during prohibition and never forgot that he made easy money then. Before he kicked off, I told him about the Dome and he laughed in my face. Now," the Colonel went on even more slowly, "now the laugh is on me. I put the top on baseball. I made my own horizon. I shut out the sky. But I've got no arms and no legs and no sons and no daughters." He took a long, long pause and rejected the pipe. The noise from the party in the outer rooms surrounded our silence. It made the Colonel's slowness even more dramatic.

"I never liked Old Jack Spenser [I was named for Grandad], and I jewed him out of his land. Fifty bucks an acre was a steal even in those days. He had liquor on his mind all the time."

While the Colonel kept pausing, I tried to remember what I actually had heard about the land on the Old Spanish Trail. I knew it had been Gramps' land, but when he went senile I was just a boy. All I remember is his crazy laugh in the Christian home. We used to have to bring him dolls when we came as if he were a baby. He died in '56, and Dad only made it two years beyond that. The liquor store was busted. Mom moved to Colorado with my sister.

"For a liquor store, he gave up this." With difficulty the Colonel made a neck gesture that suggested arms wide open. "I can't stand all these outsiders that keep coming down here. I'd like the Dome to be just for us Texans. That real-estate girl told me you wanted your own house. You're smarter than your grandad." Then the Colonel made me an offer. I thought about it overnight, asked Joanne's advice the next day. "I only think of single dwellings," she said; "the family is the unit I work with. Ask someone who knows big spaces." But without further advice I did it on my own. What was there to lose?

III

That was almost three years ago. Now, I don't work for Goodyear anymore. I don't have to. The Colonel pays me two hundred a week plus room. He only leaves the Dome to go to the doctor's office in Plaza Del Oro across the street. I have my own apartment next to his and my only real job is getting up to turn the Colonel at three each morning so he won't get bedsores. The night watchman lets me in. The Colonel is asleep on his right side. He snores quietly into his beard. Since I'm pretty tired too, it's all a blur. I pull the special pad from beneath his hips and put it on the other side of him. I grab his arms as if they're ropes and give a good hard pull, then I go back to the other side of the bed and roll his hips over. He never wakes up.

Lately Joanne has been saying that I'll inherit the Dome someday because he's got no heirs. "He picked you because you're a Texan, because he knew your grandpa. He doesn't need other reasons. What else is he going to do with it?" When she tells me how rich I'm going to be, she snuggles up close and spends an extra few minutes. The high interest rates since '73 have really hurt her business and her marriage. She doesn't talk about it too much, but things are not working out between her and Vince. "He wants to go commercial," she says; "I can't work beyond the family. He wants to use leverage. He talks about a real-estate trust. I look at houses as walls and roofs. Vince calls them instruments and units." They have filed for divorce.

This year, for the first time, Joanne bought an Astros season ticket. Sometimes I go down to watch an inning or two, and when I come back, there she is in my whirlpool. She is as fast and smooth as ever. Interest rates and marriage have not changed her. She doesn't look around for Jack Spenser's perfect house any longer. "You'll own the Dome soon," she says; "you'll call all the shots."

I don't think the Colonel is likely to make me his heir but there is no doubt that it's possible. He calls for me every few weeks just to talk. He's getting weaker but he still likes to tell me what a dumbass Grandpa was. I agree and have taken over the nurse's job with the pipe. So far it's been no real problem. If the Colonel wants to call Grandad a dumbass all the time, that's his privilege.

In most ways my life is pretty much the same, but living in the Dome has killed my interest in baseball. When I do watch an inning or two, it's only to look at the scoreboard or the mix of colors in the crowd or to listen to the sound of the bat meeting the ball. What I like to do most is walk behind the grandstand and watch the people buying refreshments. There are one hundred twenty-six places in the Dome where you can buy beer. People line up at every one of them. There are eight restaurants and six of them have liquor licenses. While Astros and Dodgers and Cubs and Giants are running the bases and hitting the balls, the Colonel is making a fortune on beer and liquor. My Grandpa, I think, wasn't such a dumbass. He just had the wrong location.

Joanne has lots of plans for later. She wants to marry me. She says that we could keep the name of her business and use all the signs she has left over from her years with Vince.

"We won't need the money," I tell her; "we'll take a vacation around the world."

"No," she says, "first we'll evict the baseball team and the conventions. We can make a big profit on these auditorium seats. Then we'll put up modern bungalows, just the kind you wanted. They'll be close to downtown and have every convenience. There's room here for dozens. Even the outdoors will be air-conditioned. We'll put good private schools in the clubhouses and lease all the corridor space for shops and supermarkets. A few condominiums down the foul lines," she says, "and a hospital in center field. The scoreboard will be the world's biggest drive-in movie."

I go along with her. She gets more passionate when she talks this way, more involved with me. She's been saying these things for quite a while now and keeping track of the Colonel's health. He is so slow these days that he falls asleep between words. I don't think he can last much longer. Joanne gets very excited when she sees his pale face being wheeled past my door. "We'll move into his place," she says, "and use this as my office." I'm sad when I think of the Colonel becoming something like my Grandpa playing with dolls, but I didn't take Joanne too seriously until a few days ago when after some drinks and a whirlpool bath she put on a long hostess gown and went back to her box behind third base. I followed because I was suspicious of the gown. She walked right over the railing onto the field. She took the third-base umpire by the arm and led him to the mound. "Let's get some sunlight in here," she yelled to the top of the Dome, "let's see what it would be like with new tenants. It's a good neighborhood. There's lots of shade and well-kept lawns, and the neighbors"—she looked at Walt Alston in the visitors' dugout—"the neighbors seem friendly and sincere." She left the umpire at the pitcher's mound and started taking her long strides toward the outfield.

"Rates can't go much higher," she told the Dodger infield,

"but if they do you'll be extra glad you bought now. A house isn't like other investments. Stocks and bonds don't give you the direct benefits of housing. There is nothing else like it on God's earth. Yearly deductions, shelter, comfort, and all of it at capital-gains rates."

"Do you have children?" she asked the second baseman, who looked on in bewilderment. "If you do you'll appreciate the lack of traffic. You can send three-year-olds to the store without any worries." By center field her stride was almost a gallop. "Don't worry," she called to the Dodgers' black left fielder, "you'll be able to live here too. It will take a few years, but the whole world is changing."

A squadron of park policemen caught up with her on the way to the bullpen. They led her back to the third-base box, where I waited alongside the manager, who knew me and told the police to let her go in my custody. The policemen were gentle with her and the crowd cheered as she put those long smooth legs easily over the high railing. She threw kisses in all directions. The scoreboard spelled out "charge" and the organist played "Funny Girl." I led her up the ramp toward the escalator. "The place will sell, Jack. Everybody loves it. That AstroTurf will save a bundle on gardening too. We can do it, Jack, I know we can. When the Colonel leaves it to you, can we go ahead with it?"

She was all motion in my apartment. I could hardly restrain her from going into the Colonel's penthouse and strangling him with a pillow. "I'm only kidding about that," she said. "We're at the top now, we can wait."

As she ran the water for another whirlpool bath to relax her I thought of my great-grandfather saying good-bye to Davy Crockett and walking out of history, his son selling out to the Colonel, and my own dad bankrupt by liquor. Far below us someone was stealing a base. Next door the Colonel was struggling for a word. Cartoons blinked from the scoreboard. I took off my clothes. "It must run in the family," I said, thinking of Gramps laughing in the empty hallway of the Christian Brothers Home. I laughed out loud too. "If I get the Dome, do anything you want with it," I said. "Just save me room for the world's largest liquor store." In the midst of bubbles, I joined her. We sparkled like champagne.

DONALD BARTHELME

I Bought a Little City

So I bought a little city (it was Galveston, Texas) and told everybody that nobody had to move, we were going to do it just gradually, very relaxed, no big changes overnight. They were pleased and suspicious. I walked down to the harbor where there were cotton warehouses and fish markets and all sorts of installations having to do with the spread of petroleum throughout the Free World, and I thought, A few apple trees here might be nice. Then I walked out this broad boulevard which has all these tall thick palm trees maybe forty feet high in the center and oleanders on both sides, it runs for blocks and blocks and ends up opening up to the broad Gulf of Mexico—stately homes on both sides and a big Catholic church that looks more like a mosque and the Bishop's Palace and a handsome red brick affair where the Shriners meet. I thought, What a nice little city, it suits me fine.

It suited me fine so I started to change it. But softly, softly. I asked some folks to move out of a whole city block on I Street, and then I tore down their houses. I put the people into the Galvez Hotel, which is the nicest hotel in town, right on the seawall, and I made sure that every room had a beautiful view. Those people had wanted to stay at the Galvez Hotel all their lives and never had a chance before because they didn't have the money. They were delighted. I tore down their houses and made that empty block a park. We planted it all to hell and put some nice green iron benches in it and a little fountain—all standard stuff, we didn't try to be imaginative.

I was pleased. All the people who lived in the four blocks surrounding the empty block had something they hadn't had before, a park. They could sit in it, and like that. I went and watched them sitting in it. There was already a black man there playing bongo drums. I hate bongo drums. I started to tell him to stop playing those goddamn bongo drums but then I said to myself, No, that's not right. You got to let him play his goddamn bongo drums if he feels like it, it's part of the misery of democracy, to which I subscribe. Then I started thinking about new housing for the people I had displaced, they couldn't stay in that fancy hotel forever.

But I didn't have any ideas about new housing, except that it shouldn't be too imaginative. So I got to talking to one of these people, one of the ones we had moved out, guy by the name of Bill Caulfield who worked in a wholesale-tobacco place down on Mechanic Street.

"So what kind of a place would you like to live in?" I asked him.

"Well," he said, "not too big."

"Uh-huh."

"Maybe with a veranda around three sides," he said, "so we could sit on it and look out. A screened porch, maybe."

"Whatcha going to look out at?"

"Maybe some trees and, you know, the lawn."

"So you want some ground around the house."

"That would be nice, yeah."

" 'Bout how much ground are you thinking of?"

"Well, not too much."

"You see, the problem is, there's only x amount of ground and everybody's going to want to have it to look at and at the same time they don't want to be staring at the neighbors. Private looking, that's the thing."

"Well, yes," he said. "I'd like it to be kind of private."

"Well," I said, "get a pencil and let's see what we can work out."

We started with what there was going to be to look at, which was damned difficult. Because when you look you don't want to be able to look at just one thing, you want to be able to shift your gaze. You need to be able to look at at least three things, maybe four. Bill Caulfield solved the problem. He showed me a box. I opened it up and inside was a jigsaw puzzle with a picture of the Mona Lisa on it.

"Lookee here," he said. "If each piece of ground was like a piece of this-here puzzle, and the tree line on each piece of property followed the outline of a piece of the puzzle—well, there you have it, Q.E.D. and that's all she wrote."

"Fine," I said. "Where are the folk going to park their cars?"

"In the vast underground parking facility," he said.

"O.K., but how does each householder gain access to his household?"

"The tree lines are double and shade beautifully paved walkways possibly bordered with begonias," he said.

"A lurkway for potential muggists and rapers," I pointed out.

"There won't be any such," Caulfield said, "because you've bought our whole city and won't allow that class of person to hang out here no more."

That was right. I had bought the whole city and could probably do that. I had forgotten.

"Well," I said finally, "let's give 'er a try. The only thing I don't like about it is that it seems a little imaginative."

We did and it didn't work out badly. There was only one complaint. A man named A. G. Bartie came to see me.

"Listen," he said, his eyes either gleaming or burning, I couldn't tell which, it was a cloudy day, "I feel like I'm living in this gigantic jiveass jigsaw puzzle."

He was right. Seen from the air, he was living in the middle of a titanic reproduction of the Mona Lisa, too, but I thought it best not to mention that. We allowed him to square off his property into a standard 60 times 100–foot lot and later some other people did that too—some people just like rectangles, I guess. I must say it improved the concept. You run across an occasional rectangle in Shady Oaks (we didn't want to call the development anything too imaginative) and it surprises you. That's nice.

I said to myself:

> Got a little city
> Ain't it pretty

By now I had exercised my proprietorship so lightly and if I do say so myself tactfully that I wondered if I was enjoying myself enough (and I had paid a heavy penny too—near to half my fortune). So I went out on the streets then and shot six thousand dogs. This gave me great satisfaction and you have no idea how wonderfully it improved the city for the better. This left us with a dog population of 165,000, as opposed to a human population of something like 89,000. Then I went down to the Galveston *News*, the morning paper, and wrote an editorial denouncing myself as the vilest creature the good God had ever placed upon the earth, and were we, the citizens of this fine community, who were after all free Americans of whatever race or creed, going to sit still while one man, *one man*, if indeed so vile a critter could be so called, etc., etc.? I gave it to the city desk and told them I wanted it on the front page in fourteen-point type, boxed. I did this just in case they might have hesitated to do it themselves, and because I'd seen that Orson Welles picture where the guy writes a nasty notice about his own wife's terrible singing, which I always thought was pretty decent of him, from some points of view.

A man whose dog I'd shot came to see me.

"You shot Butch," he said.

"Butch? Which one was Butch?"

"One brown ear and one white ear," he said. "Very friendly."

"Mister," I said, "I've just shot six thousand dogs, and you expect me to remember Butch?"

"Butch was all Nancy and me had," he said. "We never had no children."

"Well, I'm sorry about that," I said, "but I own this city."

"I know that," he said.

"I am the sole owner and I make all the rules."

"They told me," he said.

"I'm sorry about Butch but he got in the way of the big campaign. You ought to have had him on a leash."

"I don't deny it," he said.

"You ought to have had him inside the house."

"He was just a poor animal that had to go out sometimes."

"And mess up the streets something awful?"

"Well," he said, "it's a problem. I just wanted to tell you how I feel."

"You didn't tell me," I said. "How do you feel?"

"I feel like bustin' your head," he said, and showed me a short length of pipe he had brought along for the purpose.

"But of course if you do that you're going to get your ass in a lot of trouble," I said.

"I realize that."

"It would make you feel better, but then I own the jail and the judge and the po-lice and the local chapter of the American Civil Liberties Union. All mine. I could hit you with a writ of mandamus."

"You wouldn't do that."

"I've been known to do worse."

"You're a black-hearted man," he said. "I guess that's it. You'll roast in Hell in the eternal flames and there will be no mercy or cooling drafts from any quarter."

He went away happy with this explanation. I was happy to be a black-hearted man in his mind if that would satisfy the issue between us because that was a bad-looking piece of pipe he had there and I was still six thousand dogs ahead of the game, in a sense. So I owned this little city which was very, very pretty and I couldn't think of any more new innovations just then or none that wouldn't get me punctuated like the late Huey P. Long, former governor of Louisiana. The thing is, I had fallen in love with Sam Hong's wife. I had wandered into this store on Tremont Street where they sold Oriental novelties, paper lanterns, and cheap china and bamboo birdcages and wicker footstools and all that kind of thing. She was smaller than I was and I thought I had never seen that much goodness in a woman's face before. It was hard to credit. It was the best face I'd ever seen.

"I can't do that," she said, "because I am married to Sam."

"Sam?"

She pointed over to the cash register where there was a Chinese man, young and intelligent-looking and pouring that intelligent look at me with considered unfriendliness.

"Well, that's dismal news," I said. "Tell me, do you love me?"

"A little bit," she said, "but Sam is wise and kind and we have one and one-third lovely children."

She didn't look pregnant but I congratulated her anyhow, and then went out on the street and found a cop and sent him down to H Street to get me a bucket of Colonel Sanders' Kentucky Fried Chicken, extra crisp. I did that just out of meanness. He was humiliated but he had no choice. I thought:

I own a little city
Awful pretty
Can't help people
Can hurt them though
Shoot their dogs
Mess 'em up
Be imaginative
Plant trees
Best to leave 'em alone?
Who decides?
Sam's wife is Sam's wife and coveting
Is not nice.

So I ate the Colonel Sanders' Kentucky Fried Chicken, extra crispy, and sold Galveston, Texas, back to the interests. I took a bath on that deal, there's no denying it, but I learned something—don't play God. A lot of other people already knew that, but I have never doubted for a minute that a lot of other people are smarter than me, and figure things out quicker, and have grace and statistical norms on their side. Probably I went wrong by being too imaginative, although really I was guarding against that. I did very little, I was fairly restrained. God does a lot worse things, every day, in one little family, any family, than I did in that whole little city. But He's got a better imagination than I do. For instance, I still covet Sam Hong's wife. That's torment. Still covet Sam Hong's wife, and probably always will. It's like having a tooth pulled. For a year. The same tooth. That's a sample of His imagination. It's powerful.

So what happened? What happened was that I took the other half of my fortune and went to Galena Park, Texas, and lived inconspicuously there, and when they asked me to run for the school board I said No, I don't have any children.

WILLIAM BRAMMER

The Gay Place

The country is most barbarously large and final. It is too much country—boondock country—alternately drab and dazzling, spectral and remote. It is so wrongfully muddled and various that it is difficult to conceive of it as all of a piece. Though it begins simply enough, as a part of the other.

It begins, very like the other, in an ancient backwash of old dead seas and lambent estuaries, around which rise cypress and cedar and pine thickets hung with spiked vines and the cheerless festoons of Spanish moss. Farther on, the earth firms: stagnant pools are stirred by the rumble of living river, and the mild ferment of bottomland dissolves as the country begins to reveal itself in the vast hallucination of salt dome and cotton row, tree farm and rice field and irrigated pasture and the flawed dream of the cities. And away and beyond, even farther, the land continues to rise, as on a counterbalance with the water tables, and then the first faint range of the West comes into view: a great serpentine escarpment, changing colors with the hours, with the seasons, hummocky and soft-shaped at one end, rude and wind-blasted at the other, blue and green, green and gray and dune-colored, a staggered faultline extending hundreds of miles north and south.

This range is not so high as it is sudden and aberrant, a disorder in the even westerly roll of the land. One could not call it mountain, but it is a considerable hill, or set of hills, and here again the country is transformed. The land rises steeply beyond the first escarpment and everything is

40

changed: texture, configuration, blistered façade, all of it
warped and ruptured and bruise-colored. The few rivers run
deep, like old wounds, boiling round the fractures and revealing folds of slate and shell and glittering blue limestone,
spilling back and across and out of the hills toward the lower
country.

The city lies against and below two short spiny ribs of hill.
One of the little rivers runs round and about, and from the
hills it is possible to view the city overall and draw therefrom
an impression of sweet curving streets and graceful sweeping
lawns and the unequivocally happy sound of children always
at play. Closer on, the feeling is only partly confirmed,
though it should seem enough to have even a part. It is a
pleasant city, clean and quiet, with wide rambling walks and
elaborate public gardens and elegant old homes faintly ruined
in the shadow of arching poplars. Occasionally through the
trees, and always from a point of higher ground, one can see
the college tower and the Capitol building. On brilliant mornings the white sandstone of the tower and the Capitol's granite dome are joined for an instant, all pink and cream,
catching the first light.

On a midsummer morning not very long ago the sun advanced on the city and lit the topmost spines of hill, painting
the olive drab slopes in crazy new colors, like the drawing of
a spangled veil. Then the light came closer, touching the tall
buildings and the fresh-washed streets. The nearly full-blown
heat came with it, quick and palpitant. It was close to being
desert heat: sudden, emphatic, dissolving chill and outdistanc-
ing rain. . . .

It was neither first light nor early heat that caused the two
politicians to come struggling up from sleep at that hour, but
an old truck carrying migratory cotton pickers.

The younger of the two politicians was named Roy Sherwood, and he lay twisted sideways in the front seat of an automobile that was parked out front of an all-night
supermarket. Arthur Fenstemaker, the other one, the older
one, floundered in his bedcovers a few blocks distant in the
Governor's mansion.

The old truck banged along the streets, past dazzling store
fronts andthe Juicy Pig Stand and the marble façades of
small banks in which deposits were insured to ten thousand
dollars. The dozen children in the back of the truck had been
first to come awake. They pulled aside the canvas flaps and

peered out at the city, talking excitedly, whooping and hee-hawing as the old truck rolled north, straining, toward the Capitol grounds and the Governor's mansion, where Arthur Fenstemaker slept, and the supermarket where Roy Sherwood's car was parked.

The truck came to a sudden stop and began, with a terrible moaning of gears and transmission, to back into a parking space next to Roy Sherwood's car.

Roy heard the commotion and blinked his sore eyes in the early light. He struggled to untangle his long legs from between the steering wheel and seat cushion, and he was able, finally, to sit up and examine the truck. He unrolled a window and leaned his head out, taking deep breaths, blinking his eyes. The children in the truck watched him gravely for a moment and then began to giggle. Their laughter subsided abruptly when Roy called out to them *"Buena día . . ."*

There was silence and then a small voice answered back: *". . . día . . ."*

Roy smiled and opened the car door. He stood on the cool pavement for a moment, weaving slightly, trying to hold his balance. He was dizzy with fatigue and an hour's poor sleep and possibly a hangover. "One hell of an awful *día*," he muttered under his breath. The children were laughing again, and fairly soon he began to feel better. The driver of the truck climbed down and came round to Roy's side to stare at him. The fellow had a murderous look—a bandit's look. He was wearing a wrinkled double-breasted suit coat over what appeared to be a polo shirt and uncommonly dirty and outsized denim slacks. He stared at Roy with his bandit's eyes until Roy lifted his hand in a vague salute. Then the Mexican smiled, showing hilarious buck teeth, lifted his arm in the same indecisive gesture and almost immediately turned and walked toward the supermarket, flapping his feet in gray tennis shoes.

The children attempted to engage Roy in conversation. Roy came closer to the back of the truck, trying to understand some of it, cocking his head and listening carefully and interrupting now and then: *"Qué? . . . Cómo? . . . Despacio,* for chrissake, *despacio . . ."* The children giggled hysterically; two or three adults in the front cab stared at him, looking uneasy, and finally Roy gave it up and waved good-bye and wandered into the supermarket.

The inside of the store was aglow with yellow light. Every-

thing was gorgeous and brightly packaged. Only the
people—the cashier and the Mexican gathering breakfast
staples and Roy himself—seemed out of phase with the pre-
dominating illusion. Roy looked all around, examining the
market with as much wonder and concentration as might
have been demonstrated in viewing Indian cave mosaics or a
thousand-years-old cathedral. He stared all around and then
he uncapped a bottle of milk and tore open a bag of cinna-
mon buns. He wandered over the market eating and drinking,
pausing occasionally to stare enraptured at a prime cut of
beef or a phonograph album or a frozen pizza or a stack of
small redwood picnic tables. There seemed no limit to what
the market might conceivably have in stock. Roy decided the
pussy willow cuttings were his favorite; they were a little fantastic: out of season, out of habitat. . . . He wondered if the
pussy willow had been shipped fresh-frozen from the East,
like oysters or cheese blintzes. He moved on; he had something else in mind.

He located this other without difficulty—a tall pasteboard
box containing twenty-four ice-cream cones, maple flavored.
The box of cones was part of it; the plastic scoop stapled to
the outside of the box solved the next most immediate problem. He carried the cones and the scoop to the cashier and then
went back to pick up two half-gallon cartons of ice cream.

Outside again, at the back end of the truck, the children
and two or three of the older Mexicans crowded round to
watch. Roy left off serving after a while, letting one of the
older girls take his place. There were a few accented whoops
of *Ize-Cream . . . Aze Creeem,* but the children were unusu-
ally quiet for the most part, sweetly, deliriously happy waiting in line to be served. Presently, he returned to his car and
sat in the driver's seat to watch. One hell of a crazy *día,* he
reminded himself. Not to mention the *día* before and the
night or the goddam *noche* in between.

He turned now and looked in the backseat. It was all
there. . . . All of it. . . . All his art objects purchased during
his twelve hours' travel on the day before: the button-on
shoes, the iron stew pot, the corset model, the portrait of
President Coolidge, the Orange Crush dispenser with its
rusted spigot, part of an old upright piano. Everything except
. . . But he remembered now. The television set, one of the
earliest models, big as a draft animal, with a seven-inch picture tube . . . He'd left it in knee-high Johnson grass fifty

miles outside town. He grunted to himself, thinking of the television set: it was a terrible loss; he'd been blinded by the wine on the day before and thoughtlessly left the television behind. He grunted again and re-examined his treasure in the backseat.

The Mexican children were finished with their ice cream, and he could hear their singsong voices rising in volume. The elder, the old bandit in gray tennis shoes, came out of the supermarket carrying his grocery sack. He moved past Roy, nodding, showing his wonderful teeth.

"You need a stew pot?" Roy said suddenly.

The Mexican was jerked back as if suspended by a coil spring. His face twitched, but he managed to smile and mumble an incomprehensible something in Spanish.

"Stew pot," Roy repeated. "Fine piece of workmanship . . . You need one? For free . . . *por nada* . . . *Tiene usted una stew pot-to?*"

The old Mexican gasped in alarm, altogether mystified. Roy climbed out of the car and opened the back door, pointing to the soot-covered vessel. It was very much like the ones in which neighborhood washerwomen had boiled clothes during his childhood. He loved the stew pot. But now he knew he must *make the gesture*. It was part of being a public figure. He addressed the Mexican: "Here . . . You want it? Desire you the stew pot?"

Roy struggled with the pot; it was big as a washtub. The old man accepted it on faith, smiling as if vastly pleased. He bowed politely and turned toward the truck, carrying the stew pot with great dignity. The children in back greeted him with strident questions. Roy sat in the front seat of the car and watched, wondering if he ought to make a speech. They'd never understand a word, but he could make pleasant sounds. It was no matter. His Mexicans back home never understood anything, either. You just paid their poll taxes and showed them where to mark ballots when election time came round. He'd made a speech the night before. One of his best. Parked alongside a narrow river, he and the girl had lain on a picnic blanket and finished the last of the wine and the chicken. Then he had climbed a huge magnolia tree and plucked a great white bloom from the top, before descending to one of the lower limbs to make the presentation speech. He'd never been in better form. Though there had been some difficulty about addressing the girl. Using her name seemed to take all the fire out of the occasion. "Ladies . . ." he had said in the beginning, but it wasn't quite right. Nor "Fellow ladies . . ." He'd made a number of attempts: "Dear Lady" and "Most High and Mighty Ouida, Bride of My Youth, My Rock, My Fortress, My Deliverance, Horn of My Salvation and My High Tower . . ." But that had been too excessive for what, basically, was meant to be a ceremony of some dignity and restraint. He'd finally called her "My Dear Miss Lady Love. . . ."

He thought he might step outside the car and possibly stand on the Orange Crush dispenser, addressing the Mexican children briefly, but after a moment the truck started up with a great thrashing sound and began backing out of the driveway. Roy sat for a moment, rubbing his eyes, and then he got his own car started and proceeded slowly down the main street of the city behind the truck carrying the cotton pickers. After a block or so, he grew impatient with the business of waving at the children, and nodding, and blinking his lights, and waving again; and finally he raced the car's engine and passed them by. A noisy, high-pitched cry came from the children; their flapping arms caught his vision briefly through the side windows. He grinned oafishly, studying his face in the mirror. "I have a way with crowds," he said aloud to himself. "I have gifts of rare personal magnetism. . . ." He listened to the dying cheers from in back, and he thought he detected a clanging in the midst of it, a series of bell tones, deep and dull and flattish, metal on metal. My old iron stew pot, he thought . . .

Arthur Fenstemaker heard the cheers and the children's laughter and the groan of the truck's motor blended with the blows struck on the stew pot. He lay in his bed on the second floor of the Governor's mansion and listened thoughtfully. He was reminded for a moment of an old International he'd driven in the fields years before. The Mexicans were blocks away now, and he opened his eyes, still wondering over the sound from the street below. He reached for cigarettes and matches. After a moment he lay back in the bed, gasping for breath. He left the cigarette burning in a tray and pulled himself closer to Sweet Mama Fenstemaker. His right arm was pressed under his own huge weight, but he did not want to turn away just yet. Sweet Mama smelled goddam good; she nearly always perfumed herself at bedtime.

The Governor lay like that for several minutes, listening for sounds in the house or from the street, pressing his big nose against his wife's skin, until the kitchen help began to arrive downstairs. Then he rolled off the bed and went to the bathroom. He brushed his teeth and smoked another cigarette; he swallowed pills and massaged his scalp and began to stalk about the second floor of the mansion. He looked in on his brother: Hoot Gibson Fenstemaker lay sleeping quietly, knotted in bedclothes. The Governor turned back to his dressing room and stared at himself in a full-length mirror, sucking in his stomach, shifting from side to side. He slipped on gartered hose and shoes and a robe, and again stood listening, leaning over a stairwell and cocking his head. Soon he could hear the limousine being eased into position on the concrete drive. Fenstemaker strode down to the end of the hall and opened a casement window. A highway patrolman circled the car, examining tires, polishing chrome. The Governor put his head through the window and yelled: "Hidy!"

The patrolman looked up, squinting against the sun, trying to smile.

"Hah'r yew, Mist' Fenstemaker," he said.

"Nice mornin'," the Governor said, looking around.

"Hassah!" the patrolman said.

The patrolman stood on the concrete apron, gazing up at the Governor. He kicked a tire with the heel of his shoe; he patted a fender of the car. He stared at the Governor, and finally added, ". . . Sure nice one . . ."

Fenstemaker turned his head, looking over the city from the second-story window. The mansion was constructed along Georgian lines and was situated on a small rise that placed it nearly level with the Capitol dome and some of the office buildings downtown. Mist blurred the hilltops to the west, and occasionally, a mile or more away, lake water flashed in the sun. The smell of flowers, blooming in profusion in the backyard garden, was fused with the harsh bouquet of compost heaps and kitchen coffee. Fenstemaker pinched his big nose and took deep breaths. The patrolman continued to gawk at him.

"I'm not goin' anywhere right off," Fenstemaker said.

He pulled his head back inside and rang for his coffee. He sat at a desk in his study and shuffled through papers. The butler arrived with a small coffeepot, dry toast, juice, and a half-dozen newspapers.

"You had your breakfast?" Fenstemaker said. "You had your coffee?"

"Yessir," the butler said.

Fenstemaker sipped his coffee and shuffled papers.

"I hope it was better than this," he said. "Siddown and have some more."

The butler poured himself a cup and stood blowing on it, waiting.

"Siddown for Christ sake," Fenstemaker said.

"Yes sir."

"Goddam."

"Sir?"

"I'm just goddammin'."

"Yes sir."

"Let's get a new brand of coffee," Fenstemaker said. He made a face.

"I'll tell the cook."

"Nothin' tastes like it used to," Fenstemaker said. "Not even vegetables."

"Sweet potatoes especially," the butler said.

"Not even goddam sweet potatoes," Fenstemaker said.

The two of them sipped coffee. The Governor turned through the newspapers, talking but not looking up. "You think it's gettin' better?"

"What's that?"

"Bein' a colored man. You think it's any better?"

The butler looked at him desperately. "I got a good job," he said.

The Governor did not seem to pay attention. He went on talking and turning pages. "Maybe little better, I guess. . . . Discussions goin' on. . . . Least *that's* not like it used to be. Hell! I remember old Pitchfork Ben Tillman—the things he said . . ." Fenstemaker broke off momentarily, peering at the newsprint, then went on: "Of course bein' better still don't make it very good. I was thinkin' yesterday, signin' my mail, how I'd feel if I wrote a public official about, you know, my rights? I was lookin' over what I'd been sayin'. 'Well now this sure is a problem, involvin' grave emotional questions, and we can't tolerate havin' second-class citizens in this free country and I'm sure gonna do what I can. . . . Try to make reasonable progress toward a solution. . . . Sure keep your views in mind. . . .' Why *God damn!* Some cornpone Buddha say that to *me,* I'd set a bomb off under him."

The butler grinned. "I think most colored people vote for you," he said. "Even when you don't say things exact . . ." He began gathering cups and saucers.

"I'm a damned good politician," Fenstemaker said. "I know how good I am and I ain't doin' much, so what about the others not so good? Goddam and hell!"

"You want another pot?" the butler said.

"Yes," the Governor said. "Switch to that ersatz stuff—I think it's probably better than this. . . . And some fruit. They got any watermelon down there?"

"I'll see," the butler said. "They don't, we get you some."

The Governor's brother, Hoot Gibson Fenstemaker, appeared at the door. He rubbed his eyes and smiled, looking deranged. "You get me some coffee, Jimmy?" he said. The butler nodded, carrying the tray. Hoot Gibson stepped inside.

"Mornin' Arthur."

"You enjoy that party last night?" the Governor said.

"Sure did. I like parties here."

"I think you danced with every lady."

"I think I did," Hoot Gibson said. "I liked that orchestra, too. It was like Wayne King."

"I remember at college you had some Wayne King records," the Governor said, looking up from the papers. "And Henry Busse. What in hell ever happened to Henry Busse?"

"He dead?" Hoot Gibson said. He thought a moment. *"Hot Lips!* I booked old Henry Busse once for the gymnasium. A dance. Made two hundred dollars promoting old Henry Busse . . ." Hoot Gibson's eyes went cloudy, thinking about Henry Busse. He sipped from his brother's coffee cup.

Fenstemaker looked up patiently. "Don't make that noise," he said. Hoot Gibson gripped the cup with both hands and stared at the coffee. The Governor read the papers. Hoot Gibson picked up one of the sheets and glanced over the headlines. "I think I got a hangover," he said.

The Governor cleared his throat but did not comment.

"I might go back to bed awhile," Hoot Gibson said.

"Take some aspirin and sleep another hour," the Governor said.

Hoot Gibson stood and stretched and scratched himself. He loosened the drawstring on his pajamas and retied it. "I think I'll do that," he said. ". . . You got anything for me today?"

The Governor looked up and said: "You remember that fellow talkin' to me and Jay last night? Up here—out on the screen porch?"

"That new lobbyist?"

"That's the one."

"I know him. He's workin' the Capitol nearly every day now."

"Well suppose you keep an eye on him," the Governor said. "Follow him around. Or get someone to do it for you. Find out where he goes, who he's seein'. Do that today and tonight. Maybe tomorrow. Don't for God's sake let him know he's bein' watched. Give me a report—and don't come around *tellin'* me about it. Write it up."

Hoot Gibson looked vastly pleased. He vanished down the hall, humming to himself.

The Governor signed some papers. He looked at the clock—it was nearly seven; nearly nine in the East. He reached for the phone and got the long-distance operator, making notes of persons he could call in the Eastern time zone. He talked with an economist in New York. They discussed investments; Fenstemaker asked questions about the stock market; he complained that none of the big investors seemed interested in municipal bonds. "I got some mayors in trouble," he said. "They need help. You got any ideas?" He listened to the economist's ideas. They complained to each other about the goddam Republican high interest rates.

Fenstemaker rang off and placed more calls; he talked with his two senators, a union official in Philadelphia, a college professor in Boston. The professor was a nephew whom he'd put through college a half-dozen years before. "Listen," the Governor said, "those are wonderful speeches you been sendin' down—especially if I was runnin' in Oyster Bay or Newport. But I'm not, happily. Try to remember I'm way the hell down here in coonass country. . . . You forget your beginnin's? You need a little trip home? Might do you good. . . . I need some ideas. . . . You got good ideas. . . . But I want 'em in speeches that sound like Arthur Fenstemaker and not some New goddam England squire. . . ."

He completed the calls and turned back to the papers on his desk. An assistant had left him a note attached to a hand-written letter: *"This may interest you, though I advise against reading it when you're trying to shake off a low mood. It is very sad."*

He read the letter attached:

> *Sirs:*
> *We the people of the 9th grade Civics class at Hopkinsville feel that you the people of the Government should try to conquer the world here before you try to conquer outer space. We feel that there may be some kind of gas on the moon that is under the surface and if a rocket hit it, it may open the surface of the moon and these gases may escape and get into our own environment and kill us. So we feel that you should leave well-enough alone. We feel that if the Good Lord had wanted us to conquer outer space he would have put here on earth instruments instead of people. We would like to know what you think about this issue.*
>
> > *Sincerely,*
> > THE 9TH GRADE CLASS

Fenstemaker rubbed the back of his neck and pulled on his nose and sat staring at the names of the 9th Grade Class at Hopkinsville. He put the letter down and reached for the phone.

"Jay . . ."

Jay McGown's voice came to him feebly; then it got stronger. There was music being played on the radio in Jay's room. The music ended and an announcer talked about a cure for piles.

"Sir?" Jay was saying. ". . . Sir?"

"What in hell's goin' on there?"

"Sir?"

"You think we got a chance on that school bill?"

"School bill? Sure we got a chance," Jay said.

"I got your note and that letter," the Governor said.

"Ah."

"Let's take a run with that bill this week," Fenstemaker said.

"You think this week's really the best time?" Jay said. "Old Hoffman's still in the hospital. We'd need him. He wrote the damn thing. At least his name's on it."

"Who's that? Who wrote it, then?"

"A lobbyist for the schoolteachers. A lawyer from the education agency."

"Who else?"

"Me."

"Well let's take a run with it," Fenstemaker said.

"Who'll we get to floor-manage?"

"Who's on the committee?" the Governor said.

"You know that committee better than I do," Jay said.

"Name some," Fenstemaker said. "I forget."

"Who you want me to name?"

"Name some."

Jay named some of the members.

"They don't sound so good to me," the Governor said.

"They aren't," Jay said. "We'd probably end up with half a bill. Old Hoffman's not much, but he won't lose us any votes. He knows how to manage a bill."

"How 'bout Roy Sherwood?" Fenstemaker said.

"Roy's a good friend of mine," Jay said.

"So?"

"But he's not exactly one of our boys."

"Maybe he just never got invited in," the Governor said.

"He's pretty damned independent," Jay said. "And lazy. That's a bad combination."

Chimes from the college signaled the half hour. The high-way patrolman polished the limousine on the side drive. The butler came into the room with an enormous slice of water-melon. Fenstemaker broke off a piece with his hand and be-gan to eat. There was a silence on the phone while the Governor ate watermelon. Then he said: "He help write that bill? He do anything at all?"

There was another silence before Jay began to answer: "That's right. He helped a lot. Fact is, he was the only one on that lousy committee who gave a damn. With Hoffman gone."

"Well old Hoff got it reported out for us before he went to the hospital," Fenstemaker said.

"How'd you know about Roy?"

"It just sort of came to me in the night," the Governor said.

"Well I thought you might disapprove. My getting him to help us. He's a friend of mine, like I said, and we needed some help from someone on the committee. Desperately."

"All right," the Governor said. "That's just fine. I'm de-lighted. You think he could carry it?"

"I don't know. I really don't. He's never worked a bill in three terms here. I'm not even sure he'd accept the job."

"Well I'll just ask him and see."

"You think he could hold the votes we've got? He might scare some off."

"See about that, too," the Governor said. He paused, and then added: "He ain't worn himself out on Earle Fielding's wife, has he?"

There was a pause before Jay answered: "That piece of information just come to you in the night, too?"

"Everything does," the Governor said, his voice warm with pleasure. "Borne on the wind. Like a cherub. It do fly. . . . Listen . . . We'll just see how old Roy reacts. Okay? Take a little run. Pull out all the stops and try to get this thing through. Maybe tomorrow. We can't afford to wait much longer. They'll be building up opposition soon's it appears Hoffman's well. We put off any time, we lose votes and we lose hard cash in that bill. . . . You want some cash for Hopkinsville, don't you? We'll just have to get that goddam thing through in a hurry. Can't afford to have any great debates . . ."

Jay was silent on the other end of the line while Fenstemaker talked. Then the Governor rang off without formality. He dialed another number on the phone and waited during the six or seven rings. He pressed the disconnect and dialed again. After another interval, Roy Sherwood answered.

"What're you doin'?" Fenstemaker boomed.

"Sleeping," Roy Sherwood said. "Real good, too."

"Hell of a note," Fenstemaker said. "World's cavin' in all round us; rocket ships blastin' off to the moon; poisonous gas in our environment . . . Sinful goddam nation . . . laden with iniquity, offspring of evildoers. My princes are rebels and companions of thieves. . . ."

"*What?*"

". . . A horror and a hissing . . ."

"Who the hell is this?"

"Isaiah," Fenstemaker said. "The Prophet Isaiah."

"I'm going to hang up in just about three seconds," Roy said, "but first I'd really like to know who the hell this is?"

"Arthur Goddam Fenstemaker. Hah yew?"

"I think it really is," Roy said after a moment. "Governor? That you?"

"Come over the Mansion and see," Fenstemaker said. "You like watermelon? I got some damn good watermelon. You come over here and we'll break watermelon together."

Roy's response was plaintive but respectful: "It's awful early in the morning for breakfast."

"Nearly eight."

"I know," Roy said. "That gives me nearly three hours' sleep."

"Well, you're a young man. I needed five."

Roy was silent.

"You come over and talk to me about this bill?" Fenstemaker said.

"What bill's that?"

"That school thing you did for Jay. Damn good job."

"Thanks. I appreciate it. But what do you want to talk about?"

"About when you're gonna get off your ass and pass it for me."

"*Pass* it. Hell, I'm just the ghost writer. Passin' it is your—"

"I mean take charge in that madhouse."

"Hah?"

"I mean floor-manage for me."

"You sure you got the right man, Governor? I never in my life—"

"I got you, all right," the Governor said. "Roy Emerson Sherwood. Non-practicin' lawyer. Family's got cattle, little cotton. Never struck oil, though. Elected sixty-third Legislature. Reelected without opposition to sixty-fourth, sixty-fifth. Never did goddam thing here till you wrote that bill the other day. . . ."

"You got the right man, I guess," Roy said.

"You help me with that bill on the floor?"

"When you plan to bring it up?"

"Tomorrow."

"*Tomorrow!* Godalmighty—"

"Day after, maybe. Come on over here."

"Governor, I couldn't learn the *number* that bill, condition I'm in right now. Let me sleep a little. Just a little. Let me think about it."

"*Sinful* goddam nation . . . Laden with iniquity . . . My princes are—"

"All right," Roy said wearily.

"How you like your goddam eggs?" the Governor said.

JEROME CHARYN

The Catfish Man

Boomtown

1

There were nine Fannie Smiths in the Houston telephone book. I dialed them all from the air terminal and found six at home.

"Pardon me, but are you the Fannie who sold apples on top of the hill and took me for rides in your '67 Dodge? . . . Ma'am, don't call the police. It isn't necessary. I'm hanging up. . . ."

I wasn't discouraged. I copied down the addresses of the last three Fannies and rode out of the terminal in a taxi cab.

"Twenty-nine Braesbayou Yard."

That was the seventh Fannie on my list.

A boy answered the doorbell. "Grandma Fannie went to church," he said.

My Fannie couldn't have become a grandma in four years. I thanked the boy and got back into the cab.

"Driver, Little John Woods."

"Take you as far as Beechnut. Then you're on your own. Little John Woods is in Gurney. And Gurney impounds anything that moves. Got themselves one hell of a mayor. He's a pirate, that Lamar Jones."

"What is this Gurney, and why does it have its own mayor?"

54

"Ask Lamar."

He dropped me at Beechnut and I crossed over into a grassy area that was the beginning of Little John Woods. There was a sign stuck in the grass:

WELCOME TO GURNEY TOWNSHIP, USA

No Peddlers, No Paupers, No Rats,
and No Bare Feet Beyond This Point

It was like a small country of its own in the middle of Houston.

I saw Chryslers in the driveways. The houses were made of brick or wood that came from some extraordinary forest: it seemed as fierce as stone to the eye.

A cow walked in front of me with a bell on its throat.

It was a lovely, landlocked place, this Gurney, with Chryslers, cows, and no bare feet. I followed the road, thinking of Fannie Smith.

A brick-red car rattled alongside of me. I said hello. The men in the car didn't smile or touch their cowboy hats. It was the Gurney police. They scrambled out of the car, four men in brick-red shirts and rolled-up dungarees. They looked like divinity students.

"We don't allow paupers. Didn't you read the sign?"

"Who's a pauper?"

They plucked me into the car and drove me straight to city hall, which was a low building in the heart of Little John Woods, with a firehouse tacked onto it, a police barracks, a library, and a jail. I wasn't fingerprinted or anything. I was trundled over to the mayor, who was also the chief magistrate. I noticed the swelling of a pistol under his magistrate's shirt. Another divinity student, only Lamar Jones wore a mustache, like my brother Marvin.

"State your business."

"I'm in Houston to track down a friend."

"He's lying, Lamar," one of the deputies said. "I'll bet he's with the Scotch Tape Gang. . . . He walked into the woods on a scouting mission."

The mayor frowned. "Scotch Tape Gang? Does he look like a Meskin to you? Meskins don't have gray hair. But it's peculiar. . . . People never take walks in Little John Woods. Show me your driver's license."

"I don't have one. Your Honor, when I was nine and a half my father bought a car. A Plymouth. It had that emblem of a sailing ship on its hood. I sat in the back while a cousin tried to teach my father how to drive. . . . It was like being on a river. My father never learned to steer."

"You should have parked in the next township. You come waltzing in on foot, blaming your father, blabbing about this and that. That's why we have vagrancy laws. To protect us from drifters like you. The Court will please rise. . . . Jerome, I sentence you to six months in the city jail. . . . boys, get me a sandwich before I starve to death. . . . Court's adjourned."

Six months for stepping over the Gurney line?

I was thrown into a closet with a skinny Meskin by the name of Marcos. The dumb jail didn't even have a lock on the door. Marcos could wander through city hall and then return to his mattress in the closet. No wonder the deputies latched on to me. The jail wouldn't have been complete without its two convicts. The township would have to send all other vagabonds away.

Marcos was a ward of Little John Woods. He lived at the jail most of the time, as an incorrigible boy. He wasn't born in Gurney. The township had no Meskin district. He was from one of the barrios north of Little John Woods.

Convicts had to earn their keep. We were carpenters, plumbers, grocery boys, among other things. Now I understood my talk with the "judge." A driver's license wouldn't have saved my skin. Lamar would have found some excuse to hold me. He'd have made it illegal to wear yellow socks or have gray in my head. I couldn't have won against his penal code. Gurney depended on convict labor. Me and Marcos were the township's sanitation force.

Lamar didn't want to house and feed a gang of drudges that might become eyesores in Little John Woods, and destroy the rhythm of city hall. He must have figured that two slaves could run the show.

We fixed the pipes in Lamar's private tub at city hall, collected trash, painted the town's fences, mowed lawns, but our main concern was the gulley that ran through Little John Woods. Blackheart Bayou it was called, because of the bitter taste its water had. It would overflow the gulley walls during a hard rain, and the two of us would have to get down and sweep water and mud back into the bayou with enormous brooms.

The Meskin liked to call me Jeronimo, because it sounded better in his ear than Jerome. He was thirty-six, like me. He'd had a few months at Jeff Davis High, but his vocabulary was bigger than a boy from the Bronx who had catfish on his mind.

Marcos pitied me when I told him I'd never been married. He had wives in El Paso, Juarez, and Houston's Fifth Ward.

"How do you support them on a convict's pay?"

"That's easy. I have shares in nineteen oil wells."

"How much money have your wells brought in?"

The Meskin shrugged.

"Then your wives must support themselves."

"Hombre, I contribute whatever I can. . . ."

"What's this Scotch Tape Gang that Lamar's deputies tried to lay on me?"

"Bandits," Marcos said. "They murder gas station attendants and leave Scotch Tape on their mouths."

"Why Scotch Tape? Something to silence the dead?"

"Who knows? It could be a high-school trick."

I didn't care for such high schools. And I was too depressed to hunt for Fannie in my convict suit, overalls with the words PROPERTY OF LITTLE JOHN WOODS stenciled into the seat.

Stepping out of jail one morning, I looked up, and there was Fannie Brindle Smith. We'd been a few yards from each other during that first week of my labor for Lamar Jones. She hadn't noticed the hairy convict who trekked in and out of the closet, and I didn't stop to think that Fannie might be a clerk in the mayor's office.

"Fannie . . ."

Four years on the "rubber chicken circuit" must have diminished me somehow. Or was it my convict's overalls? Fannie didn't recognize the boy who'd robbed her apple barrel. But she looked again, and she laughed. She ran out from behind the mayor's counter at city hall to hug a convict with LITTLE JOHN WOODS on his ass.

We had sandwiches at the city's expense. Lamar didn't say a word. Fannie went in to have a talk with the mayor. Marcos kept winking at me.

"Hombre, he's going to give us the sewer detail for a

month. . . . That's the mayor's girl-friend you been kissing. It'll be cozy, you and Lamar sharing the same toothbrush."

"Marcos, shut up."

But the Meskin was right. Fannie didn't come out of the office. She stayed in there with Lamar. And we drove to Blackheart Bayou with our instructions for the day. We were scheduled to clear muck and dead frogs out of the gulley. The town lent Marcos its only pickup truck for our work in Little John Woods. Marcos had free use of the truck. He would ride out of Gurney and bring back an enchilada lunch.

My eyebrows were on fire. They'd burn around to the side of my head and scorch both my ears if I didn't get away from this damn township. I saw blood. I wasn't going to shovel dead frogs. "Marcos, help me escape. . . . I'll finance one of your oil wells, I swear. I have a bankbook under my pillow. It's yours."

The Meskin took black mud from the bayou and held it against my ears. My face began to cool.

"Lamar would love you to run. He'd throw a bounty on your head."

"Who's afraid of bounty hunters? Louisiana's looking for me. That's not all. There's a thug named Teddy in New York who'd chop off my nose for a nickel . . . and I'm on the navy's wanted list."

"Then why should you run, hombre, when you got a perfect hiding place in Little John Woods?"

"I'm not going to stick around while Lamar paws Fannie Smith."

2

Her eyes would lower the minute we marched into city hall. We'd come off the bayou with bags of dead frogs. I don't know what Lamar did with the frogs. The Meskin swore he had a deal with some company that turned the frogs into pocketbooks and stuffed toys.

I was out of Fannie's life. She was with that frog collector, Mayor Jones.

Why should I embarrass her with the sight of my convict's overalls? I used the jail's back door. The master wanted frogs? I dredged the bayou for those swollen-bellied creatures.

"Hombre, don't work so fast. One bag, two bags, but thirteen bags a day?"

It was the stench in my own black heart that got me to live around dead frogs. My face would disappear below the walls of Blackheart Bayou, and Marcos would have to call down into the hole.

"Eat an enchilada. It's good for you."

But I wouldn't climb out of that stinking hole. I took the enchilada and ate it with muddy fists.

"Marcos, I'm leaving Houston when my sentence is up."

"You crazy? This is boomtown. Everybody's coming here . . . and once Lamar has you, he doesn't let go. He'll give you another six months."

3

Curled up, a mattress away from Marcos, I had a dream after mucking through the bayou all afternoon. The frogs I'd bagged had come alive. They burst out of the sacks with a great push of their heads. It was raining frogs, like the bitter storms of old Egypt. Blood leaked from their bellies. And the frogs could talk.

"Jerome, come with me."

I got up off the mattress and followed that frog voice out of jail. The frog looked more and more like Fannie Smith. We crossed the woods and went into a cottage at the southern tip of Gurney.

"Sorry, Jerome. Lamar took an awful long time to pack. I couldn't invite you over with him in the house. He gets crazy when he's drunk."

We kissed like two lost children meeting in the woods. I shucked off the Gurney overalls. Then I heard a scream.

"The frogs," I said, clutching Fannie.

"It's Jessica. She's having a nightmare. She'll be all right."

I'd forgotten. Baby Jess. She stumbled out of the next room in girl's pajamas. A woman-child of eight. She didn't have chubby fingers anymore. She had crust in her eyes, and goddammit, she was hugging a teddy bear. I told myself I wasn't going to twitch over Jessica's bear. It hadn't come from my father's stock. Not all the teddy bears in the world were evil. Some of them had to be good.

"Where's Unca Lamar?" she said, measuring me with her brown eyes. Who was this old gray ears standing in his underpants in mama's living room?

"Lamar's moved out, honey. But you can see him tomorrow. . . . This is your uncle Romey. He carried you on his back a long time ago."

Uncle Romey? She didn't remember the lunatic from the Louisiana woods. Ignoring me, she took some macaroni salad from the fridge, fed herself and the teddy bear, and returned to bed. The bear had a strip of macaroni on its woolly mouth. It was nothing to smirk at. The messy face grew panther eyes in the dark.

Fannie shut the bedroom door, and we had the living room to ourselves. I sniffed the back of her neck like a prairie wolf. I'd come out of that grave in Blackheart Bayou to spend the night with Fannie. Would Lamar run a bed check at the jail? Who cares? They could come for me in the morning, bend me over the counter at city hall and break my arms and feet, as a lesson to future convicts that they were not to sully the women of Little John Woods. Let them break as many of my feet as they could find. My overalls were on Fannie's chair. My socks were in a corner of the room. I was sleeping at the cottage tonight.

El Coco

1

Funny guys in boots and pointed hats were skulking near the cottage window. You could see their shadows bump across the wall. Spotlights played on our ceiling. It was the sheriff of Harris County and his men. "What the hell are they looking for? The Russians and the Red Chinese?"

"El Coco," Fannie said.

The sheriff had mounted an invasion party at the edge of our woods for one stinking man? Who could be worth that much? Coco is wetback talk, an affectionate term for phantoms and spooks. El Coco was the leader of the Scotch Tape Gang. The sheriff's men thought the Phantom was hiding in our woods. Lamar didn't hinder their search.

Our mayor needed a friend. He'd rather walk with the sheriff than be on his own when the Houston police decided to squat at our borders in their baby-blue shirts. Stubborn bastards, they could wait six months for El Coco to come out of the woods. And we'd have a ring of cops around us.

But it didn't matter to El Coco. Baby-blue shirts or the

sheriff's men. Nobody could find him. The sheriff had blood-hounds and criminologists from Austin who understood every Chicano trick. The dogs screamed as they stepped in Black-heart Bayou. It was an unholy place for bloodhounds and men.

2

The dogs are gone, and the Meskin and me have the bayou to ourselves. We know how to skate along the surface. You have to chop with your ankles and glide with your hips, to crawl on mud. And that's when I figured the Phantom's no jerk. He's a mudcrawler too.

Marcos went off to get our enchilada lunch. And the logic of it smacked me behind the ears. There wasn't another mudcrawler in the neighborhood. Marcos was the Phantom. He had to be. While the sheriff poked with his spotlights and his dogs sank into the mud, El Coco lay on a mattress in city hall. It was a perfect cover. The Meskin would walk in and out of jail whenever he had the urge. He was Marcos the convict who did odd jobs for everybody in town.

I scrutinized El Coco after he returned. We got into our guacamole, and I said, "Does it take very long to find the right taqueria? You were in that goddamn pickup truck two hours."

The Meskin didn't answer me. He looked across the road. A tank was cruising in our woods, an old Ford with a cow-catcher in front that could have knocked a cottage down. We saw eight "roughriders" in the Ford, redneck high-school students from inside the Octopus somewhere (Octopus was the name we had for Houston in Little John Woods). They drove behind us, tossing beer cans at our heads. We ducked, and the cans fell into the bayou. They were on the prowl for wetbacks, convicts, and queers.

They charged out of their tank, grabbed us by the collar and whipped us against a tree. They took off their belts and smacked our backsides with the buckles. It was great fun. I'd have welts on my ass that Fannie could smooth with vanish-ing cream.

The roughriders made us undress. They started to judge our pricks, mocking us for the pubic hair we had, and the jiggle of our balls. I was waiting for El Coco. When the Phantom barked and jumped, I would go for their eyeballs.

The odds would shift from them to us. They had the tank with the cowcatcher, and we had the bayou. They'd be drinking black mud until their bellies burst. We would skate out of their reach while they floundered in Blackheart Bayou.

The Phantom got down on his knees. He prayed in Meskin for his deliverance. The roughriders laughed. That's when Lamar walked into the woods.

It wasn't the pistol he carried that frightened those boys. It was Lamar himself. They scuttled for their tank. "Dewey Jones," the mayor called.

A shiver went down the roughriders' backs. The mayor stopped them with a shout.

"Dewey Jones, come over here. That's public property you've been scarring up. Where's your sense of justice? Convicts aren't candy poles. Apologize. And quick. That gray boy is Jerome. And Marcos is the Mex."

"Sorry, Uncle Lamar," the tallest of them blubbered.

"Not to me, you dumb bird. Apologize to them."

The roughriders shook our hands. "Sorry, Marcos. Sorry, Jerome."

They weren't rednecks at all. They were from Little John Woods. They probably belonged to Arista, or some other honor society for youngsters from the Southwest. They loved to chase convicts, and bang into stray cows. Who was I to be so righteous about them? The Polish Baron from Music and Art. I was a hoodlum with an Arista pin for two and a half months.

Ah, I was mistaken in that Mex. El Coco wouldn't have gone down on his knees to high-school boys. Marcos was a jailbird who took long lunches, and that was it.

Maybe the Phantom was an Anglo: Lamar Jones, the mayor who robbed gas stations on the side. Goddammit, El Coco could be anybody. One of the sheriff's bloodhounds. Fannie. Or Jerome Charyn.

3

Jessica was almost nine. She couldn't get used to my presence in the cottage. She didn't say uncle, or daddy to me. I was the man who lived with her mama. The guy who belonged to Mayor Jones, her *Unca Lamar*. I was patient with her. She probably missed her true dad. Maynard the duck hunter. There were too many of her mama's boyfriends

around the cottage. First Unca Lamar. Now the convict with
mud on his pants. The forgotten one. Unca Romey.

So I decided to treat her to lunch.

"I have school today," she said.

"Come on . . . we'll go into the Mexican district. We'll
have some green sauce."

She didn't argue. But she wouldn't hold my hand. We were
both playing hooky. I should have been out on the bayou,
hunting dead frogs. The hell with it. This was Little John
Woods, where a convict could declare his own holiday.

We went into the barrio north of the woods. Never been to
these parts. All the houses were on stilts. Some of them had
refrigerators on the front porch. The roads were patches of
dirt. Children played in the shells of rusted automobiles that
rocked like squeaky carriages. No one waylaid us.

We wandered into a taqueria that existed on a sidewalk
made of wood. The taqueria was a dry-goods store as well as
a restaurant. It sold shirts and live parrots and a newspaper
called *El Norte*. You passed through a turnstile to get to the
tables. We weren't snubbed as gringos from Little John
Woods. The waitresses smiled at Jessica. And here, in this
taqueria with a wooden sidewalk, I could be her dad.

A fiddler played at lunch, a castaway from some ancient
mariachi band. He was feeble, and his elbow shook as he
scraped out his tune. He could have been a hundred or more.
The fiddler had a shiny skull. He serenaded Jessica, accompanying his fiddle with a warble he produced deep in his skinny
throat. It sounded like a rooster in agony. But Jessica enjoyed
it. He wouldn't accept a dollar from me. It was the old man's
pleasure to sing for such a pretty girl.

We had tortillas that tasted like Mexican hot dogs. Jessica
drank a glass of milk. Beer arrived in a pitcher that was dark
as the mud in our bayou. I swallowed it down with a lick of
salt, the blackest beer in the world.

A man came into the restaurant. He had a cape around his
shoulders that obscured most of his body. His head was
scrunched into the middle of the cape, and you saw eyebrows
and two ears. Those eyebrows must have revealed something.
The restaurant hushed. Men and women at the tables showed
their infants to him. He creased up his eyebrows, and the
men kissed the edges of his cape. El Coco. I didn't have to
stare at that turtlelike trundling of his head. Or his eyebrows.

And his ears. I noticed what was under the cape. He had
convict's pants.

Marcos.

That kneeling to the high-school boys was a sham. El Coco
wasn't going to give up his roost in the township to slap eight
yokels who meant nothing to him. He could have cut their
gizzards out, buried them under the cowcatcher. Then where
would he have to hide? So he trembled and prayed in Meskin
to high-school boys. And he sucked me in with that act of
his.

The Phantom sat down at one side of the taqueria. Idiot, I
should have paid the bill and run out with Fannie's daughter.
El Coco hadn't spotted us yet. But I swallowed my beer. The
cape dropped under his nose. His eyes fell on me. He was a
killer, all right. The handyman-convict had gone out of him.
The bones bristled above his jawline. He never even smiled.

Jessica wanted a beef taco. I told her shush and dragged
her through the turnstile, with the parrots near the window
squinting at us. We tramped down the wooden sidewalk and
stepped onto the road.

"Hold your horses," she said.

Could I hint that a murderer was on our tail, that I'd un-
masked the Phantom on his home grounds, and who could
tell what he might do? So I clutched her arm and pulled.

It wasn't my own craziness that compelled me out of the
taqueria, because a gang started to collect on the sidewalk.
The gang followed us. Muchachos with old, wrinkled faces.
I'd swear they were under twelve. Did they get those wrinkles
at some lost junior high? I kept pulling Jessica. "Run, run."
All I could think of was the damned Scotch Tape that went
over your mouth when you died. The streets were confusing.
I couldn't find the road that would take us back to our
woods. That little Meskin district swelled into row after row
of houses that looked the same. Refrigerators on the porches.
Stilts.

Jessica slapped at my fingers. "Let go of me."

Finally I had to carry her. The infants grew into an army.
They blocked the end of every street. I had nowhere to run
with Jessica.

Then that cape stood in front of us. El Coco. Jessica was
tired. She began to whimper out of crossness with me.

"Be still," I said. ". . . Please."

And I addressed the cape.

"Señor, she's a little girl . . . eight years old. She doesn't know a thing."

El Coco held the pockets of my shirt and shook them hard. "Pig, why did you come here?"

"Green sauce," I said. "Enchiladas . . . we wanted Mexican food."

"You should have rolled a tortilla in your backyard."

They tossed us into a beat-up station wagon. One of the infants drove. The tires bumped along the dirt, and soon we were out of the barrio. They let Jessica off a few yards from Fannie's cottage.

"Baby, go inside."

The Phantom punched me on the ear. "Shut your filthy mouth." The ear erupted into small explosions. I could feel the tremors in the roots of my nose. The tremors wouldn't stop. They were so violent, I was sure my ear and nose would break off and leave me with empty hinges on my face. The muchachos made fun of me. The tremors softened, and the wounded ear went to sleep.

The brat behind the wheel was a pro. The wagon swerved away from these woods and the independent village of Gurney, and brought us into the Octopus. We were on Bissonett. The infants shrank into their seats; this way the cops couldn't discover so many Meskins in one station wagon, and scream, "Scotch Tape Gang."

El Coco avoided Meyerland, where the Octopus could get at him from the sky with its helicopter patrols: Meyerland was where the gang had "hit" most often.

Marcos wouldn't talk to me. He was snug in that cape of his. The brat cruised round and round. Then El Coco touched his lip. He'd decided on a gas station near Houston Baptist College. I saw that attendant at the pumps. He was a boy. Blond and sweet. God, I wanted to yell. *Leave your money box and get the fuck out of there.* The Phantom shoved my face against the window.

"Look," he growled. "It's like the movies, you stupid prick." He didn't get out of the car.

The blond boy came over to the wagon. Sixteen. A sophomore somewhere. With a smile. The Phantom never had to open his door. A muchacho shoved a gun out the window. It was like a cap pistol, I swear. I heard two, three pops. Blood spilled from the side of the boy's face and splattered my window. His legs danced out from under him. That's when the

Phantom reached over me and held the dying boy by his ears, while a muchacho ran a sliver of Scotch Tape across his mouth and grabbed the money box. The Phantom let go, and the boy dropped softly to the ground. And we disappeared.

I was in some dumb fog, and then a fury ripped up out of me as we crossed the Buffalo Speedway. "Motherfuckers, tape my mouth too. . . . Go on."

"Hombre, it's not necessary," the Phantom said with a twisting smile. "You're one of us . . . our gringo accomplice."

"Why are you so sure I won't yell to the police?"

"Yell all you want . . . that nice little girl and her mama from city hall . . . hombre, do I have to show you what your yells will do?"

"Die," I said. "You and your children's army."

He laughed and put me out of his station wagon at the edge of Little John Woods.

WILLIAM EASTLAKE

The Bronc People

The two quiet Indians, resting in Z shapes, could watch and hear the shots going back and forth, back and forth, as in a Western movie. But suddenly someone was hurt and it wasn't like a Western movie now.

The two Indians had been watching from the peak of a purple New Mexican butte ever since the big white rider had driven his cattle up to the only active water hole in thirty miles and asked for water.

For two days now this forward-leaning rider with bright silvered trappings that exploded in the sun had allowed his horse to weave slowly in back of the herd; the easily distracted calves bunching to the rear, loitering then leaping ahead suddenly; the mother cows bawling for their young, turning back within the herd only to be pressed forward again in the great shove; the steers sensing the great drought ahead, pausing, tongues hanging, necks sagging, pointing rearward, red-eyed in retreat against the long dry march, quizzical, hesitant and defeated on the flank of the herd, hoping to be by-passed. The white-faced, now dust black-masked, wild-eyed heifers watched the rider, then fled frontward as his rope sang. The insulted, pride-hurt, wide-shouldered, and ball-heavy bull, forced to go now where he had not dictated to go, abused and coerced, lashed and driven toward a mad man-destiny of no water, tolling his big bellow of protest and outrage at the lead of the harem, the cows plodding, patient now, the steers following hesitant, the calves coy, tumbling,

67

skipping sometimes forward, quick and lost—they all bore the brand of the Circle Heart and they had all been without water for two days now.

"Perhaps that's true," the Indian who was on the highest part of the butte said. "But it's the other man's water. And I know the Circle Heart."

"You seem to know everything about everything," the second Indian said.

"I know how the Gran Negrito got this place and I know the Circle Heart."

"Yes, you seem to know everything about everything," the other Indian said.

"And I know how the Circle Heart will get it. They're getting it now."

The two Indians had been right in at the start of everything. They had been there when the two men had begun by talking sensibly. They were right there when they began raising their voices and they were right there when they raised their guns.

"The one who owned the water fired first."

"But not last."

The Indians had seen the man who owned the water go back in the red adobe house. They had seen the other man raise the gate to let his cattle in and they had seen the man in the house break a pane and heard him fire through the window. Then they saw the cattleman drop behind a rock and fire back. The Indians had not seen the man who went in the adobe house take a child from off the bed and put him under the bed before he started firing.

"Is the man inside the adobe house hit badly?" the Indian who was lowest on the butte asked.

"Yes."

"How can you tell?"

"Well, he seems to be firing faster," the other Indian said.

The child under the bed in the house sensed this too. Both of the men were firing much faster now. The boy's father had a lever-action Winchester and he swung the new shells in with a herky-jerky motion of his right arm. The child could not see this from under the bed but he could see the sudden brass empties that dropped around his head and he could smell the acrid gunpowder smell. He could see his father's boots moving quickly from position to new position and the floor becoming slick with something red and bright.

"Somehow I don't want to get in this one," the taller Indian said.

"Do you usually?"

"Yes, I usually do."

"Have you noticed," the shorter Indian said, "that our seat is not too good now, that the war has moved to the other side of the house? Do you think we should move with it?"

"I don't see why not."

The two Indians moved off the butte and, using the very high gray-green sage and orange, bloom-waving Cowboy's Delight for cover, got over to the other side of the rincon, where they found a good red rock to sit on. Their pants were very blue against it and their shirts were very yellow. Their wide Stetsons were so beaten up they weren't anything against anything. They both seemed tired.

"Are you bored?" the shorter Indian wanted to know.

"No."

"Have you noticed that the firing has become very irregular?"

"Yes, I've noticed that."

"Have you noticed the man on the outside seems to be winning?"

"Yes, I've noticed that."

"Do you think there'll be a result today?"

"Before the night, yes."

"Then it will be all settled today?"

"No, I don't think so."

"Can you see all right from your seat?"

"Perfectly."

The man who was supposed to be winning was firing from behind a sandstone concretion, almost round, that had come down from the Eocene cliff that circled around and made all of the firing echo. When the firing had started he told himself that all he was doing was answering back. That is, when someone insulted him he insulted back and when someone shot at him, if he had a gun, he shot back. Something like that, but actually without thought. Now he was only trying to pour enough fire, put enough shots, through the window so that he could get away with his cattle. This was the man who was supposed to be winning. He had been hit in the leg, not too badly; he could still move easily and it did not bother him at all. He had been in the last war, and in the infantry, too, but in this kind of fighting it did not help much. He had read some Western pulp stories that were supposed to be about things like this but they did not help at all. The thing he kept in mind was to fire back at the window that kept firing at him. That might stop it. Then he could trail back to the Circle Heart.

The man inside the house, who, according to the two Indians, was supposed to be losing, thought he was doing nicely. Actually, as the small boy under the bed noticed from watching the slipperiness on the floor increase, his father was not doing well at all. He had been hit seriously but did not feel it too much because he was feeling other things more. If only the intruder would leave. If only the first shot he had fired at the white man had had some effect. Now there was nothing to do except keep this up until something happened.

At the beginning he had tumbled a blue box of brass Remington 30-30 soft-point Kleen-Bore cartridges on the low oak table, and all during the fight he would pick them up in handfuls of six, which is what the lever action held, and jam them in the receiver. Now, near the ending, his wide black hand swept up the final six.

"One, two, three, four, five, six," the boy heard him say.

Actually it was the arm that had done the sweeping in of the shells. His hand did not seem to be working correctly any more. The long black arm had gathered the final shells in one big movement—sweep! At the same time a bullet hit into the adobe above the boy's head softly—thwang!

"Son? Son, it's going to be all right." The boy under the bed was too tensed to answer anyone.

The Indians had moved again and they were within a clump of sage on a small knoll now. The two Indians were Navahos and they remembered this place well from their fathers telling about it. This spring-fed, huge circle of green surrounded by mesa was where Many Cattle and Winding Water had hidden their band of Navahos in 1884. This was the place where the whites were not supposed to reach them, the place that the whites would not find. But they found it and burned everything down, the crops and the houses, and they took Many Cattle and Winding Water and their people to the stockade when they caught up with them, starving, at the Canyon de Chelly.

"Can you see all right?" the tall Indian asked. The tall Indian's name was President Taft.

"Very well," the short Indian said. The short Indian allowed the trader to call him My Prayer. They both had Indian names, too—Water Running Underneath The Ground and Walking Across A Small Arroyo. They both wore hats that were not smashed in at the top like white men's hats and they had on army surplus shoes and they both rolled cigarettes without taking their eyes off the spectacle they were watching.

"We could move down a little now, get closer now, without any danger I think," the taller Indian said. The taller Indian had just completed the manufacture of a cigarette entirely by feel and now he placed it in his mouth without ever seeing it. "Yes, I think we could move down closer."

"I guess I'm perfectly happy here," the shorter Indian said.

Inside the cabin that the Indians could see perfectly, the man was beginning to pick his shots. He was trying to place them carefully and he was trying to make each one important, as though each one were his last, which it very nearly was. He had even ceased the herky-jerky movement of throwing the shells into the chamber with a short swing of his right arm and he now worked the lever action more deliberately and certainly, as though he were opening and closing a safe containing precious things. The man he was shooting at was difficult to follow, but, despite the fact that the man was using smokeless powder, the man in the cabin could always tell where the other fired from last but never where he would fire from now, never where he was now. He could always see the two Indians, despite the fact that they kept changing their seats. They always seemed to select something on the rock balcony that gave them a perfect view no matter to which window he went. He had been tempted early in the fight to fire at least one shot close to the Indians simply because they were wherever he looked and because wherever he looked for the white man they were there, complacently, as though there were some law protecting them—two wild things out of season, or two people buying into this incident without payment. Now a shell was too expensive to waste on them. It was a silly idea anyway. Do people always get silly ideas when they are weak? Was it getting dark outside, out there, or was the weakness making everything turn to darkness?

"Son." His voice sounded weak and strange to himself. "Son, remember this." Or was the boy too small now to remember anything of this later, remember ever? "Son, remember this. Are you listening?"

No one answered him at all and then a bullet came through the window and made a strange sound as it slashed through the table.

The man who fired that shot wondered, now that the shooting had slowed down, whether that would hold things for a while, whether he might even now be able to get away, but a shot whee-ed near him as he moved quickly to new cover. He rested the New-Texan 35-caliber short-barreled Marlin saddle rifle between his knees and looked down on the house where he could see no one and wondered whether he would have to wait for darkness to escape with his animals. It was showing no signs of darkness yet. He looked hard at the windows to see if he could see someone there and then he looked up at the Indians who were always there. It would be nice to shoot at them, to do something with someone you could see. He toyed very briefly with the idea of firing at the Indians because they were there so damn comfortably as though they were two civilians inquiring the time in no-man's-land at the Battle of Gettysburg. Are people this curious? Indians are, I guess.

"Do you think it's right of us to do this?" the taller Indian said.

"Why not?"

"Watching?"

"Why not?"

"It's none of our business."

"Why not?"

"You're doing awfully well with the why nots."

"I don't think it will matter at all. I know it will not matter at all. It will come out the way it's going to come out whether we watch or not. It would not have made any difference whether anyone was watching when the whites drove us out."

"We're still here."

"I don't think we are. We're not Indians any longer."

"What are we then?"

The shorter Indian took his eyes off the battle a moment and studied his army surplus shoes. "I don't know," he said.

"Sure we're Indians."

The other Indian put his hand to his mouth and made a war-whoop noise like the one he had heard white children make in the streets of Albuquerque. "Indians! Here come the Indians!" he said.

"We speak Navaho."

"We're speaking it now."

"Then we must be Indians."

"Sure," the shorter Indian, whom the trader called My Prayer, agreed. "Sure we're Indians." And then for the first time he said something in English. "So what?" He ran it together so it sounded like some Navaho word. So whah. Sowhah. Sowah.

"I will tell you sowah," the Indian called President Taft said. "Do you know that, outside of a moving picture, they wouldn't even bother even to shoot at an Indian now?"

"That's perfectly all right with me."

"You don't understand. To them we have become nothing."

"Sowah?" the Indian called My Prayer said.

The white man who had come up fast and tired on a horse one hour ago to draw his first shot observed from his new position that he was close to the Indians. That was all right. If something happened they could testify in his favor. By moving up and over slightly to his right he could join them and find something out.

"Hi!" he said as he moved in ahead of the Indians' rock, still keeping the sage between himself and the house.

"Hello," the Indians said. They could speak four languages, through necessity: Navaho and Apache, which have the same root, Spanish, which most of the settlers were, and English, which was increasing all the time, and Zia Pueblo, which came in awfully handy in this location. That makes five languages actually, but two of these languages they spoke poorly, so they counted them as one. English and Pueblo were the two foreign languages that counted as one.

"Hello," they said in one of their poor languages.

"Hi," the white man repeated.

"It's a nice day," one of the Indians said.

"*Hace buen tiempo,*" the other Indian tried, not so sure of the white man's nation.

"No, it's a nice day," the white man said.

"It sure is," the Indian who had been correct said.

"Yeah," the white man said.

"You think it will rain?" the Indian who had been wrong said.

"It could," the white man said.

"You think it could not rain?"

"Sure it could not rain." The white man wondered what language he was speaking.

"You think it could snow?"

"Hardly, at this time of year." The white rider felt on firmer ground now.

"Yes, it could snow very hardly this time of year," President Taft said. The white man thought it would be nice if they could start all over again.

"We have been wondering what all the firing is about," the taller Indian said.

The white man pulled down on his cowboy hat. "So have I."

"Isn't it true," President Taft said, "isn't it true about all wars?"

"Isn't what true?"

"That no one knows what they're about?"

"No, it isn't," the Indian called My Prayer said. His partner, he thought, had a habit of trying to be wise by being very simple. "As long as people are involved they're about something."

"Now, that is a bright remark," the other Indian said. His partner, he thought, would go a lot farther if he did not try to be so stupid that he appeared solemn. "I can tell you what this one is about."

"What?" The white man parted the rabbit brush.

"Well, you wanted to water your cattle."

"And?" The white man picked up his gun, held the brush, and looked down on the house.

"Do you have to fire that thing here in front of us?"

"I have to fire back."

"Why?"

"So I can get away with my cattle."

The two Indians looked at each other. "All right," My Prayer said. "Fire away."

There was a soft click in front of the Indians.

"What happened?"

"A misfire."

"Try another bullet."

"The empty shell has jammed."

"Let me see the gun."

The white man below the Indian on the rock passed the gun up to My Prayer, who passed it on to President Taft, who broke off a greasewood twig and inserted this in the ejector while he hit the side of the cartridge case with the big palm of his right hand. The misfire fell out and he levered in another shell and passed the gun over to his partner, who passed it down to the white man.

"I think it should work all right now."

"Thank you," the white man said.

"It's perfectly all right. We're enjoying the show."

"But it's nice, decent of you, to take sides."

"But we're not."

"No, we're not," his partner agreed.

"You mean you'd do the same for that other—?"

"Certainly. Why not?"

"Yes, why not?" his partner said. "After all, why not?"

"I want you to try and remember who started this," the white man said from the brush. "It could be very important and I want to tell you that I don't like this at all."

"You've lost your nerve?" one of the Indians asked.

"I don't want to hurt anyone down there."

"Then why are you firing the gun?"

"So he does not fire at me."

The two Indians looked at each other.

"Oh," they said.

Below, the man that the white man above, talking to the Indians, did not want to hurt was hurt badly. But not quite so badly that he had not noticed the Indian on the rock fix a gun and pass it back down to someone in the brush. So the Indians had taken sides. Now at last he could fire at someone he could see. He raised the gun and rested it on the back of a piñon chair and got the bead right between the eyes of the tallest Indian. He could not pull the trigger. He wondered why. He tried to pull the trigger again and failed. He still had that much strength. He tested his trigger finger in the air. He still had that much strength all right. He lowered the gun and wondered why he could not shoot an Indian. He felt dizziness now and he wiped his forehead and looked around for the boy.

"Son!" he called. He could not remember now where he had put the boy. It was getting very dark. He had better light a lamp. He felt that the Coleman gasoline-pump lantern would be too much for him, so when he saw the tall, glass-chimneyed kerosene lantern, and so close too, he lighted that. He knocked the glass chimney on the floor, where it smashed, but soon he had a tall yellow flame going. Now he remembered where he had put the boy—under the bed. He had something important to tell him. He wanted to tell him to flee, run, get out, go southward again, but then, later on—finally, when he had grown, become a man—to reconquer this, to regain this—this island. This darkness. He waved the lantern weakly but it made no light. Where were all the green fields and the fresh water? Where was a small light to see the big West?

He slipped on something now and went down, the whole glass lantern smashing now where the fragile chimney had smashed before, the kerosene spreading out ahead of small pennants of flame and then licking up the walls, illumining in soft orange the books, the endless row upon row of books; tall books, wide books, thin and fat and leather books, green, red and paper books. The room, the house seemed made of books. Books, stacks of them building new rooms of books within book rooms. The flames eating upward now on books. The man on the floor wanted to tell the boy many many things but all he could say was, "Come back. Come back."

"He seems to have lighted a light."

"Yes, he's lit the light," the other Indian agreed.

"To read those books."

"What books?"

"Just books."

"What for?"

"They say he's a little crazy."

"He's got books of records too. Maybe he lit the light to play them."

"Why?"

"They say he's a little crazy."

"A houseful of books and records in the Indian Country. What's the world coming to?"

"They say he's a little crazy."

"Maybe that's why he took a shot at the white man. Maybe he thought someone was coming to do something about all those books and records."

"Yes. But I've been wondering. I been wondering why he doesn't take a shot at us."

"Why should he take a shot at us? Aren't Indians supposed to be a little crazy too?"

"I mean I fixed that gun for the white man right here in plain sight. He must have seen it." Both Indians dropped off the rock now, down behind the rock where they were out of sight. Now the white man came around the rock.

"The house is on fire!" he hollered. "Here, hold this gun. I suppose somebody's got to go down and try to get him out."

"Why?"

"God, you Indians are lunatics." The white man thrust his gun on them and took off on a long running lope down toward the burning house.

"I wonder what he meant by that?"

"Well, everyone that's different—"

"But our hogans aren't stacked with books and records."

"No, but we're Indians."

"Yes, that's true. We're Indians."

They watched as the white man rapidly approached the house and they both gave a jerk of surprise when he threw open the door and flung himself in. A wide sheet of golden flame leaped out when he opened the door but he went in anyway. Everyone was very strange today.

When the white man went in the front door the Indians noticed something run out the back. It was about the size of a good dog but it ran upright and very fast and soon it had disappeared out of sight over a small rise.

"Maybe we better catch it," the taller Indian said.

"Yes," the other Indian agreed, rising quickly. "It may be all there is left, all we have to prove to ourselves we're not absolutely—anyway, after an absolutely crazy day."

The Indians finally ran it down. They twisted and ran, twisted and ran until, at last, going up a long butte and after losing it and retracing it again and going up and down three arroyos and two mesas, they finally ran it down and carried it all the way to their wagon and put a tarp over it where it would be cool and started up their mules and were off to Canyon de Chelly.

"It's a he and he is black," the taller Indian said. "The man in the house was black so this is a black boy." He touched the tarp as the wagon bumped over a prairie-dog mound.

"Yes. And he is all that's left at the end of a very crazy day."

"We're left."

"Yes, that's true," the shorter Indian said.

"Do you think the white man is left?"

"There are plenty more."

"Yes. But what was it all about?"

"Haven't you seen a movie at the trader's? This was the same thing."

"You mean it was about nothing?"

"Not exactly. It means something to them."

"We've got to be generous."

"And understanding."

"Yes."

"I think this was about water. I think it was important to us before the white man came and the same thing is still the same and everything else is still the same."

"It's weird." He used the Spanish words, *"Es sobrenatural."*

"Yes."

"This is still the same," he said, motioning to the rocks and sky and sage around them. "And even this," he said, bending and allowing his hand to run through a wave of orange flame they rode through. "What do they call this flower?"

"Coyboy's Delight."

"They call everything by a different name but it's the same thing. And they call everything by a different time but it's the same time. Everything repeats. It would be no different if everything in every language and every time was called Cowboy's Delight."

The taller Indian realized that the shorter Indian still oversimplified a very complex thing to appear wise. Nevertheless, there was not much arguing with the idea that if a thing can happen it has happened, that if anything can go wrong it will, and there's nothing *sobrenatural* about this if you realize that there's a law governing everything, including Indians, and it's called Chance, sometimes God, but, according to this Indian, it might just as well be called Cowboy's Delight.

"That makes sense."

"Does their shooting it out back there make sense?"

"No. But maybe it makes sense to them."

"Now that they've taken it from us they'll fight over it with each other?"

"I hope there'll be some war surplus left over for us."

"There is," the Indian said, touching the bulge beneath the tarp.

"And I hope everything takes the pressure off us."

"It will," the Indian called President Taft said, staring away. "It's taken the pressure off us for quite a while now."

"Yes, that's true," the shorter Indian said.

The name of the shorter Indian was Walking Across A Small Arroyo, called My Prayer, and the taller Indian was Water Running Underneath The Ground, called President Taft. More important to them, they were going to Canyon de Chelly, but still more important, everything happened on a bright, shining, Western day, a clean, ordinary, happy, New Mexico afternoon. Even now, as the bright Indian wagon made its way through the rocks, the whole weird warp of the landscape, the entire gaudy, scintillant pattern of the West was still with them, changing yet unchanged, ending but unended. Recapitulant.

"All very well," Taft said. "But what will happen now to the Circle Heart?"

"What will happen to the Circle Heart should not happen to an Indian."

"The Circle Heart?"

"Yes. The children of the Circle Heart."

They went over a hiding undulation in the rolling sage and rock. They could see the Coyote Pass ahead, and the huge fire behind them became only a lingering pattern against the quiet blue sky.

RALPH ELLISON

Invisible Man

It goes a long way back, some twenty years. All my life I had been looking for something, and everywhere I turned someone tried to tell me what it was. I accepted their answers too, though they were often in contradiction and even self-contradictory. I was naïve. I was looking for myself and asking everyone except myself questions which I, and only I, could answer. It took me a long time and much painful boomeranging of my expectations to achieve a realization everyone else appears to have been born with: That I am nobody but myself. But first I had to discover that I am an invisible man!

And yet I am no freak of nature, nor of history. I was in the cards, other things having been equal (or unequal) eighty-five years ago. I am not ashamed of my grandparents for having been slaves. I am only ashamed of myself for having at one time been ashamed. About eighty-five years ago they were told that they were free, united with others of our country in everything pertaining to the common good, and, in everything social, separate like the fingers of the hand. And they believed it. They exulted in it. They stayed in their place, worked hard, and brought up my father to do the same. But my grandfather is the one. He was an odd old guy, my grandfather, and I am told I take after him. It was he who caused the trouble. On his deathbed he called my father to him and said, "Son, after I'm gone I want you to keep up the good fight. I never told you, but our life is a war and I

have been a traitor all my born days, a spy in the enemy's
country ever since I give up my gun back in the Reconstruc-
tion. Live with your head in the lion's mouth. I want you to
overcome 'em with yeses, undermine 'em with grins, agree
'em to death and destruction, let 'em swoller you till
they vomit or bust wide open." They thought the old man
had gone out of his mind. He had been the meekest of men.
The younger children were rushed from the room, the shades
drawn and the flame of the lamp turned so low that it sputtered on the wick like the old man's breathing. "Learn it to
the younguns," he whispered fiercely; then he died.

   But my folks were more alarmed over his last words than
over his dying. It was as though he had not died at all, his
words caused so much anxiety. I was warned emphatically to
forget what he had said and, indeed, this is the first time it
has been mentioned outside the family circle. It had a
tremendous effect upon me, however. I could never be sure
of what he meant. Grandfather had been a quiet old man
who never made any trouble, yet on his deathbed he had
called himself a traitor and a spy, and he had spoken of his
meekness as a dangerous activity. It became a constant puzzle
which lay unanswered in the back of my mind. And whenever things went well for me I remembered my grandfather
and felt guilty and uncomfortable. It was as though I was
carrying out his advice in spite of myself. And to make it
worse, everyone loved me for it. I was praised by the most
lily-white men of the town. I was considered an example of
desirable conduct—just as my grandfather had been. And
what puzzled me was that the old man had defined it as
treachery. When I was praised for my conduct I felt a guilt
that in some way I was doing something that was really
against the wishes of the white folks, that if they had understood they would have desired me to act just the opposite,
that I should have been sulky and mean, and that that really
would have been what they wanted, even though they were
fooled and thought they wanted me to act as I did. It made
me afraid that some day they would look upon me as a traitor and I would be lost. Still I was more afraid to act any
other way because they didn't like that at all. The old man's
words were like a curse. On my graduation day I delivered
an oration in which I showed that humility was the secret,
indeed, the very essence of progress. (Not that I believed
this—how could I, remembering my grandfather?—I only be-

lieved that it worked.) It was a great success. Everyone
praised me and I was invited to give the speech at a gathering
of the town's leading white citizens. It was a triumph for our
whole community.

It was in the main ballroom of the leading hotel. When I
got there I discovered that it was on the occasion of a
smoker, and I was told that since I was to be there anyway I
might as well take part in the battle royal to be fought by
some of my schoolmates as part of the entertainment. The
battle royal came first.

All of the town's big shots were there in their tuxedoes,
wolfing down the buffet foods, drinking beer and whiskey and
smoking black cigars. It was a large room with a high ceiling.
Chairs were arranged in neat rows around three sides of a
portable boxing ring. The fourth side was clear, revealing a
gleaming space of polished floor. I had some misgivings over
the battle royal, by the way. Not from a distaste for fighting,
but because I didn't care too much for the other fellows who
were to take part. They were tough guys who seemed to have
no grandfather's curse worrying their minds. No one could
mistake their toughness. And besides, I suspected that fighting
a battle royal might detract from the dignity of my speech. In
those pre-invisible days I visualized myself as a potential
Booker T. Washington. But the other fellows didn't care too
much for me either, and there were nine of them. I felt su-
perior to them in my way, and I didn't like the manner in
which we were all crowded toegther into the servants' elevator. Nor did they like my being there. In fact, as the warmly
lighted floors flashed past the elevator we had words over the
fact that I, by taking part in the fight, had knocked one of
their friends out of a night's work.

We were led out of the elevator through a rococo hall into
an anteroom and told to get into our fighting togs. Each of us
was issued a pair of boxing gloves and ushered out into the
big mirrored hall, which we entered looking cautiously about
us and whispering, lest we might accidentally be heard above
the noise of the room. It was foggy with cigar smoke. And already the whiskey was taking effect. I was shocked to see
some of the most important men of the town quite tipsy.
They were all there—bankers, lawyers, judges, doctors, fire
chiefs, teachers, merchants. Even one of the more fashionable
pastors. Something we could not see was going on up front.
A clarinet was vibrating sensuously and the men were stand-

ing up and moving eagerly forward. We were a small tight group, clustered together, our bare upper bodies touching and shining with anticipatory sweat; while up front the big shots were becoming increasingly excited over something we still could not see. Suddenly I heard the school superintendent, who had told me to come, yell, "Bring up the shines, gentlemen! Bring up the little shines!"

We were rushed up to the front of the ballroom, where it smelled even more strongly of tobacco and whiskey. Then we were pushed into place. I almost wet my pants. A sea of faces, some hostile, some amused, ringed around us, and in the center, facing us, stood a magnificent blonde—stark naked. There was dead silence. I felt a blast of cold air chill me. I tried to back away, but they were behind me and around me. Some of the boys stood with lowered heads, trembling. I felt a wave of irrational guilt and fear. My teeth chattered, my skin turned to goose flesh, my knees knocked. Yet I was strongly attracted and looked in spite of myself. Had the price of looking been blindness, I would have looked. The hair was yellow like that of a circus kewpie doll, the face heavily powdered and rouged, as though to form an abstract mask, the eyes hollow and smeared a cool blue, the color of a baboon's butt. I felt a desire to spit upon her as my eyes brushed slowly over her body. Her breasts were firm and round as the domes of East Indian temples, and I stood so close as to see the fine skin texture and beads of pearly perspiration glistening like dew around the pink and erected buds of her nipples. I wanted at one and the same time to run from the room, to sink through the floor, or go to her and cover her from my eyes and the eyes of the others with my body; to feel the soft thighs, to caress her and destroy her, to love her and murder her, to hide from her, and yet to stroke where below the small American flag tattooed upon her belly her thighs formed a capital V. I had a notion that of all in the room she saw only me with her impersonal eyes.

And then she began to dance, a slow sensuous movement; the smoke of a hundred cigars clinging to her like the thinnest of veils. She seemed like a fair bird-girl girdled in veils calling to me from the angry surface of some gray and threatening sea. I was transported. Then I became aware of the clarinet playing and the big shots yelling at us. Some threatened us if we looked and others if we did not. On my right I saw one boy faint. And now a man grabbed a silver pitcher from a table and stepped close as he dashed ice water upon him and stood him up and forced two of us to support him as his head hung and moans issued from his thick bluish lips. Another boy began to plead to go home. He was the largest of the group, wearing dark red fighting trunks much too small to conceal the erection which projected from him as though in answer to the insinuating low-registered moaning of the clarinet. He tried to hide himself with his boxing gloves.

And all the while the blonde continued dancing, smiling faintly at the big shots who watched her with fascination, and faintly smiling at our fear. I noticed a certain merchant who followed her hungrily, his lips loose and drooling. He was a large man who wore diamond studs in a shirtfront which swelled with the ample paunch underneath, and each time the blonde swayed her undulating hips he ran his hand through the thin hair of his bald head and, with his arms upheld, his posture clumsy like that of an intoxicated panda, wound his belly in a slow and obscene grind. This creature was completely hypnotized. The music had quickened. As the dancer flung herself about with a detached expression on her face, the men began reaching out to touch her. I could see their beefy fingers sink into the soft flesh. Some of the others tried to stop them and she began to move around the floor in graceful circles, as they gave chase, slipping and sliding over the polished floor. It was mad. Chairs went crashing, drinks were spilt, as they ran laughing and howling after her. They caught her just as she reached a door, raised her from the floor, and tossed her as college boys are tossed at a hazing, and above her red, fixed-smiling lips I saw the terror and disgust in her eyes, almost like my own terror and that which I saw in some of the other boys. As I watched, they tossed her twice and her soft breasts seemed to flatten against the air and her legs flung wildly as she spun. Some of the more sober ones helped her to escape. And I started off the floor, heading for the anteroom with the rest of the boys.

Some were still crying and in hysteria. But as we tried to leave we were stopped and ordered to get into the ring. There was nothing to do but what we were told. All ten of us climbed under the ropes and allowed ourselves to be blindfolded with broad bands of white cloth. One of the men seemed to feel a bit sympathetic and tried to cheer us up as we stood with our backs against the ropes. Some of us tried to grin. "See that boy over there?" one of the men said. "I want you to run across at the bell and give it to him right in the belly. If you don't get him, I'm going to get you. I don't like his looks." Each of us was told the same. The blindfolds were put on. Yet even then I had been going over my speech. In my mind each word was as bright as flame. I felt the cloth pressed into place, and frowned so that it would be loosened when I relaxed.

But now I felt a sudden fit of blind terror. I was unused to darkness. It was as though I had suddenly found myself in a dark room filled with poisonous cottonmouths. I could hear the bleary voices yelling insistently for the battle royal to begin.

"Get going in there!"

"Let me at that big nigger!"

I strained to pick up the school superintendent's voice, as though to squeeze some security out of that slightly more familiar sound.

"Let me at those black sonsabitches!" someone yelled.

"No, Jackson, no!" another voice yelled. "Here, somebody, help me hold Jack."

"I want to get at that ginger-colored nigger. Tear him limb from limb," the first voice yelled.

I stood against the ropes trembling. For in those days I was what they called ginger-colored, and he sounded as though he might crunch me between his teeth like a crisp ginger cookie.

Quite a struggle was going on. Chairs were being kicked about and I could hear voices grunting as with a terrific effort. I wanted to see, to see more desperately than ever before. But the blindfold was tight as a thick skin-puckering scab and when I raised my gloved hands to push the layers of white aside a voice yelled, "Oh, no you don't, black bastard! Leave that alone!"

"Ring the bell before Jackson kills him a coon!" someone boomed in the sudden silence. And I heard the bell clang and the sound of the feet scuffling forward.

A glove smacked against my head. I pivoted, striking out stiffly as someone went past, and felt the jar ripple along the length of my arm to my shoulder. Then it seemed as though all nine of the boys had turned upon me at once. Blows pounded me from all sides while I struck out as best I could. So many blows landed upon me that I wondered if I were not the only blindfolded fighter in the ring, or if the man called Jackson hadn't succeeded in getting me after all.

Blindfolded, I could no longer control my motions. I had no dignity. I stumbled about like a baby or a drunken man. The smoke had become thicker and with each new blow it seemed to sear and further restrict my lungs. My saliva became like hot bitter glue. A glove connected with my head, filling my mouth with warm blood. It was everywhere. I could not tell if the moisture I felt upon my body was sweat or blood. A blow landed hard against the nape of my neck. I felt myself going over, my head hitting the floor. Streaks of blue light filled the black world behind the blindfold. I lay prone, pretending that I was knocked out, but felt myself seized by hands and yanked to my feet. "Get going, black boy! Mix it up!" My arms were like lead, my head smarting from blows. I managed to feel my way to the ropes and held on, trying to catch my breath. A glove landed in my mid-section and I went over again, feeling as though the smoke had become a knife jabbed into my guts. Pushed this way and that by the legs milling around me, I finally pulled erect and discovered that I could see the black, sweat-washed forms weaving in the smoky-blue atmosphere like drunken dancers weaving to the rapid drum-like thuds of blows.

Everyone fought hysterically. It was complete anarchy. Everybody fought everybody else. No group fought together for long. Two, three, four, fought one, then turned to fight each other, were themselves attacked. Blows landed below the belt and in the kidney, with the gloves open as well as closed, and with my eye partly opened now there was not so much terror. I moved carefully, avoiding blows, although not too many to attract attention, fighting from group to group. The boys groped about like blind, cautious crabs crouching to protect their mid-sections, their heads pulled in short against their shoulders, their arms stretched nervously before them, with their fists testing the smoke-filled air like the knobbed feelers of hypersensitive snails. In one corner I glimpsed a boy violently punching the air and heard him scream in pain as he smashed his hand against a ring post. For a second I saw him bent over holding his hand, then going down as a blow caught his unprotected head. I played one group against the other, slipping in and throwing a punch then stepping out of range while pushing the others into the melee to take the blows blindly aimed at me. The smoke was agonizing and

there were no rounds, no bells at three-minute intervals to relieve our exhaustion. The room spun round me, a swirl of
lights, smoke, sweating bodies surrounded by tense white
faces. I bled from both nose and mouth, the blood spattering
upon my chest.

The men kept yelling, "Slug him, black boy! Knock his
guts out!"

"Uppercut him! Kill him! Kill that big boy!"

Taking a fake fall, I saw a boy going down heavily beside
me as though we were felled by a single blow, saw a
sneaker-clad foot shoot into his groin as the two who had
knocked him down stumbled upon him. I rolled out of range,
feeling a twinge of nausea.

The harder we fought the more threatening the men became. And yet, I had begun to worry about my speech again.
How would it go? Would they recognize my ability? What
would they give me?

I was fighting automatically when suddenly I noticed that
one after another of the boys was leaving the ring. I was surprised, filled with panic, as though I had been left alone with
an unknown danger. Then I understood. The boys had arranged it among themselves. It was the custom for the two
men left in the ring to slug it out for the winner's prize. I discovered this too late. When the bell sounded two men in tuxedoes leaped into the ring and removed the blindfold. I found
myself facing Tatlock, the biggest of the gang. I felt sick at
my stomach. Hardly had the bell stopped ringing in my ears
than it clanged again and I saw him moving swiftly toward
me. Thinking of nothing else to do I hit him smash on the
nose. He kept coming, bringing the rank sharp violence of
stale sweat. His face was a black blank of a face, only his
eyes alive—with hate of me and aglow with a feverish terror
from what had happened to us all. I became anxious. I
wanted to deliver my speech and he came at me as though he
meant to beat it out of me. I smashed him again and again,
taking his blows as they came. Then on a sudden impulse I
struck him lightly and as we clinched, I whispered, "Fake like
I knocked you out, you can have the prize."

"I'll break your behind," he whispered hoarsely.

"For *them?*"

"For *me*, sonofabitch!"

They were yelling for us to break it up and Tatlock spun
me half around with a blow, and as a joggled camera sweeps

in a reeling scene, I saw the howling red faces crouching tense beneath the cloud of blue-gray smoke. For a moment the world wavered, unraveled, flowed, then my head cleared and Tatlock bounced before me. That fluttering shadow before my eyes was his jabbing left hand. Then falling forward, my head against his damp shoulder, I whispered.

"I'll make it five dollars more."

"Go to hell!"

But his muscles relaxed a trifle beneath my pressure and I breathed, "Seven?"

"Give it to your ma," he said, ripping me beneath the heart.

And while I still held him I butted him and moved away. I felt myself bombarded with punches. I fought back with hopeless desperation. I wanted to deliver my speech more than anything else in the world, because I felt that only these men could judge truly my ability, and now this stupid clown was ruining my chances. I began fighting carefully now, moving in to punch him and out again with my greater speed. A lucky blow to his chin and I had him going too—until I heard a loud voice yell, "I got my money on the big boy."

Hearing this, I almost dropped my guard. I was confused: Should I try to win against the voice out there? Would not this go against my speech, and was not this a moment for humility, for nonresistance? A blow to my head as I danced about sent my right eye popping like a jack-in-the-box and settled my dilemma. The room went red as I fell. It was a dream fall, my body languid and fastidious as to where to land, until the floor became impatient and smashed up to meet me. A moment later I came to. An hypnotic voice said FIVE emphatically. And I lay there, hazily watching a dark red spot of my own blood shaping itself into a butterfly, glistening and soaking into the soiled gray world of the canvas.

When the voice drawled TEN I was lifted up and dragged to a chair. I sat dazed. My eye pained and swelled with each throb of my pounding heart and I wondered if now I would be allowed to speak. I was wringing wet, my mouth still bleeding. We were grouped along the wall now. The other boys ignored me as they congratulated Tatlock and speculated as to how much they would be paid. One boy whimpered over his smashed hand. Looking up front, I saw attendants in white jackets rolling the portable ring away and placing a small square rug in the vacant space surrounded by chairs. Perhaps, I thought, I will stand on the rug to deliver my speech.

Then the M.C. called to us, "Come on up here boys and get your money."

We ran forward to where the men laughed and talked in their chairs, waiting. Everyone seemed friendly now.

"There it is on the rug," the man said. I saw the rug covered with coins of all dimensions and a few crumpled bills. But what excited me, scattered here and there, were the gold pieces.

"Boys, it's all yours," the man said. "You get all you grab."

"That's right, Sambo," a blond man said, winking at me confidentially.

I trembled with excitement, forgetting my pain. I would get the gold and the bills, I thought. I would use both hands. I would throw my body against the boys nearest me to block them from the gold.

"Get down around the rug now," the man commanded, "and don't anyone touch it until I give the signal."

"This ought to be good," I heard.

As told, we got around the square rug on our knees. Slowly the man raised his freckled hand as we followed it upward with our eyes.

I heard, "These niggers look like they're about to pray!"

Then, "Ready," the man said. "Go!"

I lunged for a yellow coin lying on the blue design of the carpet, touching it and sending a surprised shriek to join those rising around me. I tried frantically to remove my hand but could not let go. A hot, violent force tore through my body, shaking me like a wet rat. The rug was electrified. The hair bristled up on my head as I shook myself free. My muscles jumped, my nerves jangled, writhed. But I saw that this was not stopping the other boys. Laughing in fear and embarrassment, some were holding back and scooping up the coins knocked off by the painful contortions of the others. The men roared above us as we struggled.

"Pick it up, goddammit, pick it up!" someone called like a bass-voiced parrot. "Go on, get it!"

I crawled rapidly around the floor, picking up the coins, trying to avoid the coppers and to get greenbacks and the gold. Ignoring the shock by laughing, as I brushed the coins off quickly, I discovered that I could contain the electricity—a contradiction, but it works. Then the men began to push us onto the rug. Laughing embarrassedly, we struggled out of their hands and kept after the coins. We were all wet and slippery and hard to hold. Suddenly I saw a boy lifted into the air, glistening with sweat like a circus seal, and dropped, his wet back landing flush upon the charged rug, heard him yell and saw him literally dance upon his back, his elbows beating a frenzied tattoo upon the floor, his muscles twitching like the flesh of a horse stung by many flies. When he finally rolled off, his face was gray and no one stopped him when he ran from the floor amid booming laughter.

"Get the money," the M.C. called. "That's good hard American cash!"

And we snatched and grabbed, snatched and grabbed. I was careful not to come too close to the rug now, and when I felt the hot whiskey breath descend upon me like a cloud of foul air I reached out and grabbed the leg of a chair. It was occupied and I held on desperately.

"Leggo, nigger! Leggo!"

The huge face wavered down to mine as he tried to push me free. But my body was slippery and he was too drunk. It was Mr. Colcord, who owned a chain of movie houses and "entertainment palaces." Each time he grabbed me I slipped out of his hands. It became a real struggle. I feared the rug more than I did the drunk, so I held on, surprising myself for a moment by trying to topple *him* upon the rug. It was such an enormous idea that I found myself actually carrying it out. I tried not to be obvious, yet when I grabbed his leg, trying to tumble him out of the chair, he raised up roaring with laughter, and, looking at me with soberness dead in the eye, kicked me viciously in the chest. The chair leg flew out of my hand and I felt myself going and rolled. It was as though I had rolled through a bed of hot coals. It seemed a whole century would pass before I would roll free, a century in which I was seared through the deepest levels of my body to the fearful breath within me and the breath seared and heated to the point of explosion. It'll all be over in a flash, I thought as I rolled clear. It'll all be over in a flash.

But not yet, the men on the other side were waiting, red faces swollen as though from apoplexy as they bent forward in their chairs. Seeing their fingers coming toward me I rolled away as a fumbled football rolls off the receiver's fingertips, back into the coals. That time I luckily sent the rug sliding out of place and heard the coins ringing against the floor and the boys scuffling to pick them up and the M.C. calling. "All right, boys, that's all. Go get dressed and get your money."

I was limp as a dish rag. My back felt as though it had been beaten with wires.

When we had dressed the M.C. came in and gave us each five dollars, except Tatlock, who got ten for being last in the ring. Then he told us to leave. I was not to get a chance to deliver my speech, I thought. I was going out into the dim alley in despair when I was stopped and told to go back. I returned to the ballroom, where the men were pushing back their chairs and gathering in groups to talk.

The M.C. knocked on the table for quiet. "Gentlemen," he said, "we almost forgot an important part of the program. A most serious part, gentlemen. This boy was brought here to deliver a speech which he made at his graduation yesterday. . . ."

"Bravo!"

"I'm told that he is the smartest boy we've got out there in Greenwood. I'm told that he knows more big words than a pocket-sized dictionary."

Much applause and laughter.

"So now, gentlemen, I want you to give him your attention."

There was still laughter as I faced them, my mouth dry, my eye throbbing. I began slowly, but evidently my throat was tense, because they began shouting, "Louder! Louder!"

"We of the younger generation extol the wisdom of that great leader and educator," I shouted, "who first spoke these flaming words of wisdom: 'A ship lost at sea for many days suddenly sighted a friendly vessel. From the mast of the unfortunate vessel was seen a signal: "Water, water; we die of thirst!" The answer from the friendly vessel came back: "Cast down your bucket where you are." The captain of the distressed vessel, at last heeding the injunction, cast down his bucket, and it came up full of fresh sparkling water from the mouth of the Amazon River.' And like him I say, and in his words, 'To those of my race who depend upon bettering their condition in a foreign land, or who underestimate the importance of cultivating friendly relations with the Southern white man, who is his next-door neighbor, I would say: "Cast down your bucket where you are"—cast it down in making friends in every manly way of the people of all races by whom we are surrounded. . . .'"

I spoke automatically and with such fervor that I did not realize that the men were still talking and laughing until my dry mouth, filling up with blood from the cut, almost strangled me. I coughed, wanting to stop and go to one of the tall brass, sand-filled spittoons to relieve myself, but a few of the men, especially the superintendent, were listening and I was afraid. So I gulped it down, blood, saliva and all, and continued. (What powers of endurance I had during those days! What enthusiasm! What a belief in the rightness of things!) I spoke even louder in spite of the pain. But still they talked and still they laughed, as though deaf with cotton in dirty ears. So I spoke with greater emotional emphasis. I closed my ears and swallowed blood until I was nauseated. The speech seemed a hundred times as long as before, but I could not leave out a single word. All had to be said, each memorized nuance considered, rendered. Nor was that all. Whenever I uttered a word of three or more syllables a group of voices would yell for me to repeat it. I used the phrase "social responsibility" and they yelled:

"What's that word you say, boy?"

"Social responsibility," I said.

"What?"

"Social . . ."

"Louder."

". . . responsibility."

"More!"

"Respon—"

"Repeat!"

"—sibility."

The room filled with the uproar of laughter until, no doubt, distracted by having to gulp down my blood, I made a mistake and yelled a phrase I had often seen denounced in newspaper editorials, heard debated in private.

"Social . . ."

"What?" they yelled.

". . . equality—"

The laughter hung smokelike in the sudden stillness. I opened my eyes, puzzled. Sounds of displeasure filled the room. The M.C. rushed forward. They shouted hostile phrases at me. But I did not understand.

A small dry mustached man in the front row blared out, "Say that slowly, son!"

"What, sir?"

"What you just said!"

"Social responsibility, sir," I said.

"You weren't being smart, were you, boy?" he said, not unkindly.

"No, sir!"

"You sure that about 'equality' was a mistake?"

"Oh, yes, sir," I said. "I was swallowing blood."

"Well, you had better speak more slowly so we can understand. We mean to do right by you, but you've got to know your place at all times. All right, now, go on with your speech."

I was afraid. I wanted to leave but I wanted also to speak and I was afraid they'd snatch me down.

"Thank you, sir," I said, beginning where I had left off, and having them ignore me as before.

Yet when I finished there was a thunderous applause. I was surprised to see the superintendent come forth with a package wrapped in white tissue paper, and, gesturing for quiet, address the men.

"Gentlemen, you see that I did not overpraise this boy. He makes a good speech and some day he'll lead his people in the proper paths. And I don't have to tell you that that is important in these days and times. This is a good, smart boy, and so to encourage him in the right direction, in the name of the Board of Education I wish to present him a prize in the form of this . . ."

He paused, removing the tissue paper and revealing a gleaming calfskin briefcase.

". . . in the form of this first-class article from Shad Whitmore's shop."

"Boy," he said, addressing me, "take this prize and keep it well. Consider it a badge of office. Prize it. Keep developing as you are and some day it will be filled with important papers that will help shape the destiny of your people."

I was so moved that I could hardly express my thanks. A rope of bloody saliva forming a shape like an undiscovered continent drooled upon the leather and I wiped it quickly away. I felt an importance that I had never dreamed.

"Open it and see what's inside," I was told.

My fingers a-tremble, I complied, smelling the fresh leather and finding an official-looking document inside. It was a scholarship to the state college for Negroes. My eyes filled with tears and I ran awkwardly off the floor.

I was overjoyed; I did not even mind when I discovered that the gold pieces I had scrambled for were brass pocket tokens advertising a certain make of automobile.

When I reached home everyone was excited. Next day the neighbors came to congratulate me. I even felt safe from grandfather, whose deathbed curse usually spoiled my triumphs. I stood beneath his photograph with my briefcase in hand and smiled triumphantly into his stolid black peasant's face. It was a face that fascinated me. The eyes seemed to follow everywhere I went.

That night I dreamed I was at a circus with him and that he refused to laugh at the clowns no matter what they did. Then later he told me to open my briefcase and read what was inside and I did, finding an official envelope stamped with the state seal; and inside the envelope I found another and another, endlessly, and I thought I would fall of weariness. "Them's years," he said. "Now open that one." And I did and in it I found an engraved document containing a short message in letters of gold. "Read it," my grandfather said. "Out loud!"

"To Whom It May Concern," I intoned. "Keep This Nigger-Boy Running."

I awoke with the old man's laughter ringing in my ears.

(It was a dream I was to remember and dream again for many years after. But at that time I had no insight into its meaning. First I had to attend college.)

HARVEY FERGUSSON

The Conquest of Don Pedro

1

The town of Don Pedro stood on the eastern edge of the lower Rio Grande Valley, where it spreads out more than a mile wide and the silver river loops and wanders through the lush green of growing crops and the bosques of cottonwood, willow and overgrown mesquite. Although its history was more a matter of legend than of record, Don Pedro was known to be a very old town. When Leo Mendes came there shortly after the Civil War it must have been at least two hundred years old. It was nearly as old as El Paso, less than a day's ride to the south, and older than Mesilla and Las Cruces, the only other towns in the region important enough to have churches. Although it now belonged to the territory of New Mexico, Don Pedro was close to both Texas and Old Mexico, as the boundaries ran then. Its proximity to the Mexican border was one thing that made it interesting to Leo Mendes.

Don Pedro had nearby neighbors there in the lower valley, but it was separated by a long and sometimes dangerous journey from the capital at Santa Fe and from the principal New Mexico settlements in the valley just south of Santa Fe. Anyone coming from the north, as Leo Mendes did, had to leave the valley at the Hot Springs of Las Palomas, where the river enters a narrow and difficult canyon, and travel for about sixty-five miles over an arid upland known as the Jornada del

95

Muerto. It was called the dead man's journey because a good many men had lost their lives there—some for lack of water and some by reason of Apache raids. It was not at all necessary to encounter such disasters, as Leo Mendes had demonstrated. A stage line now made a trip about once a month from Santa Fe to El Paso, carrying the United States mail, but Leo Mendes had driven his own burro the whole way, choosing a time when heavy rain had filled the water holes. He was not afraid of the Apaches because he had been doing business with them for several years.

New Mexico then had been a territory of the United States ever since General Kearney had run up the flag in Santa Fe after the Mexican War. There was now a Governor in Santa Fe, appointed by the President, and a duly elected legislature which deliberated in two languages, but otherwise little had changed anywhere in the territory. Most of the country was either desert or mountain or high arid plateau, so that it did not invite the plow like the fertile prairies farther east. Most of the good arable land was in the Rio Grande Valley and all of it had been privately owned and carefully cultivated for over two hundred years. For this strange country had the peculiar character of an arid wilderness with a fragment of an old civilization planted here in the heart of it, long isolated from the rest of Mexico, deriving most of its culture from the medieval Spain which had conquered it with men in armor. Here in the green valley were houses where seven generations had lived and died, and fields fertilized by the flooding river where grain had been harvested even longer. It was a place of old walls, old trees, old songs and stories, old feuds and hatreds, a place where human relations were ruled by old forms and customs too rigid for men to break.

The wilderness of mountain and desert was a hard one for pioneers to take and use, but this old and ingrown civilization was even more resistant to change and penetration. So the development and settlement of New Mexico had been slow, but pioneers had been coming in a trickle ever since the beginning of the wagon trade. Leo Mendes was one of these pioneers, but he was not one who would conquer deserts and mountains and wild Indians. Large empty spaces made him unhappy and he always crossed them in the dark if he could. He was not averse to mountains as delicate silhouettes on a distant horizon, but when he got close to them he always felt as though they were rearing to fall upon him. He regarded all forms of combat and contention as a gratuitous waste of human energy and peace of mind, and had never carried a weapon unless his walking stick could be considered one. So Leo Mendes would contribute nothing to the conquest of the wilderness, but for the business of penetrating a human society he had certain gifts which were not common among American pioneers.

2

He first saw Don Pedro from the bank of the river where he had to ford it. The town stood on slightly higher ground a few hundred yards to the east, showing only as a cluster of reddish adobe walls, with some treetops lifting above them. Beyond it the mesa, thinly grown with greasewood, was a dull and dusty olive green, reaching away toward a purple loom of mountains. It was a very hot, bright day in early September. The heat waves shimmered and danced above the old walls, as though they had stood at the bottom of a troubled, limpid sea. No human figure was anywhere in sight, nor could he hear a human sound, for it was a little past noon and the whole town was doubtless sound asleep and would be for another two hours. To these people the siesta was as sacred as prayer, and Leo had long cultivated all of their customs. So now he unpacked his burro on the sandy flood plain beside the drought-smitten river, which was nothing more than a good-sized trickle between clear pools.

Leo Mendes was a strong, stocky man of medium height with handsome heavy features, thick black eyebrows and thick curly hair. His complexion was naturally swarthy and darkened by long exposure to the sun. His blue cotton shirt and denim trousers and his wide black hat did not distinguish him from most of the natives and neither did the Apache boot-moccasins with hard cowhide soles and turned-up toes which he found the most comfortable of walking shoes. He might easily have passed for a Mexican and often did so, for he spoke Spanish not only fluently but with an instinctive mastery of native idiom, gesture and inflection. He had a gift for taking on the color of his environment without effort and without conscious intention. So he was often taken for a native, but he never pretended to be one if he was asked. By remote origin he was a Portuguese Jew and by birth a New Yorker. He looked like a Mexican and sounded like a Mexican, and sometimes briefly he even felt like a Mexican—but only briefly. At heart he was always and everywhere a stranger, with the reticence, the detachment and skepticism of the man who can mingle in any society but feels he belongs to none.

When he had dropped the two rawhide panniers on the sand and taken the wooden pack saddle off his burro, he inspected its back carefully for incipient sores. Then he plucked a bunch of grass over beside the edge of the bosque, dipped it in the water and rubbed the sweating hide to a smooth coolness. The burro turned his head slightly, as he always did when he received this attention, as though to express an incurable surprise. Perhaps no other burro in the long history of New Mexico had ever been treated with such distinguished consideration. Burros were the pack and riding animals of the poorest Mexicans and they had always been objects of abuse, execration and neglect. A burro rider used neither saddle nor bridle. He sat well toward the rump of his mount, guided him by whacking him on the side of the neck with his burro stick, and propelled him forward by a steady pounding of his rear, and by calling him all the eloquent names known to Spanish profanity. When his day's work was done a burro was turned loose anywhere and picked up his living as best he could, eating weeds, brush and even cactus when no grass was available. Yet a burro was seldom thin and many observers had noted that a dead burro was a rare sight. Burros were not immortal but they did live to a great age, and they were peculiarly immune to accidental casualty and resistant to exploitation. In the service of mankind most burros seldom exceeded a slow walk, but let one of them smell a mountain lion and he would pass anything slower than a frightened jack rabbit.

Leo's attitude toward his burro, like many of his attitudes, was a delicate blend of expediency and compassion. This was a good burro and Leo needed a good burro in his business, but he also had a deep sympathy and respect for the entire race of burros, which was a persecuted race with a great gift for passive resistance, for endurance and survival.

While his burro went foraging along the edge of the bosque, Leo stripped off his clothes and bathed luxuriously in one of the clear pools where the current poured into it and the bottom was soft, clean sand. The water was too shallow for swimming, but he washed himself carefully all over and wallowed in the cooling current with unctuous satisfaction. After he had dried in the sun and put on his clothes, leaving his feet bare, he dug into his pack and brought forth a stack of tortillas, a small round cheese, a few peaches and a bottle of native wine. Then he carefully surveyed the ground and chose a spot in the shade of a small cottonwood where the sand was smooth and a projecting root would make him a pillow. His years on the road as a peddler had made him a connoisseur of the face of the earth as a place of human repose. He spread the top cloth of his pack in the shade and sat down to his meal, slicing his white cheese to make a sandwich with the tortillas, munching his peaches for dessert and drinking exactly half his bottle of wine. It was frugal fare but his road-whetted appetite gave it relish. When he had eaten he deftly rolled a small yellow cigarette and stretched out on his back, savoring the smoke with his nose, blowing rings into the faint breeze which cooled his feet. Lying quiet he became aware of the voice of the valley, which was mostly a hum of bees, a droning of locusts and a soft chuckle of water over a sandy bed. It was like a lullaby sent to soothe him. He was full fed, supremely relaxed and comfortable. In moments such as this he always felt at home on earth, even though he was a homeless man, and at peace with himself, however difficult his fellow beings might become. What more could a man ask of life? But he knew he was now asking something more, and something other than peace. Otherwise he would not be here, camped on the edge of a settlement like an invader waiting the moment to strike.

His cigarette died between his fingers and he focused his gaze upon a great black and yellow butterfly which fluttered over him in the aimless fashion of its kind, then incredibly settled upon the tip of his big toe and sat there slowly and rhythmically opening and closing its gorgeous wings. He lay very still so as not to frighten it. When it flew away he closed his eyes and slept.

3

When he woke he knew at once by the length of the shadows that he had slept nearly an hour. The town probably would still be asleep but it would take him awhile to pack his burro and to find this man, Aurelio Beltrán, if he could find him. He knew Beltrán, being a solitary and a hunter, was much away from home, but he ought to be there on a hot day at this time of the year. If not, he would have to wait and try again. He needed an ally and all he had learned led him to believe this man was the kind of an ally he needed.

What chance had he to persuade the man to serve him? It seemed unlikely, but the conviction had grown upon him that this was the test of his luck. If he could get the kind of an arrangement he needed, then he would go ahead with his plan, and if not, well, maybe not, or maybe some other time and somewhere else. He believed a man's destiny is a thing he discovers, a mystery that unfolds, and he pursued his ends always in the spirit of inquiry rather than of heroic determination.

He had been in the valley now more than a week, going about among all the people who lived within ten miles of the town, trading with them, getting acquainted with them, asking as many questions as he could without seeming too inquisitive. He had told all of them he had a fine rifle he wanted to sell. Did they know of anyone who might be interested? All of them mentioned Augustín Vierra, the richest man in Don Pedro, the one who occupied there the position of feudal baron, owning more land and cattle than anyone else and having most of the others in debt to him. Here in the lower valley there were not such powerful families as there were farther north where the Pereas of Bernalillo were said to own half a million sheep and rule several hundred peons, but even here the order of society was a feudal order and each community was dominated by someone like Vierra. He was the only one who would have money enough to buy a good gun and he loved weapons of all kinds. Leo explained that he did no business with the *ricos*. A peddler or any other stranger could seldom get his feet inside their doors. Was there anyone else, a hunter perhaps, who would value a good gun?

He knew the man he needed would probably be a hunter. Any of these peons would work for him, but most of them would be deeply in debt to the Vierra family and he knew from long experience the strength of their allegiance to their overlords. They might hate Vierra, many of them probably did, but they would jump when he shouted, come when he called and pass on their debts from father to son like sacred heirlooms. But in every community, he knew, lived a few men of rebellious spirit, who refused to become good peons. Most of these were either bandits or thieves, specializing in the stealing of sheep, cattle or goats, according to their talents and opportunities. In fact, some form of larceny was for the poor almost the only escape from bondage except that in most communities would be found at least one professional hunter, who lived by selling meat, fresh and dried, and also hides and peltries. Most of the Mexicans, too poor to own effective arms, were not hunters, and most of the good hunters were more than half Navajo. A professional hunter would generally be a proud, fierce, restless man, who cherished his freedom and independence. Leo did not want to deal with a thief or a bandit, but he was looking for a proud and independent man who could use weapons. Instinctively, he was looking for a man who would complement himself. For if you face the hazard of violence, you must be prepared to employ violence, however little you like it.

He had inquired about this Beltrán at every house he visited, making whatever excuse he could for his curiosity, and gradually he had formed in his own mind the picture of an unusual man. Beltrán, for one thing, was unmarried, and it was very rare to find a Mexican who did not have a wife. It was said that he had married a beautiful girl when he was very young, she had died in childbirth, as so many Mexican women did, and he had lived ever since with a broken heart. That was his legend. But he had not, it appeared, taken any vow of chastity. On the contrary, he was a terror to husbands and fathers, the more so because of his great strength and truculent temper. Was he then an unreliable man? No, not at all, except that you never knew where he was. He disappeared into the mountains, sometimes for weeks at a time, had even gone as far east as the buffalo plains with his wagon, bringing it back loaded with meat and buffalo robes.

Beltrán might be hard to find, but he always kept his word. You could trust him with anything but a woman. The fact was admitted somewhat grudgingly, for Beltrán had few friends. One other thing Leo learned about him, which clinched his own conviction that this was the man he needed. Beltrán did not like the Vierras. He had a great contempt for Don Augustín and a grudge against the whole family, rooted deep in the past.

4

When Leo reached the plaza of Don Pedro there was still no sign of life except a few dogs asleep in the shade, and they did not even wake to bark at him. He sat down with his back to a wall, mopping sweat off his face with a red bandanna, surveying this place he proposed to invade. Like all Mexican towns, it was built around a public square, in this case nothing more than half an acre of sunbaked sand. The church marked its eastern limit, an old adobe church, its corners supported by heavy earthen buttresses, its bell hung in a wooden tower painted white. The Padre's residence was behind it and the two buildings were connected by high walls. The lift and droop of foliage above them suggested the Padre had created for himself a cool retreat. Not a single tree shaded the plaza, nothing grew there except a few yellow sunflowers over against the church and some gourd vines crawling over the crumbling red walls of a deserted building on the south side where Leo sat. Across the way was another tumbledown house, but evidently still in use, perhaps as a public hall where dances were held. The only sound building in sight besides the church was the long, low house on the opposite side of the plaza, with its porch supported by heavy hewn timbers, its whitewashed front wall and windows with heavy wooden bars and shutters. Treetops lifted above its roof, doubtless from the courtyard within, and the establishment reached far back toward the river in the form of a high-walled enclosure.

This, he knew, could only be the Vierra homestead, the castle which dominated this part of the valley. Somewhere behind those walls was a storeroom, where people got the few things they needed and could not produce for themselves, such as cotton cloth, needles and thread, knives and skillets. These goods were handed out to them on credit at whatever price the owner chose to ask. They all worked for him, more or less, but none of them ever worked themselves out of debt. Leo knew all about this business and he was acutely conscious of that primitive storeroom because he hoped to become its competitor, and he knew competition would not be welcomed.

At a glance the town did not look like a good place to found a business—a half-deserted place asleep in the sun and falling to pieces. But Leo was neither surprised nor discouraged. He knew that long ago this had been a much larger town, that it had been dwindling slowly for perhaps a hundred years. Apaches had raided it once, smallpox had ravaged it. When the Confederates had taken Arizona and made Mesilla their capital, many of the people had gone there because the army offered work for real money. So Don Pedro had not thriven. But Leo was not thinking primarily of the town. He had learned all about its decline before he came south. He knew if he had any success he would draw trade from all over the valley. He knew that only a few miles across the Texas border was a famous salt lake, where people came to gather salt from as much as a hundred miles away, from Sonora and Chihuahua as well as New Mexico. Under the Mexican law all usable salt deposits had been public property. Although this one now belonged to Texas, it was still open to all comers, and many of them might be customers for a good store that sold goods cheap and took almost anything in trade. Then, too, the Mexican border was nearby and a great deal of movable property always crosses a border—property of uncertain origin seeking a quick market. Best of all, Fort Selden was only eleven miles up the river, with a full company of United States Cavalry. Leo had stopped there briefly on his way south and had done a lively business in playing cards, chewing tobacco, toothbrushes and other light merchandise he had brought for that special purpose. Probably soldiers would come to his store, but that was the least of the benefits he might reap from the fort. Soldiers ate beef and horses ate corn, and he hoped to have much beef and corn to sell. Gringos in the southwest had found army contracts for beef a lucrative business. Several substantial fortunes had already been founded upon them.

So Leo did not care how dead the town might be. Perhaps he could inject a little life into it—if he was able to stay. In the northern part of the valley gringos had opened stores and some of them had succeeded and others had found it expedient to move. He had heard the story of the Schoenfelt brothers, who opened a large store in Santa Fe and received word mysteriously that if they did not move they would be quietly buried. They were men of commerce, not of battle. They had packed their goods upon three hundred burros and moved across the mountains to Las Vegas, where they still throve. So you could never tell what might happen. Leo knew of another peddler who had tried to open a store in a small town south of Albuquerque. He had been visited at night by mysterious strangers who beat him up and advised him to be gone by morning, which he was.

Leo knew he was not going to fight and win any battles, nor issue any heroic defiances. He knew that if a tense and perilous situation arose, he would depart quietly in search of peace. But he also knew that even though he faced no violence, he would inevitably meet with opposition in some form, with resentment and suspicion and dislike. This was not in the least because he was a Jew—the people of New Mexico knew almost nothing of Jews—but because he was a gringo, and even more because he would be an interloper, an innovator, a disturber of the ancient feudal peace.

Why, then, had he set out upon this adventure? Well, chiefly because now he had money. Deeply buried at the bottom of his panniers he had a canvas bag filled with the strangely assorted gold and silver coins then current in the territory, and in Santa Fe he had still more money on deposit with Wells, Fargo and Company, where he could draw on it for credit when he needed more goods. Money was a tool in his hand. He felt a need to use it.

He knew his money was pushing him into this venture and he also knew he had another and more troubling motive. In his long solitary walking he had thought it all over, questioning himself as all solitaries do. For years the proud *ricos* of the northern valley had ignored his existence. As a peddler he had never been able to get past their heavy front doors, to sell them so much as a needle. He was not an aggressive man but there was something inside him that wanted to challenge these lords of the earth, and it was in conflict with something else that wanted only peace. As a peddler he had known much of contentment. Now he had to go starting trouble for himself, risking his money if not his life. Was he then afraid? Yes, he found it necessary to admit that he was afraid and he half-enjoyed the tingle of fear, the thrill of his own temerity. One phase of his life was over and another was about to begin. He felt peculiarly alert and alive, stimulated by the mystery and hazard of new experience.

He rose and prodded his burro gently. He had named it Spinoza because his father had taught him to revere that name and he liked to utter it and to stir the memories of youth that were associated with it.

"*Vamos a ver*, Spinoza," he said. It was a common idiom of the country—"We are going to see"—reflecting the fatalism of the Mexicans, which was much like his own.

He had been told that Beltrán lived a few hundred yards from the plaza on a road running north. There he would find a long, low building, most of it empty and beginning to crumble in the weather, but at the far end a couple of rooms were kept in good repair and there lived Beltrán. It appeared that the Beltráns had once been a strong and numerous family, with a house nearly as large as that of the Vierras, but the tribe had dwindled and scattered. There were others of the name living thereabouts, but only Aurelio still lived in the ruin of the family homestead.

It was easy to find the building, and Leo noted with interest that while it was in bad shape, it could be made usable by plastering the walls and mending the roof. He went to the one good door at the far end, a heavy wooden door with a big iron latch, knocked upon it and stood waiting and listening with a sharp suspense tightening his guts, a feeling that much depended upon the next few minutes. There was a moment of silence, then he heard a slight cough, a whisper of moccasined feet across a dirt floor, and the door opened upon an impressive figure of a man. He stood well over six feet, broad-shouldered, erect and powerful, a man with no softening comfortable fat anywhere about him and no smile upon his face. It was a massively aquiline face with an imposing nose and deep-set eyes. The hair was straight and black, but Leo knew at once that this was no Indian. Beltrán was a Spaniard of the lean and taciturn breed which has been producing fighters and fanatics for a thousand years. He said, "How do you do" politely enough, but without smiling, and then after a deliberate pause, "What do you want?"

"I am a peddler," Leo said.

Beltrán considered the fact a moment.

"What do you sell?" he inquired.

"I have very beautiful colored pictures," Leo explained, "of Christ crucified, the Virgin Mary and also the Virgin of Guadelupe and most of the Saints."

Beltrán shook his head, his hand still upon the door.

"They are all safe in heaven," he said. "I see no reason to hang them on the wall."

"I have needles and thread, cotton cloth and scissors," Leo said.

Beltrán was not interested. "I have no wife," he explained.

"I have a very fine rifle," Leo ventured, feeling that he had built up to his climax. "Made by Hawken of St. Louis, with a bullet mold, a canister of powder and a bar of lead."

He could see the flash of interest in the man's eyes, but it was a very slight reaction, and he shook his head again.

"I have no money to buy a rifle," he said. "You must know that. I have buckskin and peltries, a few buffalo robes, beans and chili, but I have not seen ten silver dollars together since the soldiers left Mesilla. If you are looking for money, you have come to the wrong place."

"I take almost anything in trade," Leo said. "That is the

only way I can do business. Usually peltries and buffalo robes would be too heavy for me to handle, but I hope to be here awhile and to ship goods to Santa Fe."

Beltrán again devoted himself to thought for a long moment. At last he stepped back and opened the door wide.

"Come in," he said. "It will do no harm to look at your rifle."

Leo stepped through the door with the feeling of a conqueror who has breached the wall of a peculiarly difficult fortress. It was dark inside the room, which had only one window with wooden bars and a sheet of oiled paper. When his eyes became used to the dim light he saw that he was facing an enormous dog. It stood there looking at him, silent and motionless, except that the hair on its neck lifted a little, as though in preparation for battle. It was a yellow dog with a white splash on its throat, built much like a mastiff except that its head and ears showed a trace of hound. Leo thought it must weigh at least a hundred pounds. In spite of himself, he took a step backward. The brute looked as though it might kill a man with ease and would not be at all averse to the job.

Beltrán, relaxed for the first time, laughed a little.

"Don't be afraid of him," he said. "If you came here alone he would tear you to pieces, but as long as I am here you are safe."

He spoke a low word to the dog. It came forward slowly and with dignity, touched Leo's hand with its tongue, returned to the back of the room and lay down, its head on its paws like a couchant lion, never taking its eyes off the stranger.

"He is a very valuable dog," Beltrán explained. "He knows how to drive deer out of a canyon and how to tree bob cats and lions. He once killed a young mountain lion all alone, and a very few dogs can do that."

"He is a magnificent dog," Leo agreed. The animal's unwavering gaze made him uncomfortable, but it occurred to him that this dog might prove to be something of an asset.

"Sit down," Beltrán invited, pointing to a rolled mattress against the wall, covered with a red and black Navajo blanket. The only other furniture was a homemade chair with a rawhide seat and a massive table of hand-hewn timbers.

"First let me unpack my burro," Leo said.

He dragged his panniers into the room, dug out the rifle, which was carefully wrapped in buckskin, and laid it on the table. It was a beautiful piece with a richly figured walnut stock, a bright nickel butt-plate and a blued-steel barrel. Beltrán picked it up and brought it to his shoulder with a practiced gesture, while his cheek lovingly cuddled the polished wood. He laid it down with a sigh.

"I could never afford such a rifle as that," he said.

"You would not have to pay for it now," Leo offered. "I will give you credit."

Beltrán interrupted with an angry shake of his head.

"I am no peon," he said emphatically. "I would rather eat acorns than go into debt."

Leo saw he had made a mistake, felt he had better go straight to the point of his visit.

"You need not remain long in debt," he said. "I want to open a store in this town. I need a room, and you have empty rooms. It will take some building and plastering to make the place ready. If we can make a bargain I will pay you for the work and I will also pay you a rental."

He paused, fished in his trousers pocket, pulled out a large eight-sided gold coin called an ounce and laid it on the table.

"I have money," he explained.

Beltrán sat staring thoughtfully at the bright gold. It was evident that this double proposition had confused him and shaken his defenses. He was being asked to assume a debt and also to work, both clearly against his principles, but at the same time he was being treated as a landlord.

"So you want to open a store here," he said at length. It was hard to guess from his tone what he thought of this proposal.

Leo shrugged his shoulders and spread his hands in a gesture eloquent of man's helplessness in the face of his inscrutable destiny.

"Perhaps the Vierras will chase me out of town," he said.

"Listen!" Beltrán spoke with sudden heat. "They will not chase you out, not if I have anything to do with it."

He stopped short, evidently aware that he had committed himself more than he had intended.

"Many thanks," Leo said. "I will appreciate your friendship, whether we can do business or not." He began wrapping up the rifle. "It is time for me to go, but I will come to see you again."

Beltrán was silent a moment, watching the rifle disappear with evident reluctance.

"Where do you sleep?" he asked just as Leo was about to put it in his pack.

"I sleep anywhere," Leo said.

"You can stay here," Beltrán offered. "There is plenty of room and I have much venison."

"Well, thank you." Leo laid the rifle back on the table. "I have great pleasure."

After Beltrán had tended his horses and chopped wood they prepared a notable meal of young venison stewed with chili and beans. Leo contributed the rest of his wine and cheese and also some coffee. Before they slept that night it was understood that Leo would pay a rental of two American dollars a month for the use of a room and that Beltrán would go with his wagon to Mesilla where the Confederates had left some lumber he could buy for shelves and a counter. Although they had made no formal agreement, the store already had become a joint enterprise, a thing that existed in two imaginations.

WILLIAM GOYEN

Ghost and Flesh, Water and Dirt

Was somebody here while ago acallin for you. . . .

O don't say that, don't tell me who . . . was he fair and had a wrinkle in his chin? I wonder was he the one . . . describe me his look, whether the eyes were pale light-colored and swimmin and wild and shifty; did he bend a little at the shoulders was his face agrievin what did he say where did he go, whichaway, hush don't tell me; wish I could keep him but I cain't, so go, go (but come back).

Cause you know honey there's a time to go roun and tell and there's a time to set still (and let a ghost grieve ya); so listen to me while I tell, cause I'm in my time a tellin and you better run fast if you don't wanna hear what I tell, cause I'm goin ta tell . . .

Dreamt last night again I saw pore Raymon Emmons, all last night seen im plain as day. There uz tears in iz glassy eyes and iz face uz all meltin away. O I was broken of my sleep and of my night disturbed, for I dreamt of pore Raymon Emmons live as ever.

He came on the sleepin porch where I was sleepin (and he's there to stay) ridin a purple horse (like King was), and then he got off and tied im to the bedstead and come and stood over me and commenced iz talkin. All night long he uz talkin and talkin, his speech (whatever he uz sayin) uz like steam streamin outa the mouth of a kettle, streamin and streamin and streamin. At first I said in my dream, "Will you

do me the favor of tellin me just who in the world you can
be, will you please show the kindness to tell me who you can
be, breakin my sleep and disturbin my rest?" "I'm Raymon
Emmons," the steamin voice said, "and I'm here to stay; putt
out my things that you've putt away, putt out my oatmeal
bowl and putt hot oatmeal in it, get out my rubberboots
when it rains, iron my clothes and fix my supper . . . I never
died and I'm here to stay."

*(Oh go way ole ghost of Raymon Emmons, whisperin in
my ear on the pilla at night; go way ole ghost and lemme be!
Quit standin over me like that, all night standin there sayin
somethin to me . . . behave ghost of Raymon Emmons, behave yoself and lemme be! Lemme get out and go roun,
lemme put on those big ole rubberboots and go clompin. . . .)*

Now you shoulda known that Raymon Emmons. *There*
was *somebody*, I'm tellin you. Oh he uz a bright thang, quick
'n fair, tall, about six feet, real lean and a devilish face full of
snappin eyes, he had eyes all over his face, didn't miss a
thang, that man, saw everthang; and a clean brow. He was a
rayroad man, worked for the Guff Coast Lines all iz life, our
house always smelt like a train.

When I first knew of him he was livin at the Boardinhouse
acrost from the depot (oh that uz years and years ago), and
I uz in town and wearin my first pumps when he stopped me
on the corner and ast me to do him the favor of tellin him
the size of my foot. I was not afraid atall to look at him and
say the size a my foot uz my own affair and would he show
the kindness to not be so fresh. But when he said I only want
to know because there's somebody livin up in New Waverley
about your size and age and I want to send a birthday
present of some houseshoes to, I said that's different; and we
went into Richardson's store, to the back where the shoes
were, and tried on shoes till he found the kind and size to fit
me and this person in New Waverley. I didn't tell im that the
pumps I'uz wearin were Sistah's and not my size (when I got
home and Mama said why'd it take you so long? I said it uz
because I had to walk so slow in Sistah's pumps).

Next time I saw im in town (and I made it a point to look
for im, was why I come to town), I went up to im and said
do you want to measure my foot again Raymon Emmons,
ha! And he said any day in the week I'd measure that pretty
foot; and we went into Richardson's and he bought *me* a pair

of white summer pumps with a pink tie (and I gave Sistah's pumps back to her). Miz Richardson said my lands Margy you buyin lotsa shoes lately, are you goin to take a trip (O I took a trip, and one I come back from, too).

We had other meetins and was plainly in love; and when we married, runnin off to Groveton to do it, everybody in town said things about the marriage because he uz thirty and I uz seventeen.

We moved to this house owned by the Picketts, with a good big clothesyard and a swing on the porch, and I made it real nice for me and Raymon Emmons, made curtains with fringe, putt jardinears on the front bannisters and painted the fern buckets. We furnished those unfurnished rooms with our brand new lives, and started goin along.

Between those years and this one I'm tellin about them in, there seems a space as wide and vacant and silent as the Neches River, with my life *then* standin on one bank and my life *now* standin on the other, lookin acrost at each other like two different people wonderin who the other can really be.

How did Raymon Emmons die? Walked right through a winda and tore hisself all to smithereens. Walked right through a second-story winda at the depot and fell broken on the tracks—nothin much left a Raymon Emmons after he walked through that winda—broken his crown, hon, broken his crown. But he lingered for three days in Victry Hospital and then passed, saying just before he passed away, turnin towards me, "I hope you're satisfied. . . ."

Why did he die? From grievin over his daughter and mine, Chitta was her name, that fell off a horse they uz both ridin on the Emmonses' farm. Horse's name was King and we had im shot.

Buried im next to Chitta's grave with iz insurance, two funerals in as many weeks, then set aroun blue in our house, cryin all day and cryin half the night, sleep all broken and disturbed of my rest, thinkin oh if he'd come knockin at that door right now I'd let him in, oh I'd let Raymon Emmons in! After he died, I set aroun sayin who's gonna meet all the hours in a day with me, whatever is in each one—*all those hours*—who's gonna be with me in the mornin, in the ashy afternoons that we always have here, in the nights of lightnin who's goan be lyin there, seen in the flashes and makin me feel as safe as if he uz a lightnin rod (and honey he *wuz*); who's gonna be like a light turned on in a dark room when I go in, who's gonna be at the door when I open it, who's goin to be there when I wake up or when I go to sleep, who's goin to call my name? I cain't stand a life of just me and our furniture in a room, who's gonna *be* with me? Honey it's true that you never miss water till the well runs dry, tiz truly true.

Went to talk to the preacher, but he uz no earthly help, regalin me with iz pretty talk, he's got a tongue that will trill out a story pretty as a bird on a bobwire fence—but meanin what?—sayin "the wicked walk on every hand when the vilest men are exalted"—now what uz that mean?—; went to set and talk with Fursta Evans in her Millinary Shop (who's had her share of tumult in her sad life, but never shows it) but she uz no good, sayin "Girl pick up the pieces and go on. . . . Here try on this real cute hat" (that woman had nothin but hats on her mind—even though she taught me *my* life, grant cha *that*—for brains she's got hats). Went to the graves on Sundays carryin potplants and cryin over the mounds, one long wide one and one little un—how sad are the little graves a childrun, childrun ought not to have to die it's not right to bring death to childrun, they're just little toys grown-ups play with or neglect (thas how some of em die, too, honey, but won't say no more bout that); but all childrun go to Heaven so guess it's best—the grasshoppers flyin all roun me (they say graveyard grasshoppers spit tobacco juice and if it gets in your eye it'll putt your eye out) and an armadilla diggin in the crepe-myrtle bushes—sayin "dirt lay light on Raymon Emmons and iz child," and thinkin "all my life is dirt I've got a family of dirt." And then I come back to set and scratch aroun like an armadilla myself in these rooms, alone; but honey that uz no good either.

And then one day, I guess it uz a year after my famly died, there uz a knock on my door and it uz Fursta Evans knockin when I opened it to see. And she said "Honey now listen I've come to visit with you and to try to tell you somethin: why are you so glued to Raymon Emmons's memry when you never cared a hoot bout him while he was on earth, you despised all the Emmonses, said they was just trash, wouldn't go to the farm on Christmas or Thanksgivin, wouldn't set next to em in church, broke pore Raymon Emmons's heart because you'd never let Chitta stay with her grandparents and when you finely did the Lord punished you

for bein so hateful by takin Chitta. Then you blamed it on
Raymon Emmons, hounded im night and day, said he killed
Chitta, drove im stark ravin mad. While Raymon Emmons
was live you'd never even give him the time a day, wouldn't
lift a hand for im, you never would cross the street for im, to
you he uz just a dog in the yard, and you know it, and now
that he's dead you grieve yo life away and suddenly fall in
love with im." Or she tole me good and proper—said "You
never loved im till you lost im, till it uz too late," said, "now
set up and listen to me and get some brains in yo head,
chile." Said, "Cause listen honey, I've had four husbands in
my time, two of em died and two of em quit me, but each
one of em I thought was goin to be the *only* one, and I took
each one for that, then let im go when he uz gone, kept goin
roun, kept ready, we got to honey, left the gate wide open for
anybody to come through, friend or stranger, ran with the
hare and hunted with the hound, honey we got to *greet* life
not grieve life," is what she said.

"Well," I said, "I guess that's the way life is, you don't
know what you have till you don't have it any longer, till
you've lost it, till it's too late."

"Anyway," Fursta said, "little cattle little care—you're beginnin again now, fresh and empty handed, it's later and it's
shorter, yo life, but go on from *here* not *there*," she said.
"You've had one kind of a life, had a husband, putt im in iz
grave (now leave im there!), had a child and putt her away,
too; start over, hon, the world don't know it, the world's fresh
as ever—it's a new day, putt some powder on yo face and
start goin roun. Get you a job, and try that; or take you a
trip. . . ."

"But I got to stay in this house," I said. "Feel like I cain't
budge. Raymon Emmons is here, live as ever, and I cain't get
away from im. He keeps me fastened to this house."

"Oh poot," Fursta said, lightin a cigarette. "Honey you're
losin ya mine. Now listen here, put on those big ole rubberboots and go clompin, go steppin high and wide—cause listen
here, if ya don't they'll have ya up in the Asylum at Rusk
sure's as shootin, specially if you go on talkin about this
ghost of Raymon Emmons the way you do."

"But if I started goin roun, what would people say?"

"You can tell em it's none of their beeswax. Cause listen
honey, the years uv passed and are passin and you in ever
one of em, passin too, and not gettin any younger—yo hair's

gettin bunchy and the lines clawed roun yo mouth and eyes
by the glassy claws of cryin sharp tears. We got to paint ourselves up and go on, young *outside*, anyway—cause listen
honey the sun comes up and the sun crosses over and *goes
down*—and while the sun's up we got to get on that fence
and crow. Cause night muss fall—and then thas all. Come
on, les go roun; have us a Sataday night weddin ever Sataday
night; forget this old patched-faced ghost I hear you talkin
about. . . ."

"In this town?" I said. "I hate this ole town, always rain
fallin—'cept this ain't rain it's rainin, Fursta, it's rainin mildew. . . ."

"O deliver me!" Fursta shouted out, and putt out her cigarette. "You won't do. Are you afraid you'll *melt?*"

"I wish I'd melt—and run down the drains. Wish I uz rain,
fallin on the dirt of certain graves I know and seepin down
into the dirt, could lie in the dirt with Raymon Emmons on
one side and Chitta on the other. Wish I uz dirt. . . ."

"I wish you are just crazy," Fursta said. "Come on, you're
gonna take a trip. You're gonna get on a train and take a
nonstop trip and get off at the end a the line and start all
over again new as a New Year's Baby, baby. I'm gonna see
to that."

"Not on no train, all the king's men couldn't get me to ride
a train again, no siree. . . ."

"Oh no train my foot," said Fursta.

"But what'll I use for money please tell me," I said.

"With Raymon Emmons's insurance of course—it didn't
take all of it to bury im, I know. Put some acreage tween you
an yo past life, and maybe some new friends and scenery too,
and pull down the shade on all the water that's gone under
the bridge; and come back here a new woman. Then if ya
went tew you can come into my millinary shop with me."

"Oh," I said, "is the world still there? Since Raymon Emmons walked through that winda seems the whole world's
gone, the whole world went out through that winda when he
walked through it."

Closed the house, sayin "good-bye ghost of Raymon Emmons," bought my ticket at the depot, deafenin my ears to
the sound of the tickin telegraph machine, got on a train and
headed west to California. Day and night the trainwheels on
the traintracks said *Raymon Emmons Raymon Emmons Ray-*

mon Emmons, and I looked through the winda at dirt and desert, miles and miles of dirt, thinkin I wish I uz dirt I wish I uz dirt. O I uz vile with grief.

In California the sun was out, wide, and everbody and everthang lighted up; and oh honey the world *was* still there. I decided to stay awhile. I started my new life with Raymon Emmons's insurance money. It uz in San Diego, by the ocean and with mountains of dirt standin' gold in the blue waters. A war had come. I was alone for a while, but not for long. Got me a job in an airplane factory, met a lotta girls, met a lotta men. I worked in fusilodges.

There uz this Nick Natowski, a brown clean Pollock from Chicargo, real wile, real Satanish. What kind of a life did he start me into? I don't know how it started, but it did, and in a flash we uz everwhere together, dancin and swimmin and *everthang.* He uz in the war and in the U.S. Navy, but we didn't think of the war or of water. I just liked him tight as a glove, in iz uniform, I just liked him laughin, honey, I just liked him *ever* way he was, and that uz all I knew. And then one night he said, "Margy I'm goin to tell you somethin, goin on a boat, be gone a long long time, goin in a week." Oh I cried and had a nervous fit and said, "Why do you have to go when there's these thousands of others all aroun San Diego that could go?" and he said, "We're goin away to Coronada for that week, you and me, and what happens there will be enough to keep and save for the whole time we're apart." We went, honey, Nick and me, to Coronada, I mean we really *went.* Lived like a king and queen—where uz my life behind me that I thought of onct and a while like a story somebody was whisperin to me?—laughed and loved and I cried; and after that week at Coronada, Nick left for sea on his boat, to the war, sayin I want you to know baby I'm leavin you my allotment.

I was blue, so blue, all over again, but this time it uz diffrent someway, guess cause I uz blue for somethin live this time and not dead under dirt, I don't know; anyway I kept goin roun, kept my job in fusilodges and kept goin roun. There was this friend of Nick Natowski's called George, and we went together some. "But why doesn't Nick Natowski write me, George?" I said. "Because he cain't yet," George said, "but just wait and he'll write." I kept waitin but no letter ever came, and the reason he didn't write when he could of, finely, was because his boat was sunk and Nick Natowski in it.

Oh what have I ever done in this world, I said, to send my soul to torment? Lost one to dirt and one to water, makes my life a life of mud, why was I ever put to such a test as this O Lord, I said. I'm goin back home to where I started, gonna get on that train and backtrack to where I started from, want to look at dirt awhile, can't stand to look at water. I rode the train back. Somethin drew me back like I'd been pastured on a rope in California.

Come back to this house, opened it up and aired it all out, and when I got back you know who was there in that house? That ole faithful ghost of Raymon Emmons. He'd been there, waitin, while I went aroun, in my goin roun time, and was there to have me back. While I uz gone he'd covered everythang in our house with the breath a ghosts, fine ghost dust over the tables and chairs and a curtain of ghost lace over my bed on the sleepinporch.

Took me this job in Richardson's Shoe Shop (this town's big now and got money in it, the war 'n oil made it rich, ud never know it as the same if you hadn't known it before; and Fursta Evans married to a rich widower), set there fittin shoes on measured feet all day—it all started in a shoestore measurin feet and it ended that way—can you feature that? Went home at night to my you-know-what.

Comes ridin onto the sleepinporch ever night regular as clockwork, ties iz horse to the bedstead and I say hello Raymon Emmons and we start our conversation. Don't ask me what he says or what I say, but ever night is a night full of talkin, and it lasts the whole night through. Oh onct in a while I get real blue and want to hide away and just set with Raymon Emmons in my house, cain't budge, don't see daylight nor dark, putt away my wearin clothes, couldn't walk outa that door if my life depended on it. But I set real still and let it all be, claimed by that ghost until he unclaims me—and then I get up and go roun, free, and that's why I'm here, settin with you here in the Pass Time Club, drinkin this beer and tellin you all I've told.

Honey, why am I tellin all this? Oh all our lives! So many thangs to tell. And I keep em to myself a long long time, tight as a drum, won't open my mouth, just set in my blue house with that ole ghost agrievin me, until there comes a time of tellin, a time to tell, a time to putt on those big ole rubberboots.

Now I believe in *tellin*, while we're live and goin roun; when the tellin time comes I say spew it out, we just got to tell things, things in our lives, things that've happened, things we've fancied and things we dream about or are haunted by. Cause you know honey the time to shut you mouth and set moultin and mildewed in yo room, grieved by a ghost and fastened to a chair, comes back roun again, don't worry honey, it comes roun again. There's a time ta tell and a time ta set still ta let a ghost grieve ya. So listen to me while I tell, cause I'm in my time atellin, and you better run fast if you don wanna hear what I tell, cause I'm goin ta tell. . . .

The world is changed, let's drink ower beer and have us a time, tell and tell and tell, let's get that hot bird in a cole bottle tonight. Cause next time you think you'll see me and hear me tell, you won't: I'll be flat where I cain't budge again, like I wuz all that year, settin and hidin way . . . until the time comes roun again when I can say oh go way ole ghost of Raymon Emmons, go way ole ghost and lemme be!

Cause I've learned this and I'm gonna tell ya: there's a time for live things and a time for dead, for ghosts and for flesh 'n bones: all life is just a sharin of ghosts and flesh. Us humans are part ghost and part flesh—part fire and part ash—but I think maybe the ghost part is the longest lastin, the fire blazes but the ashes last forever. I had fire in California (and water putt it out) and ash in Texis (and it went to dirt); but I say now, while I'm tellin you, there's a world both places, a world where there's ghosts and a world where there's flesh, and I believe the real right way is to take our worlds, of ghosts or of flesh, take each one as they come and take what comes in em: take a ghost and grieve with im, settin still; and take the flesh 'n bones and go roun; and even run out to meet what worlds come in to our lives, strangers (like you), and ghosts (like Raymon Emmons) and lovers (like Nick Natowski) . . . and be what each world wants us to be.

And I think that ghosts, if you set still with em long enough, can give you over to flesh 'n bones; and that flesh 'n bones, if you go roun when it's time, can send you back to a faithful ghost. One provides the other.

Saw pore Raymon Emmons all last night, all last night seen im plain as day.

JOHN GRAVES

The Last Running

They called him Pajarito, in literal trader-Spanish interpretation of his surname, or more often Tom Tejano, since he had been there in those early fighting days before the Texans had flooded up onto the plains in such numbers that it became no longer practical to hate them with specificity.

After the first interview, when he had climbed down from the bed where an aching liver held him and had gone out onto the porch to salute them, only to curse in outrage and clump back into the house when he heard what they wanted, the nine of them sat like grackles about the broad gray-painted steps and talked, in Comanche, about Tom Texan the Little Bird and the antique times before wire fences had partitioned the prairies. At least, old Juan the cook said that was what they were talking about.

Mostly it was the old men who talked, three of them, one so decrepit that he had had to make the trip from Oklahoma in a lopsided carryall drawn by a piebald mare, with an odd long bundle sticking out the back, the rest riding alongside on ponies. Of the other six, two were middle-aged and four were young.

Their clothes ran a disastrous gamut from buckskin to faded calico and blue serge, but under dirty Stetsons they wore their hair long and braided, plains style. Waiting, sucking Durham cigarettes and speaking Comanche, they sat about the steps and under the cottonwoods in the yard and ignored those of us who drifted near to watch them, except the one or two whom they considered to have a right to their attention. Twice a day for two days they built fires and broiled unsymmetrical chunks of the fat calf which, from his bed, furiously, Tom Bird had ordered killed for them. At night—it was early autumn—they rolled up in blankets about the old carryall and slept on the ground.

"They show any signs of leaving?" Tom Bird asked me when I went into his room toward evening of the second day.

I said, "No, sir. They told Juan they thought you could spare one easily enough, since all of them and the land too used to be theirs."

"They didn't used to be nobody's!" he shouted.

"They've eaten half that animal since they got here," I said. "I never saw anybody that could eat meat like that, and nothing but meat."

"No, nor ever saw anything else worth seeing," he said, his somber gray eyes brooding. He was one of the real ones, and none of them are left now. That was in the twenties; he was my great-uncle, and he had left Mississippi in disgust at sixteen to work his way out on the high plains to the brawling acquisitive Texas frontier. At the age of eighty-five he possessed—more or less by accident, since cattle rather than land had always meant wealth to him—a medium-large ranch in the canyon country where the Cap Rock falls away to rolling prairies, south of the Texas Panhandle. He had buried two wives and had had no children and lived there surrounded by people who worked for him. When I had showed up there, three years before the Comanches' visit, he had merely grunted at me on the porch, staring sharply at my frail physique, and had gone right on arguing with his manager about rock salt in the pastures. But a month later, maybe when he decided I was going to pick up weight and live, we had abruptly become friends. He was given to quick gruff judgments and to painful retractions.

He said in his room that afternoon, "God damn it. I'll see them in hell before they get one, deeper than you can drop an anvil."

"You want me to tell them that?"

"Hell, yes," he said. "No. Listen, have you talked any with that old one? Starlight, they call him."

I said that neither Starlight nor the others had even glanced at any of us.

Tom Bird said, "You tell him you're kin to me. He knows a lot, that one."

"What do you want me to say about the buffalo?"

"Nothing," he said and narrowed his eyes as a jab of pain shot through him from that rebellious organ which was speaking loudly now of long-gone years of drinking at plains mudholes and Kansas saloons. He grunted. "Not a damn thing," he said. "I already told them."

Starlight paid no attention at all when I first spoke to him. I had picked up a poor grade of Spanish from old Juan in three years but was timid about using it, and to my English he showed a weathered and not even disdainful profile.

I stated my kinship to Tom Bird and said that Tom Bird had told me to speak to him.

Starlight stared at the fourteen pampered bison grazing in their double-fenced pasture near the house, where my great-uncle could watch them from his chair in the evenings. He had bred them from seed stock given him in the nineties by Charles Goodnight, and the only time one of them had ever been killed and eaten was when the governor of the state and a historical society had driven out to give the old man some sort of citation. When the Comanches under Starlight had arrived, they had walked down to the pasture fence and had looked at the buffalo for perhaps two hours, hardly speaking, studying the cows and the one calf and the emasculated males and the two bulls—old Shakespeare, who had killed a horse once and had put innumerable men up mesquite trees and over fences, and his lecherous though rarely productive son, John Milton.

Then they had said, matter-of-factly, that they wanted one of the animals.

Starlight's old-man smell was mixed with something wild, perhaps wood smoke. His braids were a soiled white. One of the young men glanced at me after I had spoken and said something to him in Comanche. Turning then, the old Indian looked at me down his swollen nose. His face was hexagonal and broad, but sunken where teeth were gone. He spoke.

The young man said in English with an exact accent, "He wants to know what's wrong with old Tom Bird, not to talk to friends."

All of them were watching me, the young ones with more affability than the others. I said Tom Bird was sick in the liver and patted my own.

Starlight said in Spanish, "Is he dying?"

I answered in Spanish that I didn't think so but that it was painful.

He snorted much like Tom Bird himself and turned to look again at the buffalo in the pasture. The conversation appeared to have ended, but not knowing how to leave I sat there on the top step beside the old Comanche, the rest of them ranged below us and eyeing me with what I felt to be humor. I took out cigarettes and offered them to the young man, who accepted the package and passed it along, and when it got back to me it was nearly empty. I got the impression that this gave them amusement, too, though no one had smiled. We all sat blowing smoke into the crisp evening air.

Then, it seemed, some ritual biding time had passed. Old Starlight began to talk again. He gazed at the buffalo in the pasture under the fading light and spoke steadily in bad Spanish with occasional phrases of worse English. The young Indian who had translated for me in the beginning lit a small stick fire below the steps. From time to time one of the other old men would obtrude a question or a correction, and they would drop into the angry Comanche gutturals, and the young man, whose name was John Oak Tree, would tell me what they were saying.

The story went on for an hour or so; when Starlight stopped talking they trooped down to the carryall and got their blankets and rolled up in them on the ground. In the morning I let my work in the ranch office wait and sat down again with the Comanches on the steps, and Starlight talked again. The talk was for me, since I was Tom Bird's kinsman. Starlight did not tell the story as I tell it here. Parts I had to fill in later in conversation with Tom Bird, or even from books. But this was the story.

Without knowing his exact age, he knew that he was younger than Tom Bird, about the age of dead Quanah Parker, under whom he had more than once fought. He had come to warrior's age during the big fight the white men had had among themselves over the black men. Born a Penateka or Honey Eater while the subtribal divisions still had meaning, he remembered the surly exodus from the Brazos reservation to Oklahoma in 1859, the expulsion by law of the Comanches from all of Texas.

But white laws had not meant much for another ten years or so. It was a time of blood and confusion, a good time to be a Comanche and fight the most lost of all causes. The whites at the Oklahoma agencies were Northern and not only tolerated but sometimes egged on and armed the parties striking down across the Red, with the full moon, at the line of settlements established by the abominated and tenacious Texans. In those days, Starlight said, Comanches held Texans to be another breed of white men, and even after they were told that peace had smiled again among whites, they did not consider this to apply to that race which had swarmed over the best of their grass and timber.

In the beginning, the raids had ritual formality and purpose; an individual party would go south either to make war, or to steal horses, or to drive off cattle for trading to the New Mexican *comancheros* at plains rendezvous, or maybe just reminiscently to run deer and buffalo over the old grounds. But the distinctions dimmed. In conservative old age Starlight believed that the Comanches' ultimate destruction was rooted in the loss of the old disciplines. That and smallpox and syphilis and whiskey. And Mackenzie's soldiers. All those things ran in an apocalyptic pack, like wolves in winter.

They had gone horse raiding down into the Brazos country, a dozen of them, all young and all good riders and fighters. They captured thirty horses here and there in the perfect stealth that pride demanded, without clashes, and were headed back north up the Keechi Valley near Palo Pinto when a Texan with a yellow beard caught them in his corral at dawn and killed two of them with a shotgun. They shot the Texan with arrows; Starlight himself peeled off the yellow scalp. Then, with a casualness bred of long cruelty on both sides, they killed his wife and two children in the log house. She did not scream as white women were said to do, but until a hatchet cleaved her skull kept shouting, "Git out! Git, git, git."

And collecting five more horses there, they continued the trek toward the Territory, driving at night and resting at known secret spots during the days.

The leader was a son of old Iron Shirt, Pohebits Quasho, bullet-dead on the Canadian despite his Spanish coat of mail handed down from the old haughty days. Iron Shirt's son said that it was bad to have killed the woman and the children, but Starlight, who with others laughed at him, believed even afterward that it would have been the same if they had let the woman live.

What was certain was that the Texans followed, a big party with men among them who could cut trail as cleanly as Indians. They followed quietly, riding hard and resting little, and on the third evening, when the Comanches were gathering their herd and readying themselves to leave a broad enclosed creek valley where they had spent the day, their sentry on a hill yelled and was dead, and the lean horsemen with the wide hats were pouring down the hillside shouting the long shout that belonged to them.

When it happened, Starlight was riding near the upper end of the valley with the leader. The only weapons with them were their knives and Starlight's lance, with whose butt he had been poking the rumps of the restive stolen horses as they hazed them toward camp below. As they watched, the twenty or more Texans overrode the camp, and in the shooting and confusion the two Comanches heard the end of their five companions who had been there afoot.

"I knew this," the leader said.

"You knew it," Starlight answered him bitterly. "You should have seen the sentry, Know-much."

Of the other two horse gatherers, who had been working the lower valley, they could see nothing, but a group of the Texans rode away from the camp in that direction, yelling and firing. Then others broke toward Starlight and the leader a half mile above.

"We can run around them to the plain below," the son of Iron Shirt said. "Up this creek is bad."

Starlight did not know the country up the creek, but he knew what he felt, and feeling for a Comanche was conviction. He turned his pony upstream and spurred it.

"Ragh!" he called to the leader in farewell. "You're dirty luck!" And he was right, for he never saw the son of Iron Shirt again. Or the other two horse gatherers either.

But the son of Iron Shirt had been right, too, because ten minutes later Starlight was forcing his pony among big fallen boulders in a root tangle of small steep canyons, each of which carried a trickle to the stream below. There was no way even to lead a horse up their walls; he had the feeling that any one of them would bring him to a blind place.

Behind him shod hoofs rang; he whipped the pony on, but a big Texan on a bay horse swept fast around a turn in the canyon, jumping the boulders, and with a long lucky shot from a pistol broke Starlight's pony's leg. The Comanche fell with the pony but lit cat-bouncing and turned, and as the Texan came down waited crouched with the lance. The Texan had one of the pistols that shot six times, rare then in that country. Bearing down, he fired three times, missing each shot, and then when it was the moment Starlight feinted forward and watched the Texan lurch aside from the long bright blade, and while he was off balance, Starlight drove it into the Texan's belly until it came out the back. The blade snapped as the big man's weight came onto it, falling.

Starlight sought the pistol for a moment but not finding it ran to the canyon wall and began climbing. He was halfway up the fifty feet of its crumbling face when the other Texan rode around the turn and stopped, and from his unquiet horse, too hastily, fired a rifle shot that blew Starlight's left eye full of powdered sandstone.

He was among swallows' nests. Their molded mud crunched under his hands; the birds flew in long loops, chittering about his head. Climbing, he felt the Texan's absorbed reloading behind and below him as the horse moved closer, and when he knew with certainty that it was time, looked around to see the long caplock rifle rising again.

The bullet smashed through his upper left arm, and he hung only by his right, but with the long wiry strength of trick horsemanship he swung himself up and onto the overhanging turf of the cliff's top. A round rock the size of a buffalo's head lay there. Almost without pausing he tugged it loose from the earth and rolled it back over the cliff. It came close. The Texan grabbed the saddle as his horse reared, and dropped his rifle. They looked at each other. Clutching a blood-greasy, hanging arm, the Comanche stared down at a big nose and a pair of angry gray eyes, and the young Texan stared back.

Wheeling, Starlight set off trotting across the hills. That night before hiding himself he climbed a low tree and quavered for hours like a screech owl, but no one answered. A month later, an infected skeleton, he walked into the Penateka encampment at Fort Sill, the only one of twelve to return.

That had been his first meeting with Tom Bird.

When telling of the fights, Starlight stood up and gestured

in proud physical representation of what he and the others
had done. He did not give it as a story with a point; it was
the recountal of his acquaintance with a man. In the bug-
flecked light of a bulb above the house's screen door the old
Indian should have looked absurd—hipshot, ugly, in a greasy
black hat and a greasy dark suit with a gold chain across its
vest, the dirty braids flying as he creaked through the motions
of long-unmeaningful violence.

But I did not feel like smiling. I looked at the younger Indians expecting perhaps to find amusement among them, or
boredom, or cynicism. It was not there. They were listening,
most of them probably not even understanding the Spanish
but knowing the stories, to an ancient man who belonged to a
time when their race had been literally terrible.

In the morning Starlight told of the second time. It had
been after the end of the white men's war; he was a war
chief with bull horns on his head. Thirty well-armed warriors
rode behind him when he stopped a trail herd in the Territory for tribute. Although the cowmen were only eight, their
leader, a man with a black mustache, said that four whoa-
haws were too many. He would give maybe two.

"Four," Starlight said. "Texan."

It was an arraignment, and the white man heard it as such.
Looking at the thirty Comanches, he said that he and his
people were not Texans but Kansas men who were returning
home with bought cattle.

"Four whoa-haws," Starlight said.

The white man made a sullen sign with his hand and spoke
to his men, who went to cut out the steers. Starlight watched
jealously to make certain they were not culls, and when three
of his young men had them and were driving them away, he
rode up face to face with the white leader, unfooled even
though the mustache was new.

"Tejano," he said. "Stink sonabitch." And reached over
and twisted Tom Bird's big nose, hard, enjoying the rage
barely held in the gray eyes. He patted his scarred left biceps
and saw that the white man knew him, too, and reached over
to twist the nose again, Tom Bird too prudent to stop him
and too proud to duck his head aside.

"Tobacco, Texan," Starlight said.

Close to snarling, Tom Bird took out a plug. After sam-
pling and examining it and picking a bit of lint from its sur-

face, Starlight tucked it into his waistband. Then he turned his horse and, followed by his thirty warriors, rode away.

In those days revenge had still existed.

He had been, too, with Quanah Parker when that half-white chief had made a separate peace with Tom Bird—Tom Tejano the Pajarito now, looming big on the high plains—as with a government, on the old Bird range up along the Canadian. There had been nearly two hundred with Quanah on a hunt in prohibited territory, and they found few buffalo and many cattle. After the peace with Tom Bird they had not eaten any more wing-branded beef, except later when the Oklahoma agency bought Bird steers to distribute among them.

They had clasped hands there in Quanah's presence, knowing each other well, and in the cowman's tolerant grin and the pressure of his hard fingers Starlight had read more clearly the rout of his people than he had read it anywhere else before.

"Yah, Big-nose," he said, returning the grip and the smile. Tom Bird rode along with them hunting for ten days and led them to a wide valley twenty miles long that the hide hunters had not yet found, and they showed him there how their fathers had run the buffalo in the long good years before the white men. November it had been, with frosted mornings and yellow bright days; their women had followed them to dress the skins and dry the meat. It was the last of the rich hunting years.

After that whenever Tom Bird passed through Oklahoma he would seek out the Indian who had once pulled his nose and would sometimes bring presents.

But Starlight had killed nine white men while the fighting had lasted.

Dressed, Tom Bird came out onto the porch at eleven o'clock, and I knew from the smooth curve of his cheek that the liver had quit hurting. He was affable and shook all their hands again.

"We'll have a big dinner at noon," he told Starlight in the same flowing pidgin Spanish the old Comanche himself used. "Juan's making it especially for my Comanche friends, to send them on their trip full and happy."

Still unfooled, Starlight exhumed the main topic.

"No!" Tom Bird said.

"You have little courtesy," Starlight said. "You had more once."

Tom Bird said, "There were more of you then. Armed."

Starlight's eyes squinted in mirth, which his mouth did not let itself reflect. Absently Tom Bird dug out his Days O' Work and bit a chew, then waved the plug apologetically and offered it to the Comanche. Starlight took it and with three remaining front teeth haggled off a chunk and pretended to put it into his vest pocket.

They both started laughing, phlegmy, hard-earned, old men's laughter, and for the first time—never having seen Tom Bird outargued before—I knew that it was going to work out.

Tom Bird said, "Son of a coyote, you . . . I've got four fat *castrados,* and you can have your pick. They're good meat, and I'll eat some of it with you."

Starlight waggled his head mulishly. "Those, no," he said. "The big bull."

Tom Bird stared, started to speak, closed his mouth, threw the returned plug of tobacco down on the porch, and clumped back into the house. The Indians all sat down again. One of the other older men reached over and picked up the plug, had a chew, and stuck it into his denim jacket. Immobility settled.

"Liberty," Starlight said out of nowhere, in Spanish. "They speak much of liberty. Not one of you has ever seen liberty, or smelled it. Liberty was grass, and wind, and a horse, and meat to hunt, and no wire."

From beyond the dark screen door Tom Bird said, "The little bull."

Starlight without looking around shook his head. Tom Bird opened the door so hard that it battered back against the house wall, loosening flakes of paint. He stopped above the old Indian and stood there on bowed legs, looking down. "You rusty old bastard!" he shouted in English. "I ain't got but the two, and the big one's the only good one. And he wouldn't eat worth a damn."

Starlight turned his head and eyed him.

"All right," Tom Bird said, slumping. "All right."

"Thank you, Pajarito," Starlight said.

"Jimmy," the old man said to me in a washed-out voice, "go tell the boys to shoot Shakespeare and hang him up down by the washhouse."

"No," John Oak Tree said.

"What the hell you mean, no?" Tom Bird said, turning to him with enraged pleasure. "That's the one he wants. What you think he's been hollering about for two whole days?"

"Not dead," John Oak Tree said. "My grandfather wants him alive."

"Now ain't that sweet?" the old man said. "Ain't that just beautiful? And I can go around paying for busted fences from here to Oklahoma and maybe to the God damn Arctic Circle, all so a crazy old murdering Comanche can have him a pet bull buffalo."

Starlight spoke in Spanish, having understood most of the English. "Tom Tejano, listen," he said.

"What?"

"Listen," Starlight said. "We're going to kill him, Tom Tejano. We."

"My butt!" said Tom Bird, and sat down.

In the afternoon, after the fried chicken and the rice and mashed beans and the tamales and the blistering chili, after the courteous belching and the smoking on the porch, everyone on the ranch who could leave his work was standing in the yard under the cottonwoods as the nine Comanches brought their horses up from the lot, where they had been eating oats for two days, and tied them outside the picket fence, saddled.

After hitching Starlight's mare to the carryall, without paying any attention to their audience they began to strip down, methodically rolling their shed clothes into bundles with hats on top and putting them into the back of the carryall. Starlight reeled painfully among them, pointing a dried-up forefinger and giving orders. When they had finished, all of them but he wore only trousers and shoes or moccasins, with here and there scraps of the old bone and claw and hide and feather paraphernalia. John Oak Tree had slipped off the high-heeled boots he wore and replaced them with tennis sneakers.

A hundred yards away, gargling a bellow from time to time, old Shakespeare stood jammed into a chute where the hands had choused him. Between bellows, his small hating eye peered toward us from beneath a grayed board; there was not much doubt about how *he* felt.

The Indians took the long, blanketed bundle from the carryall and unrolled it.

"For God's sake!" a cowboy said beside me, a man named Abe Reynolds who had worked a good bit with the little buffalo herd. "For God's sake, this is nineteen damn twenty-three?"

I chuckled. Old Tom Bird turned his gray eyes on us and glared, and we shut up. The bundle held short bows, and quivers of arrows, and long, feather-hung, newly reshafted buffalo lances daubed with red and black. Some took bows and others lances, and among the bowmen were the two old men younger than Starlight, who under dry skins still had ridged segmented muscles.

"Those?" I said in protest, forgetting Tom Bird. "Those two couldn't . . ."

"Because they never killed one," he said without looking around. "Because old as they are, they ain't old enough to have hunted the animal that for two whole centuries was the main thing their people ate, and wore, and made tents and ropes and saddles and every other damn thing they had out of. You close your mouth, boy, and watch."

Starlight made John Oak Tree put on a ribboned medal of some kind. Then they sat the restless ponies in a shifting line, motley still but somehow, now, with the feel of that old terribleness coming off of them like a smell, and Starlight walked down the line of them and found them good and turned to raise his hand at Tom Bird.

Tom Bird yelled.

The man at the chute pulled the bars and jumped for the fence, and eight mounted Indians lashed their ponies into a hard run toward the lumpy blackness that had emerged and was standing there swaying his head, bawling-furious.

Starlight screeched. But they were out of his control now and swept in too eagerly, not giving Shakespeare time to decide to run. When the Indian on the fastest pony, one of the middle-aged men, came down on him shooting what looked like a steady jet of arrows from beside the pony's neck, the bull squared at him. The Indian reined aside, but not enough. The big head came up under the pony's belly, and for a moment horse and rider paused, reared against the horns and went pinwheeling backward into the middle of the onrushing others.

"Them idiots!" Abe Reynolds said. "Them plumb idiots!"

One swarming pile then, one mass with sharp projecting heads and limbs and weapons, all of them yelling and pounding and hacking and stabbing, and when old Shakespeare shot out from under the pile, shrugging them helter-skelter aside, he made a run for the house. Behind him they came yipping, leaving a gut-ripped dead horse on the ground beside the chute and another running riderless toward the northeast. One of the downed hunters sat on the ground against the chute as though indifferently. The other—one of the two oldsters—was hopping about on his left leg with an arrow through the calf of his right.

But I was scrambling for the high porch with the spectators, those who weren't grabbing for limbs, though Tom Bird stood his ground cursing as Shakespeare smashed through the white picket fence like dry sunflower stalks and whirled to make another stand under the cottonwoods. Some of the Indians jumped the fence and others poured through the hole he had made, all howling until it seemed there could be no breath left in them. For a moment, planted, Shakespeare stood with arrows bristling brightly from his hump and his loins and took someone's lance in his shoulder. Then he gave up that stand, too, and whisked out another eight feet of fence as he leveled into a long run down the dirt road past the corrals.

They rode him close, poking and shooting.

And finally, when it was all far enough down the road to have the perspective of a picture, John Oak Tree swung out leftward and running parallel to the others pulled ahead and abruptly slanted in with the long bubbling shriek, loud and cutting above all the other noise, that you can call rebel yell or cowboy holler or whatever you want, but which deadly exultant men on horseback have likely shrieked since the Assyrians and long, long before. Shakespeare ran desperately free from the sharp-pointed furor behind him, and John Oak Tree took his dun pony in a line converging sharply with the bull's course, and was there, and jammed the lance's blade certainly just behind the ribs and pointing forward, and the bull skidded to his knees, coughed, and rolled onto his side.

"You call that fair?" Abe Reynolds said sourly.

Nobody had. It was not fair. Fair did not seem to have much to do with what it was.

Starlight's carryall was headed for the clump of horsemen down the road, but the rest of us were held to the yard by the erect stability of Tom Bird's back as he stood in one of the gaps in his picket fence. Beside the chute, Starlight picked up the two thrown Indians and the saddle from the dead horse, the old hunter disarrowed and bleeding now, and drove on to where the rest sat on their ponies around Shakespeare's carcass.

Getting down, he spoke to John Oak Tree. The young Indian dismounted and handed his lance to Starlight, who hopped around for a time with one foot in the stirrup and got up onto the dun pony and brought it back toward the house at a run, the lance held high. Against his greasy vest the big gold watch chain bounced, and his coattails flew, but his old legs were locked snugly around the pony's barrel. He ran it straight at Tom Bird where he stood in the fence gap, and pulled it cruelly onto its hocks three yards away, and held out the lance butt first.

"I carried it when I pulled your nose," he said. "The iron, anyhow."

Tom Bird took it.

"We were there, Tom Tejano," Starlight said.

"Yes," my great-uncle said. "Yes, we were there."

The old Comanche turned the pony and ran it back to the little group of his people and gave it to John Oak Tree, who helped him get back into the carryall. Someone had caught the loose pony. For a few moments all of them sat, frozen, looking down at the arrow-quilled black bulk that had been Shakespeare.

Then, leaving it there, they rode off down the road toward Oklahoma, past the fences of barbed steel that would flank them all the way.

A cowhand, surveying the deadly debris along the route of their run, said dryly, "A neat bunch of scutters, be damn if they ain't."

I was standing beside old Tom Bird, and he was crying. He felt my eyes and turned, the bloody lance upright in his hand, paying no heed to the tears running down the sides of his big nose and into his mustache.

"Damn you, boy," he said. "Damn you for not ever getting to know anything worth knowing. Damn me, too. We had a world, once."

ROBERT HENSON

Billie Loses Her Job

When I come out of prison in 1936, a man named Jax was waiting at the gate to sign me up for a personal appearance tour with his carnival: "Jax Shows—Pre-eminent in the Field."

I said I didn't have nothing to tell. "Besides," I said, "he's been dead two years."

"Oh, Billie," he said, "if I could just show you the newspaper clippings, the magazine articles, even the movies! Ever hear of this new guy, Humphrey Bogart?—it's him right down to the grin! What's the biggest draw at the FBI in Washington, D.C.?—his .38, the straw hat he was wearing, his sun glasses. John Dillinger's a legend, Billie, an American hero!"

I said it was news to me.

"The lodge where him and the FBI shot it out—Little Bohemia, remember?—that guy's got a gold mine, tourists beating a path up there just to look at the bullet holes!"

"I wasn't there," I said. "That's what I mean."

I was going to Neopit, Wisconsin, to visit my mother, then on to Chicago to find work. Inside I'd learned how to *do* something for the first time in my life, even if it was only cutting shirtwaist patterns. My supervisor told the parole board I was the best worker she ever had. But . . . outside it was still hard times—especially for women, Indians, and ex-cons. How'd you like to be all three? When Mr. Jax looked me up again several months later, I'd left Chicago. I was back in Neopit.

He didn't have the look white men usually had when they knocked on a door on the reservation. He said, "I knew I was in the right place as soon as I saw that teepee." He meant the fake teepee refreshment stand for tourists that was in the middle of town. Indians were just show business to him.

"Actually I'm only half Menomini," I told him. "Of course, it's the half that shows."

"You got a nice smile, Billie," he said. "You got beautiful eyes. I still want you to join the midway. People'd take to you if you didn't do nothing but smile and say, Hello, I'm Billie Frechette. Crowds are one thing I *know* about."

They'd been playing lots in Illinois for a month and were fixing to loop down through Missouri, Kansas, and Oklahoma. "If you joined us now you'd have a whole month before we start hitting the fairs and the big crowds. However," he said, "in case you're still hesitating, I've got this great big ace up my sleeve. Guess who you'll be on the platform with? John Dillinger, *Senior!* Just signed!"

I couldn't think of what to say. We were sitting at the kitchen table, wind blowing straight through the house from front to back. My mother never closed a window from June to November. Mr. Jax looked at the wall behind me where there was an old calendar picture of Lindberg in his aviator's cap.

"An American hero, Billie, just like Lindy!"

"I've met Mr. Dillinger," I said.

"All the better! Did you know he started going out two weeks after Johnny was killed? Vaudeville, midways, he's even given talks at Little Bohemia. Don't that tell you something? But *this*—his dad and his only true love on the same bill! We'll pack 'em in! Don't get me wrong," he said. "This here'll be an office attraction—that means my own personal management. It won't be no freak show, I promise you."

I wasn't thinking about that.

Sure enough, before we ever got to the fair dates, he called me in for a talk. "Billie, Billie, Billie," he says, shaking his head, "you could go down in history as the *one woman* in John Dillinger's life. But you know what's gonna happen? The Woman in Red's gonna take your place. Not the woman that stuck by him, but the one that sold him out! How could you let that happen?

"I'm gonna have to let you go, Billie," he says.

The way he used to shake his head and say my name over always reminded me of Louis Piquett, Johnny's mouthpiece. "Billie, Billie, Billie," he'd say, "Johnny wants to *marry* you! Doesn't that mean anything to you?"

Well, he wanted to marry me as soon as he met me. I was working hat check in a nightclub in Chicago. The first time he come in he leaned across the counter and said, "Know something?—you got beautiful eyes." The next two nights we had drinks on my break. He said he was from Indianapolis and had to go back on business but he'd send for me if I'd come.

"What kind of business?"

He opened his billfold and took out some clippings from Indiana newspapers, all about a daring new bank robber who'd walked in with a straw hat tipped over one eye, announced a stickup and then—instead of pushing open the teller's door—jumped up on the ledge and vaulted right over the cage.

"Why'd you do that?" I asked.

He said he didn't know why, he didn't even think about it—"All at once I was just flying through the air. Will you come if I send for you? I know we've just met but, baby, I've fallen for you in a great big way. Say razzberries, but to me that means just one thing. I want to be with you for-ever. . . ."

He always did talk like a popular song. It wasn't what he *said* that made me go to Indianapolis a few months later. In fact, I told him right off that I was married and couldn't get a divorce because my husband had been sent up for fifteen years and I didn't know where. He gave Louis Piquett a standing order: "Find the louse."

Louis had contacts in every pen in the forty-eight states, but finding Sparks wasn't that easy. He told me in private it was hard to believe I didn't know where my own husband had been sent.

I said, "Well, he wasn't tried in Chicago, it was in St. Louis. So I couldn't be there."

"And he never *once* got in touch with you after he was sentenced?"

"I guess he was ashamed."

*   *   *

When I first met the man I married, I asked why everyone called him Sparks instead of George. He said it was because he was an electrician.

I was crazy about baseball in those days. On Saturdays I used to hitch a ride into Shawano with my girl friend. Usually we'd just stand around, but if there was a baseball game that's where I'd be. He turned up one summer playing first base for the Shawano team. He was Menomini but he'd gone away to Haskell Indian School in Kansas, then did odd jobs around the country.

He took me to Chicago after we were married. There was supposed to be a lot of work for electricians because of the World's Fair coming up: "A Century of Progress." That sounded good to me. Next thing I knew he caught fifteen for armed robbery.

A friend of his took me on at the nightclub. He was the one that changed my name to Billie, said it went better with Frechette. He used to tell people I was French and Indian— "French where you want her to be French, and Indian where you want her to be Indian." I was used to the jokes. Before long I had me a Persian lamb coat and a long bob, and I'd learned how to cover smallpox scars with makeup.

Louis finally tracked Sparks down in Leavenworth and gave him Johnny's message. "What're you telling me for?" Sparks says. "We ain't married. I didn't even know she was using my name."

"Billie, Billie, Billie . . . you've lied to me so much," Louis says, "trying to keep me from finding this so-called husband of yours. Why did you give me all those names—George Welton, Welton Sparks, George Sparks? Why didn't you just tell me to look for George Welton Frechette, nicknamed Sparks? Why did you let me think Frechette was your maiden name?"

"All I'm asking you to do is check on his story before you say anything to Johnny."

"All right, tell me again where you were married."

"Chicago."

"Not Shawano?"

"We stood up in front of a preacher in Shawano, then when we got to Chicago, we went to city hall to make sure it was legal."

"So you were married in Wisconsin *and* Illinois."

"And one or the other's bound to have a record of it," I said, "if you just keep looking."

He always liked me, Louis did, but Johnny was the one he'd do anything for. He served time for the same rap as me—harboring a fugitive. I seen him just once after we both got out. He still looked like a kewpie doll with his big round eyes and round face. "I never told him, Billie," he said. "At least I spared him that." I couldn't figure out what he meant.

"He died not knowing that you could have married him *any time. . . .*" Tears actually rolled down his cheeks when he said it.

Mr. Dillinger always introduced me as Johnny's wife—at least until he got sore and stopped introducing me at all. "I first met the little lady *you're* waiting to meet," he'd say after his own talk, "back in April 1934. My son brought her to the farm. He had many women friends, so they tell me, but only two he ever brought to get his Dad's blessing.

"I warned him against the first one. I said, 'That girl will not stick by you,' which proved correct as he later admitted to me. But when he come leading this little lady by the hand—never mind state troopers watching the road, and G-men watching the house—I said, 'She's the one for you, Johnny,' and he said, 'Dad, I'm glad to hear that because I want you to meet the sweetest little wife in the world—Billie Frechette!'

That was my cue to step out on the platform.

He knew from experience what people liked to hear, but I never doubted he believed every word he said, especially if it was something Johnny told him. He was supposed to have been strict in earlier days. Wouldn't lift a finger to save Johnny from his first long stretch—wouldn't pay for a lawyer—wouldn't even go to the trial. Prison didn't change Johnny, except to make him a pro. The month he got out he robbed ten banks in a row. It was Mr. Dillinger that caved in. He used to tell audiences, "My boy lived longer in forty minutes than I did in forty years"—something Johnny said once to a bunch of reporters.

*   *   *

I never knew my own father—he was gone before I had the chance. If I'd met him later, I wouldn't have cared two hoots in hell what he thought about me. Johnny was just the opposite. I couldn't get over the way he beamed when Mr. Dillinger took me around at a family reunion introducing me as "Johnny's wife" and "my new daughter-in-law." I was dying for a cigarette. "No—he don't believe in women smoking!" Johnny whispered, nearly paralyzing my elbow with his thumb and finger. His sister Audrey had to sneak me out behind the barn. I was twenty-four years old!

There were relatives and friends from all around Mooresville at that reunion. Naturally no one expected Johnny to show up—it hadn't been six weeks since he busted out of Crown Point jail with his "wooden gun," and the FBI had just promoted him to Public Enemy No. 1. But when he got word from Audrey that there was going to be a reunion, nothing could keep him away. "Fix yourself up," he says. "I'm taking you to meet my dad."

We drove down from Chicago a day early, got there just before dark. State police had the turn-off to the farm staked out, but he said he had a secret way to get to the house that he'd used since he was a kid. Nobody knew about it except him.

No wonder. We left the car on a back road, crawled through a barbed-wire fence, and started off through this maze of gullies and ravines, some so deep I could see tree roots over my head. He was carrying his Tommy, so I had to carry the overnight bag. I was wearing a skirt flared at the bottom but tight around the hips, a blouse with a lace collar, bolero jacket, and high-heeled shoes with ankle straps. Fix myself up!

"The least you could've done was warn me to bring another pair of shoes," I said.

"Go barefoot."

The gullies were sandy but with a lot of little flat rocks. I remember thinking how tender my feet had got. Time was I could walk on cockleburrs and not feel a thing.

Mr. Dillinger nearly had a heart attack when he answered the back door, but right then, I'm sure, is when he took a liking to me. Not when Johnny got around to introducing me, but when he seen me following him barefoot.

State troopers and FBI cruised back and forth all the next

day but didn't have no reason to come onto private property. There was just local people coming and going. Audrey and the others set up a big chicken dinner out back where Johnny could keep out of sight while everyone else let themselves be seen walking around and acting natural.

Afterward Johnny told everyone to gather around, he had a big surprise. He reached in his pocket and pulled out a wooden gun blacked with shoe polish. "Here it is, folks—the gun that locked up eight deputies and twelve trusties at Crown Point! Audrey," he says, "I'm turning this over to you. Don't you part with it for any price. Keep it and pass it on to your kids!"

For some reason Audrey flickered me a glance. I was hoping I didn't look more surprised than anybody else.

They all got out their Kodaks and begged him to pose with the gun. He said he'd do even better. He went in the house and got his Tommy. Mr. Dillinger stopped him on the porch. I don't know what he said but Johnny answered in a voice *everyone* could hear, "This Tommy's as harmless as that wooden gun. Sure I keep it loaded, but I never shoot except to throw a scare into someone that's trying to shoot *me*. That's one thing you don't have to worry about, Dad. I've never killed a man and I never will."

That night I asked him where he got the wooden gun. He gave me a hard look. "Why?"

"Well, you never showed it to *me*."

"I made it in jail, just like I said."

"I don't think Audrey bought the story."

"Did she say anything to you?"

"No."

"Well, don't judge everyone by yourself."

Newspapers and public officials raised a terrible stink about that reunion. All those good people knowing the where-abouts of John Dillinger on that day, and not a one calling the law! He was still collecting newspaper clippings about himself. Only one thing bothered him—the way they kept referring to me as an "unidentified female companion."

"Now Dad will think I lied to him."

Moorseville people got their backs up at being called pro-crime. They sent a petition to the governor asking him to give Johnny a full pardon if he turned himself in. They said banks were as guilty as he was of taking people's money, only banks never got punished. They also said he wasn't violent, which was proved by the fact that he'd never killed a man. They wanted him to be given a chance to start over.

He was shook up by the petition. He said he'd written to some of the very same people at the time of his parole hearing, asking for letters of recommendation. "Not a fucking one answered! Now they see they were wrong—they want to make it up to me. They're good people."

I said, "I guess you're going to turn yourself in, huh?"

For a second I thought he was going to punch me—he couldn't stand not to be taken seriously. But all he done was say with kind of a sneer, "Why don't you wake up, Billie—broaden your horizons." A remark I haven't figured out to this day.

Once down in Florida he beat me up so bad Pete Pierpont had to drag him off me. That was Christmas Day 1933. Two black eyes, kicked my leg so hard I could barely walk, busted my lip. Red Hamilton, Boobie Clark, Chuck Makley, and Pete were downstairs, them and their girl friends, having breakfast. It's funny Pete should be the only one to help me—his girl started the trouble, Mary Kinder.

She was a tiny little thing but red-haired and mean. Johnny had gone down to the table and found his place wasn't set. In front of all the men, Mary said her and the other girls were tired of doing my work, said I never done my share, said she bet I was still putting on my makeup that very minute. Which happened to be true because of the smallpox scars.

I knew about how much good it'd do to me to say that or anything else when he come slamming into the room yelling at me to get my ass downstairs and fix his breakfast! I said, "Well, what are you having?"

"Whatever the others are having!"

"Well, I hope it's bread and gravy, because if there are drippings I can make gravy, but that's all I know how to cook and I've told you that before."

"Then start learning!"—and he sends my makeup crashing to the floor.

I grabbed my long nail file. "I'm not starting *anything* just to please those bitches downstairs, and especially that one bitch!"

He swung on me, caught me in the mouth. Twisted my

arm to make me drop the nail file. I went down on my knees to get it and he kicked me on the leg two or three times, hard. When I tried to stand up, I fell sideways on the bed. I went limp. I covered up my face with my arms and said, "Go ahead, show what a big man you are, prove you got power! The worst mistake of my life was to believe it myself!"

Then he begun accusing me of fooling around with someone else. That's what he always brought it down to. He never knew what I meant by power. "Tell me who it is or I'll kill you!"

So I said, "Charles Lindbergh."

He jumped on me like a mad dog, and I believe he would have killed me if Pete hadn't run in and stopped him. He was Johnny's best friend from prison, the only one he would ever listen to. Pete managed to get him out of the room into the hall. I didn't even care what they were saying, I was busy sopping blood from my lip with a wadded-up corner of the sheet.

Pretty soon Johnny came back alone. Didn't say a word. Grabbed me by the arm and made me sit up. Took my suitcase out of the closet and threw it on the bed, threw down a roll of bills. "Go back where you came from," he said, and walked out.

About an hour later I was limping down the stairs. Halfway down I heard Mary sing out, "Come on, everybody, let's open our presents!"

They were standing around the tree when I went by in the hall—taking their cue from Johnny and pretending not to notice me. Just as I got to the front door, Pete broke away. He said, "Wait on the porch. I'll call a taxi."

I said in a loud voice, "Don't bother, I got a car," and I jingled the keys to Johnny's new Ford. He'd left them lying on the bureau.

Pete stood there like he was frozen. After a couple of seconds Johnny said, "Let her have it."

So I went back where I came from—Neopit, not Chicago.

I could be gone a year and my mother wouldn't act no more surprised than if she'd seen me the day before. She'd always say she was expecting me because of a dream she'd had. I used to tease her. I'd say, "Oh, you're getting just like Grandmaw!" She thought she'd turn her back on the old ways, but she believed in dreams to the point where she didn't even say she *dreamed* this or that last night, but this or that *happened* last night. She looked down on the people over at Zoar, where they still lived in bark huts and belonged to the Medicine Lodge. She turned Catholic, she married a white man, she wanted overstuffed furniture, linoleum, and running water in the house, like the people over at Keshena. Still, there wasn't nothing she liked better than getting together with her cronies to swap tales about love powders and witches. On State 47, Neopit's right in between Zoar and Keshena.

When I drove into the yard she said, "I knew it was you. I seen your face in the water last night, so I knew you'd be crossing Wolf River today." I said, "Oh, you dreamed that because you want running water so bad." She pretended to think for a minute, then said deadpan, "I believe you're right, Evelyn, and I seen your face because you're going to pay for it."

She was teasing me back. Other girls left the reservation and worked and come back with money to buy nice things. I usually showed up with nothing but the clothes on my back. This time, though, I had the Ford and the roll of bills.

I hadn't even counted it. She sat down and counted it first thing. Almost a grand.

"Well, it's all yours," I said. "Buy yourself a radio, get some furniture, have the front door fixed."

She acted uneasy. "I'll put it away and use it a little at a time." She wasn't worried about where it come from, only about being witched if someone got jealous.

A few days later snow begun to fall. "What are you going to do with that car?" she said.

"Leave it where it is, I guess."

Made no difference to me if it was buried in the snow. It got me where I was going, I didn't have no more use for it.

She went and borrowed a tarpaulin from a neighbor. "*You're* the one that's like Grandmaw," she said.

Mr. Dillinger used to tell people that Johnny was just an average American boy except for not having a mother after the age of three. He said Johnny liked to read Wild West stories, especially about Jesse James. He admired Jesse for fighting railroads and the money boys back East. Jesse was the one, he said, that inspired Johnny to respect women.

While he was giving his talk, he used to hold up baby

clothes and a toy car he said was Johnny's favorite plaything and copies of Wild West magazines and family photographs in frames and souvenirs he said Johnny had sent him from different places, like a pillow with "A Century of Progress" painted on it. Then, at the end, with the crowd as quiet and respectful as church, he would unfold the suit he said Johnny was wearing the day he was shot. When he held it up you could hear people catch their breath because of all the bullet holes.

"That old man's a natural," Mr. Jax said. "Pay attention to what he does."

Because when I went out it was just like air leaking out of a balloon. Pretty soon I'd hear people muttering, "That ain't Billie Frechette." Crowds would get smaller after a few days, and by the end of the run there'd be hecklers. Mr. Dillinger could make people blubber, but it was me they were waiting to hear from.

Not long ago a woman reporter told me something about Johnny as a kid. The summer he turned thirteen he organized a gang-bang for some of his pals. He didn't know any more about sex than they did—it was probably his first time. But he found the girl, gave a demonstration as best he could, then stood lookout while the others took their turns.

She asked if he'd ever mentioned this to me. I said no, but it didn't surprise me. I was wishing I'd known about it when me and Mr. Dillinger had our blowup. Just an average American boy!

Mr. Dillinger was plenty upset as it was. I said, "If you knew as much as you think you do, you'd know he lied to you about being married."

"You're the liar," he says.

"I was already married. And even if I *had* married him he would definitely have been second or third choice."

"Liar!"

I said, "You call me a liar again and I'm going to forget you're an old man and do something we'll both be sorry for!"

Mr. Jax had to step in between us.

Later he said, "Sometimes the Indian in you really comes out." I'd heard that before too. It could mean anything.

People didn't want to listen to another set talk after Mr. Dillinger got finished. They had to ask questions or bust.

What was his favorite sport? What was his favorite song? Questions were tame back then. Usually they knew the answers better than I did. The first time someone wanted to know his favorite song, I said, "Home on the Range," and a half a dozen people called out, "What about 'Happy Days Are Here Again'?" "Well," I said, "can't a fella have more then one favorite?" I couldn't remember anything special about the way he dressed. I don't think I *ever* knew what he liked to eat. Things like that didn't make no impression on me.

Mr. Dillinger would get mad enough to have a stroke. "My son's eyes was blue—not brownish-green or greenish-gray or any other color except *blue!* He dressed in style, he had a ruby ring and a five-hundred-dollar gold watch! Bread and gravy's what *you* like to eat," he said. "You're the one that likes 'Home on the Range' and baseball games!"

"Is that true?" Mr. Jax said. "Is that what you've been doing? Christ, Billie," he says, "it's only been two years. How could you forget? Those were the days!"

Louis visited me right after I was sentenced. Johnny had just made headlines again, shooting his way out of Little Bohemia Lodge. Six people dead or wounded, something like that. President Roosevelt went on radio to tell people not to glorify criminals. Everyone knew who he meant. Louis said J. Edgar Hoover put him up to it because Johnny kept making the FBI look like fools.

But Johnny was depressed, Louis said. "He's had enough, Billie, he wants out. This time he means it. First he has to have plastic surgery. While that's going on, I'll file your appeal. He wants you out in time to go with him to Mexico."

"Don't do it," I said.

He wasn't listening. "Even if we lose, he'll be waiting for you when you do get out. He said to tell you that. He said to tell you he'll do whatever has to be done. You're the only woman he ever loved, Billie."

He looked more like a kewpie doll than ever. I said, "Well, tell him to take care of himself."

"Take care of himself! Is that the only message you have to send?"

"It's a good message for him."

Which it was. Two months later he was lying dead in the alley by the Biograph Theater.

One afternoon someone asked me how I felt about the Woman in Red—"him taking up with her and all that while you was in jail. . . ."

People had Anna Sage and Polly Hamilton mixed up then, or rolled into one. I wasn't clear about them myself. He walked out of the Biograph with two women, but one dropped out of sight so fast hardly anyone noticed her. Actually she was his new girl friend—a call girl Anna had been using for bait. But it was Anna, wearing that red dress and fighting to collect the reward, that stuck in everyone's mind.

I said, "Well, I never expected him not to have another girl just because I was in jail, so I don't have no feelings about her one way or another. I never did have," I said.

Mr. Jax was waiting for me in the tent, shaking his head. We were getting near the Oklahoma line by then, "heading into real Dillinger country," Mr. Jax said. "We've got to get your act in shape."

I said, "Tell me what you want me to say and I'll say it."

"Next time someone asks about the Woman in Red, don't say you weren't *never* jealous, say in this case you didn't have no *reason* to be. Say you know from reliable sources that the Woman in Red was just a friend, someone that encouraged him to think of her as an older sister he could talk to and trust. She let him hide out in her place, then betrayed him— for money! Say you'd forgive him even if there was more to it than that: 'All of us have faced temptation and fallen. I will not cast the first stone. But I truly believe I have nothing to forgive him for. He was betrayed by a woman, yes! but not by the woman he loved!' "

"Well," I said deadpan, "if you want me to remember all that you'd better write it down. I'd never think of it by myself."

He lost his temper. "You claim you can't remember the color of his eyes, you claim you never got jealous! What the hell *do* you remember? What kind of feelings *did* you have?"

I don't know why everyone expected me to be jealous, like a witch. It was always the other way around. We hadn't been together two months before he took it in his head that I was making eyes at Eddie Shouse, a driver they sometimes used. Good-looking fellow, always had a girl on each arm and another one waiting in the car. I liked him but never paid no attention to his flirting. That's just the way he was.

But one day Johnny come storming in and pulled his .38 on me. "Get your hat and coat, you're going for a ride."

This was in Chicago. We were sharing an apartment with Pete and Mary. They heard him yelling at me, and come out into the hall in time to see him prodding me along with that .38. Pete says, "Use your common sense, Johnny. Shouse'll make a pass at anything in skirts. That ain't Billie's fault."

"She's leading him on. He wouldn't have the guts."

"What if she is?" Mary says. "She has a right to go for any guy she pleases. If she likes him, who are you to stop her?"

Which might sound like she was on my side, but really she was trying to stir him up more. It wasn't the first time.

He made me drive to a deserted stretch on the lakefront and park. "You got anything to say?"

"No."

"You don't seem to realize you're gonna *die*, sister!"

I didn't answer, just stared out the window on my side and thought about the wind blowing through the house, bare floors, bare walls, like sitting in the cockpit of a plane.

He said, "Remember what I told you when we met—that if you'd be on the level I'd give everybody the go-by for you?"

I said, "Well, I've been on the level. I can't help it if you don't believe me."

"I told you if you couldn't feel the same towards me as I felt towards you, then not to come when I sent for you—remember?"

"Yes."

"Why'd you come?" I couldn't think of any answer that wouldn't make things worse.

He said, "It's not enough for me if you just respect me, Billie. If you can't love me, I'd be better off not ever seeing you again."

I went on looking out the window. I wasn't going to beg.

"What's Ed Shouse got? What do you dames see in him? What makes you get all wet between the legs just because a guy's good-looking and has a fancy line?"

I turned and stared at him, disgusted.

He started rambling—all the women that'd let him down . . . his wife divorcing him while he was in the pen . . . a girl breaking off their engagement because she didn't want to settle down . . . another one skipping town with a square . . . he thought I was different, he was planning to take me to meet his Dad, etc., etc.

I thought, "Maybe he'll get it out of his system"—and sure enough, he trailed off after a while and lowered the gun and just set there. Then he all of a sudden grinned. "One thing I will say, kiddo, you don't lose your head easy."

I said, "Well, you ought to know that from just last week." I meant being with him in the Terraplane when he ditched four police cars—the wildest chase Chicago had ever seen. "I didn't lose my head because I know you're a good driver. You take chances, but I never yet seen you wreck a car."

"Put that in your purse till we get home," he says, handing me the .38.

He parked in front of the building and put his arm around my shoulder as we went up the walk. He rung the bell instead of using his key so Pete would have to look through the peephole. Pete really whooped: "They're back safe!"

"What happened?" Mary said. Johnny put on his best shit-kicking grin. "I couldn't do it. . . ."

I went on down the hall and into the bedroom. Mary followed me. I don't know what she had in mind, but before she could open her mouth I pulled the .38 out of my purse and pointed it right in her face. "Say one more word against me, bitch—*ever*—and there'll be some dead snatch around here!"

She backed out of the room, white as dough. She knew I wasn't kidding—and knew I wasn't talking about Eddie Shouse neither.

She was at it again, though, in Florida. And twenty years later still at it. One July a Chicago newspaper run an "anniversary story" on Johnny's death, and reporters rustled her up for an interview. Not that it was ever hard to do. They asked if she knew what'd become of me. "Oh no," she said, "she dropped out of sight. Billie was a very unusual person," she said. "She didn't have a single good feature except her eyes. She didn't know how to dress or use makeup or do her hair. The rest of us couldn't understand what Johnny seen in her—except he was always for the underdog. . . ."

I asked him to stop teaming up with Pete. When the gang rented more than one hideout, him and Pete always went in together. I said, "I can't get along with her in the same *house*, much less the same *bedroom*."

"What are you talking about?" he said. "You and her don't do nothing."

"Well, neither do you and Pete, so what's the point?"

"The point is, he's my pal—and he likes company."

The questions the reporter asked made me realize how much times had changed. She looked like she hadn't been out of college more than a couple of years. Pretty too. But right away she wanted the dirt. "Was there any group sex in the gang?" I said I didn't think what we done could be called that—just sometimes we'd be in the same bedroom. "Was that Dillinger's idea?" I said it was the men's. "Did you detect any homosexual overtones?" No. "Did he force you to continue after you objected?" No.

And didn't force me to go to Tucson neither when he come after me all the way from Florida. "*That's* what people want to hear," Mr. Jax said. "Not how you wouldn't cook his goddamn breakfast!"

He drove into the yard and honked the horn. I looked out the door. "I'm here to repossess my car," he says.

"Well, it's right there in front of you, and the keys are in it."

"Who's gonna drive this one back to Chicago, that's what I want to know."

It was the first time he'd ever seen Neopit, and vice versa. My mother didn't have no idea who he was, even after I introduced him, but she said, "I knew somebody was coming. Last night Evelyn took the tarp off the car. I asked her what she was doing, I said it might snow. 'I know,' she said, 'but I feel restless.' "

He looked funny because the tarp hadn't been taken off the car, it was still there—but "restless" was just what he wanted to hear. He followed me into the kitchen. The first thing he saw was that picture of Lindbergh. "Nice-looking fella," he grins. Then started in on me to go with him to Arizona. The others were already on the way there from Florida. "I told 'em I had to go by way of Wisconsin. . . ."

"What's in Arizona?"

"A new life, Billie. I got fifty thousand in cash. I've made my mark. Out there we'll be just a hop, skip, and jump from the border. After that . . . well, what do you say?"

It wasn't the money, it wasn't Mexico. I can't explain what flashed through my mind, but clear as daylight I saw that what was going to happen had already happened, and now I had to go through with it or it would always be waiting for me.

He'd dropped Red Hamilton off in Chicago. He went back to pick him up. They were supposed to meet me in three days in Aurora.

Instead he come by himself. We started driving day and night without stopping. I forget just where we picked up a paper with the headline, DILLINGER WANTED FOR MURDER. It turned out him and Red had robbed a bank in East Chicago but had been surprised by the police. In the shooting, Red was hurt, so was a cop. Now the cop had died. So it had finally come around. "That makes three of you," I said.

"Yeah, but they ain't got a case against *me*."

No use reminding him that the only reason they had a case against Pete and Chuck was because they killed a sheriff springing *him* from Lima jail. He was too busy gloating over witnesses that were coming to his defense in East Chicago. "Listen to this: 'A woman who was cashing a check started to hand her money over to Dillinger but he refused it, saying politely that he was robbing a bank, not the people.' . . ."

All the papers played up how he turned back when Red was hit and helped him to the car. ("Hell yes," he says, "he was carrying the money!") " 'Four policemen had a clear shot at him during those moments when he refused to desert his accomplice, but as usual he was miraculously untouched in the hail of bullets.' . . ."

Things like that sent him sky-high: "Miraculously untouched! That's me!"

What they couldn't do in Chicago, Indianapolis, or Minneapolis–St. Paul, they done in Tucson. Someone recognized Boobie Clark from a picture in the post office. The cops spent a day trailing us around, picking us off one or two at a time. No big gun battles, just a wipeout of the whole gang except Red Hamilton.

Three states wanted Johnny; Indiana finally got him. They took him to Crown Point because a new wing had just been added to the jail there, guaranteed escape-proof. To make sure, they put extra guards on duty around the clock.

The girls were packed off to Indianapolis—all except me. I suddenly found myself on the street, and Louis was handing me some money and a railroad ticket to St. Paul. "Rent an apartment and keep in touch. Johnny's orders." That's all he'd tell me.

The girls served thirty days. The fellows never made the street again. They were tried in Lima for killing that sheriff. Pete and Chuck got the chair, Boobie got life.

Johnny was charged with murder too. I went to St. Paul and sent the address. It wasn't over yet. I knew I'd see him again.

A month later he was knocking on the door.

There wasn't nothing miraculous about the escape. He had a real gun.

"Billie, Billie," Mr. Jax says, "how could anyone smuggle a real gun into the jail where *John Dillinger* was being held! It's against common sense."

"Well, how could anyone smuggle enough guns into Pendleton that Pete, Chuck, Boobie, and six others could bust out? But Johnny fixed it—the biggest break the state pen ever had. He fixed that, and Louis fixed this. Money," I said. *"That's* what's common sense."

He took two hostages and drove off in the sheriff's own car. He'd grabbed a machine gun by that time, but when he turned the two men loose at the edge of town, he reached in his pocket and flashed a .45 in front of their eyes. "Want to see what got me downstairs, boys? Wood and shoe polish!"

They made the mistake of telling this to the newspapers. They said they thought he was pulling their leg—it looked like a real .45 to them. The tier guard that'd had it poked in his stomach said the same thing. Nobody else got a good look at it. As soon as he got to the ground floor and a machine gun, he put it in his pocket. Pretty soon, though, everybody was talking about that wooden gun. It was *his* story they believed.

In St. Paul, I asked him to show it to me. He said he'd left it with Louis in Chicago—didn't want to lose it—someday it'd be valuable. "I suppose you think it's a lot of hooey," he said.

"Well, seeing's believing."

I was joking and thought he was too, but all of a sudden he got sore. "You'll see it," he says. "Don't judge everyone by yourself."

At the reunion Audrey slipped over to me. "I hope you don't mind him giving this to me."

"Oh no."

She had a funny little smile. "Did you know I'm thirteen years older than Johnny?"

"No. Why?"

"Oh, no reason. I'm the only mother he ever had," she said.

I told Mr. Jax I couldn't prove it, but in my opinion that wooden gun was a cover story for Louis. Louis knew people thought Johnny could do anything. If he said he rounded up eight deputies with a wooden gun, you could forget about anyone suspecting a fix.

Mr. Jax got as sore as Johnny. "That gun's part of American history! But if it *was* a cover story—which I don't believe—then it's to his credit that he didn't tell you."

No use saying that wasn't the reason.

I said, "Know who else he didn't tell? Pete and Chuck. They tried the same thing on Death Row, using soap instead of wood. Chuck was shot to pieces, and Pete burned right on schedule."

He said, "Billie, if you want people to like and respect you, you better get over trying to debunk John Dillinger. That's not what you're getting paid for," he said.

Funny, but the night before that reporter was due I was sitting at the kitchen table and all at once I could remember letter-perfect everything Mr. Jax and Mr. Dillinger ever wanted me to say. I thought, "Well, better late than never." I needed an operation for a little growth on my neck—I was hoping she'd help me out, me giving her an exclusive interview and all. I was ready to start with how it was love at first sight when Johnny walked in the nightclub, and go on from there.

She was polite but she set me straight in the first ten minutes. "Billie," she said, "I'm not here to get the same old Robin Hood line. The angle I'm working on is the truth behind the macho legend."

He had a gun in St. Paul I hadn't seen before. It wasn't wood, though—it was a pistol-sized machine gun that he could hide under his coat. He'd had it made special. He tried it out on jobs in Iowa and South Dakota while they were still looking for him in Chicago, and he used it when they finally caught up with us early one morning in St. Paul. He fired through the door, driving them back, then tore the hall to pieces while I flew down the back stairs wearing nothing but my slip and Persian lamb. I backed the car out of the garage, but he wouldn't get in—he kept shooting up the rear end of the building. "For God's sake, get in!" I screamed. He didn't care who he killed.

He was bleeding in one leg, so I had to drive. How we got to Minneapolis I'll never know. All I can remember is what a relief it was to see daylight again. In St. Paul we had to keep the shades drawn, couldn't go out till after dark, had to sneak down the back stairs. I never did get used to hiding out.

He was stretched out on the backseat. I heard him mumble, "You're okay, kid."

"Thanks."

"Yeah—you too," he says after a second.

I looked around. He'd been talking to that gun.

This reporter had her own ideas about guns. She brought up Clyde Barrow, George Kelly, Baby Face Nelson. The only one I knew was Baby Face. Kelly's wife, though, was on my tier in Milan. She had it in for me until she saw I wouldn't pull rank on her. I never talked about Johnny at all; she talked about George all the time—mostly trying to convince us that she'd been the real brains of the Kelly gang, and if he'd listened to her, they'd be out "drinking good beer," as she used to say, instead of doing life. She liked to read his letters from Alcatraz out loud and make fun of the mushy parts. She said she didn't know how he ever got the name "Machine Gun" Kelly—people might *think* he could write his name on the wall with bullets, but he couldn't even *hit* a wall. Her name was Kathryn.

I was picked up not long after Nelson joined the new gang, so I didn't know him very well—though as well as I wanted to. A mean killer. It was worth your life to call him Baby Face. As far as I could tell, his wife was crazy about him.

*   *   *

Johnny took him in after Crown Point, along with some others of the same kind. The only one left from the old gang was Red. On the Iowa and South Dakota jobs he shot out windows, kicked hostages, cursed at women, and went out of his way to kill. "I don't like it no better than you do," Johnny says to Red, "but that's the way they want it." By "they" he meant the cops, the FBI, the banks. The same line he peddled at the reunion.

Red wasn't fooled. "Johnny won't have to worry about his rep," he said to me on the sly, "as long as he's got Baby Face."

It was Baby Face the public got down on. Once when they were using two cars, someone threw tacks under his tires but not Johnny's. He died in a ditch. The body wasn't even claimed.

Johnny was laid out in state in the morgue. Lines a quarter of a mile long. Someone selling pieces of cloth they said had been dipped in the blood in the alley. Mr. Dillinger went to get the body. Lines outside the funeral parlor in Mooresville. Big mob at the cemetery. Couldn't hardly get the coffin out of the hearse. Tombstone chipped to bits as quick as it was put up. Mr. Dillinger said he had to have the casket dug up and set in concrete, then concrete slabs poured in the dirt over it. "People wouldn't believe he was dead, they wanted to see with their own eyes."

You couldn't feel sorry for him——he was too pleased and proud. "Audrey chased two fellers back to their car one day and seen California license plates!"

From Minneapolis we went to Chicago, then to the reunion, then to Indianapolis, then back to Chicago. I could almost feel the wind at my back. We shouldn't have gone near Chicago——the heat was on worse than any place. But he was in an ugly mood, he wanted to see Louis in person. "I'll give him one more chance. And then——" He cocked his finger at his temple. He was hell-bent on making good that lie about us being married.

Louis tried to get out of meeting him; he was sure he'd be followed. But Johnny wouldn't take no for an answer and wouldn't explain what he wanted on the phone. Finally Louis agreed to meet him in a bar on North State Street about ten P.M.

I knew he'd spill the beans if I didn't get to him first, so when Johnny was parking the car I said, "Let me go in ahead of you to see if the coast is clear."

He looked at me kind of funny—I didn't usually volunteer—and besides that, the Feds now wanted me for harboring. Then he said, "Okay, but if he ain't there, *scram!* Don't hang around."

The place was crowded—I couldn't see him—but I hung around for a few minutes in case he was in the men's or something. I heard a car horn blasting away—I don't know why it didn't register sooner. I beat it for the door—I could hear a motor being gunned—tires squealing. I run right into the big paws of the FBI.

"What's the matter?" I said to Mr. Jax. "Does it sound like I'm blaming him for making his getaway? Tell me what you want me to say. It wasn't his fault; I done it to myself."

He wouldn't answer, just looked at me.

"Well, not on *purpose*," I said, "if that's what you think."

We hit a spell of cyclone weather down near the corner of Missouri, Arkansas, and Oklahoma. Twisters like rattlesnakes all through that section. We'd be coming to a town and see a rooftop hanging in a tree, or a telephone pole sticking through the side of a barn like a toothpick. Everybody's nerves were on edge.

One afternoon—I remember how sultry and still it was—a woman asked me how many scars Johnny had on his body. I'd never been asked that before, maybe it seemed too personal; but whether it was that or the weather or what, I went blank. I said, "Well, he had a scar from climbing a barbed-wire fence as a boy. . . ."

There was some shuffling around, people cutting their eyes at each other. "She means from the times he was shot," a man said.

"Well, he was pretty lucky, you know. He got creased a lot of times but he didn't really have what you'd call scars—no, not that I remember."

"She ain't Billie Frechette. . . ."

Mr. Dillinger had been laying off me for a while—now he landed with both feet. "My son was hunted and hounded and cut down in cold blood, and you tell people he didn't have no scars! I was the one identified the body, I *seen*—" He broke clear down.

"Well, I didn't say *no* scars, just none I could remember."

"If you can't remember, who can?" Mr. Jax said.

All of a sudden I screamed, "Anybody'd think I spent my whole life with John Dillinger instead of one piss-ant year!"

Mr. Dillinger turned and walked out. "I won't be on the same platform with her no more."

Mr. Jax didn't run after him. He knew who was leaving and who was staying. "Billie, Billie, Billie . . . you're just not making 'em believe that you were the love of his life."

"Or vice versa."

He wasn't interested in that, never had been. "I'm gonna have to let you go, Billie."

He was right about one thing—the Woman in Red took my place. When I left the carnival, I pledged not to talk about John Dillinger again. Every now and then someone would track me down, but I stuck to my rule for forty years.

I didn't mention money until this reporter was in the house. "I've had to scramble these past few years. Take a look around," I said, wishing I hadn't had my hair touched up—her eyes went right to it.

She was interested in what I told her about Kathryn Kelly. "Mightn't she have been saying he wasn't so hot in bed— 'couldn't hit a wall' with his gun?"

"She was disappointed in him, but *brains* was what he didn't have."

She asked if Johnny had anything to "compensate for." "Was he underendowed, for instance?"

"That'd have to be in his opinion, wouldn't it?"

"Not necessarily. *Was* it his opinion?"

I said I didn't know.

"What about Harry Pierpont?"

"Pete? How would I know? Ask Mary Kinder."

"She's been saying for a number of years that they weren't lovers, more like brother and sister."

"Well, that's news to me."

"Did you ever sense that Johnny was showing off for Pete—to help him along?" I thought if any of this was true, no wonder Mary Kinder hated me!

I wasn't surprised when she begun to lose patience with me. I could read her mind a mile off—I was one of those women that men make doormats out of. Half Indian besides—probably didn't care much about sex, just laid there. My opinion of her was she had a one-track mind.

"Listen," I said, "I'd like to help you, I could use some money, but as far as I'm concerned you're barking up the wrong tree."

She asked what I thought her angle should be. I couldn't explain. I kept wanting to say, "Well, he was deceitful in the way the old people say evil spirits are. He didn't really have a shape of his own, he could only *take* shapes." I thought, "The older I get, the more I go blanket, just like Maw. . . ."

When I was in the hospital with my neck, I found a book by Lindbergh's wife on the book cart—diaries and letters telling how they met and such. I felt sad seeing pictures of him looking the way he looked on my wall. He had a smile that lifted right off the page, the clearest eyes. I remember when I first tacked his picture up. I was seventeen. My mother said, "Who's that?" Without even thinking I said, "Someone that's got Power."

"What do you know about Power?"

She never had told me about it, of course, but I must have picked it up somewhere. "I don't know if it's the same," I said, "but if a white man can have it, he's got it. I can tell by the eyes."

His wife saw it too. Oh, she fell hard when she met him. She told herself she wasn't going to be taken in, but something burned like a bright fire in his eyes. He made her feel like he could do anything. The minute he proposed she said yes. She didn't expect it, didn't want the kind of life he was offering, but what could she do? There he was, she said—she had to go.

My mother studied that picture several days before she said anything. Then all of a sudden she started talking about the old ways. "When I was a girl, I went out in the woods and fasted so that I would see the future. Back then young girls who seen the sun or wind believed they'd find happiness, they'd get a good husband. But in my dream the wind was pressing like a hand against my back, pushing me faster and faster along a road until I was almost skimming. I turned my head and seen a tall dark shape, but I couldn't make out any feature except his eyes—cold and blue as ice, but at the same time they burned. I told my mother and she said I'd seen the Wandering Man, a spirit who never rests but goes round and round the earth with a burden on his back. He takes many different shapes, but when you see him, it means misfortune unless you perform special ceremonies."

"Did you perform them?"

"I started to, but I quit because I was in school; I was afraid to ask the Sisters for time off."

"About payment—" this woman said.

"Forget it," I said, to save her the trouble. "I never could make anything out of John Dillinger."

DOROTHY M. JOHNSON

Lost Sister

Our household was full of women, who overwhelmed my Uncle Charlie and sometimes confused me with their bustle and chatter. We were the only men on the place. I was nine years old when still another woman came—Aunt Bessie, who had been living with the Indians.

When my mother told me about her, I couldn't believe it. The savages had killed my father, a cavalry lieutenant, two years before. I hated Indians and looked forward to wiping them out when I got older. (But when I was grown, they were no menace anymore.)

"What did she live with the hostiles for?" I demanded.

"They captured her when she was a little girl," Ma said. "She was three years younger than you are. Now she's coming home."

High time she came home, I thought. I said so, promising, "If they was ever to get me, I wouldn't stay with 'em long."

Ma put her arms around me. "Don't talk like that. They won't get you. They'll never get you."

I was my mother's only real tie with her husband's family. She was not happy with those masterful women, my Aunts Margaret, Hannah and Sabina, but she would not go back East where she came from. Uncle Charlie managed the store the aunts owned, but he wasn't really a member of the family—he was just Aunt Margaret's husband. The only man who had belonged was my father, the aunts' younger brother.

157

And I belonged, and someday the store would be mine. My mother stayed to protect my heritage.

None of the three sisters, my aunts, had ever seen Aunt Bessie. She had been taken by the Indians before they were born. Aunt Mary had known her—Aunt Mary was two years older—but she lived a thousand miles away now and was not well.

There was no picture of the little girl who had become a legend. When the family had first settled here, there was enough struggle to feed and clothe the children without having pictures made of them.

Even after army officers had come to our house several times and there had been many letters about Aunt Bessie's delivery from the savages, it was a long time before she came. Major Harris, who made the final arrangements, warned my aunts that they would have problems, that Aunt Bessie might not be able to settle down easily into family life.

This was only a challenge to Aunt Margaret, who welcomed challenges. "She's our own flesh and blood," Aunt Margaret trumpeted. "Of course she must come to us. My poor, dear sister Bessie, torn from her home forty years ago!"

The major was earnest but not tactful. "She's been with the savages all those years," he insisted. "And she was only a little girl when she was taken. I haven't seen her myself, but it's reasonable to assume that she'll be like an Indian woman."

My stately Aunt Margaret arose to show that the audience was ended. "Major Harris," she intoned, "I cannot permit anyone to criticize my own dear sister. She will live in my home, and if I do not receive official word that she is coming within a month, I shall take steps."

Aunt Bessie came before the month was up.

The aunts in residence made valiant preparations. They bustled and swept and mopped and polished. They moved me from my own room to my mother's—as she had been begging them to do because I was troubled with nightmares. They prepared my old room for Aunt Bessie with many small comforts—fresh doilies everywhere, hairpins, a matching pitcher and bowl, the best towels and two new nightgowns in case hers might be old. (The fact was that she didn't have any.)

"Perhaps we should have some dresses made," Hannah suggested. "We don't know what she'll have with her."

"We don't know what size she'll take, either," Margaret

pointed out. "There'll be time enough for her to go to the store after she settles down and rests for a day or two. Then she can shop to her heart's content."

Ladies of the town came to call almost every afternoon while the preparations were going on. Margaret promised them that, as soon as Bessie had recovered sufficiently from her ordeal, they should all meet her at tea.

Margaret warned her anxious sisters. "Now, girls, we mustn't ask her too many questions at first. She must rest for a while. She's been through a terrible experience." Margaret's voice dropped way down with those last two words, as if only she could be expected to understand.

Indeed Bessie had been through a terrible experience, but it wasn't what the sisters thought. The experience from which she was suffering, when she arrived, was that she had been wrenched from her people, the Indians, and turned over to strangers. She had not been freed. She had been made a captive.

Aunt Bessie came with Major Harris and an interpreter, a half-blood with greasy black hair hanging down to his shoulders. His costume was half army and half primitive. Aunt Margaret swung the door open wide when she saw them coming. She ran out with her sisters following, while my mother and I watched from a window. Margaret's arms were outstretched, but when she saw the woman closer, her arms dropped and her glad cry died.

She did not cringe, my Aunt Bessie who had been an Indian for forty years, but she stopped walking and stood staring, helpless among her captors.

The sisters had described her often as a little girl. Not that they had ever seen her, but she was a legend, the captive child. Beautiful blonde curls, they said she had, the big blue eyes—she was a fairy child, a pale-haired little angel who ran on dancing feet.

The Bessie who came back was an aging woman who plodded in moccasins, whose dark dress did not belong on her bulging body. Her brown hair hung just below her ears. It was growing out; when she was first taken from the Indians, her hair had been cut short to clean out the vermin.

Aunt Margaret recovered herself and, instead of embracing this silent stolid woman, satisfied herself by patting an arm and crying, "Poor dear Bessie, I am your sister Margaret.

And here are our sisters Hannah and Sabina. We do hope you're not all tired out from your journey!"

Aunt Margaret was all graciousness, because she had been assured beyond doubt that this was truly a member of the family. She must have believed—Aunt Margaret could believe anything—that all Bessie needed was to have a nice nap and wash her face. Then she would be as talkative as any of them.

The other aunts were quick-moving and sharp of tongue. But this one moved as if her sorrows were a burden on her bowed shoulders, and when she spoke briefly to answer to the interpreter, you could not understand a word of it.

Aunt Margaret ignored these peculiarities. She took the party into the front parlor—even the interpreter, when she understood there was no avoiding it. She might have gone on battling with the major about him, but she was in a hurry to talk to her lost sister.

"You won't be able to converse with her unless the interpreter is present," Major Harris said. "Not," he explained hastily, "because of any regulation, but because she has forgotten English."

Aunt Margaret gave the half-blood interpreter a look of frowning doubt and let him enter. She coaxed Bessie. "Come, dear, sit down."

The interpreter mumbled, and my Indian aunt sat cautiously on a needlepoint chair. For most of her life she had been living with people who sat comfortably on the ground.

The visit in the parlor was brief. Bessie had had her instructions before she came. But Major Harris had a few warnings for the family. "Technically, your sister is still a prisoner," he explained, ignoring Margaret's start of horror. "She will be in your custody. She may walk in your fenced yard, but she must not leave it without official permission.

"Mrs. Raleigh, this may be a heavy burden for you all. But she has been told all this and has expressed willingness to conform to these restrictions. I don't think you will have any trouble keeping her here." Major Harris hesitated, remembering that he was a soldier and a brave man, and added, "If I did, I wouldn't have brought her."

There was the making of a sharp little battle, but Aunt Margaret chose to overlook the challenge. She could not overlook the fact that Bessie was not what she had expected.

Bessie certainly knew that this was her lost white family,

but she didn't seem to care. She was infinitely sad, infinitely removed. She asked one question: "Ma-ry?" and Aunt Margaret almost wept with joy.

"Sister Mary lives a long way from here," she explained, "and she isn't well, but she will come as soon as she's able. Dear sister Mary!"

The interpreter translated this, and Bessie had no more to say. That was the only understandable word she ever did say in our house, the remembered name of her older sister.

When the aunts, all chattering, took Bessie to her room, one of them asked, "But where are her things?"

Bessie had no things, no baggage. She had nothing at all but the clothes she stood in. While the sisters scurried to bring a comb and other oddments, she stood like a stooped monument, silent and watchful. This was her prison. Very well, she would endure it.

"Maybe tomorrow we can take her to the store and see what she would like," Aunt Hannah suggested.

"There's no hurry," Aunt Margaret declared thoughtfully. She was getting the idea that this sister was going to be a problem. But I don't think Aunt Margaret ever really stopped hoping that one day Bessie would cease to be different, that she would end her stubborn silence and begin to relate the events of her life among the savages, in the parlor over a cup of tea.

My Indian aunt accustomed herself, finally, to sitting on the chair in her room. She seldom came out, which was a relief to her sisters. She preferred to stand, hour after hour, looking out the window—which was open only about a foot, in spite of all Uncle Charlie's efforts to budge it higher. And she always wore moccasins. She never was able to wear shoes from the store, but seemed to treasure the shoes brought to her.

The aunts did not, of course, take her shopping after all. They made her a couple of dresses; and when they told her, with signs and voluble explanations, to change her dress, she did.

After I found that she was usually at the window, looking across the flat land to the blue mountains, I played in the yard so I could stare at her. She never smiled, as an aunt should, but she looked at me sometimes, thoughtfully, as if measuring my worth. By performing athletic feats, such as walking on my hands, I could get her attention. For some reason, I valued it.

She didn't often change expression, but twice I saw her scowl with disapproval. Once was when one of the aunts slapped me in a casual way. I had earned the slap, but the Indians did not punish children with blows. Aunt Bessie was shocked, I think, to see that white people did. The other time was when I talked back to someone with spoiled, small-boy insolence—and that time the scowl was for me.

The sisters and my mother took turns, as was their Christian duty, in visiting her for half an hour each day. Bessie didn't eat at the table with us—not after the first meal.

The first time my mother took her turn, it was under protest. "I'm afraid I'd start crying in front of her," she argued, but Aunt Margaret insisted.

I was lurking in the hall when Ma went in. Bessie said something, then said it again, peremptorily, until my mother guessed what she wanted. She called me and put her arm around me as I stood beside her chair. Aunt Bessie nodded, and that was all there was to it.

Afterward, my mother said, "She likes you. And so do I." She kissed me.

"I don't like her," I complained. "She's queer."

"She's a sad old lady," my mother explained. "She had a little boy once, you know."

"What happened to him?"

"He grew up and became a warrior. I suppose she was proud of him. Now the army has him in prison somewhere. He's half Indian. He was a dangerous man."

He was indeed a dangerous man, and a proud man, a chief, a bird of prey whose wings the army had clipped after bitter years of trying.

However, my mother and my Indian aunt had that one thing in common: they both had sons. The other aunts were childless.

There was a great to-do about having Aunt Bessie's photograph taken. The aunts, who were stubbornly and valiantly trying to make her one of the family, wanted a picture of her for the family album. The government wanted one too, for some reason—perhaps because someone realized that a thing of historic importance had been accomplished by recovering the captive child.

Major Harris sent a young lieutenant with the greasy-haired interpreter to discuss the matter in the parlor. (Margaret, with great foresight, put a clean towel on a chair and saw to it the interpreter sat there.) Bessie spoke very little during the meeting, and of course we understood only what the half-blood *said* she was saying.

No, she did not want her picture made. No.

But your son had his picture made. Do you want to see it? They teased her with that offer, and she nodded.

If we let you see his picture, then will you have yours made?

She nodded doubtfully. Then she demanded more than had been offered: If you let me keep his picture, then you can make mine.

No, you can only look at it. We have to keep his picture. It belongs to us.

My Indian aunt gambled for high stakes. She shrugged and spoke, and the interpreter said, "She not want to look. She will keep or nothing."

My mother shivered, understanding as the aunts could not understand what Bessie was gambling—all or nothing.

Bessie won. Perhaps they had intended that she should. She was allowed to keep the photograph that had been made of her son. It has been in history books many times—the half-white chief, the valiant leader who was not quite great enough to keep his Indian people free.

His photograph was taken after he was captured, but you would never guess it. His head is high, his eyes stare with boldness but not with scorn, his long hair is arranged with care—dark hair braided on one side and with a tendency to curl where the other side hangs loose—and his hands hold the pipe like a royal scepter.

That photograph of the captive but unconquered warrior had its effect on me. Remembering him, I began to control my temper and my tongue, to cultivate reserve as I grew older, to stare with boldness but not scorn at people who annoyed or offended me. I never met him, but I took silent pride in him—Eagle Head, my Indian cousin.

Bessie kept his picture on her dresser when she was not holding it in her hands. And she went like a docile, silent child to the photograph studio, in a carriage with Aunt Margaret early one morning, when there would be few people on the street to stare.

Bessie's photograph is not proud but pitiful. She looks out

with no expression. There is no emotion there, no challenge, only the face of an aging woman with short hair, only endurance and patience. The aunts put a copy in the family album.

But they were nearing the end of their tether. The Indian aunt was a solid ghost in the house. She did nothing because there was nothing for her to do. Her gnarled hands must have been skilled at squaws' work, at butchering meat and scraping and tanning hides, at making tepees and beading ceremonial clothes. But her skills were useless and unwanted in a civilized home. She did not even sew when my mother gave her cloth and needles and thread. She kept the sewing things beside her son's picture.

She ate (in her room) and slept (on the floor) and stood looking out the window. That was all, and it could not go on. But it had to go on, at least until my sick Aunt Mary was well enough to travel—Aunt Mary who was her older sister, the only one who had known her when they were children.

The sisters' duty visits to Aunt Bessie became less and less visits and more and more duty. They settled into a bearable routine. Margaret had taken upon herself the responsibility of trying to make Bessie talk. Make, I said, not teach. She firmly believed that her stubborn and unfortunate sister needed only encouragement from a strong-willed person. So Margaret talked, as to a child, when she bustled in:

"Now there you stand, just looking, dear. What in the world is there to see out there? The birds—are you watching the birds? Why don't you try sewing? Or you could go for a little walk in the yard. Don't you want to go out for a nice little walk?"

Bessie listened and blinked.

Margaret could have understood an Indian woman's not being able to converse in a civilized tongue, but her own sister was not an Indian. Bessie was white, therefore she should talk the language her sisters did—the language she had not heard since early childhood.

Hannah, the put-upon aunt, talked to Bessie too, but she was delighted not to get any answers and not to be interrupted. She bent over her embroidery when it was her turn to sit with Bessie and told her troubles in an unending flow. Bessie stood looking out the window the whole time.

Sabina, who had just as many troubles, most of them emanating from Margaret and Hannah, went in like a martyr, firmly clutching her Bible, and read aloud from it until her time was up. She took a small clock along so that she would not, because of annoyance, be tempted to cheat.

After several weeks Aunt Mary came, white and trembling and exhausted from her illness and the long, hard journey. The sisters tried to get the interpreter in but were not successful. (Aunt Margaret took that failure pretty hard.) They briefed Aunt Mary, after she had rested, so the shock of seeing Bessie would not be too terrible. I saw them meet, those two.

Margaret went to the Indian woman's door and explained volubly who had come, a useless but brave attempt. Then she stood aside, and Aunt Mary was there, her lined white face aglow, her arms outstretched. "Bessie! Sister Bessie!" she cried.

And after one brief moment's hesitation, Bessie went into her arms and Mary kissed her sun-dark, weathered cheek. Bessie spoke. "Ma-ry," she said. "Ma-ry." She stood with tears running down her face and her mouth working. So much to tell, so much suffering and fear—and joy and triumph, too—and the sister there at last who might legitimately hear it all and understand.

But the only English word that Bessie remembered was "Mary," and she had not cared to learn any others. She turned to the dresser, took her son's picture in her work-hardened hands, reverently, and held it so her sister could see. Her eyes pleaded.

Mary looked on the calm, noble, savage face of her half-blood nephew and said the right thing: "My, isn't he handsome!" She put her head on one side and then the other. "A fine boy, sister," she approved. "You must"—she stopped, but she finished—"be awfully proud of him, dear!"

Bessie understood the tone if not the words. The tone was admiration. Her son was accepted by the sister who mattered. Bessie looked at the picture and nodded, murmuring. Then she put it back on the dresser.

Aunt Mary did not try to make Bessie talk. She sat with her every day for hours, and Bessie did talk—but not in English. They sat holding hands for mutual comfort while the captive child, grown old and a grandmother, told what had happened in forty years. Aunt Mary said that was what Bessie was talking about. But she didn't understand a word of it and didn't need to.

"There is time enough for her to learn English again,"

Aunt Mary said. "I think she understands more than she lets on. I asked her if she'd like to come and live with me, and she nodded. We'll have the rest of our lives for her to learn English. But what she has been telling me—she can't wait to tell that. About her life, and her son."

"Are you sure, Mary dear, that you should take the responsibility of having her?" Margaret asked dutifully, no doubt shaking in her shoes for fear Mary would change her mind now that deliverance was in sight. "I do believe she'd be happier with you, though we've done all we could."

Margaret and the other sisters would certainly be happier with Bessie somewhere else. And so, it developed, would the United States Government.

Major Harris came with the interpreter to discuss details, and they told Bessie she could go, if she wished, to live with Mary a thousand miles away. Bessie was patient and willing, stolidly agreeable. She talked a great deal more to the interpreter than she had ever done before. He answered at length and then explained to the others that she had wanted to know how she and Mary would travel to this far country. It was hard, he said, for her to understand just how far they were going.

Later we knew that the interpreter and Bessie had talked about much more than that.

Next morning, when Sabina took breakfast to Bessie's room, we heard a cry of dismay. Sabina stood holding the tray, repeating, "She's gone out the window! She's gone out the window!"

And so she had. The window that had always stuck so that it would not raise more than a foot was open wider now. And the photograph of Bessie's son was gone from the dresser. Nothing else was missing except Bessie and the decent dark dress she had worn the day before.

My Uncle Charlie got no breakfast that morning. With Margaret shrieking orders, he leaped on a horse and rode to the telegraph station.

Before Major Harris got there with half a dozen cavalrymen, civilian scouts were out searching for the missing woman. They were expert trackers. Their lives had depended, at various times, on their ability to read the meaning of a turned stone, a broken twig, a bruised leaf. They found that Bessie had gone south. They tracked her for ten miles. And then they lost the trail, for Bessie was as skilled as they were.

Her life had sometimes depended on leaving no stone or twig or leaf marked by her passage. She traveled fast at first. Then, with time to be careful, she evaded the followers she knew would come.

The aunts were stricken with grief—at least Aunt Mary was—and bowed with humiliation about what Bessie had done. The blinds were drawn, and voices were low in the house. We had been pitied because of Bessie's tragic folly in having let the Indians make a savage of her. But now we were traitors because we had let her get away.

Aunt Mary kept saying pitifully, "Oh, why did she go? I thought she would be contented with me!"

The others said that it was, perhaps, all for the best.

Aunt Margaret proclaimed, "She has gone back to her own." That was what they honestly believed, and so did Major Harris.

My mother told me why she had gone. "You know that picture she had of the Indian chief, her son? He's escaped from the jail he was in. The fort got word of it, and they think Bessie may be going to where he's hiding. That's why they're trying so hard to find her. They think," my mother explained, "that she knew of his escape before they did. They think the interpreter told her when he was here. There was no other way she could have found out."

They scoured the mountains to the south for Eagle Head and Bessie. They never found her, and they did not get him until a year later, far to the north. They could not capture him that time. He died fighting.

After I grew up, I operated the family store, disliking storekeeping a little more every day. When I was free to sell it, I did, and went to raising cattle. And one day, riding in a canyon after strayed steers, I found—I think—Aunt Bessie. A cowboy who worked for me was along, or I would never have let anybody know.

We found weathered bones near a little spring. They had a mystery on them, those nameless human bones suddenly come upon. I could feel old death brushing my back.

"Some prospector," suggested my riding partner.

I thought so too until I found, protected by a log, sodden scraps of fabric that might have been a dark, respectable dress. And wrapped in them was a sodden something that might have once been a picture.

The man with me was young, but he had heard the story

of the captive child. He had been telling me about it, in fact. In the passing years it had acquired some details that surprised me. Aunt Bessie had become once more a fair-haired beauty, in this legend that he had heard, but utterly sad and silent. Well, sad and silent she really was.

I tried to push the sodden scrap of fabric back under the log, but he was too quick for me. "That ain't no shirt, that's a dress!" he announced. "This here was no prospector—it was a woman!" He paused and then announced with awe, "I bet you it was your Indian aunt!"

I scowled and said, "Nonsense. It could be anybody."

He got all worked up about it. "If it was *my* aunt," he declared, "I'd bury her in the family plot."

"No," I said, and shook my head.

We left the bones there in the canyon, where they had been for forty-odd years if they were Aunt Bessie's. And I think they were. But I would not make her a captive again. She's in the family album. She doesn't need to be in the family plot.

If my guess about why she left us is wrong, nobody can prove it. She never intended to join her son in hiding. She went in the opposite direction to lure pursuit away.

What happened to her in the canyon doesn't concern me, or anyone. My Aunt Bessie accomplished what she set out to do. It was not her life that mattered, but his. She bought him another year.

LOUIS L'AMOUR

The Strong Shall Live

The land was fire beneath and the sky was brass above, but throughout the day's long riding the bound man sat erect in the saddle and cursed them for thieves and cowards. Their blows did not silence him, although the blood from his swollen and cracked lips had dried on his face and neck.

Only John Sutton knew where they rode and only he knew what he planned for Cavagan, and John Sutton sat thin and dry and tall on his long-limbed horse, leading the way.

Nine men in all, tempered to the hard ways of an unforgiving land, men strong in the strengths needed to survive in a land that held no place for the weak or indecisive. Eight men and a prisoner taken after a bitter chase from the pleasant coastal lands to the blazing desert along the Colorado River.

Cavagan had fought on when the others quit. They destroyed his crops, tore down his fences, and burned his home. They killed his hired hand and tried to kill him. When they burned his home he rebuilt it, and when they shot at him he shot back.

When they ambushed him and left him for dead, he crawled into the rocks like a wounded grizzly, treated his own wounds, and then caught a horse and rode down to Sutton's Ranch and shot out their lights during the victory celebration.

Two of Sutton's men quit in protest, for they admired a

169

game man, and Cavagan was winning sympathy around the country.—

Cavagan was a black Irishman from County Sligo. His mother died on the Atlantic crossing and his father was killed by Indians in Tennessee. At sixteen Cavagan fought in the Texas war for independence, trapped in the Rockies for two years, and in the war with Mexico he served with the Texas Rangers and learned the value of a Walker Colt.

At thirty he was a man honed by desert fires and edged by combat with fist, skull, and pistol. Back in County Sligo the name had been O'Cavagan and the family had a reputation won in battle.

Sutton's men surrounded his house a second time thinking to catch him asleep. They fired at the house and waited for him to come out. Cavagan had slept on the steep hillside behind the house and from there he opened fire, shooting a man from his saddle and cutting the lobe from Sutton's ear with a bullet intended to kill.

Now they had him, but he sat straight in the saddle and cursed them. Sutton he cursed but he saved a bit for Beef Hannon, the Sutton foreman.

"You're a big man, Beef," he taunted, "but untie my hands and I'll pound that thick skull of yours until the yellow runs out of your ears."

Their eyes squinted against the white glare and the blistering heat from off the dunes, and they tried to ignore him. Among the sand dunes there was no breeze, only the stifling heaviness of hot, motionless air. Wearily their horses plodded along the edge of a dune where the sand fell steeply off into a deep pit among the dunes. John Sutton drew rein. "Untie his feet," he said.

Juan Velasquez swung down and removed the rawhide thongs from Cavagan's feet, and then stood back, for he knew the manner of man that was Cavagan.

"Get down," Sutton told Cavagan.

Cavagan stared his contempt from the slits where his eyes peered through swollen, blackened flesh, then he swung his leg across the saddle, kicked his boot free of the stirrup and dropped to the ground.

Sutton regarded him for several minutes, savoring his triumph, then he put the flat of his boot against Cavagan's back and pushed. Cavagan staggered, fought for balance, but the sand crumbled beneath him and he fell, tumbling to the bottom of the hollow among the dunes.

With his hands tied and his body stiff from the beatings he had taken he needed several minutes to get to his feet. When he stood erect he stared up at Sutton. "It is what I would have expected from you," he said.

Sutton's features stiffened, and he grew white around the mouth. "You're said to be a tough man, Cavagan. I've heard it until I'm sick of it, so I've brought you here to see how much is tough and how much is shanty Irish bluff. I am curious to see how tough you will be without food or water. We're leaving you here."

Hannon started to protest. He had himself tried to kill Cavagan, but to leave a man to die in the blazing heat of the desert without food or water and with his hands bound . . . a glance at Sutton's face and the words died on his lips.

"It's sixty miles to water," he managed, at last.

John Sutton turned in his saddle and measured Hannon with a glance, then deliberately he faced front and started away. Reluctantly, the others followed.

Juan Velasquez looked down into the pit at Cavagan. He carried a raw wound in his side from a Cavagan bullet, but that pit was seventy feet deep. Slowly, thinking as he did it, Juan unfastened his canteen and was about to toss it to Cavagan when he caught Sutton's eyes on him.

"Throw it," Sutton suggested, "but if you do you will follow it."

Juan balanced the canteen on his palm, tempted beyond measure. Sixty miles? With the temperature at one hundred and twenty degrees? Reluctantly, he retied the canteen to his saddle horn. Sutton watched him, smiling his thin smile.

"I'll remember that, Juan," Cavagan said. "It was a good thought."

John Sutton turned his square thin shoulders and rode away, the others following. Hannon's shoulders were hunched as if expecting a blow.

When the last of them had disappeared from sight, Cavagan stood alone at the bottom of the sand pit.

This was 1850 and even the Indians avoided the sand hills. There was no law west of Santa Fe or east of the coast mountains. Cavagan had settled on land that Sutton considered his, although he had no legal claim to it. Other would-be settlers had been driven off, but Cavagan would not be driven. To make matters worse he courted the girl Sutton had marked for himself.

Cavagan stood in the bottom of the sand pit, his eyes closed against the glare of the sun on the white sand. He told himself, slowly, harshly, that he would not, he must not die. Aloud he said, *"I shall live! I shall see him die!"*

There was a burning fury within him but a caution born of experience. Shade would come first to the west side of the pit, so with his boot he scraped a small pit in the sand. There, several inches below the surface, it was a little cooler. He sat down, his back to the sun, and waited.

More than seven hours of sunlight remained. To attempt climbing from the pit or even to fight the thongs on his wrists would cause him to perspire profusely and lessen his chances of ultimate survival. From this moment he must be patient, he must think.

Sweat dripped from his chin, his throat was parched and the sun on his back and shoulders was like the heat from a furnace. An hour passed, and then another. When at last he looked up there was an inch of shadow under the western lip of the pit.

He studied the way his wrists were bound. His hands had been tied to the pommel, so they were in front of him. He lifted his wrists to his teeth and began ever so gently to work at the rawhide knots. It took nearly an hour, but by the time his wrists were free the shade had reached the bottom of the pit. He coiled the rawhide and slipped it into his pocket.

The east slope was somewhat less steep, with each step he slid back, but with each he gained a little. Finally he climbed out and stood in the full glare of the setting sun.

He knew where the nearest water hole lay but knew Sutton would have it guarded. His problem was simple. He had to find water, get out of the desert, then find a horse and weapons. He intended to destroy Sutton as he would destroy a rabid wolf.

Shadows stretched out from the mountains. To the north the myriad pinnacles of the Chocolate Mountains crowned themselves with gold from the setting sun. He started to walk.

It was not sixty miles to the nearest water, for Cavagan knew the desert better than Sutton. West of him, but in a direction he dare not chance, lay Sunset Spring. Brackish water, and off the line for him.

Twenty-five miles to the northwest among the pinnacles of

the Chocolates were rock tanks that might contain water. A Cahuilla Indian had told him of the natural reservoir, and upon this feeble chance he rested his life.

He walked northwest, his chances a thousand to one. He must walk only in the early hours of the morning and after sundown. During the day he must lie in the shade, if he found any, and wait. To walk in the sun without water was to die.

The sand was heavy and at each step he sank to his ankles. Choosing a distant peak in the Chocolates he pointed himself toward it. When the stars came out he would choose a star above it for a guide. At night landmarks have a way of losing themselves and what was familiar by day becomes strange and unfamiliar in the darkness.

To reach the vicinity of the rock tanks was one thing, to find them quite another. Near such tanks in the Tinajas Altas men had died of thirst within a few feet of water, unaware of its presence. Such tanks were natural receptacles catching the runoff from infrequent rains, and so shaded, that evaporation was slow. As there was no seepage there was no vegetation to indicate the presence of water.

The shadows grew long and only a faint afterglow remained in the sky. On his right and before him lay the valley dividing the dunes from the Chocolate Mountains. Now the air was cool and here and there a star appeared. Desert air is thin and does not retain the heat, hence it soon becomes cool, and in the middle of the night, actually cold. These were the hours Cavagan must use.

If he could not find the tanks, or if there was no water in them, he would die. Cavagan was a man without illusion. His great strength had been sapped by brutal treatment, and he must conserve what strength remained. Locating his peak and a star above it, he walked on. A long time later, descending from the last of the dunes, he took a diagonal course across the valley. Twice he paused to rest, soaking up the coolness. He put a small pebble in his mouth to start the saliva flowing. For a time it helped.

Walking in heavy sand he had made but two miles an hour, but on the valley floor he moved faster. If he reached the *tinajas* and they held water he would have achieved one goal. However, he had no way of carrying water and the next water hole was far. Not that one can place reliance on any desert water hole. Often they were used up or had gone dry.

His battered face throbbed with every step and his head ached. The pinnacles of the Chocolates loomed nearer, but he was not deceived. They were miles away.

An hour before dawn he entered a wash that came down from the Chocolates. He was dead tired, and his feet moved awkwardly. In eleven hours he had probably traveled no more than twenty-three or -four miles and should be near the tanks. He found a ledge that offered shade and stretched out. He was soon asleep.

The heat awakened him. His mouth was dry as parchment and he had difficulty in moving his tongue, which seemed awkward and swollen. A glance at the sun told him it was noon or nearly so. According to the Cahuilla he should be within a few yards of water, certainly within a mile or so. In that maze of cliffs, boulders, rock slabs, and arroyos, cluttered with canelike clumps of ocotillo, he would be fortunate to find anything.

Animals would come to water but many desert creatures lived without it, getting what moisture they needed from succulent plants or cacti. Some insects sought water, and he had noticed bees flying past taking the straight line that usually led to hive or water.

His throat was raw and his mind wandered. Far off, over the desert he had recently crossed, lay a lovely blue lake, shimmering among the heat waves . . . a mirage.

Lying down again he waited for dusk. He was sweating no longer and movement was an effort. He had been almost thirty hours without water and in intense heat.

It was almost dark when he awakened again. Staggering to his feet he started to climb. The coolness refreshed him and gave him new strength. He pushed on, climbing higher. His vision was uncertain and his skull throbbed painfully, but at times he felt an almost delirious gaiety, and then he would scramble up rocks with zest and abandon. Suddenly he sat down. With a shock of piercing clarity he realized he could die.

He rarely thought of dying, although he knew it was expected of him as of all men, yet it was always somebody else who was dying. Suddenly he realized he had no special dispensation against death and he could die now, within the hour.

It was faintly gray in the east when he started again. Amazingly, he found the tanks.

A sheep track directed him. It was a half-sheltered rock tank, but it was dry. Only a faint dusting of sand lay in the bottom.

A few minutes later, and a little higher up, he found a second tank. It was bone-dry.

Soon the sun would rise and the heat would return. Cavagan stared at the empty tanks and tried to swallow, but could not. His throat was raw, and where it was not raw it felt like old rubber. His legs started to tremble, but he refused to sit down. He knew if he sat now he might never get up. There was a queerness in him, a strange lightness as if he no longer possessed weight. Through the semi-delirium induced by heat, thirst, and exhaustion there remained a hard core of resolution, the firmness of a course resolved upon and incomplete. If he quit now John Sutton would have won. If he quit now the desert would have defeated him, and the desert was a friendly place to those who knew how to live with it.

Cunning came to him. To those who knew how to live *with* it, not against it. No man could fight the desert and live. A man must move with it, give with it, live by its rules. He had done that, so what remained?

His eyes peered into the growing light, refusing to focus properly, his thoughts prowling the foggy lowlands of his mind, seeking some forgotten thing.

Think back . . . the rock tanks of the Chocolates. The Chocolates. The Chocolates were a range running parallel to the dunes which the Mexicans called the *algodones*. Bit by bit his thoughts tried to sort out something he knew, but something was missing. Something else the Cahuilla had said. It came to him then like the Indian's voice in his ears. *"If there is no water in the tanks, there is a seep in the canyon."*

Almost due west was the canyon through which ran the old Indian trail . . . maybe five miles.

It was too far. And then he got up without decision and walked away. He walked with his head up, his mind gone off somewhere, walking with a quick, lively step. When he had walked for some distance he fell flat on his face.

A lizard on a rock stared at him, throat throbbing. Something stirred Cavagan's muscles, and he got his hands under him and pushed himself to his knees. Then he got up, weaving a little. It was daylight.

A bee flew past.

He swayed a little, brow puckered, a bee flying straight

. . . hive or water or a hive near water? He took a few hesitant steps in the direction the bee had flown, then stopped. After a bit another droned past and he followed, taking a sight on a clump of ocotillo some distance off. He stumbled and fell, scarcely conscious of it until he arose and stared at his palms, lacerated by the sharp gravel.

When he fell again he lay still for what must have been a considerable time, finally becoming aware of a whistling sound. He pushed himself up, listening. The sound reminded him of a cricket, yet was not a cricket. He listened, puzzled yet alerted for some reason he did not understand.

He moved then, and under a clump of greasewood something stirred. He froze, thinking first of a rattler, although the heat was too great for one to be out unless in a well-shaded position. And then his eye caught a movement, and he knew why the sound had alerted him. It was a tiny red-spotted toad.

Long ago he had learned that the red-spotted toad always lived within the vicinity of water and never got far from it.

Awkwardly he got to his feet and looked carefully around. His eyes could not seem to focus properly, yet down the canyon he glimpsed some galleta grass and walked toward it, coming upon the seep quite suddenly.

Dropping to his knees he scooped water in his palm and drank it. A cold trickle down his throat was painful on the raw flesh. With gentle fingers he put water on his lips, bathed his cheeks and face with it, then drank a little more.

Something inside was crying out that he was safe, but he knew he was not. He drank a little more, then crawled into the shade of a rock and lay on his back and slept.

When he awakened he crawled out and drank more and more, his water-starved body soaking up the moisture. He had found water but had no means of carrying it with him, and the canyon of the seep might well become his tomb, his open tomb.

Cavagan got out the rawhide with which his wrists had been bound and rigged a snare for small game. In placing the snare he found some seeds, which he ate. He drank again, then sat down to think his way forward.

From where he now sat there were two possible routes. Northeast toward the Colorado was Red Butte Spring, but it was at least twenty-five miles away and in the wrong direction.

The twelve miles to Chuckawalla Spring began to loom very large, and leaving the water he had found worried him. The Chuckawalla Mountains were a thin blue line on the northern horizon, and even if he reached them the next spring beyond was Corn Springs, just as far away. Yet the longer he waited the more his strength would be drained by lack of food. He had never known such exhaustion, yet he dare not wait.

On the second morning his snare caught a kangaroo rat, which he broiled over a small fire. When he had eaten he got up abruptly, drank some more, glanced at the notch in the Chuckawallas and started walking.

At the end of an hour he rested, then went on at a slower pace. The heat was increasing. In midafternoon he fell on his face and did not get up.

More than an hour must have passed before he became aware of the intense heat and began to crawl like a blind mole, seeking shade. The plants about him were less than a foot high, and he found nothing, finally losing consciousness.

He awakened, shaking with chill. The moon cast a ghostly radiance over the desert, the clustered canes of the ocotillo looking like the headdresses of gigantic Indians. He got to his feet, aware of a stirring in the night. He waited, listening. A faint click of a hoof on stone and then he saw a desert bighorn sheep walk into the wash and then he heard a faint splash. Rising, he walked down to the wash and heard a scurry of movement as the sheep fled. He almost walked into the spring before he saw it. He drank, then drank again.

Late the next afternoon he killed a chuckawalla with a well-thrown stone. He cooked the big lizard and found the meat tender and appetizing. At dusk he started again, crossing a small saddle to the north side of the mountains. It was twelve miles this time, and it was daybreak before he reached Corn Springs. He recognized it by the clump of palms and mesquite in the wash before reaching the spring, some clumps of *baccharis*, clusters of small twigs rising two to three feet. And then he found the spring itself. After drinking he crawled into the shade and was asleep almost at once.

He opened his eyes, aware of wood-smoke. Rolling over quickly, he sat up.

An old man squatted near a kettle at a fire near the spring, and on the slope a couple of burros browsed.

"Looks to me like you've had a time of it," the old man commented. "You et anything?"

"Chuckawalla . . . had a kangaroo rat a couple of days ago."

The old man nodded. "Et chuck a time or two . . . ain't as bad as some folks might figger."

Cavagan accepted a bowl of stew and ate slowly, savoring every bite. Finally, placing the half-empty bowl on the ground he sat back. "Don't suppose a man with a pipe would have a cigarette paper?"

"You started that Mex way of smokin'? Ain't for it, m'self. Give me a pipe ever' time." The old man handed him his tobacco pouch and dug into his duffle for a rolled up newspaper. "Don't tear the readin' if you can he'p. A body don't find much readin' in the desert and sometimes I read through a newspaper five or six times."

Cavagan wiped his fingers on his pants and rolled a smoke with trembling fingers. Then he put the cigarette down and ate a few more bites before lighting up.

"Come far?"

"Fifty-five, sixty miles."

"An' no canteen? You had yourself a time." The old man said his name was Pearson. He volunteered no more than that. Nor did he ask questions. There were not four white men between the San Jacintos and the Colorado River.

"I've got to get to that hot spring this side of the pass, up there by the San Jacintos," Cavagan said. "I can get a horse from the Cahuillas."

The old man stirred his fire and moved the coffeepot closer. "You listen to me you won't go back."

"You know who I am?"

"Got no idea. Figgered you didn't get where you was by chance. Six years I been prospectin' hereabouts an' I ain't seen nobody but a Chemehuevi or a Cahuilla in this here country. A man would have himself an outfit, gun, knife, canteen. Strikes me somebody left you out here apurpose."

"If you could let me have a canteen or a water sack. Maybe a knife."

"How d'you figger to get out of here?"

"West to the Hayfields, then Shaver's Well and the Yuma stage road."

Pearson studied him out of shrewd old eyes. "You ain't no

pilgrim. You made it this far on nerve an' savvy, so mayhap you'll go all the way."

He tamped his pipe. "Tell you something. You fight shy of them Hayfields. Seen a couple of gents settin' on that water with rifles. A body could figger they was waitin' for somebody."

The old man helped Cavagan to more stew. He rarely looked directly at Cavagan.

"Are they on the Hayfields or back up the draw?"

Pearson chuckled. "You do know this country. They're on the Hayfields, an' could be they don't know the source of that water. Could be you're figurin' a man might slip around them, get water, and nobody the wiser."

"If a man had a water sack he might get as far as Hidden Spring."

The old man looked up sharply. "Hidden Spring? Never heard of it."

"Southwest of Shaver's . . . maybe three miles. Better water than Shaver's."

"You must be Cavagan."

Cavagan did not reply. He finished the stew, rinsed the bowl, then filled his coffee cup.

"Nobody knows this country like Cavagan. That's what they say. Nobody can ride as far or shoot as straight as Cavagan. They say that, too. They also say Cavagan is dead, left in the *algodones* with his hands tied. Lots of folks set store by Cavagan. Them Californios, they like him."

Cavagan slept the day away, and the night following. Pearson made no move to leave, but loafed about. Several times he cooked, and he watched Cavagan eat.

Cavagan found him studying some Indian writing. "Can't make head nor tail of it," Pearson complained. "If them Cahuillas can, they won't say."

"This was done by the Old Ones," Cavagan said, "the People Who Went Before. I've followed their trails in the mountains and across the desert."

"They left trails?"

. "A man can go from here to the Cahuilla village at Martinez. The trail follows the canyon back of the village and goes back to Sheep Mountain. There's a branch comes down back of Indian Wells and another goes to the Indian village at the hot spring at the entrance to San Gorgonio Pass. There's a way over the mountains to the coast, too."

Back beside the fire Cavagan added coffee to what was in the pot, then more water before putting it on the fire. Pearson watched him. "Met a damn fool once who throwed out the grounds . . . throwed away the mother. Never seen the like. Can't make proper coffee until she's two, three days old."

He lit his pipe. "A man like you, he might know a lot about water holes. Worth a lot to a man, knowin' things like that."

"The rock tanks in the Chocolates are dry this year," Cavagan said, "but there's a seep in Salvation Pass." He poked twigs under the coffeepot. "Twenty, twenty-two miles east of Chuckawalla there's a red finger of butte. Maybe a quarter of a mile east of that butte there's a little canyon with a seep of water comin' out of the rock. Good water."

"Place like that could save a man's life," Pearson commented. "Good to know things like that."

"The Cahuillas used the old trails. They know the springs."

Wind was rustling the dry palm leaves when Cavagan crawled out in the early dawn and stirred the coals to life to make coffee.

Pearson shook out his boots, then put on his hat. When he had his boots on he went to the limb where his pants were hung and shook them out. A scorpion about four inches long dropped from a trouser leg and scampered away.

"Last time it was a sidewinder in my boot. A body better shake out his clothes before he puts 'em on."

Pearson slipped suspenders over his shoulders. "Figger you'll hit the trail today. If you rustle through that stuff of mine you'll find you a water sack. Crossin' that ol' sea bottom out there, you'll need it." He hitched his shoulders to settle his suspenders. "Still find shells along that ol' beach."

"Cahuillas say a ship came in here once, a long time ago."

"If they say it," Pearson said, "it did."

Cavagan filled the bag after rinsing it, then dipped it in water from the spring. Evaporation would keep it cool.

Pearson took a long knife from his gear. "Never catered to that one m'self, but a body never knows when he'll need an extry."

Cavagan shouldered the sack and thrust the knife into his belt. "Look me up some time," he said. "Just ask for Cavagan."

Pearson's back was turned, packing gear, when Cavagan spoke. He let him take a dozen steps, and then said, "You get to Los Angeles, you go to the Calle de los Negros. Ask for Jake. He owes me money an' I expect he might have a pistol. Get whatever you need."

John Sutton sat at dinner at one end of a long table in his ranch house at Calabasas. The dinner had been enhanced by a turkey killed the day before at a *cienaga* a few miles away. He was restless, but there was no reason for it. Almost a month had gone by. His men had returned to the algodones but found no trace of Cavagan. Nor had they expected to. He would have died out on the desert somewhere.

Juan Velasquez saw the rider come up the canyon as he loafed near the gate, standing guard. At the gate the rider dismounted and their eyes met in the gathering dusk. "Buenas noches, Señor," Juan said. "I had expected you."

"So?"

"I have an uncle in Sonora, Señor. He grows old, and he asks for me."

"Adios Juan."

"Adios, Señor."

Cavagan walked up the steps and into the house where John Sutton sat at dinner.

TIM McCARTHY

The Windmill Man

What was the premonition? It had been with him at least since the day old Clayton Hobbs fell off the mill and killed himself. Nearly a month ago now. Clayton had been astride the tail pouring fresh oil into that gear case. The simplest of jobs. But Clayton was over seventy years old and had vowed never to climb another windmill tower. "Hang it all. I ain't going to drag Justus across forty miles of desert just to pour a few quarts of oil into a gear case." Those might have been his words, talking to himself in the way of the lonely, tobacco juice bubbling at his lip, bursting, staining his mustache. The simplest of jobs, yet something went wrong. The old man lost his balance, or his heart kicked up on him—something! He fell sixty feet to the ground. No one found him for three days, after the ravens and the coyotes had got to him, an oil can crushed in his fist. Justus sent flowers: "Condolences. Justus Knight." And that night he crept out of bed while his wife slept, went out and leaned against the windmill down by the corral, and cried.

For fifty years Clayton had been a windmill man in that part of the state and clear over into Arizona. He had been one of many to begin with. But gradually the others had died off or been killed or crippled, and no one had showed up to fill their shoes. Clayton was alone. In those last years he taught Justus everything he knew about windmills—including how to fear and love them, if such things can indeed be taught. Justus had the ten sections his father left him, but they were mostly sand and creosote bush and they wouldn't carry fifty head without feeding extra. He also had two daughters and a wife who wanted her slice of the American pie, so he had to find some other way to earn money. The neighbors laughed at him when he finally went into the windmill business on his own. Windmills were on the way out; he would never make a living. That was six years ago. Clayton had referred his dwindling trade to Justus and now the younger man had more work than he could handle. Six years had brought changes that were astonishing to most people. Gas was short, electricity threatened or curtailed. You couldn't buy anything when you wanted it, and what you did get hold of cost twice what it was worth. The country was going to pot, and some of its people were turning back to the things they could more or less rely upon. Things like the windmill, a machine as simple as it was old upon the earth. And the wind to drive it, which for all its capriciousness was free and full of power. Now Clayton was dead, and Justus was the only good windmill man for a long way around.

He should have been content, and he supposed that for the most part he was. Until a month ago at least. He was keeping his wife happy. She had a new pickup, and they had recently moved from the adobe ranch house his father had built into a shiny, air-conditioned mobile home that had arrived in two sections and was designed to look like a house. It almost succeeded, too, when it was set on a concrete foundation and surrounded by a trim lawn. A year of work and watering had turned the place into a regular oasis, with the towering antenna for the colored television filling in for a palm tree. Justus was glad that his wife liked the place, and he always felt cool and clean there himself. But there were days when he still preferred the corral and pens and old adobes down across the arroyo to the rear. Usually such things didn't trouble him one way or the other. He was on the road most of the time. He had his work and he liked it. There was a solid, straightforward satisfaction in building a windmill from the ground up—lowering the drop pipe, cylinder, and sucker rod two, three, or even four hundred feet toward the bowels of the earth, cementing the anchor posts, and coaxing the tower up stage by stage until the stub tower clamped into its peak and you could set the gin pole to haul the mill up. Then before long he could throw the furl lever and watch that towering creation groan to life. Those first strokes never failed to pump up an edge of tension, of anticipation, that drew his belly a little tight. For after all those years, all those windmills, he had not overcome the wonder, the sudden thrill he felt every time that first jet of water spurted from the lead pipe. That was the kind of satisfaction a man could stand upon, could build his life upon from the ground up.

If anyone had ever succeeded in getting Justus to talk seriously about his work, he probably would have told him something of the sort. Yet even that much was unlikely. Justus was a reserved man, a little shy in his ways. He thought he knew himself pretty well. He was small and trim, with light brown eyes and a straight look. His round chin bulged from a squarish face and he kept his sandy hair cropped so close that from a distance he appeared bald. On the ground his manner was tight, even stiff at times. He didn't smoke, swear, or drink. His voice was an even drawl, subdued, almost a hush, as if there were something deep within himself that he feared to awaken. But once up on a windmill tower his whole body and bearing seemed to relax, to run with life. He swung out free as a wild thing, silent and sure, and often those who watched from below clamped their awe-hung jaws for fear of giving themselves away. What most men found dangerous Justus experienced as a kind of liberation.

That was his secret. He was hardly conscious of it himself, but even if he had been able to articulate it down to its last wind-torn detail, he never would have done so. Justus was not the kind of man to give so precious a thing away. He kept what was his to himself and let others think what they would. There was a kind of sideways satisfaction even in that. Anyway it all held for him until the day Clayton Hobbs fell off the mill. What was the premonition? At first it was only a shadow, a certain darkness that he could all but feel in his chest, as if a cloud had come between him and his heart. Then he got the job of erecting what he had come to call the Royal Don windmill, and the shadow began to take shape. It was as if that windmill were the voice of his premonition, an articulation of it shaping itself girt by girt, angle brace by angle brace into the sky.

The Royal Don windmill fought him from the start. Clayton had warned him that might happen. "Cussed things can get so ornery they might as well as be human," he said. The mill was to pump a domestic well on a newly purchased piece of land up off the old Royal Don Mine road. Once you left the shade of the giant cottonwoods along the Mimbres there was nothing up there but rocks and hills, rugged arroyo-slashed rangeland, flood-heaved, wind-dried, and sun-cracked. Oak, juniper, mesquite. No one had ever lived on it before— no white man at any rate—then along came Jesse Pruit and drilled a well on an impossible hill. Why in God's name would anyone ever want to live out here? That was Justus's first reaction as he turned off the mine road onto Pruit's track. But the place had its pull. Even Justus felt it, and he was a man who usually saw land only in terms of wind, water, and grazing potential. There was a subdued, even subtle grandeur to it, if you can imagine such a thing. It stretched north to the brooding Black Range, west and south along the coppery Santa Rita hills, then past the granite jut of Cooke's Peak and clear into Mexico. A long, lonely landscape that could tumble your heart and in the next breath ache low in your belly with the spirit of a half-forgotten place, an old memory you could not quite catch and conquer. Justus hopped out of his pickup, turned a quick circle, then let his gaze come to rest on the rough, raw pyramid called Cooke's Peak, monumental, anchoring the Mimbres Range to the plain. "Nice place you got here," he said. Jesse Pruit seemed to ponder this. He looked sideways at the ground, shoved his hands in his jeans with his thumbs thrusting free, hunched his hulking shoulders, spit, shifted his plug, lurched Justus a straight look, and said, "Yup." Jesse had come over from Texas, but Justus didn't hold that against him. He liked the man from the start. Though Jesse was over fifty, you could tell at a glance that he was still a working fool. He looked to have been carved from oak, the whole of him, from his salted sideburns to his down-at-the-heel boots. Solid. You would have had to roast him an hour to get an ounce of fat off of him. His cap was the only whimsical touch. He favored the same floppy, polka-dotted affair that Justus liked to wear on the job. Justus had a sign reading "I work alone" taped to the toolbox in the back of his truck. But when Jesse offered to give him a hand, he did not hesitate to accept. Good thing he did, too! He needed all the help he could get with the Royal Don windmill.

It wasn't just the windmill, either. The land itself seemed to resent the intrusion. It offered them about a foot of stony topsoil, then crumbled to a rock-ribbed grainy substance that looked more like ashes than dirt. It was like digging into the record of some primordial conflagration deep as the earth. The more you dug, the more there was to dig; the hole never got any deeper. They finally had to drench it with river water so they could take the anchor holes down to four feet. From there the first two sections of the tower went up easily. Justus began to feel better. But the ground around the well sloped two ways, and they had a devil of a time squaring and leveling those sections so they could cement them down. They'd get one leg right only to throw another one off. Round and round they wrestled it through an afternoon of ninety-degree heat, a vicious circle that brought them both to the edge of cursing. They kept looking to the west for wind but none came, and they counted themselves lucky on that score. At five they got it leveled and went down to Jesse's trailer for a drink of cold water. Suddenly—out of a sky so calm that even the ravens had forsaken it—a fierce wind gusted up, rocked into the hill, snapped sotol stalks, swooshed like sixty through the juniper, and died. In the silence that whirled like a second, soundless wind into its wake both men turned to face the hill, knowing full well what they would see. For a moment, neither could draw a breath. There was no air! Up there on the hill the tower lay on its side like the skeleton of some prehistoric beast. Jesse spit and looked sideways at the ground. Justus yanked off his polka-dotted cap and swabbed his glistening pate.

And that's the way it went with the Royal Don windmill. Two anchor posts were bent beyond use. Parts were hard to find. There was a delay of three days before they could heave the tower back into place. Then they took it up, section by section, girt by girt, fighting, it seemed, for every bolt and nut they could punch or hammer home. After what seemed a month of Sundays, Justus pried the ill-fitted stub tower close enough to clamp, then worked the wooden platform down over it. The tower was up! Justus looked down at the other man and almost smiled. Jesse had been watching every move, shading his eyes with a big brown hand, one cheek bulging with tobacco. Now he looked aslant and rotated his shoulders, the way a boxer does sometimes to loosen up, spat, then knelt by one corner post to chain a block into place. With luck they would haul the mill up before quitting time. But the first time Justus swung up onto the platform he knocked a wrench off. "Watch it!" The shout was too late. Jesse's forearm was gashed to the bone, the wrench bloody by his knee. Justus had to drive him into Silver for stitches. Another day shot. He began to hate that windmill the way he would never have allowed himself to hate another man. He'd already lost money on it. Now it had cost him his helper. Next thing he knew he would be losing his temper—something no windmill man could safely allow himself to do.

The next day they got the tailbone, vane, and motor assembled and the whole works onto the tower—Justus handling the tackle and a somewhat wan Jesse backing the pickup with one hand. But of course the wind had gusted up at the very moment Justus was anchoring the block on top of the gin pole. He rocked there forty feet in the air, fighting for balance, clinging like a lover to that wavering plastic pole, his heart punching into his throat. And then the motor wouldn't slip plump onto the mill pipe. Justus wrestled it every which way until his belly burned with anger and the blood surged hot into his head. He could barely see for the sweat smarting his eyes. Finally he gripped the rim of the gear case, braced both feet against the motor and wrenched his whole weight into it, time after time, hunched parallel to the ground like some lesser primate raging at the mesh of his cage, heaving, twisting, until Jesse heard him screech something that sounded like shhee-at! and the motor clunked home. Jesse smiled, looked sideways at the ground, and spat.

The wheel went on without undue trouble, arm after arm, tediously but true, which for this windmill was something of a small miracle. By sunset the sucker rod was bolted to the pump pole, the connection made between the towering mill and the short brass cylinder three hundred feet into the earth. The wind was still up. Justus threw the furl lever, but for the first time that he could remember he did not keep watch for that first jet of water. He put his ear to the drop pipe, and as soon as he heard that both check valves were working properly, he turned his back on the clicking, clanking mill, hopped into his pickup and began to make out Jesse's bill. For all he cared that windmill could spin itself off the face of the earth—even if he would have to replace it under his usual guarantee.

What was the premonition? It weighed heavy in him again as he crossed the divide into Silver City that afternoon. Jesse had caught up with him by phone at the Carlton ranch outside of Lordsburg: "That windmill of yours has gone crazy.

Furl wire's broken, storm's coming, tank's full, and the water's wasting all over the ground."

My windmill. The protest rose in Justus's throat but he forced it down. His heart fell, quaked. In a small, quiet voice he said, "I'm real busy right now. Can't you climb up there and brake it?"

There was a long silence. For a moment he thought Jesse had hung up. Then he pictured him looking slantwise at the floor, one hand holding the phone, the other stuffed in his pocket, thumb thrusting free. He waited, fought to gird his heart for what he knew he was about to hear. Finally Jesse spoke: "I could . . . but I'm not about to. Not the way that thing's turning . . . You *do* guarantee your work, don't you?"

"I'll be there directly."

Now he had crossed the Santa Ritas and was heading down the valley. He drove mechanically, watching the road but not really seeing it. He tried not to think, to imagine. The few thoughts that forced themselves upon him seemed to come from somewhere outside his head. Echoes. But always it was there. The premonition. Towering into a roiling sky. A runaway windmill. He hadn't realized until that afternoon how hard he had been fighting to put the Royal Don windmill behind him. Now it was there. A runaway. A premonition.

It hadn't rained for nearly a year. The grass was burned beyond feeding, the ground cracked like a dead skin. Today the first rain of the season was brewing over the Black Range. A runaway windmill was bad enough. But a runaway with lightning, a shifting wind . . . Justus shrugged and felt a little better. It would be, *had* to be that way with the Royal Don windmill.

He was almost through the village before he realized where he was. Haphazard adobes, most of them unplastered, rusted tin roofs, mud walls bellying above crumbling stone foundations, a rickety store with a single gas pump in front, a squat bar, its one small window bright with a neon beer sign. Only two miles to the turn. Not a soul in sight. Newspapers blowing down a dirt street. An election poster on a fence post, half the candidate's head flapping in the wind. A dying place. Yet up there in the hills a few miles above the valley Jesse Pruit was staking a claim on life. With a pick and shovel, some rocks and mud, he was starting the whole circle all over again. A man ought to take hope from that. Justus could not. His belly turned with dread.

Water was running in the Mimbres. First time in months. Justus took note as he crossed the bridge. Must have been raining in the mountains for hours. As he crossed the first cattle guard up from the valley the wind nearly tore the steering wheel from his hand, jolting him from his daze. He had to pull himself together. Get this job done. Go home and watch TV from a big chair, with the first rain clicking on the trailer roof. The image settled him somewhat. And then he caught sight of it. The Royal Don windmill. About a mile to the west across that humping time-slashed land. Barely visible against the lowering day, the roiling blackness of the sky. He looked away, his stomach tightening again, as he turned onto Jesse's track.

Jesse was waiting at the foot of the tower, beneath the whir of the great wheel, in the swift fourbeat click-click-clank-click of the mill, the wind beating his yellow slicker about his legs. The moment Justus hopped from the pickup it began to rain. Cooke's Peak had vanished in the storm. Lightning jagged in a sudden simultaneous row of four across the Black Range. All the land—the hills, the canyons, the arroyos, and the valley—between the Emory Pass and Caballo Blanco in the Santa Rita range was wind-rocked and thundered, heaving with sound. The wind tore at Jesse's hill, wrenched the junipers nearly flat to the rocks. Justus was soaked in the ten steps it took him to reach the tower. "Where's it broke at?" he shouted in response to Jesse's nod.

Jesse spat, the wind smearing his tobacco spit against the storage tank behind. He seemed to consider the question for a moment then shouted his response. "Right at the furl lever. Only way you can hitch it is from the platform."

"We'll see," said Justus setting his jaw. But as he spoke the wind shifted, gusted south, violently. The great wheel heaved round, its tail thrashing, wind-whipped, as if the mill were some monstrous sea creature beached in the storm. Justus stared at it, rain drilling his face, and he realized that what he felt swelling into his heart from the very pit of him was fear.

With a quick, slashing motion he turned and stepped to the pickup, dug a short iron bar from the jumble in back. Maybe he could pry the furl lever home from below the platform, brake the wheel. Supporting the bar like a stubby lance

against his hip, he advanced on the tower. "We'll get her," he
said with a glance toward Jesse. But the wind snatched his
words, smashed them back past his own ear, and Jesse,
unhearing, spat and looked aslant. Justus's polka-dotted cap
was smeared to his head and pulled so far down over his ears
that nothing could blow it off. He tugged at it one last time,
then shoved the heavy bar into his belt and scampered up the
corner post ladder.

The wind seemed to redound, redouble as he climbed the
shuddering tower. The upper cross braces hummed and
rattled. The four-beat rhythm of the mill, louder, more immediate, click-click-clank-click. And the wheel, always the
wheel, whirring louder, fiercer, until those whirling arms
cleaved just above his head. He wrapped his legs around the
stub tower and hitched himself around beneath the platform
until he could arch the bar up over and probe for a hold on
the furl lever. The bar, the tower, everything was slick and
slippery in his hands. There! He'd almost had it. Again.
Again. But no. It was no good. The wheel was going too fast.
He'd never be able to brake it with the bar. Damn this windmill anyway. Damn it all to hell. He would have to attach the
furl wire then have Jesse brake the mill from below. Lightning thundered onto the valley, blazing, blinding deep behind
his eyes—a cold, white heat. *Rising.* Damn you! Damn you!
He heaved himself up and beat at the furl lever with the bar.
Beat at it. Beat at it. Damn you! Damn you! But nothing. He
could barely hear the iron strike home. He was breathless, exhausted, trembling. He hurled the useless bar out into the
blackness of the storm and inched back to the ladder. For a
few moments he clung there, motionless, feeling foolish and
afraid, despising himself to the edge of tears, breathless,
gathering strength. He would have to go up.

His breath was returning. He raised his head above the
platform, so close to the raging wheel that its breath felt
more powerful than the wind itself. He gauged his move,
concentrating so hard that for a moment both the windmill
and the storm faded to the recesses of his hearing. If the
wind didn't decide to shift he would be all right. He turned
his attention to the wind, gauging it, feeling it out. But that
voice howling out of the back was dumb, deep as madness,
and he could not hear its intent. Now, Justus! He heaved
himself onto the platform and in almost the same motion
caught the furl lever with one boot and from that foothold

swung up onto the tail. At first he merely held on for dear life, straddling that cold, ribbed giant as if it were some towering, insensible mutation of the horse. Then he gradually got his bearings. The wind clubbed and ripped at him, rain stung his face, but he felt he had firm hold. The wheel couldn't touch him here. He was on top! He had been there before, a thousand times, wind or no wind. Here the wheel's whir was a fiercesome roar. Its twelve-foot span whirled so fast that the curving, cleaving blades were one. No. Faster yet! There was a tail of speed, of motion, an aureole of velocity ringing the wheel, making it appear larger than life. But suddenly he was not afraid. His cap was planted firmly, safely upon his ears. He felt light, almost happy—the way he used to feel in the old days, when Clayton was alive. He glanced confidently down at Jesse. The other man's face was in shadow, his slicker a yellow blur. Only his hands stood forth. They looked huge and very white on the corner post. Even from that height Justus could see that their grip was hard, immovable, as if Jesse alone were holding up the tower. Justus clucked his tongue and twisted his upper body down toward the furl lever, the toe of one boot snagged in the ribbing for support. His heart thrilled to the whir and race of the wind. He had been here before! He had the wire hitched in a jiffy. "Brake the wheel!" he shouted as he arched himself back onto the tail. Then a blast of lightning, thunderous blaze. For a blink of time Justus felt himself burned black against the jagging light. His arms were already flailing, as if he sensed the shift before it came. It came. A clubbing crosswind out of the black. Whipping the tail round, flipping the man off like so much jetsam. He turned once in the air, his body loosely awry, as if it were already limp and lifeless. Yet he landed on his hands and knees—at the last trying to rise even as he fell. The shock was tremendous. His insides seemed to explode against his spine, then collapse into his belly in a mush. Only the polka-dotted cap held true.

What was the premonition? He felt it looming there in the descending black, heard it above the storm in the four-beat rhythm of the mill, in the great wheel whirring as if it would turn forever. He had been there before. He puked a blackish gob, smearing his mouth, the darkening earth, dying, dying out, the windmill man.

LARRY McMURTRY

Terms of Endearment

1

Royce Dunlup was lying in bed with a cold can of beer balanced on his stomach. The phone by the bed began to ring and he reached over and picked the receiver up without disturbing the can of beer. He had a big stomach, and it was no real trick to balance a can of beer on it, but in this instance the can was sitting precisely over his navel, and keeping it there while talking on the phone was at least a little bit of a trick.

Since leaving Rosie and taking up, more or less formally, with his girl friend Shirley Sawyer, Royce had learned a lot of new tricks. For one thing, Royce had learned to have sex lying flat on his back, something he had never done in all his conservative years with Rosie. Nobody had ever tried to teach Royce anything like that before, and at first he made a nervous pupil, but Shirl soon broke him in. While she was in the process of breaking him in she talked to him about something called fantasy, a concept she had picked up in her one year of junior college in Winkelburg, Arizona. Fantasy, as Shirley explained it, meant thinking about things you really couldn't do, and her own favorite fantasy involved having sex with a fountain. In particular, Shirley wanted to have it with Houston's new Mecom fountain, a splendid new gusher of water right in front of the equally splendid Warwick Hotel. At night the Mecom fountain was lit up with orange lights, and Shirley insisted that she couldn't think of anything better

192

than seating herself right on top of a great spurt of orange water, right there in front of the Warwick Hotel.

That wasn't possible, of course, so Shirley had to make do with the next best, which was seating herself every night or two on what she primly referred to as Royce's "old thing." About all that was required of Royce at such times was to keep still, while Shirley jiggled around and made little spurting sounds in imitation of the fountain she imagined herself to be sitting on. Royce's only worry was that someday Shirley might lose her balance and fall backwards, in which case his old thing was bound to suffer, but so far it hadn't happened and Royce had never been one to look too far ahead.

His own favorite fantasy was simpler, and involved sitting the beer can on his navel. What Royce liked to pretend was that the beer can had a little hole in its bottom and his navel a secret hole in its top, so that when he put the can of beer over his navel a nice stream of cold beer squirted right down into his stomach with no effort on his part at all. That way the two pleasantest things in life, sex and beer drinking, could be accomplished without so much as lifting a hand.

Shirley evidently liked sitting on his old thing so much that she was willing to support him to keep it handy, so Royce had become a man of substantial leisure. His memory had never been very keen, and in three weeks he managed to forget Rosie and his seven children almost completely. Now and then longings for his darling Little Buster would come over him, but before they got too strong Shirley would come home and set a cold beer on his navel and the memory would subside. Shirley lived in a three-room house on Harrisburg, right next door to a used-tire center, and Royce spent much of his day staring happily out the window at a mountain of some 20,000 worn-out tires. For activity he could walk two blocks down Harrisburg to a 7-Eleven and buy some more beer, or, if he was especially energetic, walk another block and spend an afternoon happily playing shuffleboard at a bar called the Tired-Out Lounge, the principal hangout of his old friend Mitch McDonald.

Mitch was a retired roustabout who had had a hand pinched off in an oil field accident years before. It had been him, in fact, who had introduced Royce to Shirley. She had been Mitch's girl friend for years, but they had had a falling out that started (Shirley later told Royce) because Mitch's old thing acquired the bad habit of falling out of Shirley just at the wrong time. Despite this, Mitch and Shirley had decided to stay friends, and in a moment of lethargy Mitch handed his friend Shirley over to his friend Royce. He himself regarded Royce as being far too crude for Shirley, and he was very upset when they happened to hit it off. It was his own doings, however, and he managed to keep quiet about how wrong it all was, except to Hubbard Junior, the nervous little manager of the Tired-Out Lounge. Mitch frequently pointed out to Hubbard Junior that Royce and Shirley couldn't last, and Hubbard Junior, a very neat man who had the bad luck to own a bar that was only two blocks from a tire factory, always agreed, as he did with everybody, no matter what they said.

Still, on the surface, Royce and Mitch were still buddies, and it was no great surprise to Royce that it was Mitch who rang him up on the phone.

"What's up, good buddy?" Mitch asked when Royce said hello.

"Restin'," Royce said. "Havin' a few beers."

"You're gonna need something stronger than that when you hear what I got to say," Mitch said. "I'm over here at the J-Bar Korral."

"Aw, yeah?" Royce said, not much interested.

"It's this here East-Tex Hoedown," Mitch went on. "They have it ever' Friday night, unescorted ladies free. The pussy that walks around loose over here ain't to be believed."

"Aw, yeah?" Royce repeated.

"Anyhow, guess who just come in," Mitch said.

"John F. Kennedy," Royce guessed, feeling humorous. "Or is it old LBJ?"

"Nope," Mitch said. "Guess again."

Royce racked his brain. He could think of nobody they both knew who might be likely to turn up at the East-Tex Hoedown. In fact, in his relaxed state, he could not even think of anybody they both knew.

"Too tired to guess," Royce said.

"All right, I'll give you a hint," Mitch said. "Her name starts with an R."

Mitch expected that crucial initial to burst like a bombshell in Royce's consciousness, but once again he had miscalculated.

"Don't know nobody whose name starts with an R," Royce

said. "Nobody 'cept me, an' I ain't hardly even got out of bed today."

"Rosie, you dumb shit," Mitch said, exasperated by his friend's obtuseness. "Rosie, Rosie, Rosie."

"Rosie who?" Royce said automatically, all thought of his wife still far from his mind.

"Rosie Dunlup!" Mitch yelled. "Your wife Rosie, ever hear of her?"

"Oh, Rosie," Royce said. "Ask her how Little Buster's doin', will you?"

Then the bombshell finally burst. Royce sat up abruptly, spilling the can of beer off his navel. He didn't notice it until the cold liquid began to leak underneath him. Then, since when he sat up his stomach hid the can, he thought the sudden shock must have caused him to wet the bed.

"Rosie?" he said. "You don't mean Rosie?"

"Rosie," Mitch said quietly, savoring the moment.

"Go tell her I said to go home," Royce said. "What's she think she's doin' over there at a dance with all them sluts?

"She oughtn't to be out by herself," he added.

"She ain't out by herself," Mitch said. It was another moment to savor.

Royce stuck his finger in the puddle he was sitting in, and then smelled the finger. It smelled like beer rather than piss, so at least he was rid of one anxiety. Dim memories of his married life began to stir in him, but only vaguely, and when Mitch dropped his second bombshell the room of Royce's memory went black.

"Whut?" he asked.

Mitch adopted a flat, informative tone and informed Royce that Rosie had arrived with two short men, one of whom wore a mustache. The other was a well-known oil man who drove a white Lincoln.

There was silence on the line while Royce absorbed the information. "Fuck a turkey," he said finally, running his fingers through his hair.

"Yeah, don't that beat all?" Mitch said. "I guess what they say is true: While the cat's away, the mouse will play."

"Why, what does she mean, goin' off an' leavin' the kids?" Royce said. A sense of indignation was rising in him.

"She's a married woman," he added forcefully.

"She sure ain't actin' like one tonight," Mitch said. "Her an' that Cajun's dancin' up a storm."

"Don't tell me no more. You're just makin' it hard for me to think," Royce said. He was trying to keep in mind a paramount fact: Rosie was his wife, and she was in the process of betraying him.

"You comin' over?" Mitch asked.

In his agitation, Royce hung up the phone before he answered. "You goddamn right I'm coming over," he said to no one. Problems lay in his way, however. One of his shoes was lost. Shirley had a scroungy little mongrel named Barstow, after her hometown, and Barstow was always dragging Royce's shoes off into corners so he could nibble at the shoestrings. Royce found one shoe in the kitchen, but the other one was completely lost. While he was looking for it, though, he found a bottle of Scotch he had forgot they had, a good deal of which he gulped down while he was looking for the shoe. The shoe refused to turn up, and Royce, tormented by the thought of what his wife was getting away with, grew more and more frantic. He turned the bed upside down, thinking it might be under there. Then he turned the couch upside down. Then he stepped outside to kick the shit out of Barstow, who had vanished as neatly as the shoe.

As the minutes ticked by, Royce's desperation increased, and his fury with it. Finally he decided the shoe was nonessential; he could do what he had to do with one shoe on. He rushed out into the street and jumped into his delivery truck, but unfortunately, thanks to a month of inactivity, the truck's battery was dead. Royce felt like turning the truck over, as he had the bed and the couch, but sanity prevailed. After trying vainly to flag down a couple of passing cars he hobbled rapidly up to the Tired-Out Lounge. Everybody got a good laugh at the sight of him with one shoe on and one shoe off, but Royce scarcely heard the uproar.

"Shirley's damn turd hound stole it," he said to silence speculation. "Got an emergency. I need somebody to come help me jump-start my truck."

Nothing wins friends in a bar like someone else's emergency, and in no time Royce was getting a jump-start from a '58 Mercury, his shoe problem forgotten. Five or six tire experts from the used-tire center stood around idly kicking at the tires of Royce's truck while the jump-start took place. Several of them tried not too subtly to find out what the emergency was. After all, they had left their drinking to participate in it and had done so with the expectation—always a reasonable one on Harrisburg—of gunshots, screaming women, and flowing blood. A used potato chip truck with a rundown battery was a poor substitute, and they let Royce know it.

"What the fuck, Dunlup," one said. "Your old lady's house ain't even on fire."

Royce was not about to admit the humiliating truth, that his wife was out honky-tonking with other men. He silenced all queries by slamming his hood down and roaring away, although the hood popped up again before he had gone a block, mainly because in his haste he had neglected to remove the battery cables and had slammed it down on them.

The men who had helped him watched him go with a certain rancor. "The son of a bitch is too ignorant even to put on both shoes," one of them said. They were hoping maybe he'd have a car wreck before he got out of sight, but he didn't and they were left to straggle back to the bar without even a story to tell. "Dumb bastard," another tire whanger said. "I wouldn't help him next time if a snappin' turtle had a holt of his cock."

2

Over at the J-Bar Korral, meanwhile, a colorful evening was in progress. A group called the Tyler Troubadours was flailing away at a medley of Hank Snow favorites, and the customers had divided themselves roughly into three equivalent groups: those who came to drink, those who came to dance, and those who hoped to accomplish a little of both. Brylcream and Vitalis gleamed on the heads of those men who bothered to take their Stetsons off, and the women's hair was mostly upward coiffed, as if God had dressed it himself by standing over them with a comb in one omnipotent hand and a powerful vacuum cleaner in the other.

Everybody was happy and nearly everybody was drunk. One of the few exceptions to both categories was Vernon, who sat at a table smiling uncomfortably. He was not sober on purpose, but then neither was he unhappy on purpose. Both states appeared to belong to him, which was just as well, since as near as he could tell nobody else wanted them.

Certainly Rosie didn't. She had immediately flung herself into dancing, figuring that was the easiest way to keep her mind off the fact that she was out on a date with F.V.

d'Arch. It was very clear to her that it was a date, since at the last minute she had let him pay for her ticket; beyond that, her imagination refused to take her. She had more or less forgotten why she had been so determined to drag poor Vernon along, but she was glad that she had, anyway, just in case problems arose with F.V.

Fortunately, though, F.V. had shown himself to be a model of comportment. He flung himself into dancing just as eagerly as Rosie had, mostly to keep his mind off the fact that he couldn't think of anything to say to Rosie. For years the two staples of their conversation had been Bossier City, Louisiana, and Packard engines, and neither seemed quite the right thing to talk about on their first date.

Also, looming in both their minds was the specter of Royce Dunlup. Despite the fact that he had not been heard from in weeks, and might be in Canada, or even California, both Rosie and F.V. secretly assumed that somehow he would find them out and turn up at the dance. They also secretly assumed that by their being there together they were guilty—probably in the eyes of God and certainly in the eyes of Royce—of something close to adultery, although they had as yet to exchange even a handshake. Both were sweaty before they had danced a step, from guilt and nervousness, and the dancing proved to be an enormous relief. At first F.V. danced with great Cajun suavity, from the hips down, never moving his upper body at all, which struck Rosie as slightly absurd. She was used to lots of rocking and dipping and hugging when she danced, and while she didn't especially want F.V. to try any hugging she did expect him to at least turn his head once in a while. Right away she poked him in the ribs to make her point.

"Loosen up there, F.V.," she said. "We ain't standin' in no boat, you know. You're gonna be a dead loss when they play one of them jitterbugs if you can't twist no better'n that."

Fortunately a little practice and five or six beers and the fact that there was no sign of Royce did wonders for F.V.'s confidence, and Rosie had no more cause for complaint. F.V. had her on the floor for every dance and they were only cut in on twice, both times by the same massive drunk, who couldn't seem to get over the fact that Rosie was as short as she was. "Ma'am, you're plumb *tiny*," he said several times.

"That's right. Be careful you don't fall on me. I'd just be a smear on the floor if you was to," Rosie said, charitable in her happiness at finding out she could go about in the world and dance with various men without any lightning bolts striking her dead.

In her happiness, and because the inside of the J-Bar Korral was roughly the temperature of a bread oven, she began to drink beer rapidly during the intermissions. F.V. drank beer rapidly too, and Vernon bought beer as rapidly as they drank it. The top of their table was a puddle from all the moisture that had dripped off the bottles, and Vernon amused himself while they danced by soaking up the puddle with napkins.

"F.V., we ort to of been doing this years ago," Rosie said during one intermission. She was feeling more and more generous toward F.V. The fact that he had gotten up the nerve to mumble, "Wanta go?" that morning was the beginning of her liberation.

"We ort, we ort," F.V. said. "Wanta come next week?"

"Oh, well," Rosie said, fanning herself with a napkin. The "oh, well" was a delaying tactic she had picked up from listening to Aurora.

"They have these dances ever' week," F.V. said. He paused. "Ever' week on the dot," he added, in case Rosie doubted it.

"That's sweet," Rosie said vaguely, looking around the room in such a way as to leave in question as much as possible. It was rather vulgar of F.V. to rush her so, she felt, and the thought of having to commit herself to something a whole week away was scary.

"It's the same band all the time," F.V. persisted.

"Vernon, you ought to try a dance or two," Rosie said, hoping to slip quietly off the spot she was on.

"I was raised Church of Christ," Vernon explained. "They ain't partial to dancing."

Vernon was not going to be any help, Rosie saw. He was merely waiting politely for the evening to be over. Meanwhile, F.V.'s dark Cajun eyes were shining and he was waiting to find out if he had a date for next week.

"Well, if Little Buster ain't been kidnapped, or the sky don't fall . . ." Rosie said and let her sentence trail off.

That was enough for F.V. Anything less crushing than blank refusal had always been enough for F.V. He leaned back and drank beer while Vernon ate pretzels.

Vernon felt like he was still in a state of backward drift.

Old Schweppes, the baseball fan, would have said that life had thrown him a curve, the curve being Aurora, but to Vernon it felt more like the road of his life had just suddenly forked, giving him no time to turn. He had left the old straight road of his life, probably forever, on the impulse of an instant, yet it did not surprise him very much that the fork had so quickly led him into the sand. He did not expect to get back on the old road, and to him the sweat and the roar of the J-Bar were just part of the sand. He watched and ate his pretzels rather disconnectedly, mild in his dullness, not thinking of much.

None of them knew that outside in the far reaches of the J-Bar parking lot a baby blue delivery truck was revving up. Royce Dunlup had arrived and was preparing his vengeance.

He had not, however, parked his truck. On the way over he had had the feeling that a few beers might clear his head, so he had stopped at an all-night grocery and bought two six-packs of Pearl. To his annoyance, everyone in the store had laughed at him because he had on only one shoe. It was beginning to seem to Royce that he must be the first person in the history of the world to have a shoe carried off by a girl friend's dog.

The cashier at the grocery store, no more than a pimply kid, had felt obliged to crack a joke about it. "What happened, hoss?" he asked. "Did you forget to put the other one on, or forget to take this one off?"

Royce had taken his six-packs and limped to his truck, followed by the rude jeers of several onlookers. The incident set him to brooding. People seemed to assume that he was some kind of nut, a kind who only liked to wear one shoe. If he went limping into a big dance like the East-Tex Hoedown wearing only one shoe hundreds of people would probably laugh at him; his whole position would be automatically undermined. For all he knew, Rosie could have him committed to an insane asylum if he showed up at a dance with only one shoe on.

It was a thorny problem, and Royce sat in his truck at the far end of the J-Bar parking lot and drank his way rapidly through a six-pack of beer. It occurred to him that if he waited patiently enough some drunk was sure to stagger out and collapse somewhere in the parking lot, in which case it would be no trouble to steal a shoe. The only risky part about such a plan was that Rosie and her escorts might leave before he could find a collapsed drunk. In light of the seriousness of it all, the matter of the missing shoe was a terrible irritation, and Royce made up his mind to strangle Barstow the next time he came home, Shirley or no Shirley. He drank the second six-pack even more rapidly than the first. Drinking helped keep him in a decisive mood. The J-Bar was only a cheap prefabricated dance hall, and Royce could hear the music plainly through the open doors. The thought that his own wife of twenty-seven years was in there dancing with a low-class Cajun put him in a stomping mood, but unfortunately he had nothing but a sock on his best stomping foot.

Then, just as he was finishing his twelfth beer, a solution to the whole problem accidentally presented itself. Royce had about decided to wait in the truck and try to run over Rosie and F.V. when they came out to leave. He killed his motor and prepared to lie in wait, and just as he did the solution appeared in the form of two men and a woman, all of whom seemed to be very happy. When they stepped out of the door of the J-Bar they had their arms around one another and were singing about crawfish pie, but by the time they had managed to stagger the length of the building the party mood had soured. One of the men was large and the other small, and the first sign of animosity Royce noticed came when the big man picked up the little man by his belt and abruptly flung him at the rear wall of the J-Bar Korral.

"Keep your fuckin' slop bucket mouth shut around my fiancée, you little turd you," the big man said, just about the time the little man's head hit the wall of the J-Bar Korral. Royce couldn't tell if the little man heard the command or not. Instead of answering he began to writhe around on the concrete, groaning out indistinct words.

The woman paused briefly to look down at the small writhing man. "Darrell, you never need to done that," she said calmly. "I've heard the word 'titty' before anyway. I got two of 'em, even if they ain't the biggest ones in the world."

The big man evidently didn't think her comment deserved an answer, because he grabbed her arm and stuffed her into a blue Pontiac without further ado. The two of them sat in the Pontiac for a while watching the little man writhe; then, somewhat to Royce's surprise, the big man started the car and drove away, without bothering to run over the little man. The little man finally managed to get one foot under himself. The other foot evidently wouldn't go under him, because he hopped on one leg right past Royce's potato chip truck and on into the darkness of the parking lot.

Royce scarcely gave him a glance. He had just had an inspiration. When the little man struck the building, it seemed to Royce that the building had crunched. He had distinctly heard a crunching sound. Obviously the building was flimsy; it was probably only made of plywood and tarpaper. There was no reason for him to wait half the night so as to run over Rosie and F.V. in the parking lot. A building that would crunch under the impact of a small dirty-mouthed man wouldn't stand a chance against a six-year-old potato chip truck in excellent condition. He could drive right through the wall and run over Rosie and F.V. while they were actually dancing together.

Without further contemplation, Royce acted. He drove his truck up parallel to the rear wall and leaned out and punched the wall a time or two with his fist. It felt like plywood and tarpaper to him, and that was all he needed. He chose as his point of entry a spot right in the center of the rear wall, backed up so as to give himself about a twenty-yard run at it, revved his engine for all it was worth, and, with blood in his eye, drove straight into the wall.

The J-Bar Korral was a big place, and at first only those customers who happened to be drinking or dancing at the south end of the building noticed that a potato chip truck was in the process of forcing its way into the dance. The first impact splintered the wall and made a hole big enough for the nose of the truck, but it was not big enough for all the truck and Royce was forced to back up and take another run at it. A couple from Conroe were celebrating their first wedding anniversary at a table only a few yards from where the nose of the truck broke through, and the young couple and their friends, while mildly surprised to see the wall cave in and the nose of a truck appear, took a very mature attitude toward the whole thing.

"Look at that," the husband said. "Some sorry son of a bitch missed his turn an' hit the wall."

Everybody turned and watched, curious to see whether the truck was going to break on through. "I hope it ain't a nigger," the young wife said. "I'd hate to see a nigger while we're celebratin', wouldn't you, Goose?" Goose was her pet name for her husband. He didn't like for her to use it in company, but the sight of the truck caused her to forget that temporarily. Her first name was Beth-Morris and that's what everybody called her, including her husband's best friend, Big Tony, who happened to be sitting right next to her at the table, helping her celebrate her first anniversary. No sooner had she uttered the forbidden nickname than Big Tony gave her a best-friendly hug and began to make goose talk right in her little white ear. "Shit, your husband's already too drunk to cut the mustard. Let's you an' me sneak out to the car and play a little goosey-gander," Big Tony said.

Before Beth-Morris could take a firm stance Royce and his truck burst right into the J-Bar Korral. Annoyed at being stopped the first time, Royce had backed halfway across the parking lot for his second run. Beth-Morris looked up just in time to see a potato chip truck bearing right down on their table. She screamed like a banshee, spoiling everyone's anniversary mood. Big Tony instantly had all thoughts of goosey-gander driven from his mind. He had just time to fling his beer at Royce's windshield before the edge of the front bumper hit his chair and knocked him under the table.

For a brief moment there was a lull. The people in the south end of the dance hall stared at Royce and his truck, unwilling to believe what they were seeing. Royce turned on his windshield wipers, to get Big Tony's beer off his windshield, at which point people began to scream and push back their chairs. Royce knew he had no time to lose. Rosie and F.V. might escape him in the confusion. He let out his clutch and roared right out on the dance floor, scattering tables like matchsticks.

Of the people Royce sought, F.V. was the first to see him. He and Rosie were dancing near the bandstand. They had both heard the first screams, but screams were not uncommon at a big dance, and they didn't immediately stop dancing. At the sound of gunfire they would have stopped dancing, but screams ordinarily just meant a fist fight, and fist fights were not worth stopping for.

Thus it was a severe shock to F.V. to complete what he thought was a nicely executed step and look up to see Royce Dunlup's potato chip truck driving straight toward the bandstand. If shocks really froze blood, his circulatory system would have achieved a state of immediate deep freeze. As it was, except for a couple of involuntary jerks, he managed to control himself rather well.

"Don't look now," he said to Rosie. "Royce is here. Don't look now."

Rosie felt instantly weak. It was not a surprise, though; the only thing surprising was that she seemed to hear the sound of a truck. It was bound to be her imagination, however, and F.V.'s tone had more or less convinced her that her life depended on keeping her head down, so she did. She assumed Royce was stalking through the dancers, probably with a gun in his hand; since she had nowhere else to put it, she reposed her trust in F.V. Perhaps he could steer them out the door so they could make a run for it.

But F.V. had stopped dancing and stood stock still, and the sound of a truck got louder; then the sound of screams got far too loud to be the result of a fist fight, and the musicians suddenly lost the beat. "My gawd," the vocalist said, and Rosie looked up just in time to see her husband driving past in his familiar baby blue delivery truck.

For a moment Rosie suddenly felt deeply happy. There was Royce in his delivery truck, driving with both hands on the wheel, just like he always did. Probably all that had happened had been a dream. Probably she was not at a dance but home in bed; the dream would be over any minute and she would be back in the life she had always lived.

A happy relief swelled in her as she stood there expecting to wake up. Then, instead of her waking up, Royce's truck hit the bandstand, flinging musicians left and right. The drummer's drums all fell on top of him and the vocalist was knocked completely off the platform into the crowd. To make matters worse, Royce backed the truck up and went at the bandstand again. The drummer, who had just managed to get to his feet, was once again knocked sprawling into his drums. The second crash did something bad to the electrical system. It spluttered and flashed a very white light, and the electric guitar, which was lying off by itself in a corner, suddenly emitted a horrible scream, frightening everyone in the place so badly that all the women screamed too. All the musicians picked themselves up and fled except one, the bull fiddle player, a tall gangly fellow from Port Arthur who preferred death to cowardice. He leapt over the fallen drummer and smashed at the potato chip truck with his bull fiddle. "Son of a bitch bastard!" the bull fiddle player yelled, raising the fiddle on high.

Royce was mildly surprised at the stance the bull fiddle

player took, but he was far from daunted. He backed up a few feet and went at the bandstand a third time. The gallant from Port Arthur got in one tremendous swing before being flung backward into the drums and the drummer. The fight was not gone from him, though; he rose to his knees and flung a cymbal at the truck, cracking Royce's windshield.

"Security, security, where's the goddamn security?" the vocalist yelled from the midst of the crowd.

As to that, no one knew, least of all the two owners of the J-Bar, Bobby and John Dave, who had run out of their office to watch the destruction of their place of business. They were both middle-aged businessmen, long accustomed to dealing with rowdiness, but the spectacle that confronted them was more than they had bargained for.

"How'd that get in here, John? Dave?" Bobby asked, astonished. "We never ordered no potato chips."

Before John Dave could answer, Royce was off again. He was largely satisfied with the destruction of the bandstand, and whirled the truck around to face the crowd. He began a fast trip around the perimeter of the dance hall, honking as loud as he could in order to scatter the many bunches of people. It worked too; the people scattered, hopping around like grasshoppers over the many fallen chairs. In order to block the exit Royce then began to use his truck like a bull-dozer, pushing chairs and tables into the one door and then smashing them into a kind of mountain of nails and splinters.

Vernon, ever a cool head in an emergency, had rushed to Rosie's side as soon as he figured out what was happening, and the two of them were concentrating on trying to keep F.V. from panicking, which might give their position away. The fact that they were all short gave them some advantage, though it didn't seem so to F.V. "Good as dead, good as dead," he kept saying.

"Damn the luck," he added mournfully.

"It ain't luck, it's justice," Rosie said grimly. She was not especially calm, but she was a long way from panic. She had not lived with Royce twenty-seven years without learning how to take care of herself when he was mad.

Vernon watched the little blue truck chug around the room smashing what few tables it hadn't already smashed. The three of them had taken refuge behind the huge man who had danced with Rosie; fortunately he was with his equally huge wife. The two of them seemed to be enjoying the spectacle enormously.

"That's a pretty little blue truck," the huge lady said. "Whyn't we get one of them to haul the kids in?"

At that very moment the pretty little blue truck veered their way. "Here's what you do. You two run for the ladies' room," Vernon said. "Run, run!"

Rosie and F.V. broke for it and the moment they did Royce spotted them. He braked in order to get an angle on where they were going, and while he was slowed down six drunks rushed out of the crowd and grabbed his rear bumper. The huge man decided to get in on the sport and ran right over Vernon, who had just moved in front of him to try to get in the truck. Royce jerked the truck into reverse and flung off all but two of the drunks; then he shot forward again and the last two let go. As the truck went by, the huge man threw a table at it, but the table only hit one of the drunks.

F.V. outran Rosie to the ladies' room, only to remember at the last second that he wasn't a lady. He stopped and Rosie ran into him.

"Ooops, where's the men's room?" F.V. asked.

Rosie looked around and saw that the crowd had parted and that Royce was bearing down on them. There was no time for commentary. She shoved F.V. through the swinging door and squeezed in behind him about two seconds before the truck hit the wall.

The part of the J-Bar where the rest rooms were had once been the projection area when the J-Bar had been a drive-in theater rather than a dance hall. It had cinderblock walls. Royce had expected to plow right through into the ladies' john, but instead he was stopped cold. He even bumped his head on his own windshield.

His confusion at finding a wall he couldn't drive through was nothing, however, to the confusion inside the rest room. Most of the women who had been using it were blissfully ignorant of what was going on out on the dance floor. They had heard some screaming, but they had just assumed it was a bigger than usual fight and more or less resolved to stay where they were until it was over. Several were in the process of combing their hair upwards, one or two were regluing false eyelashes, and one, a large redhead named Gretchen who had just finished getting laid out in the parking lot, had one leg propped up over a lavatory and was douching.

"Lord knows the trouble it saves," she remarked, to general agreement, and the conversation, such as it was, was largely concerned with the question of unwanted pregnancies. A woman who was sitting in one of the toilets was regaling everyone with a story about unwanted triplets when with no warning at all a small male Cajun popped through the door and right into their midst. The appearance of F.V. was so startling that no one noticed the small frightened-looking redhead who was right on his heels; but the shock that followed when the truck hit the wall was nothing anyone could miss. Gretchen fell right off the lavatory, and a blonde named Darlene opened her mouth to scream and dropped a false eyelash in it. F.V., off balance to begin with, had the bad fortune to fall right on top of Gretchen.

"It's a monster, get him away," Gretchen screamed. She assumed she was about to be raped and rolled on her belly and kept screaming. A couple of women rolled out from under the doors of the toilet stalls. They assumed a tornado had struck, but when they saw F.V. they began to scream for the police. Rosie had her ear to the door, and could hear the wheels of the truck spinning on the slick dance floor. When she looked around she saw that F.V. was in real trouble. Five or six women had leaped on him to keep him from raping Gretchen, and a particularly tough-looking young brunette was trying to strangle him with a tubular syringe.

"Naw, naw," Rosie said. "He ain't out to hurt nobody. He just run in here to hide. My husband tried to run over him in a truck."

"He dove at me," Gretchen said.

"You mean there's a truck loose in this dance?" the young brunette said. "That's the dumbest thing I ever heard of."

She hurried over and peeked out the door. "Aw," she said, "it's just a little truck. I thought you meant a cattle truck, or something like that. Anyway, it's driving off."

Gretchen was still looking at F.V. with burning eyes. The news that a truck was loose in the dance hall seemed to mean nothing to her at all. "I still think he's an ol' sex fiend," she said, looking at F.V. "A man that waits till he's right between my legs to fall down may fool you, honey, but he ain't fooling me."

F.V. decided Royce was the lesser of two evils. He ran out

the door, with Rosie close behind him. On the dance floor a scene of pandemonium reigned. Royce had a headache from bumping his windshield, and had decided to go back to his original plan, which had been to run over the two sinners in the parking lot. To make that work he had to get back to the parking lot, and it wasn't proving easy. The patrons of the J-Bar had had time to size up the situation, and a number of the drunkest and most belligerent began to throw things at the truck—beer bottles particularly. The outraged vocalist had managed to locate the two security policemen, both of whom had been taking lengthy craps when the trouble started. The two policemen rushed onto the dance floor with guns drawn, only to discover that the criminal was in retreat.

Royce ignored the rain of beer bottles and plowed on across the dance floor, honking from time to time. The two policemen, plus Bobby and John Dave and the vocalist, began to chase the truck. Neither of the policemen was the sort to enjoy having a crap interrupted, though, and they weren't running their best. When a small man jumped out at them and yelled "Stop!" they stopped.

"Don't stop," the vocalist yelled, very annoyed.

Rosie joined Vernon. "It's all right, it's all right," she assured the policemen. "It's my husband. He's crazed with jealousy, that's all."

"I knowed it, Billy," one of the policemen said. "Just another goddamn family fight. We could have stayed where we was."

"Family fight, my Lord in heaven," John Dave said. "Lookit this dance hall! Hurricane Carla never done us this much damage."

"No problem, no problem," Vernon said quickly, pulling out his money clip. He peeled off several hundred dollars. "The man's my employee and I'll make good your damages," he assured them.

At that moment there was the sound of a car wreck. Despite the bottles and an occasional chair, Royce had managed to drive more or less calmly down the length of the dance floor and out the hole he had made coming in. It was just after he got out that the wreck occurred. The large man in the blue Pontiac had thought it all over and decided to come back and throw the little man against the wall again, and he was driving along slowly, looking for him, when Royce drove through his hole. Darrell, the large man, was not expecting anyone to drive out of the wall of the dance hall and was caught cold. The impact threw Royce out the door of his truck and onto the asphalt of the parking lot.

The next thing Royce knew he was looking up at a lot of people he didn't know, all of whom were looking down at him. The surprising thing was that there was one person in the crowd he did know, namely his wife Rosie. The events of the evening, particularly the unexpected car wreck, had confused Royce a good deal, and he had for the moment completely forgotten why it was he had come to the J-Bar Korral in the first place.

"Royce, just keep still now," Rosie said. "Your ankle's broken."

"Aw," Royce said, looking at it curiously. It was the ankle belonging to the foot on which he had no shoe, and the sight of his sock, which wasn't even particularly clean, made him feel deeply embarrassed.

"I never meant to come with just one shoe on, Rosie," he said doing his best to meet his wife's eyes. "The reason is Shirley's damn old dog carried the other one off."

"That's all right, Royce," Rosie said. She saw that Royce had forgotten her little indiscretion for the moment; he just looked tired, drunk, and befuddled, as he often did on Friday night, and squatting down beside him in the parking lot, with hundreds of excited people around, was indeed a little bit like waking up from a bad dream, since the man before her was so much like the same old Royce instead of the strange new hostile Royce she had been imagining for several weeks.

Royce, however, felt a little desperate. It seemed very important to him that Rosie understand he had not deliberately set out to embarrass her. Long ago his own mother, a stickler for cleanliness, had assured him that if he didn't change his underwear at least twice a week he was sure to be killed in a car wreck someday wearing dirty underwear, a fact that would lead inevitably to the disgrace of his whole family. A dirty sock and one shoe was maybe not so bad as dirty underwear, but Royce still felt that his mother's prophecy had finally been fulfilled, and he needed to do what he could to assure Rosie it hadn't really been his fault.

"Looked ever'where for it," he said morosely, hoping Rosie would understand.

Rosie was plain touched. "That's all right, Royce, quit worryin' about that shoe," she said. "Your ankle's broke an'

you wouldn't be able to wear it anyhow. We got to get you to
a hospital."

Then, to Royce's great surprise, Rosie put her arm around
him. "Little Buster asked about you, hon," she said softly.

"Aw, Little Buster," Royce said, before relief, embarrassment, fatigue, and beer overwhelmed him. Soon, though, he
was completely overwhelmed. He put his head on his wife's
familiar slate-hard breastbone and began to sob.

In that he was not alone for long. Many of the women and
even a few of the men who had gathered around forgot that
they had come out to tear Royce limb from limb. At the
sight of such a fine and fitting reunion the urge for vengeance
died out in the crowd's collective breast. A number of women
began to sob too, wishing they could have some kind of reunion. Darrell, the owner of the ill-fated Pontiac, decided to
forgive Royce instead of stomping him, and went off with his
girl friend to continue the argument they were having over
whether "titty" was an okay word. Bobby and John Dave
shook their heads and accepted ten of Vernon's one-
hundred-dollar bills as collateral against whatever the damages might total up to be. They realized that, once again, the
East-Tex Hoedown had been a big success. The two policemen went back to their bowel movements, Vernon started an
unsuccessful search for F.V., and Mitch McDonald, Royce's
best buddy, immediately went to a phone booth to call Shirley and tell her Royce had gone back to his wife. He made it
clear that he had nothing but forgiveness in his heart, and
hinted rather broadly that his own, very own, old thing was
aching to have Shirley come and sit on it again. To which
Shirley, who was filling beer pitchers with her free hand at the
time, said, "Sit on it yourself, you little tattletale. I got better
things to do if you don't mind."

Rosie knelt by her husband, gratefully receiving the warm
sentiments of the crowd. Many a woman leaned down to tell
her how happy she was that she and her husband had got it
all straightened out. Royce had cried himself to sleep against
her breast. Soon an ambulance with a siren and a revolving
red light screamed up and took Royce and Rosie away, and
then two big white wreckers came and got the Pontiac and
the potato chip truck. Some of the crowd straggled back
through the hole in the wall to talk things over, others drifted
off home, and many stayed where they were—all of them
happy to have witnessed for once, such passion and compas-

sion. Then, when all was peaceful, a spongy raft of clouds blew in from the Gulf, hiding the high wet Houston moon, and the clouds began to drop a soft, lulling midnight drizzle on the parking lot, the cars, and the happy, placidly milling crowd.

DURANGO MENDOZA

The Woman in the Green House

He came on horseback, riding slowly up the dirt road from the corner, his old saddle creaking and his body swaying slightly with the gait. The horse's hooves chipped rough crescents into the hard earth beneath the layer of dust with clopping sounds, and it began to plod slower until it stopped before the small green tar-paper house.

The sky was high and cloudless above, and the sparse trees and few houses stood quiet and submissive under the afternoon. The man's heavy shoulders sagged forward a little, and the wide-brimmed hat that he wore pulled to one side shadowed his face. It was a broad square face, and the sunlight off the road made it, reddish-brown already, seem even more flushed. He spoke gruffly to his horse, and they started again along the road toward town.

Inside the house the woman moved away from the window and sat down on the edge of the bed. A hot breath of air lifted the filmy curtains above the bed, and she looked down on her children. They were spread apart on the sheeted mattress, and their small faces and limbs glowed with warm dampness.

She picked up a towel and flicked away some flies come to settle and continued to wave it slowly over her children. After a time she lay down beside the youngest who was three and rested her head on her arm. Instinctively, the little boy pushed against her. She spoke softly and rubbed his damp hair back from his forehead.

When they woke up, she sent them out into the yard to play, and soon they disappeared among the weeds toward the old abandoned barn where they often played. The woman moved around the two rooms and gathered up clothing to mend. And all the rest of the afternoon she sat near the door and worked alone. Periodically one of the children would come puffing up to the door wanting water, and would linger only for moments after drinking to lean against her lap to see what she was doing. Then she would become restless and pace around the rooms as if looking for something.

It had been bad at first, and later it seemed to have become less important, but now she could not help but remember, and she waited in anticipation. On some nights she began to let her youngest nurse, although she had no milk to give. She became conscious of her clothes—not their appearance, but how they felt upon her body. Then one day she walked into town without underwear, but had become ashamed and fled back to her house where she spent the rest of the day alternately forgetting her children and then suddenly turning upon them and hugging them to her.

Evening came thick and warm and settled its darkness over the small town and filled the woman's house. The dust upon the roads began to cool, and its harsh daytime odor became richer. The trees and grass seemed to relax, and the sky was the last to darken. Lights came on reluctantly along the sparse streets, and the stars grew brighter and began to stare or glimmer. Atop the water tower the red blinker came on, although few airplanes ever passed and none so low.

The woman filled the wash tub on the back stoop and called her children from the supper table to bathe them. She stood them each in turn in the tub and scrubbed their small bodies as they laughed and splashed or cried when soap got in their eyes. Then they stood around wrapped in towels until she emptied the tub along the fence line and hurried before her into the lamp-lit house. She dressed them in clean underwear and carried the little boy to the bed as the other two scrambled to beat them there.

The night air was still hot, and she fanned them lightly with a piece of cloth as they talked of childish things until they began to mumble and drowse, wanting to stay awake but unable to do so. The youngest had already fallen asleep against his mother and heard nothing, as none of them did except the mother when the man on horseback paused again before their house and then moved on into the darkness.

Above the thin rippled clouds the moon was like a luminous stone in clear water, shining its pale wash into the two rooms of the woman's house.

After the war the man had driven tractor at twenty dollars a week for the man who owned the hardware store and much of the land near the town. He worked alone and could be seen riding the machine slowly back and forth across the wide fields, plowing, discing, and planting throughout the long hot days. He sat slumped a little in the seat, wearing a rumpled dirty hat cocked to one side and grasping the back of the seat to brace himself as he turned to look back over the furrows. He thought often of the war but said little about it or anything else. In the evening he went home to his old mother in the country.

One day as he struggled silently in the heat with a jammed attachment, a chain snapped and lashed him across the forehead, and in the red and black of his pain the war seemed again to crush upon him. It seemed also that the devil laughed beside him and became the one who had struck him.

They found him later lying upon the broken ground with his blood dried and dark upon his face and soaked into the loose earth.

He could not work for a time after the accident, and he rode often by the little green house and puzzled over the woman who lived there. As did most Chicanos in the community, he knew the basic situation of every other Chicano adult and their families. He knew that this woman and her three sisters had gone away to the city and had returned with a child apiece out of wedlock, except for the woman, who had married and had had three children. He knew also that they lived on welfare, for he had seen one day the women behind the stores grasping the potatoes that her children discovered among the discarded crates and burlap sacks. He had seen how the children acted as if they were playing a game, but what pleased him most was the woman as she stood among them. After that, he watched for them and saw them often along the streets or at church meetings.

Many times as he rode, the war entered his mind and blurred the minutes until the horse would slow down, then stop, and his big shoulders would seem to hunch forward, and the healing scar on his forehead would tighten with pain.

One day he appeared to the woman before her house, sitting on his horse in the heat and sun like a drooping statue. He heard a screen door slap shut and later saw her standing above him.

You are sick, she was telling him. Come inside. It is the heat and your riding and the cut upon your forehead. Come inside.

She had watched him lying there on his back, and her eyes hid what she thought, if she thought at all, and her posture was timid. Almost reluctantly, she reached out and touched him. She stroked him and felt him begin to swell when he woke up with the war still vague behind his eyes. And then they were inside the little green house, and almost automatically he pulled her upon him.

When the woman woke up, the man still slept. The heat in the room was close, and when she sat up on the edge of the bed, she saw her youngest sitting on a chair with his legs hanging off the side, looking at her through the lattice backing. She started to pick him up, but he slipped away from her and ran outdoors. She saw him through the screen with his small arms bent and his hands held up shoulder high, trotting in the sunlight toward the high grass and the old barn.

To get married they traveled to a town beyond the low surrounding hills and left the children with a friend of the woman's to go to the courthouse. But the youngest would not stop crying and clung to his mother when she tried to leave until finally she diverted him long enough to get away. And when he found out that he had been deceived he cried even louder and would not be approached.

Finally the other children took him outside with them where they were coasting down a hill on a tricycle. They tried to coax him to try it, but he wouldn't until they all struggled to put him on. Then, speeding down the sidewalk hill with the others screaming and laughing beside him, his crying changed to laughter without a pause between them. And when the new couple kissed in the mornings, he stood with the other two and giggled shyly, too. And like them, he was glad when the man left for work. But when he returned at dusk, they became quiet and avoided him.

Those kids, the man told the woman one night while they were in bed, they don't want me here.

Oh, she said, but they aren't used to having a father. Their daddy—

You shut up about their daddy, the man said. I don't want to hear nothing about the son of a bitch.

All right, said the woman, and that night she dreamed of the children's daddy. She dreamed of the times they had had.

In the night the three little ones played in the darkness on their bed, quietly, stopped every so often to listen to the man's rumbling voice as he spoke of the war to their mother. When he was loud, they looked at each other in the darkness.

When fall came the woman began to swell and grow larger through the winter. The children would gather around and feel the tiny kicks in her belly. The man began to help the children dress and wash in the mornings. The little boy thought it was strange. The oldest would become stiff when the man approached her, and the middle boy said nothing and tried to help himself as much as possible.

One morning the children woke up in a cold house. They felt immediately that no one was home, but they didn't stir from the bed. Instead they began to exhale their breath to make round whistling noises. Then sunlight touched the frosted panes, and they saw the old man crouching in the corner. He had been watching them. His long chapped hands hung over his knees and flapped once when he saw that they had seen him. They could not remember ever having seen him before.

The oldest spoke first: Where's Mama? she said.

Where Mama? said the youngest. Where Mama, ol' man?

The old man unfolded himself, but didn't straighten when he stood. Instead he shuffled into the other room where their mother's bed was. They heard him open the door and felt the walls tremble when it slammed. The yellow jewels of sunlight danced in the window frost. As time passed, the frost began to fade and the wind began to blow.

A fat woman came out of the other room. It just wasn't time, she said after she told them.

I felt it kick, said the middle boy.

Yes, said the girl.

But your daddy will be back pretty soon and take you to see your mama.

There, daddy, said the little boy when the man came to the door and entered the house.

The fat woman told him: Your kids are all ready to go see their mother now.

Those ain't my kids, he told her, and went on into the other room.

There, daddy, said the little boy.

You hush your mouth, the girl whispered fiercely. You hear? You just hush up.

The little boy began to whimper, and the fat woman took him on her knee. After a while he pressed against her, and she sat with him there. He looked at his sister and made a face. Suddenly she began to cry, and he jerked and became afraid. But the fat woman held him closer and called him poor baby, and he felt better. The middle boy said nothing and held onto the woman's sleeve and watched his sister standing slumped near the door with her coat on.

N. SCOTT MOMADAY

The Way to Rainy Mountain

They lived at first in the mountains. They did not yet know of Tai-me, but this is what they knew: There was a man and his wife. They had a beautiful child, a little girl whom they would not allow to go out of their sight. But one day a friend of the family came and asked if she might take the child outside to play. The mother guessed that would be all right, but she told the friend to leave the child in its cradle and to place the cradle in a tree. While the child was in the tree, a redbird came among the branches. It was not like any bird that you have seen; it was very beautiful, and it did not fly away. It kept still upon a limb, close to the child. After a while the child got out of its cradle and began to climb after the redbird. And at the same time the tree began to grow taller, and the child was borne up into the sky. She was then a woman, and she found herself in a strange place. Instead of a redbird, there was a young man standing before her. The man spoke to her and said: "I have been watching you for a long time, and I knew that I would find a way to bring you here. I have brought you here to be my wife." The woman looked all around; she saw that he was the only living man there. She saw that he was the sun.

After that the woman grew lonely. She thought about her people, and she wondered how they were getting on. One day she had a quarrel with the sun, and the sun went away. In her anger she dug up the root of a bush which the sun had warned her never to go near. A piece of earth fell from the root, and she could see her people far below. By that time she had given birth; she had a child—a boy by the sun. She made a rope out of sinew and took her child upon her back; she climbed down upon the rope, but when she came to the end, her people were still a long way off, and there she waited with her child on her back. It was evening; the sun came home and found his woman gone. At once he thought of the bush and went to the place where it had grown. There he saw the woman and the child, hanging by the rope half-way down to the earth. He was very angry, and he took up a ring, a gaming wheel, in his hand. He told the ring to follow the rope and strike the woman dead. Then he threw the ring and it did what he told it to do; it struck the woman and killed her, and then the sun's child was all alone.

The sun's child was big enough to walk around on the earth, and he saw a camp nearby. He made his way to it and saw that a great spider—that which is called a grandmother—lived there. The spider spoke to the sun's child, and the child was afraid. The grandmother was full of resentment; she was jealous, you see, for the child had not yet been weaned from its mother's breasts. She wondered whether the child were a boy or a girl, and therefore she made two things, a pretty ball and a bow and arrows. These things she left alone with the child all the next day. When she returned, she saw that the ball was full of arrows, and she knew then that the child was a boy and that he would be hard to raise. Time and again the grandmother tried to capture the boy, but he always ran away. Then one day she made a snare out of rope. The boy was caught up in the snare, and he cried and cried, but the grandmother sang to him and at last he fell asleep.

> Go to sleep and do not cry.
> Your mother is dead, and still you feed
>   upon her breasts.
> Oo-oo-la-la-la-la, oo-oo.

The years went by, and the boy still had the ring which killed his mother. The grandmother spider told him never to throw the ring into the sky, but one day he threw it up, and it fell squarely on top of his head and cut him in two. He looked around, and there was another boy, just like himself, his twin. The two of them laughed and laughed, and then they went to the grandmother spider. She nearly cried aloud when she saw them, for it had been hard enough to raise the one. Even so, she cared for them well and made them fine clothes to wear.

Now each of the twins had a ring, and the grandmother spider told them never to throw the rings into the sky. But one day they threw them up into the high wind. The rings rolled over a hill, and the twins ran after them. They ran beyond the top of the hill and fell down into the mouth of a cave. There lived a giant and his wife. The giant had killed a lot of people in the past by building fires and filling the cave with smoke, so that the people could not breathe. Then the twins remembered something that the grandmother spider had told them: "If ever you get caught in the cave, say to yourselves the word *thain-mom,* 'above my eyes.'" When the giant began to set fires around, the twins repeated the word *thain-mom* over and over to themselves, and the smoke remained above their eyes. When the giant had made three great clouds of smoke, his wife saw that the twins sat without coughing or crying, and she became frightened. "Let them go," she said, "or something bad will happen to us." The twins took up their rings and returned to the grandmother spider. She was glad to see them.

JOHN NICHOLS

The Milagro Beanfield War

Amarante Córdova had had thirteen children. That is, he and his wife, Elizabeth—known as Betita—had had thirteen children, who either still were or had been Nadia, Jorge, Pólito, María Ana, Berta, Roberto, Billy, Nazario, Gabriel, Ricardo, Sally, Patsy, and Cipriano. Betita, who had never been sick a day in her life, died in 1963, on November 22, on the same day as President Kennedy, but not from a bullet in the head. She had been outside chopping wood during a lovely serene snowstorm when suddenly she set down the ax and began to walk along the Milagro-García spur onto the mesa. In recalling her death later Amarante would always tell his listeners, "You cannot imagine how beautiful it was that afternoon. The snow falling was as serene as the white feathers of a swan. When the ravens sailed through it they made no sound. You looked up and the big black birds were floating through the snowflakes like faint shadows of our forefathers, the first people who settled in the valley. The tall sagebrush was a lavender-green color because there had been a lot of rain in the autumn, and that was the only color on the otherwise black and white mesa, the pale lavender-green of the sage on which snow had settled. You remember, of course, that Betita's hair was as white as the snow, and she was wearing a black dress and a black woolen shawl that Sally, our daughter who was married to the plumber from Doña Luz, knitted for her on a birthday long ago."

Slowly, taking her time, Betita walked across the mesa to the rim of the gorge. "And there she stood on the edge looking down," Amarante said. "For a long time she was poised there like a wish afraid to be uttered. The walls of the gorge created a faded yellow glow to the flakes falling eight hundred feet down to the icy green river below. Ravens were in the air, circling, their wings whispering no louder than the snow falling. It was very peaceful. I was at the house, I never saw her leave. But when she didn't come in with the wood after a while, I saddled up that lame plow horse we used to have called Buster, and went after her, following her tracks in the snow. Just as I left the road to enter the chamisal an owl dropped out of the darkening sky, landing on a cedar post not ten yards away. An owl is a sure sign from the dead, you know, and it was right then I knew she had disappeared into the gorge. When I arrived at the rim an enormous raven was standing where she had last stood, and when he saw me he spread his wings, which were wider than my outstretched arms, and floated up like a good-bye kiss from my wife into the lazy storm. Next day we opened the church, only the second time that year it was used, not to say prayers for Betita, but to burn candles and shed our tears for the President who had died in Dallas. But I lit my candles for Betita, and nobody noticed. Three months later her body was discovered on the bank of the river two miles below Chamisaville."

The Córdova sons and daughters had scattered, as the saying goes, to the four winds. Or actually, only to the three winds, eastward being anathema to the children of Milagro, whose Mississippi was the Midnight Mountains, that chain running north and south barely a mile or two from all their backyards.

Nadia, a waitress most of her life, first in Doña Luz, then Chamisaville, wound up in the Capital City barrio, dying violently (and recently) at the age of sixty-one in a lover's quarrel. Jorge emigrated to Australia where he tended sheep, same as at home. Pólito, who spent his life wandering around, getting married three or four times and taking care of sheep in Wyoming, Montana, and Utah, had died young of the flu. María Ana wanted to be a dancer, took the train to San Francisco, and after years of strenuous work, heartbreak, and small roles in the city ballet company, she hurt her back and wound up teaching in an Arthur Murray studio. Berta married an Anglo who raised lemons in California, and, curiously, they never had any children. Roberto, Billy, and Nazario became farm workers, mechanics, truck drivers, dishwashers, and short-order cooks in and around Los Angeles; they all raised large families, and although between them they'd had nine sons in Vietnam, only one of Billy's kids, Rosario, had been killed. Gabriel, who miraculously metamorphosed into a run-of-the-mill featherweight boxer in the army, turned pro after his discharge, was known as the Milagro Mauler during his short and undistinguished prime, and died in a plane crash in Venezuela. Ricardo had stayed on as a rancher in Milagro, although he spent half his life in the lettuce, sugar beet, or potato fields of southern Colorado, or else with the big sheep outfits up in Wyoming and Montana. Two of his sons, Elisardo and Juan, had died in Vietnam; another boy was stationed in Germany. Sally married a plumber in Doña Luz and had eleven kids herself, one of whom became a successful pop singer in Mexico City, but never sent any money home, not even after the plumber died when a black widow bit him while he was creeping around somebody's musty crawl space on a job. Patsy, the most beautiful and the sharpest in school, ran west to join a circus, became an Avon lady instead, and died with her husband and all their children except Peter (who was in a Japanese hospital at the time recovering from wounds received in Vietnam) in a head-on car crash in Petaluma. And little Cipriano, the baby of the family, born in 1925, who went farther than everyone else in his education, and, in fact, had just obtained a full scholarship to Harvard when he was drafted, was vivisected by a German machine gun during the first eighteen seconds of the Normandy D-day landings.

All his life Amarante had lived in the shadow of his own death. When he was two days old he caught pneumonia, they gave him up for dead, somehow he recovered. During his childhood he was always sick, he couldn't work like other boys his age. He had rheumatic fever, chicken pox, pneumonia three or four more times, started coughing blood when he was six, was anemic, drowsy all the time, constantly sniffling, weak and miserable, and—everybody thought—dying. At eight he had his tonsils out; at ten, his appendix burst. At twelve he was bitten by a rattlesnake, went into a coma, survived. Then a horse kicked him, breaking all the ribs on his left side. He contracted tuberculosis. He hacked and stumbled around, hollow-eyed, gaunt and sniffling, and folks crossed themselves, murmuring Hail Marys whenever he staggered into view. At twenty, when he was already an alcoholic, scarlet fever almost laid him in the grave; at twenty-three malaria looked like it would do the job. Then came several years of amoebic dysentery. After that he was constipated for seventeen months. At thirty, a lung collapsed; at thirty-four, shortly after he became the first sheriff of Milagro, that old devil pneumonia returned for another whack at it, slowed his pulse to almost nothing, but like a classical and very pretty but faint-hearted boxer, couldn't deliver the knockout punch. During the old man's forties a number of contending diseases dropped by Amarante's body for a shot at the title. The clap came and went, had a return bout, was counted out. The measles appeared, as did the mumps, but they did not even last a full round. For old time's sake pneumonia made a token appearance, beat its head against the brick wall that evidently lined Amarante's lungs, then waved a white flag and retreated. Blood poisoning blew all his lymph nodes up to the size of golf balls, stuck around for a month, and lost the battle.

Amarante limped, coughed, wheezed; his chest ached; he spat both blood and gruesome blue-black lungers, drank until his asshole hurt, his flat feet wailed; arthritis took sledgehammers to his knees; his stomach felt like it was bleeding; and all but three of his teeth turned brown and toppled out of his mouth like acorns. In Milagro, waiting for Amarante Córdova to drop dead became like waiting for one of those huge sneezes that just refuses to come. And there was a stretch during Amarante's sixties when people kept running away from him, cutting conversations short and like that, because everybody *knew* he was going to keel over in the very next ten seconds, and nobody likes to be present when somebody drops dead.

In his seventies Amarante's operations began. First they removed a lung. By that time the citizens of Milagro had gotten into the irate, sarcastic, and not a little awed frame of mind which had them saying: "Shit, even if they took out that old bastard's other lung he'd keep on breathing."

A lump in his neck shaped like a miniature cow was removed. After that a piece of his small intestine had to go. There followed, of course, the usual gallbladder, spleen, and kidney operations. People in Milagro chuckled. "Here comes the human zipper," whenever Amarante turned a corner into sight. His friends regarded him with a measure of respect and hatred, beseeching him to put in a good word for them with the Angel of Death, or whoever it was with whom he held counsel, even as they capsized over backward into the adobe and caliche darkness of their own graves.

But finally, at seventy-six, there loomed on Amarante's horizon a Waterloo. Doc Gómez in the clinic at Doña Luz sent him to a doctor at the Chamisaville Holy Cross Hospital, who did a physical, took X rays, shook his head, and sent the old man to St. Claire's in the capital, where a stomach specialist, after doing a number of tests and barium X rays and so forth, came to the conclusion that just about everything below Amarante's neck had to go, and the various family members were notified.

The family had kept in touch in spite of being scattered to the three winds, and those that were still living, including Jorge from Australia, returned to Milagro for a war council, and for a vote on whether or not they could muster the money to go ahead with their father's expensive operation. "If he doesn't have this operation," the Capital City doctor told them, "your father will be dead before six months are out."

Now the various members of the family had heard that tune before, but all the same they took a vote: Nadia, María Ana, Berta, Sally, and Billy voted for the operation; Jorge, Roberto, Nazario, and Ricardo voted against it. And so by a 5–4 margin Amarante went under the knife and had most of his innards removed. He recuperated for several weeks, and then, under Sally's and Ricardo's and Betita's care, went home to Milagro.

But it looked as if this time was really *it*. Slow to get back on his feet, Amarante had jaundice and looked ghastly. He complained he couldn't see anymore, and they discovered he had cataracts in both eyes, so Ricardo and Sally and Betita took him back to St. Claire's and had those removed. Thereafter, he had to wear thick-lensed glasses which made him look more like a poisoned corpse than ever before. His slow, creeping way of progressing forward made snails look like Olympic sprinters. The people of Milagro held their collective breath; and if they had been a different citizenry with a different culture from a different part of the country, they probably would have begun to make book on which day *it* would happen. In fact, the word had spread, so that down in

Chamisaville at the Ortega Funeral Home, which handled most of the death from Arroyo Verde to the Colorado border, it became common for Bunny Ortega, Bruce Maés, and Bernardo Medina to wonder, sort of off the cuff during their coffee breaks, when Amarante's body would be coming in. And eventually, although she did not go so far as to have Joe Mondragón or one of the other enterprising kids like him dig a grave out in the camposanto, Sally did drop by Ortega's in order to price coffins and alert the personnel as to what they might expect when the time came.

One gorgeous autumn day when all the mountain aspens looked like a picture postcard from heaven, Amarante had a conversation with Sally. "I guess this old temple of the soul has had it," he began with his usual sly grin. "I think you better write everybody a letter and tell them to come home for Christmas. I want to have all my children gathered around me at Christmastime so I can say good-bye. There won't be no more Navidades for me."

Sally burst into tears, she wasn't quite sure whether of relief or of grief. And, patting her father on the back once she had loudly blown her nose, she said, "Alright, Papa. I know everybody who's left will come."

And *that* was a Christmas to remember! The Celebration of 1956. Jorge came from Australia with his wife and their five children. Nadia journeyed up from the capital with her lover. María Ana took off from the Arthur Murray studios in San Francisco, flying in with her husband and four children. Berta and the lemon grower took a train from the San Jose Valley. Roberto, Billy, and Nazario, their wives and fourteen children and some grandchildren, drove in a caravan of disintegrating Oldsmobiles from L.A. And Sally and the remaining two of her brood still in the nest motored up every day from Doña Luz. People stayed at Ricardo's house, at what was left of Amarante's and Betita's adobe, and some commuted from Sally's in Doña Luz.

They had turkeys and pumpkin pie, mince pie and sour cream pie; they had chili and posole, corn and sopaipillas and enchiladas and empanaditas, tequila and mescal, Hamms and Coors and Old Crow, and in the center of it all with the screaming hordes revolving happily about him, chest-deep in satin ribbons and rainbow-colored wrapping paper, so drunk that his lips were flapping like pajamas on a clothesline during the April windy season, sat the old patriarch himself, dying but not quite dead, and loving every minute of it. His children hugged him, whispered sweet nothings in his ear, and waited on his every whim and fancy. They pressed their heads tenderly against his bosom, muttering endearing and melodramatic lovey-doveys, even as they also anxiously listened to see if the old ticker really was on its last legs. They took him by the elbow and held him when he wished to walk somewhere, they gazed at him sorrowfully and shed tears of both joy and sadness, they squeezed his feeble hands and reminisced about the old days and about the ones who were dead, about what all the grandchildren were doing, and about who was pregnant and who had run away, who was making a lot of money and who was broke and a disgrace, who was stationed in Korea and who was stationed in Germany . . . and they joined hands, singing Christmas carols in Spanish, they played guitars and an accordion, they wept and cavorted joyously some more, and finally, tearfully, emotionally, tragically, they all kissed his shrunken cheeks and bid him a fond and loving adios, told their mama Betita to be strong, and scattered to the three winds.

Three years later when Jorge in Australia received a letter from Sally in Dõna Luz, he replied:

What do you mean he wants us all to meet again for Christmas so he can say good-bye? What am I made out of, gold and silver? I said good-bye two winters ago, it cost me a fortune! I can't come back right now!

Nevertheless, when Sally a little hysterically wrote that this time was really *it*, he came, though minus the wife and kiddies. So also did all the other children come, a few minus some wives or husbands or children, too. At first the gaiety was a little strained, particularly when Nazario made a passing remark straight off the bat to Berta that he thought the old man looked a hell of a lot better than he had three years ago, and Berta and everyone else within hearing distance couldn't argue with that. But then they realized they were all home again, and Milagro was white and very beautiful, its juniper and piñon branches laden with a fresh snowfall, and the smell of piñon smoke on the air was almost like a drug making them high. The men rolled up their sleeves and passed around the ax, splitting wood, until Nazario sank the ax into his foot, whereupon they all drove laughing and drinking beer down to the Chamisaville Holy Cross Hospital where the doctor on call proclaimed the shoe a total loss, but only had to take two stitches between Nazario's toes. Later that same afternoon there was a piñata for the few little kids—some grandchildren, a pocketful of great-grandchildren—who had come, and, blindfolded, they pranced in circles swinging a wooden bat until the papier-mâché donkey burst, and everyone cheered and clapped as the youngsters trampled each other scrambling for the glittering goodies. Then the kids stepped up one after another to give Grandpa sticky candy kisses, and he embraced them all with tears in his eyes. Later the adults kissed Grandpa, giving him gentle abrazos so as not to cave in his eggshell chest. "God bless you," they whispered, and Amarante grinned, flashing his three teeth in woozy good-byes. "This was in place of coming to the funeral," he rasped to them in a quavering voice. "Nobody has to come to the funeral." Betita started to cry.

Out of the old man's earshot and eyesight his sons and daughters embraced each other, crossed themselves, crossed their fingers, and, casting their eyes toward heaven in supplication, murmured, not in a mean or nasty way, but with gentleness and much love for their father:

"Here's hoping . . ."

When, five years later, Jorge received the next letter from Sally, he wrote back furiously:

NO! I just came for Mama's funeral!

On perfumed pink Safeway stationery she pleaded with him to reconsider, she begged him to come. For them all she outlined their father's pathetic condition. He'd had a heart attack after Betita's death. He had high blood pressure. His veins were clotted with cholesterol. His kidneys were hardly functioning. He had fallen and broken his hip. A tumor the size of an avocado had been removed from beside his other lung, and it was such a rare tumor they didn't know if it was malignant or benign. They thought, also, that he had diabetes. Then, most recently, a mild attack of pneumonia had laid him out for a couple of weeks. As an afterthought she mentioned that some lymph nodes had been cut from his neck for biopsies because they thought he had leukemia, but it turned out he'd had an infection behind his ears where the stems of his glasses were rubbing too hard.

Jorge wrote back:

What is Papa trying to do to us all? I'm no spring chicken, Sally. *I* got a heart condition. *I'm* blind in one eye. *I* got bursitis so bad in one shoulder I can't lift my hand above my waist. And I've *got* diabetes!

He returned, though. He loved his father, he loved Milagro. Since the last time, Nadia had also died. The other surviving children came, but none of the grandchildren or great-grandchildren showed up. Times were a little tough, money hard to come by. And although maybe the old man was dying, he looked better than ever, better even than some of them. His cheeks seemed to have fleshed out a little, they were even a tiny bit rosy. Could it be their imagination, or was he walking less stooped over now? And his mind seemed sharper than before. When Jorge drove up the God damn old man was outside chopping wood!

They shared a quiet, subdued celebration. Most of them had arrived late and would leave early. And after they had all kissed their father good-bye again, and perhaps squeezed him a little harder than usual in their abrazos (hoping, maybe, to dislodge irrevocably something vital inside his body), the sons and daughters went for a walk on the mesa.

"I thought he said he was dying," Jorge complained, leaning heavily on a cane, popping glycerin tablets from time to time.

"I wrote you all what has happened," Sally sighed. "I told you what Papa said."

"How old is he now?" asked Berta.

"He was born in 1880, qué no?" Ricardo said.

"That makes him eighty-four," Billy said glumly. "And already I'm fifty."

"He's going to die," Sally said sadly. "I can feel it in my bones."

And those that didn't look at her with a mixture of hysteria and disgust solemnly crossed themselves. . . .

For the Christmas of 1970 only Jorge came. He bitched, ranted, and raved at Sally in a number of three-, four-, and five-page letters, intimating in no uncertain terms that he couldn't care less if his father *had* lost all the toes on one foot plus something related to his bladder, he wasn't flying across any more oceans for any more Christmases to say good-bye to the immortal son of a bitch.

But he came.

The airplane set down in the capital; he took the Trailways bus up. Ricardo, who was recovering from stomach surgery but slowly dying of bone cancer anyway, met him at Rael's store. Sally came up later. Jorge had one blind askew eye and poor vision in the other, he was bald, limping noticeably, haggard and frail and crotchety. He felt that for sure this trip was going to kill him, and did not understand why he kept making it against his will.

Then, when Jorge saw Amarante, his suspicions were confirmed. His father wasn't growing old: he had reached some kind of nadir ten or twelve years ago and now he was growing backward, aiming toward middle age, maybe youth. To be sure, when Amarante lifted his shirt to display the scars he looked like a banana that had been hacked at by a rampaging machete-wielding maniac, but the light in his twinkling old eyes, magnified by those glasses, seemed like something stolen from the younger generation.

The next day, Christmas Day, in the middle of Christmas dinner, Jorge suffered a heart attack, flipped over in his chair, his mouth full of candied sweet potato, and died.

Bunny Ortega, Bruce Maés, and the new man replacing Bernardo Medina (who had also died), Gilbert Otero, smiled sadly but with much sympathy when Sally and Ricardo accompanied the body to the Ortega Funeral Home in Chamisaville.

"Well, well," Bunny said solicitously. "So the old man finally passed away."

"No-no-no," Sally sobbed. "This is my brother . . . his son! . . ."

"Ai, Chihuahua!"

And here it was, two years later more or less, and Joe Mondragón had precipitated a crisis, and Amarante Córdova had never been so excited in his life.

One day, during his Doña Luz daughter's weekly visit, Amarante told her, "Hija, you got to write me a letter to all the family."

Sally burst into tears. "I can't. I won't. No. You can't make me."

"But we have to tell everyone about what José has done.

They must see this thing and take part in it before they die. Tell them the shooting is about to start—"

So Sally dutifully advised her surviving siblings about what Joe Mondragón had done; she informed them that the shooting was about to start.

Maybe they read her letters, maybe they only looked at the postmark, but to a man jack they all replied: "Send us your next letter *after* Papa is dead!"

"That's the trouble with this younger generation," Amarante whined petulantly. "They don't give a damn about anything important anymore."

CAROLYN OSBORN

My Brother Is a Cowboy

My daddy used to advise my brother and me, "Don't tell everything you know." This was his golden rule. I keep it in mind as I constantly disregard it. I've been busy most of my life telling everything I know. My brother Kenyon took it to heart. He tells nothing, not even the most ordinary answers to questions about his everyday existence. If my mother asks when he'll be home for supper, he says, "I don't know." The nearest he'll come to giving the hour for when he'll come in or go out is "Early" or "Late." His common movements, the smallest events of his day, are secret.

Mother follows these like a female detective. "Kenyon left the bread out this morning and the pimento cheese. I wonder if he had pimento cheese for breakfast, or took sandwiches for lunch, or both?" If, after she counts the remaining bread slices, sandwiches seem a possibility, she wonders where he has to go that's so distant he needs to take lunch with him. The names of surrounding towns come to her mind. "He won't be going anywhere near Lampasas because they have good barbeque there and he wouldn't take pimento cheese if he could get barbeque." She has an advantage over Daddy; at least she's observed Kenyon's eating habits through the years and can spend hours happily trying to guess what he's going to do about lunch and whether or not he's going to turn up for supper.

Daddy doesn't care about where Kenyon eats lunch. What

he wants to know is how many ranches Kenyon is leasing, how his sheep, goats, and cattle are doing, if he's making money or not.

We all want to know if he's ever going to get married. Does he have a girl? Does he want to marry? He is almost thirty, taller than my father's six feet, though how much we don't know, for he won't stand and be measured. He has dark hair that curls when he forgets to get it cut, which is most of the time. The curls come over his forehead and disgust him so much he is forever jamming his hat down low to cover his hair. When we were children he made me cut the front curls off. I was spanked for doing it. His nose is long and straight. There is a small slanting scar just missing his eye running over his left eyebrow. His eyes are brown. His mouth is wide and generally closed.

When we ask if he's ever going to marry, and nothing will stop us from asking, he says, "Find me a girl who'll live out in the country, cook beans, and wash all day." He runs his hands over the creases in his clean blue jeans, sticks the shirttail of his clean shirt in, and laughs. Mother gets angry then. She's responsible for all his clean clothes and feels sometimes this is the only reason he shows up at the house. Often she says, "He doesn't need a wife! He needs a washer-woman!" Not once, however, has she ever said this to him, fearing he'll put on his boots and walk out the door to some unknown café one last time.

She isn't curious about where I'm going to eat. Everybody in town knows I eat lunch every day at the Leon High School cafeteria. I'm the singing teacher. Wouldn't you know it! Since I've already told you Kenyon's almost thirty, you might as well know I'm almost twenty-six. At least nobody asks me when I'm going to get married, not to my face anyway. Being related and having practically no heart at all, Kenyon has the gall to wonder out loud if I'm ever going to catch a man. When he does this, I tell him I have as much right to uphold the long tradition of old-maidhood as he has to represent the last of the old West. My brother is a cowboy.

I tell him, "You're the last of a vanishing breed, the tail end of the roundup of the longhorn steers, the last great auk alive, a prairie rooster without a hen!"

All he replies to this is, "Sister, there ain't no substitute for beef on the hoof." He gets out real quick before I can go on about helicopters substituting for horses and feed lots replacing the open range.

Since the wires have been cut between Kenyon and his family, we have to depend on other sources of information, the weekly newspaper for instance. That's where we found out he'd been riding bulls in rodeos the summer after he flunked out of college. He got his picture on the front page for falling off a Brahma bull headfirst. The photographer caught the bull still doubled up and Kenyon in midair, his hands out in front of him right before he hit the dirt. My daddy strictly forbade any more bull-riding on the grounds he wasn't going to have his son associating with a bunch of rodeo bums.

Kenyon said, "These bums are the best friends I got and I'll associate with whoever I want."

"You are going to kill yourself and me too." Daddy put his hand over his heart like he was going to have an attack that minute. "And, furthermore, I'm going to cut you out of my will if you keep up this fool riding." Then he laid down on the bed and made me take his blood pressure. I was home on vacation from nursing school in Galveston.

Kenyon smiled, showing he still had all his teeth, and the next thing we read in the newspaper was he'd gone off and joined the paratroopers, joined of his own free will, mind you, for three years. Daddy, who'd been in the infantry in WW II, was half proud and half wild. "He doesn't have enough sense to keep his feet on the ground! If he isn't being thrown from a bull, he's throwing himself out of airplanes!" He wrote an old army buddy of his who'd retired, like he did, near his last post—except the post was up in Tennessee where Kenyon was stationed instead of Texas where we are. This old buddy wrote back saying:

Dear Willie,

Your boy is doing fine. I talked to his C.O. yesterday. He told me Pvt. Kenyon K. Lane is making a good soldier.

Yours truly,
Henry C. Worth, Lt. Col., Ret.

P.S. He told me Kenyon inspires good morale because he jumps out of planes with a wad of tobacco in his mouth and spits all the way down.

Your friend,
Lt. Col. Henry C. Worth, Ret.

I think Daddy was happy for a while. He showed the letter to me before he went downtown to show it to some of his friends at the drugstore where they all meet for coffee. By the time he came home, Mother was back from the grocery.

"William, how can you go around showing everybody that letter when I haven't read it!" She read it and was crying before she finished. "Who taught him how to chew tobacco? He'll ruin his teeth. He was such a nice clean boy."

"Ruin his teeth!" Daddy shouted. "You've got to worry about his teeth when he's falling out of airplanes every day!"

"He's not falling," I said. "He's jumping and he's doing it of his own free will."

"Free will nothing!" Daddy turned on me. "Don't you be telling me about free will in the U.S. Army. I know about the army. I spent twenty years in the army."

I had to take his blood pressure after that. He spent the next three years writing to his army buddies near whatever post my brother happened to be on, and getting news of Kenyon from them. All his letters were signed Col. William K. Lane, Ret.

I spent those years finishing my education, they thought. In the daytime I was. I wore a white uniform and low white shoes and went to nursing school in Galveston. Friday and Saturday nights I put on a red sequined dress and a pair of red high heels and went to sing at one of the nightclubs. My stage name was Gabriella and I wore so much makeup nobody from Leon would have known it was me. I had learned something from Kenyon, not to tell everything I knew and to follow my own free will. It worked too. When I was home I took Daddy's blood pressure and Mother's temperature; when I was in Galveston I was singing two nights a week.

Don't get any ideas either—singing and wearing a red dress was all I was doing. The men in the combo I sang with were more strict with me than they would have been with their own daughters if they had had any. I could drink soda pop only, and I had to sit with one of them while I was drinking. Except for the sequins I might as well have been in a convent. I sang songs like "I Can't Say No" without ever having a chance to not say it. Still, I was satisfied. Singing was what I wanted. I thought if I could support myself by nursing, I could gradually work my way into show biz and up to New York. So I was down in Galveston nursing and singing while my brother was on some army post jumping out of airplanes, I supposed.

One Friday night I was giving out with "Zip-Pah-De-Do-Dah" trying to cheer up a few barflies when in walks Kenyon. He knows me right away, red sequins, makeup, and all. He is wearing a tight-fitting paratrooper's uniform, his pants tied up in his boots, which laced to the knee practically. Very spiffy and clean. Mother would have been happy to see him.

"My, oh, my, what a wonderful day!" I finish. The barflies applaud. My brother just stands quietly while I slink off the platform. It's time for the break, so Tiny the drummer, who is actually a big fat man, married with a wife and baby he calls every night in Dallas, takes me by the arm to a table. Kenyon comes right over. I can see immediately he has gotten himself all shined up for one reason—to get roaring drunk—to the disgrace of family and country. He's just off the reservation and ready to howl. Obviously, I'm in his way.

I smile at him and say, "Hi. What are you doing down here? Are you AWOL?"

"No," he grins, "I'm on leave. You're the one that's AWOL."

Tiny says, "Scram, soldier boy."

"It's my brother, Tiny. He's in the paratroopers. He jumps out of airplanes."

"Gay Baby, don't pull the brother bit on me."

"But he is," I insist. "Show him your birthmark or something, Kenyon."

"Jump on out of here, fly boy," says Tiny.

"If I go, you go too, Gay Baby," says Kenyon with a merciless smirk.

"I'm not going anywhere till I finish here tonight. You sit down and behave yourself. Have a beer."

"You're leaving right now. My sister isn't going to hang around no honky-tonk." With this he grabs me by the arm and I scream at him, "Let go!" But he doesn't and by this time I'm furious. "You auk! You dodo! You idiot!"

Tiny rises like a giant blimp slowly filling with air. Before he can signal to the other fellows though, Kenyon pulls me to my feet. The other four members of the combo—Louie, the piano player; Max, the bass; Joe, the sax; and Evans, the trumpet—run to assist us.

Kenyon turns the table on its side. "She's going with me," he says.

I peek between the fingers of my free hand to see if he's got a six-shooter in his free hand. He's got nothing, nothing but swagger. Pretty soon he has a cut over his left eye—Tiny did it with a chair—and I have not one red cent left of all my savings from singing nights. My going-to–New York money has gone to bail Dangerous Dan Kenyon McGrew out of the Galveston jail.

"Listen, Kenyon," I tell him, "this is not Leon and this is not the nineteenth century. It's the second half of the twentieth in case you haven't noticed it from your airplane riding! There is nothing wrong with me singing in a quiet respectable bar."

"No sister of mine—"

"You just pretend I'm not any sister of yours. We're so different one of us must have been left on the doorstep."

"You think I'm a bastard?"

"Well, you're the one calling the cards," I said and flounced out of the jail. I was mad and in a hurry to get home to bed. All I cared about right then was sleep. That particular Saturday I had to work the 7:00 A.M. shift at the hospital. Kenyon being such a zipper-lip type, I certainly wasn't worrying about him telling anybody I was working in a nightclub and him spending some time in jail. I should have let him stay in jail. He got in his car that very same night and drove straight to Leon. And, when he got there early the next morning, he told. He told everything he knew.

They didn't give me any warning, not a phone call—nothing. Daddy appeared in full uniform, the old army pinks and greens with eagles flapping on both shoulders. He had been getting ready to leave for a battalion reunion at Ft. Sam Houston when Kenyon showed up, and he didn't waste time changing clothes. He should have. His stomach had expanded some since WW II so his trousers were lifted an inch too high over his socks.

The first thing I said when I saw him was, "Daddy, what on earth are you doing down here in your uniform? It's non-reg. They don't wear that kind anymore."

"Sister, don't you tell me about the U.S. Army regulations. I gave twenty years of my life to them."

"Well, they are likely to slap you in the loony bin here for walking around dressed up like that."

"If I was you, I wouldn't be talking about how other people are dressed."

"Daddy, there is nothing wrong with my uniform," I said. I'd been wearing it for eight hours and hadn't spilt a thing on it. There was nothing wrong with the way I looked at all except for the circles under my eyes from staying up till 2:00 A.M. getting a certain person out of jail. I was just about dead from exhaustion.

"I hear you've got another dress, a red one."

We were talking in the lobby of the hospital and when he said that I wanted to call for a stretcher.

"No daughter of mine is going to hang around with gangsters at nightclubs."

I don't know where he got the gangsters, probably from the last time he was in a nightclub.

"This isn't 1920 and I don't know any gangsters. The fellows Kenyon got in a fight with are musicians. They were trying to protect me." He wasn't listening. He didn't want to hear my side. His mind was already made up.

"You go and get your things," he told me. "No daughter of mine is going to be corrupted by jazz and booze."

What could I do? I'd spent all my savings getting Kenyon out of jail. I went with Daddy back to Leon thinking it would all blow over after a while. Mother, at least, would be on my side since she knew what it was to live with a husband who still thought he was in the first half of the twentieth century and a son who hadn't progressed past 1900. When we got to Leon though, I found out different. The very first thing Mother did was to show me mine and Kenyon's birth certificates.

"Look here, young lady, neither you nor your brother was left on anybody's doorstep. I hope this is proof enough for you." She shoved the yellowed pages with their loopy-de-loop handwriting in my face and started crying before I could say I never really meant it.

I stayed home that weekend and the rest of that semester. Good-bye nursing. I wasn't so crazy about it anyway. I guess what happened to me could happen to anybody, but I wonder how many girls end up teaching a bunch of high-school kids to sing "Sweet Adeline" after they started out with a great career in show biz. Daddy took me completely out of school. In January he let me enroll in a Baptist church college only forty miles from Leon. I got my teacher's certificate there in music education and that's all I got. They had a short rope on me.

When I finished I was twenty-three, due to the interruption in my education. Daddy had a heart attack that year and I went home to help Mother nurse him and to teach singing in Leon High School.

My brother, when he was through with the paratroopers, came home too. He started working on ranches and slowly saved enough to lease places of his own. He hadn't paid me back the bail money yet. I hadn't paid him back either, but I was planning on how I was going to. Someday, I thought, he is going to find some girl who wants to quit riding the barrel races in rodeos and get married. When he brings this cutie home in her embroidered blouse and her buckskin fringes, I am going to tell everything I know, not about him being in jail. The fact he spent a few hours in the Galveston jail wouldn't bother her. Galveston's a long way from Leon.

I wasn't going to tell this rodeo queen Kenyon was bound to drag home about his past; I was going to predict her future. I was going to let this little girl know she might as well throw away her western breeches and get into a skirt that hit the floor. And, I was going to tell her she'd better wave goodbye forever to the bright lights, the crowd, the band, and the Grand Entry Parade because all that was in store for her was a pot of beans to stir and blue jeans to wash at home on the range. She wasn't to expect any modern appliances to help her out either, because I knew Kenyon. He wouldn't buy her a single machine, not even a radio. If she wanted to hear any music she'd have to invite me out to sit on the front porch and sing "Zip-Pah-De-Do-Dah" as the sun sank slowly in the west.

I had it all planned out, a feeble sort of revenge, but at least I'd have my say—me, the Cassandra of Leon, prophesying a terrible future for a fun-loving cowboy's sweetheart. Of course, like a lot of too well-planned revenges, it didn't turn out that way. I got restless sitting around in the teacher's lounge, going to the movie every Saturday night with a man I'd known since we were both in high school, Alvin Neeley, the band director. We weren't anything to each other but companions in boredom, chained together by what everyone thought was our common interest, music. We were supposed to be a perfect couple because we could both read notes. Everyone imagined we were sitting on the piano bench warbling duets, but we weren't.

Alvin was a marcher. He kept in step even when we were walking a few blocks down the street, and believe me, he wasn't marching to the sound of any distant drum. Alvin had his own drum in his head, and when he puckered his lips, I knew he wasn't puckering up for me; he was puckering up for Sousa. Sometimes, just for diversion, I'd refuse to march in step with him. If he put his left foot forward, I'd start out on my right, but he'd always notice and with a quick little skip in the air, he'd be in step with me. Off we'd go marching to the movie to the tune of "The Stars and Stripes Forever" every Saturday. And all this time Kenyon was stomping in and out of the house bird-free, intent on his own secret purposes.

Mother would come and sit on the foot of my bed after I got home from a date with Alvin. "Did you have a good time?" she'd say.

"All right." I wasn't going to tell her I'd had a bad time. She had enough troubles as it was. Since his heart attack my daddy spent most of his time sitting around the house with his right hand on the left side of his chest the way actors used to indicate great pain in the old silent films.

She'd ask me what movie we saw and I'd tell her, *Monsters of the Slimy Green Deep* or whatever it was. Nothing but Grade B movies ever made it to Leon, and Alvin and I went regularly no matter what was showing—like taking a pill on schedule.

"Well, how is Alvin getting along?"

She wasn't interested in Alvin's health. What she wanted to know was how Alvin and I were getting along. I'd say all right to that too. I kept on saying the same thing till one night she said, "I sure would like to have some grandchildren."

"Mother, you better get Kenyon to work on that because you're not going to get any grandchildren out of me and Alvin Neeley."

"Why not?"

"I'd have to marry him—that's why, and I'm not going to even if he asks, and he's not going to ask. He can barely hold a conversation anyway. All he can do is whistle—and march." I was sitting across the room from her rubbing my aching legs.

"Why do you keep on going out with him then?"

"I don't see anybody else bashing the door down to ask me to a movie. I go out with Alvin because he takes me. It's one way of getting away from this house, a way of getting out of Leon even if it's to go to the *Slimy Green Deep*."

"You worry me," said Mother.

"I worry myself," I told her and I did. I was stuck with Alvin Neeley in Leon. I'd done what they all wanted me to do and now they were stuck with me. They had me on their hands.

Mother evidently spoke to Kenyon about my miserable unwed existence and insisted he find somebody for me. I say Mother did it, put the idea in Kenyon's head that he find somebody for me, because, left to himself, Kenyon was not at all bothered by an old-maid sister. He thought he'd saved me from the gutter. From there on I was supposed to be continually thankful and permanently respectable.

When I got home early one Saturday night I was told, before I had time to say anything, that he'd "fixed up" a date for me the following Saturday.

"Who with?"

"Fellow named Frank Harwell from Lampasas. He ranches out west of town. He's going to take you dancing."

"He's from a big family. I know some of them. Harwells are spread all over Lampasas," Mother said happily.

"He served in Korea, in the infantry," said Daddy as if he'd just pinned the Distinguished Conduct Medal on somebody.

They all knew what they wanted to know about Frank Harwell and I didn't know a thing. "How old is he? Is he short or tall, skinny or fat, intelligent or ignorant, handsome or ugly?" I could have gone on all night throwing questions at them, but I quit. They were all sitting there looking so smug.

"He's the best I could do," said Kenyon. "You'll like him. All the girls do."

"Where are we going dancing?" Since Leon's in a dry county there's not a real nightclub within twenty miles.

"We'll go out to the VFW Club," Kenyon said.

"We? Are you going too? Who do you have a date with?"

"Nobody. I'm just going along for the ride."

"Kenyon, I'm twenty-five years old going on twenty-six,

and I'll be damned if you're going anywhere as my chaperone."

"Sister, watch your language," said Daddy. "Is he a good dancer, Kenyon?"

"Daddy, what do you care if he's a good dancer or not? You're not the one who's going to be dancing with him."

"I don't want my daughter marrying some Valentino. Good dancers make bad husbands."

"Daddy! You are hopelessly behind times! If you'd turn on your TV set you'd see people dancing without even touching each other. The Valentinos are all gone. Anyway, I'm not going to my wedding Saturday night. I'm going to the VFW Club!"

They had me. I was trapped into having a date with Frank Harwell just to prove to Daddy he wasn't a Valentino. I didn't mind so much. After all, I'd endured a long dry march in the desert with Alvin Neeley. And, I wanted to know what Kenyon did with himself when he wasn't riding the range.

On Saturday night I pranced into the living room in my best and fullest skirt. You have to have plenty of leg room for country dances. Kenyon was standing talking to Frank Harwell, who looked like a cowboy straight out of a cigarette advertisement, lean, tanned, and terribly sure of himself. He was every young girl's dream, and old girl's too. My knees were shaking a little when he looked me over. For a minute I wished I hadn't worn a sensible dress. I wished I was all togged out in my red sequins and red high heels again.

We all three got in Frank's pickup. He and Kenyon did most of the talking. We hadn't gone two blocks before Kenyon insisted he had to stop and look at some stock at the auction barn on the way to the VFW.

"Fine," said Frank in a grand, easygoing way. He was the most totally relaxed man I'd ever seen. He drove his pickup through town with one hand on the wheel, guiding it to the right and left as if he were reining a horse.

When we got to the auction barn Kenyon shot out of the truck, leaving the door open behind him.

"Always in a hurry," said Frank and leaned over me to pull the door shut. I felt like a huge old cat had fallen in my lap.

"You don't seem to be."

"Naw." He eased himself up, pulled out a package of cigarettes, lit one, then leaned back and blew smoke out. I kept expecting to hear an announcer's voice saying something about how good cigarettes were so I waited a minute before saying anything myself. Finally, I asked him about his ranch. He told me about his spring roundup, how much mohair had been clipped from his goats, how many cows had calved, the number of rattlesnakes he'd killed, how much a good rain would help, and other interesting things like that. We sat there, with Frank worrying about his wells running dry and the miles of fence he needed to repair; I was worrying about whether we'd ever get to the dance. The VFW Club was on top of a hill behind the auction barn. We could have walked up there, but it could have been in the next county as far as Frank was concerned. He got a bottle of bourbon out of the glove compartment and took a long swallow from it. When Kenyon came back he passed the bottle to him. Neither one of them offered me a swallow and I knew I'd have to be seventy and taking whiskey for medicinal purposes before either one of those two would dream of offering a girl a drink.

Kenyon was excited about a bull he'd seen. "He's that same old Brahma that throwed me. I'd know him anywhere. Gentle as he can be outside the ring, but let somebody get on his back and he goes wild. Wonder why they're selling him. He's a good rodeo bull."

"Getting old maybe," Frank drawled. They both laughed as if he'd said the most hilarious thing in the world. Then they both took another drink so *they* were in a good mood when we got to the VFW at 9:30 P.M. The hall was an old WW II army surplus barracks the veterans had bought and painted white. Judging from the noise coming out of the place, the men standing around cars outside talking and sneaking drinks, and the two cops at the doorway, it was wilder than any Galveston club on a Saturday night. The cops nodded at us as we went in. The girl who was selling tickets to the dance warned Frank and Kenyon to hold on to them because nobody was allowed to come back in without one.

Frank swung me out on the dance floor and that was the last I saw of Kenyon for a while except for a glimpse of him out of the corner of my eye. He was dancing with one of my ex-students, a not so bright one, who'd somehow managed to graduate the year before. Every once in a while Frank would excuse himself to go out and take a swig from his bottle. I sat at a table by myself drinking soda pop and thinking about my Galveston days when I at least had the company of some grown men when I was drinking. The musicians at the VFW that night, by the way, hardly deserved the name. They sawed and wheezed through their whole repertory which consisted of about fifteen songs, all sounding alike. It's fashionable now to like what everyone calls "country music," but if you had to sit out in the VFW and listen to it, you'd get pretty tired of the music and the country.

After a while I caught sight of Frank strolling in the front door. He stopped by another table for a minute to pat a girl on the top of her frizzy blonde head, then he ambled on over to me.

"Where's Kenyon?" I was tired of listening to the whining songs, tired of being flung around the dance floor. The new dances I'd told Daddy about hadn't gotten to Leon yet—they probably never will get to Frank Harwell. The more he drank the harder he danced, not on my toes, but stomping hard on the floor taking great wide steps and swinging me around in circles. It was 1:00 A.M., time to go home. Nobody else seemed to think so though. The hall was even more packed than when we first came in.

"Last time I saw him Kenyon was outside arguing with the cops. He's lost his ticket and they won't let him back in."

"Why doesn't he buy another one?"

"He thinks they ought to take his word he already bought one. You know he's got high principles and—"

"I know about his principles all right. He's got high principles and no scruples!!"

"Aw, don't be too hard on your brother."

I was getting ready to tell him that Kenyon had been hard on me when we both turned our heads to see what was causing all the shouting down by the door. It was my brother leading that gentle old Brahma bull by a rope around his neck. The crowd was parting before him. Some of them were jumping out the windows and everybody else was headed for the back door. The blonde Frank had patted on the head was standing on top of a table screaming, "Help! Somebody do something!" Nobody was doing anything but getting out. Kenyon staggered through the hall with a mean grin on his face, drunk as the lord of the wild frontier and cool as a walking ice cube. Behind the bandstand the musicians were crawling out the windows. The bass fiddler tried to throw his fiddle out first, but it got stuck. He left it there, half in, half out, and wriggled through another window. A man following him didn't watch where he was going and caught his foot in the middle of a drum.

Behind Kenyon the bull, uncertain of his footing on the slippery floor, was trying to adjust himself. He slid along, his tail lashing frantically, his hooves skidding in all directions. When Kenyon slowed down a little to get past some tables the Brahma snorted and jumped—like Alvin Neeley doing his little skip in mid-air to keep in step.

"Come on. We can't stand here gawking. Somebody's going to get hurt if Kenyon lets that old bull go." Frank grabbed my hand and we headed for the back door. By the time we got out Kenyon and the bull had the VFW Club to themselves.

We waited out back. The cops waited too. Kenyon appeared in the doorway. The bull nudged up behind him. He turned and scratched the bull's head.

"I told you," Kenyon hollered at the cops, "I already bought one ticket." Then he walked down the steps carefully leading the bull, talking to him all the way. "Watch your step, old buddy. That's right. Easy now."

The cops let Kenyon put the bull back in the auction pen, and when he was finished, they put him in their car. He was laughing so hard he couldn't fight very well, but he tried.

"Oh Lord!" Frank sighed lazily from the safety of his pickup. "If he wouldn't fight, they'd let him go. Those boys were ready for that dance to break up anyway."

"Aren't you going to help him?"

"Naw. He took this on hisself. You want us both in jail?"

"In jail?"

"Yeah," Frank drawled and hoisted his big handsome self across the seat toward me.

"Shouldn't we follow them?"

"Look at that moon."

There wasn't a moon in sight, not a sliver of one. Gorgeous Frank Harwell was so sleepy drunk he mistook somebody's headlights for the moon. All the excitement on top of all the dancing we'd done was too much for him I guess, because the next thing I knew he'd passed out. I lifted his head off my shoulder, propped it up against the window, and climbed into the driver's seat.

I got to the jail in time to hear them book Kenyon for being drunk and disorderly and disturbing the peace. He paid his own way out this time, but the only reason they didn't lock him up for the night was I was there to take him home. Of course, I couldn't take him home in his condition. Daddy would have had an attack and Mother would have probably fainted at the sight of him. Her clean-cut, hard-working, tight-lipped boy was a living mess. He looked like he'd been riding the bull rather than leading him. I managed to brush most of the dust off of him. The cops gave him back his hat. We stopped at Leon's one open-all-night café, where I went in and got a quart of black coffee. When he'd finished this he was sober enough to go in the men's room and wash his face. Frank slept through the whole rehabilitation.

Kenyon wanted to park the pickup on the square across from the jail and walk home, leaving Frank there snoring. "Maybe the cops will come out and get him," he said.

"It's not any use to get mad at Frank. It was your idea to bring that animal into the dance hall."

"You taking up for him?"

"I got you out of jail, didn't I?"

Kenyon nodded. I went in the café to get some more coffee for Frank. When I came back out Kenyon started shaking him, but before he got him awake he turned to me and said, "Sister, don't tell everything you know."

"Why not? Mother and Daddy are going to find out anyway. By church time tomorrow everybody in town will be talking—"

"I'd rather they get it second-hand."

By this time I was so mad I jabbed Frank with my elbow, handed him the coffee, and lit into Kenyon. "You'd rather everybody get everything second-hand. Nobody is supposed to do anything but you."

"What are you talking about?"

"Never mind! You wouldn't understand if I kept talking till sunup, but I'll tell you this, Kenyon—I'm not going to devote the rest of my life to keeping you out of jail. From now on you are on your own."

"Sister, I've always been on my own."

How contrary can a person be? Here I'd just saved him from a night in the Leon County jail, not to mention the time I got him out of the Galveston jail. I didn't argue with him though. I knew if I told him he wasn't on his own till he left home, he wouldn't wait a minute before telling me the same thing—with Frank Harwell sitting right next to me taking in every word.

"You want me to drive?" Kenyon asked him.

"Naw, you have got in enough trouble tonight, you and that dancing bull. I'll make it."

They both laughed. Frank even tried to slap my knee, but I dodged him.

"I want to go home," I said.

"Gal, that's where we're going."

It was 2:30 A.M. I could imagine Daddy sitting on the front porch wrapped in his overcoat with his M-1 stretched across his knees. For once, we were lucky. Mother and Daddy were both in bed asleep. Kenyon and I tiptoed to our rooms without waking either one of them. When they asked us the next morning where we'd been so late, Kenyon said, "Dancing." Since they were used to short answers from him he didn't have to say anything else. Of course Mother came and sat on the foot of my bed and asked me all about Frank Harwell.

"Mother, Frank is a very handsome man and no doubt all the other girls like him, but he is a cowboy and I think one cowboy is enough in the family."

Then I told her. "In June I'm going down to San Antonio and look for a job in one of the schools there."

"You can't—"

"Yes, I can. If I don't leave home now, I'll be right here the rest of my days."

"She might as well," Kenyon said. He was leaning in the doorway, eavesdropping to see whether I was going to tell on him. "She's too uppity for anybody in Leon." With that he turned around and left. He didn't know it, but it was the best thing he could have said. Daddy blamed himself for giving me too much education and Mother was so anxious to be a grandmother I think she'd have been happy to see me off to New York.

In June I went to San Antonio and found a job at one of the high schools. I found a husband, too, a fine doctor who sings in the chorus during opera season. That's where I met him—in the chorus. We were rehearsing for *La Traviata*. His name is Edward Greenlee. Dr. Edward Greenlee.

"Can he rope?" Kenyon asked.

"Can you tie a suture?"

"What branch of the army was he in?"

"He was in the navy, Daddy."

"Is he from a large family?"

"Mother, there are Greenlees all over San Antonio."

We had a June wedding in the First Methodist in Leon. Daddy gave me away. Kenyon was an usher. He looked handsome in his white tux jacket, the only one he'd ever worn in his life. I told him so when I got to the church in my bridal finery. He said thanks and grinned his tight-lipped grin. I looked down. The black pants covered all of the stitching decorating the tops, but I could plainly see, and so could everybody else at my wedding, that Kenyon had his boots on.

I guess he'll go on being true to the code and die with them on. He's living out on one of his ranches now, fifteen miles from the nearest town and ninety miles from San Antonio. Sometimes on Sunday afternoons Edward and I take the children and drive up to see him. There's no way of letting him know we're coming because he doesn't have a telephone. We don't have to worry about inconveniencing anybody though; Kenyon lives by himself.

The last time we were there we missed him. My five-year-old boy, William, walked around on the bare floors and said, "Doesn't he have any rugs?"

When we were checking the cupboards in the almost bare kitchen Cynthia, our three-year-old, wailed, "Doesn't he have any cookies?"

"No, he doesn't have any rugs and he doesn't have any cookies. But he does have a bathtub, hot and cold running water, a bed, a fire, three cans of chili, a sack of flour, two horses, a sheep dog, and a whole lot of sheep, goats, and cattle."

"Why doesn't he have any cookies?"

"This sure is a lumpy old chair," said William. He should have known. He was sitting in the only one in the room. "Is Uncle Kenyon poor?"

"All of your Uncle Kenyon's money is tied up in stock, the sheep, and goats and cattle," said Edward, who always tries to explain things.

"Uncle Kenyon is a cowboy," I said, which was really the only explanation.

OPAL LEE POPKES

Zuma Chowt's Cave

In 1903 an Indian named Chowt followed a pack of rats through Dume Canyon, north of Santa Monica. To Chowt, the wind-scarred canyon was not Dume Canyon (a white-man name) but was called Huyat, something white people would have laughed at had they known its meaning.

But the white man chasing Chowt was less interested in the terrain than in proving his superiority to a fleeing Indian. Chowt had learned devious methods of avoiding capture. He tried to tell them the truth. He was following a rat, which was the truth. The white man stopped chasing, and sat down to laugh so long and hard that Chowt escaped and continued to follow the trail of the rat.

Chowt did not particularly care for his diet of small animals unless he was near starvation, but at that moment he was. He was also thirsty.

1903 was a dry year, when rats in prolific numbers left their haunts in search of water. In fact, the year was so dry they said even that a rat with an itch could start a fire with the shine of his eyes. Rubbing two blades of grass sparked a conflagration.

The rats searched for water. Chowt hungered for the fresh coolness of spring water. So he followed the rats through Dume Canyon, along the splitrock cliffs beside the Pacific Ocean. There was plenty of ocean to drink, but the rats knew as well as Chowt to scamper down the ocean edge, to other places, darting back and forth. Chowt sat down on a rock and waited for them to make up their minds. The little water wands didn't seem to be in any great hurry.

Chowt was a little man, small even as Indians go, and appeared to be a large bird poised on the rock, with his tiny legs drawn up under him.

The rats angled up a burned slope. Chowt followed. They ignored him. He was too far away to be attacked, but close enough to see the hundreds of gray bits of coarse fur, slipping in and out among the rocks, clinging with long tails and claw feet, always upward on the smooth slope, bypassing the boulders, going around the steep upward crags, speckling the side of the hill. They angled back and forth, but their general direction was to the north, from where even Chowt could smell water.

It took them two days to reach the top of the hill. They drank the meager dew at night, ate the same wild oats Chowt ate, and chewed on the same berry bushes. Chowt's body craved meat, but he waited patiently for them to find water before he would devour the water wands.

Chowt could see higher hills, even a few mountains to the north, but the rats seemed to prefer this particular hill, which climbed abruptly toward the ocean, ending in a sharp, high cliff facing the Pacific. Chowt knew the hill also ended in an abrupt cliff on the north side. The south slope was covered with gray vegetation, burned by wind, salt, and sun. Toward the east, the hills meandered into other, taller hills. But the rats went north, where a five-hundred-foot drop awaited them.

They continued onto a rock jutting out ten feet or so above the northeast canyon floor and disappeared. Others traveled over the top until all the rats had disappeared. None fell into the canyon, therefore Chowt knew they had found their gold.

Chowt waited patiently, in case the rats came out. During the night he heard them scurrying about, eating grass seeds, and then hiding again before the sun lightened the sky.

Chowt waited for the sun to come up, to evaporate any dew that might make the rocks slick. Then he walked casually to the top of the boulder, squatted, leaned over to see a small cave entrance large enough for any midget Indian named Zuma Chowt.

Slowly he swung himself down, with nothing but a half thousand feet of air below him, and clung to the rock with lichen tenacity, hanging by the sweat of his fingers. His feet swung blindly toward the rocky lip below the cave entrance. With a mighty swing he heaved himself, feet first, into the cave.

He crawled backward, listening, hearing the gush of liquid echoing in the silent cave. Every few feet he swept his short arms above him, judging the ever-increasing height of the cave ceiling. Then he stood erect in the damp stillness.

Dark encircled him completely as he felt along the side of the cave until water splashed onto his hand. He smelled the water before he drank, then felt with his feet to find where the spring splashed from the cave wall; he stood under the cold water and murmured pleasures. On hands and knees he followed the stream to its outlet in the rocks.

The next few weeks Chowt spent trying to get out of the cave. He made the inside of the mountain into a molehill in his desperate struggle for survival. He pounded the walls, listening for the dull, flat sound that said dirt instead of rock, a place to dig for an opening, an escape.

Using his strong, thin fingers, he clawed and dug at the dirt that faced the ocean, because a deep cleft in the rock floor indicated that at one time the water had emptied into the ocean through a waterfall which had been shunted aside during some past earthquake. Somewhere in that rocky cliff there must still be an opening.

When hunger gnawed at him, he sat quietly, waiting for the rats to attack. Then he pounced and came out the victorious diner. But the supply of rats was rapidly becoming exhausted, and still he had not found an exit.

Then one day Chowt's raw and bleeding hands dug into dirt and returned filled with nothing but salty ocean air. He peeked through the hole to see the sun setting on a brilliant ocean. He ripped his clothing apart, made a rope, and swung down.

In the months that followed, Chowt decided that the better part of valor—eluding the white man—would be to make the cave his home. He stole ropes and spades from nearby villages and returned to the cave.

He would sit on the top of the hill and contemplate his home and stare for long hours at the ocean which crashed against the cliff below. Then one day he shoved a few stones here and there, placing them carefully at the top of the hill where the cracked stone layered beneath the thin vegetation. Then he swung down to the bottom of the cliff and stood in the surf, looking upward. Carefully he shoved stones here and about. Though the rocks appeared to be shoved at random, he had a plan.

When he went topside again, he broke small stones loose from beside and beneath the larger ones, and suddenly it seemed that the whole cliff was tumbling into the ocean.

He waited until the dust had subsided, then looked down at the debris he had created. The top of the hill was now reasonably flat, and as the stones and boulders had fallen they had crashed into the smaller ones he'd placed so carefully, thus changing the course of the stones so they landed in a haphazard V in the ocean.

He sat for a long time in the cliff opening, waiting for the tide to come in, and when it did the water roared into his inlet with a vengeance. He tossed out a long piece of twine with a fishhook on the end.

But along with the man-made fishing hole came an unexpected problem. The tide rushed into the V-shaped inlet and, with nowhere else to go, rose with a roar, splashing water halfway up the cliff. During storms the waves would expend themselves, with a mighty heave, into the cave itself.

Luckily, however, storms were infrequent, and with his stolen spade he dug dirt from inside his new home, moved rocks, chiseled, and finally fashioned a commodious place which, though dark and cool, was periodically washed by ocean storms.

He dug out the other veins of the cave. He stopped fighting the white man long enough to settle peaceably in Dume Canyon.

Once or twice a year he walked to Oxnard to earn or steal oddments of clothing. He was past the time when the pecking between races excited him, and, too, the white man had become bored and embarrassed by the continual harassment of the remnants of Indian bands.

His female Indian acquaintances wanted nothing to do with itinerant Indians. They had jobs as servants, or returned to the reservations.

During the hot California summers he walked throughout the state, wherever he pleased, looking not unlike a tiny Mexican—except for the fold of skin across his eyelids and his thin mouth—dressed in a pair of boy's overalls. In winter he improved his quarters.

Dume Canyon, squatting halfway between Santa Monica

and Oxnard, improved with the help of Chowt. He trimmed dead branches for firewood, used the dead brush for bedding, trapped the wild animals that harassed the ranchers, cleaned the cliffs of dangerous rock that might fall on him, or unsuspecting cowboys, and developed the water source in the cave. He learned to harness the black gold which dripped and disappeared between the rocks inside his cave—and in the discovery, made quite by accident, he almost buried himself alive.

Few people knew that Chowt lived in a cave in Dume Canyon. After two white men fell off the cliff trying to get to him, they decided he was a monument to the judiciousness of the new laws that said Indians hurt nobody.

A few years after Chowt arrived, the state built a road along the ocean, cutting through the rocks at the foot of his cliff home. The builders never realized Chowt was watching them from behind the dead branches that camouflaged his cave opening.

Civilization closed in on Chowt after that first road was built. It hurt him to see a wagon and team of mules, then eventually a car or two, drive past, filled with people. Though he mellowed and became like a bonsai—tiny, pruned, seeming to live forever as an unseen gray ghost—civilization hurt him. When there had been no one, it had been easier; now he felt an ache, like a missing leg, a missing arm; he longed for human laughter, a human voice.

One day he returned to the cave with a friend, a fellow Indian, but after a year or two the friend couldn't stand the solitude and loneliness, and left. Chowt tried bringing a squaw to live with him, but she couldn't stand him. So he built, and struggled on, until loneliness overwhelmed him again.

One day when Chowt was seventy-five, he raided the home of an Oxnard banker, kidnapped the Indian servant girl, and took her for a wife. The older people in Oxnard remembered him then and laughed at the romance of such an old codger. Newspaper people searched old files and reprinted the old stories about him. A master's thesis was written about the one remaining Indian in the area, the goat of the hills. One doctor's dissertation was begun, but when the doctor-to-be tried to climb up to Chowt's cave for an interview, he fell off, after which people decided to leave Chowt alone. Indians were no longer being punished for white men's clumsiness.

And much to everyone's surprise, including Chowt's, the Indian girl stayed with him.

By 1944 he was completely forgotten by the younger generation. He was ninety years old, but still active and well. He had learned a few English phrases from his wife and still made a few trips into Oxnard, but most of his time was spent happily with his wife and daughter, whom he taught to survive in the best way he knew how—through his old Indian ways. His fortress was inaccessible, his life was secure, and he saw no reason to change his ways for himself or his little family. His cave was situated on public land, so no person harassed him about it.

Once a scoutmaster shepherding his troop through the area thought he saw a gray ghost of a woman swinging across the cliffs on a rope, but he refused to admit it to his scouts, and instead told them about Tarzan. A motorist swore he heard a mermaid singing off key, but the motorist had liquor on his breath. An intrepid teenage rock hound told people how he caught his foot in a trap and a dark woman with a hairy body opened the trap and set him free. But the teenager gave up rock collecting and did not return for a second look.

A man named Leo Corrillo offered to finance a public park out of the area, but nobody wanted useless rocks and a cruel surf.

Also in 1944, Chowt's daughter turned fifteen. Her brown skin blackened from the sun, she was a thin shadow climbing over rocks and through bushes, with wild, uncombed black hair and a bloodcurdling scream that practiced peculiar English to the Pacific Ocean. She would swing on a wet seaweed rope firmly anchored inside the cave, or use one Chowt had stolen at Oxnard. Any person seeing her thus move over the face of the rocky cliffs would have sworn he had seen a mountain goat skipping nimbly. And with good reason. She wore garments of fur or skins, having made them according to Chowt's instructions. She balanced herself with the agility of a mountain goat, having learned that from her father too. He taught her how to squat high up in the rocks in the sun, like a gray wildcat, to watch the ocean for food. He taught her everything he knew, and her mother taught her pidgin English.

The Indian girl squatted on a rock far up on the cliff to watch what appeared to her to be a log drifting in to shore.

She spread her leather skirt about her legs, dug her toes against the rock, and pondered what she could do with that log.

It wasn't the same kind of log one chopped down green or picked up from a dead tree. Driftwood was hard and light.

"I want that log." In her mind she devised various uses for it. She could cut it in half and make two stools. She could burn out the center and make a dugout canoe. She could split it, burn it, make fence posts, a seat, or even a ladder out of it. No, it wasn't a scrubby pine or a limber sapling. It would be pretty, too. She could even float on it out into the ocean and catch fish.

She swung down the cliff on her rope, ran across the rutted road to the beach, and dived into the breakers, her leather skirt clinging to her body like a second skin. As she swam closer she saw a person clinging to the driftwood and as she came up to him he smiled wanly, thinking help was arriving. The girl slapped him across the side of the head, sending him tumbling into the breakers. With one hand grasping the log, she swiftly outdistanced the weary man.

He pleaded, but she was already nearing the beach. Salt water filled his mouth. He sputtered. He turned on his back to float, letting the surf carry him toward the beach, until finally he lay like a half-drowned rat amid the litter of rusty cans, half-buried old fire holes, broken bottles, soggy paper cartons. All with a stench to match.

"Fuckin' bastard!" He lay there shivering, the sand filtering over him in the strong wind, as he waited for his breath to return. He looked about for a place to hide in case the military was searching for him. Down the coastline, shrouded in September heat, he could see the outlines of a military post. He judged the distance to be about five or ten miles. "Goddamn! I didn't desert just to be shot for a deserter!"

The entire beach was as silent as the day Chowt had first stepped upon it. Seagulls perched or stood at the water's edge, backing away when the surf nibbled at their feet. Then they followed the water as it went out again, leaving bits of smelly sewage. They clustered in groups that flew upward to avoid the incoming water, searching to find fish, because they had already picked the rusty cans clean or eaten the last bit of discarded meat. No sunbathers came to this beach anymore, because of the garbage and also because its surf dumped clumps of oil and tar from a sunken tanker a few miles offshore.

Sand whirled and dribbled over the rock, only to be captured by the water as the surf pounded forward. There was a smell of tar and oil everywhere.

When the man finally staggered to an upright position, the seagulls fled. "I wonder where that damn dame come from," he said aloud, but his words drifted into the wind and smashed on the red-rock canyon walls leaning in layers for miles down the deserted shoreline.

He could see the road clinging to the edge of the ocean. But there was no car in sight. "Gas rationing," he said, glad no civilian was about to intrude on his freedom. The eroded stone peaks stood defiantly against the ocean, with only the ribbon of road hanging between.

He stared at the cliffs. No vegetation except bunches of dead bushes dotting the cliffs. Nothing but broken rock—pocked, burned black by wind and sun, or bleached red. No life. To the south, through the haze, he could see what he thought was Santa Monica.

He crossed the road and stood beneath the canyon cliff, where the wind was less fierce. Breakers followed him obediently to the road, fell back. Huge boulders lay to either side of him.

He saw a car coming so he hid among the coarse rocks. There, warm, resting in a pocket of sun, he moaned, laid his head on a bunch of dry grass, and waited for the car to pass. Then he sighed, leaned more comfortably into the warm afternoon sun, closed his eyes, and went to sleep.

Several jeeps full of military police drove slowly back and forth, and had Private Nelson Winks been awake he would have heard them say, "Probably sharks got him." And, "Don't see how he had the strength to make it. Probably drowned."

The girl hid above in the cave, and when Private Winks awoke, the beach once more seemed vacant and captured in silence. He rummaged in his pockets for food, found nothing but a chewed wad of gum and a wet cigarette package. He laid the package of cigarettes on the rocks to dry and popped the gum into his mouth, chewing lint and gum together. The gum still contained its spearmint flavor.

He climbed up onto one of the boulders. Just as he reached the top he fell back, but not before he had seen a service station down the road. "Coupla miles. And I don't see no MPs." His intention was to walk to the service station, but he changed his mind when he heard a jeep nearing from the north.

"Damn, they ain't gonna find me!" He hid behind a boulder. "Thousand miles of water in front of me, and rocks behind me. No better than a cornered rat."

But the jeep drove by, and his confidence returned. He said aloud, "I can make it to the service station before dark."

Seagulls once more perched around him. Then he heard a noise above. Thinking it was a seagull, he looked up, preparing to duck, but he saw the figure of a girl dressed from head to foot in skins.

"Rat's ass!" he exclaimed, sheltering his head from the shower of rocks. "I know that's a girl," he muttered, "but she don't look like no broad I ever seen." He moved aside as a large rock bounced where his head had been a moment before. "That's the same priss that tried to bash my head in and stole my log. How the hell did she get way up there? She must be half mountain goat!"

She was brushing rocks off the ledge, and they fell like bullets around Winks. He clasped his hands together over his head. "Damn you, you she-ass. I ain't gonna take that!" He reached for a rock and slung it upward. She plucked a rock out of a crevice and threw it at him. He ducked. The rock missed his head but slammed into his leg, knocking him sideways, so that he hit his head against the cliff and crumpled down, unconscious, on a jagged seat.

She sat on the ledge, dangling her feet over the side, now and then nonchalantly peering down at his prone figure. She was very dark, and her long black hair was plaited into a pigtail that coiled like a snake beside her on the ledge.

She heard a call from above, and the face of a woman appeared out of the cave. Her mother said something in her native tongue to the girl and it was ignored as the girl casually swung her feet back and forth. The woman repeated her demand and the girl said, in English, defiantly. "I won't!" It wasn't the kind of flat, angry "won't" a white girl might have uttered, in that there was no stubbornness to her tone of speech. Rather, her voice was coarse and untrained, oddly singsong, as though she'd learned English that had been tuned in to the wind, moving up and down as though the notes had been blown across the top of a bottle. Actually, that was indeed why she spoke English that way—because it had come to her from across the cave entrance.

"You will!" said the older woman, in a softer English than the girl, for the mother had learned her English from people accustomed to speaking it.

"I won't!" said the girl. "Kill him." She picked up another rock, aimed it down at Winks.

The mother said patiently, "I tell you it is a man. A man like your father. It is a man like a husband. It is not an animal to be slaughtered for food. It is a man. A man!"

"White man?" she asked, and the words were strangely harsh against the cliff.

"White man," said the mother.

"Kill, kill, kill, kill," she singsonged. "Kill, kill, kill, kill."

The mother reverted to her native tongue. *"Ubayi na Chowt, na Chowt."* Then she lowered a rope.

The girl pouted, muttered angrily, but climbed down the rope, barely touching the rocks as she swung in and out, shoving with her toes like a ballet dancer. Then she stood beside Winks, looked down at his limp figure, picked up a rock, and pulled back her arm for a good hard aim.

The woman let loose a blistering string of words, clearly condemning the girl. She kept scolding her, chattering like an angry bird, while the reluctant girl tied the rope about Winks. Then the woman began pulling him up the side of the cliff to the cave above.

The girl made no attempt to move the soldier's limp, unconscious body out of the way of the sharp rocks which ripped into his flesh; his blood marked his ascent up the wall.

Then the girl shoved him into the mouth of the cave, tossed the rope in, and went away to sulk on the ledge hewn out of the wall inside the cave. She watched her mother take long thin leaves from a plant and lay them on Winks's bleeding back, on the open wounds the rocks had cut into his shoulders, and where his head had banged against the cliff. She tied the leaves on with green seaweed strings around his head, waist, and chest. She tied his hands together and his feet; then she too went to the ledge and sat down beside her daughter.

They argued, jabbered, chattered—first in their native tongue, then in sprinkles of Spanish, English, whatever language the woman had picked up in the kitchens of her past.

There was even a "*mais oui*." However, English came more easily.

The old woman said, "When I came here there were no soldiers, no roads, nothing but water and rock and Henry's tree. Now we got dirty beach and rocks. Trash on beach."

"Trash on beach," echoed the girl. "Trash on beach."

"I sen' you to Mrs. Eli. She teach you white ways of white man," said the mother, not knowing the woman called Eli had been dead for ten years.

"But Dowdy says stay here where Henry only kill," argued the girl. "Henry" was the name they had deciphered from a cross Chowt had once stolen from a church. The cross now occupied a revered niche next to the drops of oil that fell continually onto a rock where, once lit, they burned steadily like a candle might—a spot where the family did its cooking and odd worshiping.

Winks opened his eyes, rolling them in an arc that took in the whole room with a quick glance. On seeing the two women, he yelled. They answered coolly, in quiet words that, even though spoken in English, had a wild quality, perhaps because they blended with the pounding surf. "Pray to Henry," the old woman was saying.

They watched Winks struggle with his seaweed bonds, screaming at them. They did not stir, even when he wriggled across the stone floor to the cave entrance and looked down at the road below. He moaned, inched himself backward, sliding, dragging a seaweed mat they had placed under him.

For a long time he stared at them, the gloom of the cave broken by a single shaft of light from the cave opening, then he whispered in an agonized voice through his pain. "You ain't niggers. You ain't got them flat noses or wide lips, and they ain't got your kind of hair. I know now. I'm on Guadalcanal, and you're natives, and I'm about to be dumped in a stew pot." He began to whimper. The two women did not move.

"Who are you?" he pleaded. They ignored him but continued their jabbering to each other while he tried to add them up to something. "Let me see. . . . I was near Santa Monica when I dove overboard. I know I wasn't rescued. I couldn't have drifted down to Old Mexico because I never lost sight of that string of mountains. But you can't be Americans, because people like you don't live in the U.S.A."

His head hurt, and he wondered if they had smashed it.

His hands were tied. They had even knotted the seaweed between his fingers, spreading them until they felt like crabs. The rough weeds with which the old woman had treated his wounds felt like spikes. He looked toward the little oil flame beside the cross. The slow drip would fall on the rocky niche, burn furiously, then almost go out before another drop ignited it again, and the smoke curled up to disappear mysteriously.

"This is a cave," he argued to himself. "I must be near Santa Monica. I remember. I looked up and something knocked me down. You—dressed in skins. Skins! Indians! You Indians? I'll be damned. Indians!"

The old woman looked steadily at him and nodded as she picked up a flat, hollowed-out rock.

He said, "Well, you ain't friendly Indians. How in the hell did people like you keep from gettin' civilized? Where you been? Don't you know there's a world out there?"

The girl picked up another rock, a long flat one shaped like a fence picket.

He ducked, expecting to be smashed. "Cut me loose?" he asked.

The old woman got up and went over to him, her long black cotton skirt swishing. She reached over him and untied a few of the knots that held his hands and arms.

"She understands, I think," he murmured. He picked some of the leaves from his head, smelled them, muttered, and threw them on the floor. "Wonder what kind of junk they doused me with? They must have beat me up."

He sat up and could see more clearly that the cave was fairly well lighted from the large entrance, beside which was set a cross of wood on which were tied bushes, with their roots sticking out into the cave: a removable camouflaging door.

The room extended backward into darkness, but there appeared to be another source of light where the rocks jutted out to semienclose this particular large room, which was about fifteen feet wide and barely tall enough for a man of Winks's size to stand up. He wished he could.

The floor of the cave was covered intermittently with seaweed mats, tightly woven. Here and there throughout this front area, and in the semidarkness beyond, rocks jutted up two or three feet from the floor; they were hewn flat across the top and crudely made articles were set upon them.

His head began to pain him again. "Damn if that junk didn't have some kind of medicine in it." He felt the side of his face, covered with dried blood. It hurt, so he reached for the leaf he'd thrown away and reinserted it under the seaweed strings.

Here and there on the floor he could see reflections of light playing, as though reflected from water, and he wondered if escape would be possible. As his eyes became more accustomed to the gloom, he saw other things—a crude loom made of tree branches that leaned against a wall near the cliff entrance, bearskins and woven mats hanging neatly from wooden pegs in the rock walls.

The old woman slipped up behind him, grabbed his hands, and looped the seaweed around them so quickly Winks could not protest.

"Damn you to hell. If I wasn't aching in every bone I'd bat you one."

The girl walked away into the depth of the cave. The old woman sat down and silently watched him.

Then Winks became aware of the light sounds of tinkling water falling, bubbling, gurgling, dripping. Yet he saw nothing.

The girl returned, having taken off her wet leather skirt, and was wearing a very short, ragged skirt and a sleeveless cotton shirt. As she moved around he saw she wore no underclothing at all, and there was not a hair on her body. The soles of her feet were white and the palms of her hands were white, in contrast to the deep brown of the rest of her.

I hope they ain't cannibals, he thought. Then, expecting no answer, he said, "How long you lived here?"

The girl said nothing, but the old woman said, in her strange singsong voice that flirted up and down like a flute, "Chowt came here fifty years ago."

"Forty, Mowma," said the girl. Winks could scarcely understand either of them because of the way they trilled and spilled their words like water.

"I'll be damned. What do you want to live here for?" He could smell the salt in the air. Ocean air. "How come your old man picked this place to hole up in?"

The old woman turned to the girl, and they threw his words back and forth, trying to translate them. Then the girl said, in a surly manner, "He followed the rats."

"Rats follow water," explained the old woman.

After having listened to their meager conversation, he was beginning to make out their language. They acted as though their oldest friends were the sun, the wind, the stars. There was no human touch about them. They were people in name only.

"How far to Santa Monica?" he asked. "Why don't you live there? I'd go on relief before I'd live here."

They seemed to tire of him suddenly, because the girl walked away to the place where the little pool of oil burned and returned with what appeared to him to be pieces of tiny tree limbs, which she shared with her mother.

"I'm hungry," he said. He might as well have been one of the rocks protruding from the floor of the cave. "I'm hungry!" he shouted. "Is that a stove? What you got cookin'? I want something to eat." His fear of the woman waned as his pain eased, so he shouted, "You goin' to let me lay here and starve? Gimme one of them sprouts to eat."

The woman bit them off, chewing slowly, ignoring him. "Chowt come and you eat," said the old woman.

Winks thought about her words. "Shout come and you eat?" But he'd been shouting and nothing had happened.

Then the woman went to the kitchen niche again and by the light of the burning oil he could see her pick dishes from between the rocks in the wall. She returned with a tray made of seaweed, on which were a few chipped dishes and some coarse spoons whittled from wood.

She set the tray on one of the protruding floor-rocks near him. He could identify pepper-tree twigs among the woven seaweed of the tray. She set her table.

"You goin' to untie me?" asked Winks.

She returned to the niche for more dishes, this time of metal. She plucked more dishes from a woven bag hanging from a peg between two rocks on the wall. These dishes had the appearance of tarnished, unpolished silver.

Winks turned his attention again to his wounds, which were completely covered by the long strips of leaves and bark. "Whatever medicine man you got, he's better than what they gave me at the dispensary. I'll bet these leaves would even cure the clap!" He looked closely for a long time at his bandages. Then suddenly he said, "You got a bathroom?"

Surely they understood *that* word. The girl looked at her mother, then sat down at the crude table and bit off a piece of stick. She began to chew.

"I gotta go to the john," he repeated. The girl glared, picked up a smooth round stone from a basket filled with rocks, and threw it at him. It missed only because he ducked.

"I gotta go," he said, wondering how Robinson Crusoe had managed. In all his reading about shipwrecks or people abandoned on desert islands this basic bodily function had never been a problem.

He could feel the salt caking on his body, the dried blood. He grunted, imitating a bodily function, hoping. In answer the girl picked up a handful of stones and slammed them at him.

"You are the throwinest female," he muttered.

"I kill him?" the girl asked her mother.

"No. Mrs. Eli had white husband. You have white husband too, and I have grandbaby."

CHARLES PORTIS

Dog of the South

"What line of work are you in, Speed?"

"I'm back in college now. I'm trying to pick up some education hours so I can get a teaching certificate."

"What you are then is a thirty-year-old schoolboy."

"I'm twenty-six."

"Well, I don't guess you're bothering anybody."

"The Civil War used to be my field."

"A big waste of time."

"I didn't think so. I studied for two years at Ole Miss under Dr. Buddy Casey. He's a fine man and a fine scholar."

"You might as well loiter for two years. You might as well play Parcheesi for two years."

"That's a foolish remark."

"You think so?"

"It's dumb."

"All right, listen to me. Are you a reader? Do you read a lot of books?"

"I read quite a bit."

"And you come from a family of readers, right?"

"No, that's not right. That's completely wrong. My father doesn't own six books. He reads the paper about twice a week. He reads fishing magazines and he reads the construction bids. He works. He doesn't have time to read."

"But you're a big reader yourself."

"I have more than four hundred volumes of military history in my apartment. All told, I have sixty-six lineal feet of books."

"All right, now listen to me. Throw that trash out the window. Every bit of it."

He reached into his grip and brought out a little book with yellow paper covers. The cellophane that had once been bonded to the covers was cracked and peeling. He flourished the book. "Throw all that dead stuff out the window and put this on your shelf. Put it by your bed."

What a statement! Books, heavy ones, flying out the windows of the Rhino apartment! I couldn't take my eyes from the road for very long but I glanced at the cover. The title was *With Wings as Eagles* and the author was John Selmer Dix, M.A.

Dr. Symes turned through the pages. "Dix wrote this book forty years ago and it's still just as fresh as the morning dew. Well, why shouldn't it be? The truth never dies. Now this is a first edition. That's important. This is the one you want. Remember the yellow cover. They've changed up things in these later editions. Just a word here and there but it adds up. I don't know who's behind it. They'll have Marvin watching television instead of listening to dance music on the radio. Stuff like that. This is the one you want. This is straight Dix. This is the book you want on your night table right beside your glass of water, *With Wings as Eagles* in the yellow cover. Dix was the greatest man of our time. He was truly a master of the arts, and of some of the sciences too. He was the greatest writer who ever lived."

"They say Shakespeare was the greatest writer who ever lived."

"Dix puts William Shakespeare in the shithouse."

"I've never heard of him. Where is he from?"

"He was from all over. He's dead now. He's buried in Ardmore, Oklahoma. He got his mail in Forth Worth, Texas."

"Did he live in Fort Worth?"

"He lived all over. Do you know the old Elks Club in Shreveport?"

"No."

"Not the new one. I'm not talking about the new lodge."

"I don't know anything about Shreveport."

"Well, it doesn't matter. It's one of my great regrets that I never got to meet Dix. He died broke in a railroad hotel in Tulsa. The last thing he saw from his window is anyone's guess. They never found his trunk, you know. He had a big tin trunk that was all tied up with wire and ropes and belts and straps, and he took it with him everywhere. They never found it. Nobody knows what happened to it. Nobody even knows what was in the trunk."

"Well, his clothes, don't you think?"

"No, he didn't have any clothes to speak of. No *change* of clothes. His famous slippers of course."

"His correspondence maybe."

"He burned all letters unread. I don't want to hear any more of your guesses. Do you think you're going to hit on the answer right off? Smarter people than you have been studying this problem for years."

"Books then."

"No, no, no. Dix never read anything but the daily papers. He *wrote* books, he didn't have to read them. No, he traveled light except for the trunk. He did his clearest thinking while moving. He did all his best work on a bus. Do you know that express bus that leaves Dallas every day at noon for Los Angeles? That's the one he liked. He rode back and forth on it for an entire year when he was working on *Wings*. He saw the seasons change on that bus. He knew all the drivers. He had a board that he put on his lap so he could spread his stuff out, you see, and work right there in his seat by the window."

"I don't see how you could ride a bus for a year."

"He was completely exhausted at the end of that year and he never fully recovered his health. His tin trunk had a thousand dents in it by that time and the hinges and latches were little better than a joke. That's when he began tying it up with ropes and belts. His mouth was bleeding from scurvy, from mucosal lesions and suppurating ulcers, his gums gone all spongy. He was a broken man all right but by God the work got done. He wrecked his health so that we might have *Wings as Eagles*."

The doctor went on and on. He said that all other writing, compared to Dix's work, was just "foul grunting." I could understand how a man might say such things about the Bible or the Koran, some holy book, but this Dix book, from what I could see of it, was nothing more than an inspirational work for salesmen. Still, I didn't want to judge it too quickly. There might be some useful tips in those pages, some Dix thoughts that would throw a new light on things. I was still on the alert for chance messages.

I asked the doctor what his mother was doing in British Honduras.

"Preaching," he said. "Teaching hygiene to pickaninnies."

"She's not retired?"

"She'll never retire."

"How does she happen to be in British Honduras?"

"She first went down there with some church folks to take clothes to hurricane victims. After my father died in 1950, she went back to help run a mission. Then she just stayed on. The church bosses tried to run her off two or three times but they couldn't get her out because she owned the building. She just started her own church. She says God told her to stay on the job down there. She's deathly afraid of hurricanes but she stays on anyway."

"Do you think God really told her to do that?"

"Well, I don't know. That's the only thing that would keep me down there. Mama claims she likes it. She and Melba both. She lives in the church with her pal Melba. There's a pair for you."

"Have you ever been down there?"

"Just once."

"What's it like?"

"Hot. A bunch of niggers."

"It seems a long way off from everything."

"After you get there it doesn't. It's the same old stuff."

"What does your mother do, go back and forth to Louisiana?"

"No, she doesn't go back at all."

"And you haven't seen her but once since she's been there?"

"It's a hard trip. You see the trouble I'm having. This is my last shot."

"You could fly down in a few hours."

"I've never been interested in aviation."

"I'm going down there after a stolen car."

"Say you are."

He kept twisting about in the seat to look at the cars approaching us from behind. He examined them all as they passed us and once he said to me, "Can you see that man's arms?"

"What man?"

"Driving that station wagon."

"I can see his hands."

"No, his arms. Ski has tattoos on his forearms. Flowers and stars and spiders."

"I can't see his arms. Who is Ski?"

He wouldn't answer me and he had no curiosity at all about my business. I told him about Norma and Dupree. He said nothing, but I could sense his contempt. I was not only a schoolboy but a cuckold too. And broke to boot.

He nodded and dozed whenever I was doing the talking. His heavy crested head would droop over and topple him forward and the angle-head flashlight on his belt would poke him in the belly and wake him. Then he would sit up and do it over again. I could see a tangle of gray hair in his long left ear. I wondered at what age that business started, the hair-in-the-ear business. I was getting on myself. The doctor had taken me for thirty. I felt in my ears and found nothing, but I knew the stuff would be sprouting there soon, perhaps in a matter of hours. I was gaining weight too. In the last few months I had begun to see my own cheeks, little pink horizons.

I was hypnotized by the road. I was leaning forward and I let the speed gradually creep up and I bypassed Mexico City with hardly a thought for Winfield Scott and the heights of Chapultepec. To pass it like that! Mexico City! On the long empty stretches I tried to imagine that I was stationary and that the brown earth was being rolled beneath me by the Buick tires. It was a shaky illusion at best and it broke down entirely when I met another car.

A front tire went flat in a suburb of Puebla and I drove on it for about half a mile. The spare was flat too, and it took the rest of the afternoon to get everything fixed. The casing I had driven on had two breaks in the sidewall. I didn't see how it could be repaired but the Mexican tire man put two boots and an inner tube in the thing and it stood up fine. He was quite a man, doing all this filthy work in the street in front of his mud house without a mechanical tire breaker or an impact wrench or any other kind of special tool.

We found a bakery and bought some rolls and left Puebla in the night. Dr. Symes took a blood-pressure cuff from his grip. He put it on his arm and pumped it up and I had to drive with one hand and hold the flashlight with the other so he could take the reading. He grunted but he didn't say whether it pleased him or not. He crawled over into the back seat and cleared things out of his way and said he was going to take a nap. He threw something out the window and I realized later it must have been my Zachary Taylor book.

"You might keep your eye peeled for a tan station wagon," he said. "I don't know what kind it is but it's a nice car. Texas plates. Dealer plates. Ski will be driving. He's a pale man with no chin. Tattoos on his forearms. He wears a little straw hat with one of those things in the hatband. I can't think of the word."

"Feather."

"No, I can think of feather. This is harder to think of. A brass thing."

"Who is this Ski?"

"Ted Brunowski. He's an old friend of mine. They call him Ski. You know how they call people Ski and Chief and Tex in the army."

"I've never been in the service."

"Did you have asthma?"

"No."

"What are you taking for it?"

"I don't have asthma."

"Have you tried the Chihuahua dogs in your bedroom at night? They say it works. I'm an orthodox physician but I'm also for whatever works. You might try it anyway."

"I have never had asthma."

"The slacker's friend. That's what they called it during the war. I certified many a one at a hundred and fifty bucks a throw."

"What do you want to see this fellow for?"

"It's a tan station wagon. He's a pale man in a straw hat and he has no more chin than a bird. Look for dealer plates. Ski has never been a car dealer but he always has dealer plates. He's not a Mason either but when he shakes your hand he does something with his thumb. He knows how to give the Masonic sign of distress too. He would never show me how to do it. Do you understand what I'm telling you?"

"I understand what you've said so far. Do you want to talk to him or what?"

"Just let me know if you see him."

"Is there some possibility of trouble?"

"There's every possibility."

"You didn't say anything about this."

"Get Ski out of sorts and he'll crack your bones. He'll smack you right in the snout, the foremost part of the body. He'll knock you white-eyed on the least provocation. He'll teach you a lesson you won't soon forget."

"You should have said something about this."

"He kicked a merchant seaman to death down on the ship channel. He was trying to get a line on the Blackie Steadman mob, just trying to do his job, you see, and the chap didn't want to help him."

"You should have told me about all this."

"Blackie was hiring these merchant seamen to do his killings for him. He would hire one of those boys to do the job on the night before he shipped out and by the time the body was found the killer would be in some place like Poland. But Ski got wise to their game."

"What does he want you for?"

"He made short work of that sailor. Ski's all business. He's tough. He's stout. I'm not talking about these puffy muscles from the gymnasium either, I'm talking about hard thick arms like bodark posts. You'd do better to leave him alone."

All this time the doctor was squirming around in the back trying to arrange himself comfortably on the seat. He made the car rock. I was afraid he would bump the door latch and fall out of the car. He hummed and snuffled. He sang one verse of "My Happiness" over and over again, and then, with a church quaver, "He's the Lily of the Valley, the bright and morning star."

I tuned him out. After a while he slept. I roared through the dark mountains, descending mostly, and I thought I would never reach the bottom. I checked the mirror over and over again and I examined every vehicle that passed us. There weren't many. The doctor had given me a tough job and now he was sleeping.

The guidebook advised against driving at night in Mexico but I figured that stuff was written for fools. I was leaning forward again and going at a headlong pace like an ant running home with something. The guidebook was right. It was a nightmare. Trucks with no taillights! Cows and donkeys and bicyclists in the middle of the road! A stalled bus on the crest of a hill! A pile of rocks coming down the road. An overturned truck and ten thousand oranges rolling down the road! I was trying to deal with all this and watch for Ski at the same time and I was furious at Dr. Symes for sleeping through it. I no longer cared whether he fell out or not.

Finally I woke him, although the worst was over by that time.

"What is it?" he said.

"I'm not looking for that station wagon anymore. I've got my hands full up here."

"What?"

"It's driving me crazy. I can't tell what color these cars are."

"What are you talking about?"

"I'm talking about Ski!"

"I wouldn't worry about Ski. Leon Vurro is the man he's looking for. Where did you know Ski?"

"I don't know Ski."

"Do you want me to drive for a while?"

"No, I don't."

"Where are we?"

"I don't know exactly. Out of the mountains anyway. We're near Veracruz somewhere."

I kept thinking I would pull over at some point and sleep until daylight but I couldn't find a place that looked just right. The Pemex stations were too noisy and busy. The doctor had me stop once on the highway so he could put some drops in his red eye. This was a slow and messy business. He flung his elbows out like a skeet shooter. I held the army flashlight for him. He said the drops were cold. While I was at it, I checked the transmission fluid and there were a lot of little blue flashes playing around the engine where the spark-plug cables were cracked and arcing.

He napped again and then he started talking to me about Houston, which he pronounced "Yooston." I like to keep things straight and his movements had me confused. I had thought at first that he came to Mexico direct from Louisiana. Then it was California. Now it was Houston. Ski was from Houston and it was from that same city that the doctor had departed in haste for Mexico, or "Old Mexico" as he called it.

"Who is this Ski anyway?"

"He's an old friend of mine. I thought I told you that."

"Is he a crook?"

"He's a real-estate smarty. He makes money while he's sleeping. He used to be a policeman. He says he made more unassisted arrests than any other officer in the colorful history of Harris County. I can't vouch for that but I know he made plenty. I've known him for years. I used to play poker with him at the Rice Hotel. I gave distemper shots to his puppies. I removed a benign wart from his shoulder that was as big as a Stuart pecan. It looked like a little man's head, or a baby's head, like it might talk, or cry. I never charged him a dime. Ski has forgotten all that."

"Why did you tell me he was looking for you?"

"He almost caught me at Alvin. It was nip and tuck. Do you know the County Line Lounge between Arcadia and Alvin?"

"No."

"The Uncle Sam Muffler Shop?"

"No."

"Shoe City?"

"No."

"Well, it was right in there where I lost him. That traffic circle is where he tore his britches. I never saw him after that. He has no chin, you know."

"You told me that."

"Captain Hughes of the Rangers used to say that if they ever hanged old Ski they would have to put the rope under his nose."

"Why was he after you?"

"Leon Vurro is the man he really wants."

The highways of Mexico, I thought, must be teaming with American investigators. The doctor and I, neither of us very sinister, had met by chance and we were both being more or less pursued. What about all the others? I had seen some strange birds down here from the States. Creeps! Nuts! Crooks! Fruits! Liars! California dopers!

I tried not to show much interest in his story after the way he had dozed while I was telling mine. It didn't matter, because he paid no attention to other people anyway. He spoke conversational English to all the Mexicans along the way and never seemed to notice that they couldn't understand a word he said.

The story was hard to follow. He and a man named Leon Vurro had put out a tip sheet in Houston called the *Bayou Blue Sheet*. They booked a few bets too, and they handled a few layoff bets from smaller bookies, with Ski as a silent partner. They worked the national time zones to their advantage in some way that I couldn't understand. Ski had many other interests. He had political connections. No deal was too big or too small for him. He managed to get a contract to publish a directory called *Stouthearted Men*, which was to be a collection of photographs and capsule biographies of all the county supervisors in Texas. Or maybe it was the county clerks. Anyway, Ski and the county officers put up an initial sum of $6,500 for operating expenses. Dr. Symes and Leon Vurro gathered the materials for the book and did some work on the dummy makeup. They also sold advertisements for it. Then Leon Vurro disappeared with the money. That, at any rate, was the doctor's account.

"Leon's an ordinary son of a bitch," he said, "but I didn't think he was an out-and-out crook. He said he was tired. Tired! He was sleeping sixteen hours a day and going to the picture show every afternoon. I was the one who was tired, and hot too, but we could have finished that thing in another two weeks. Sooner than that if Leon had kept his wife out of it. She had to stick her nose into everything. She got the pictures all mixed up. She claimed she had been a trapeze artist with Sells-Floto. Told fortunes is more like it. Reader and Adviser is more like it. A bullwhip act is more like it. She looked like a gypsy to me. With that fat ass she would have broke the trapeze ropes. Gone through the net like a shot. We had to work fast, you see, because the pictures were turning green and curling up. I don't know how they got wet. There's a lot of mildew in Houston. You can bet I got tired of looking at those things. I wish you could have seen those faces, Speed. Prune Face and BB Eyes are not in it with those boys."

"You must think I'm a dope," I said. "You never intended to publish that book."

"No, it was a straight deal. Do you know the Moon Publishing Company?"

"No."

"They have offices in Palestine, Texas, and Muldrow, Oklahoma."

"I've never heard of it."

"It's a well-known outfit. They do job printing and they put out calendars and cookbooks and flying-saucer books and children's books, books on boating safety, all kinds of stuff. *A Boy's Life of Lyndon B. Johnson*. That's a Moon book. It was a straight enough deal."

"How much money did Leon Vurro get?"

"I don't know. Whatever was there, he cleaned it out. It's a shame too. We could have finished that thing in two weeks. We were already through the M's and that was halfway. More, really, because there wouldn't be many X's and Z's. You never know. Maybe Leon was right. You have to know when to lay 'em down. It was a weekend deal, you see. There's a lot of mischief on weekends and not just check-kiting either. Leon cleared out the account on Friday afternoon. I was in San Antonio trying to sell ads for that fool book. The word got out fast on Leon but it didn't get to me. It didn't reach the Alamo City. I got back in my room in Houston on Sunday night. I was staying at Jim's Modern Cabins out on Galveston Road. My cabin was dark and the window was open. You had to leave your windows open. Jim doesn't have air conditioning except in his own office. He's got a big window unit in his office that will rattle the walls. I walked by my front window and I could smell Ski's fruity breath. He has diabetes, you see. These young doctors tell everybody they have diabetes but Ski really has it. I knew he was waiting inside that cabin in the dark and I didn't know why. I left with hardly any delay and then it was nip and tuck in south Houston. I made it on down to Corpus and traded my car for that hippie bus at the first car lot that opened up. I knew I didn't have any business driving a car forty feet long but that was the only unit on the lot the fellow would trade even for. I thought it might make a nice little home on the road. Your top gospel singers all have private buses."

"Why would Ski be after you if Leon Vurro got the money?"

"Leon's wife was behind all that. Bella set that up. I never said she was dumb."

"How do you know all that stuff if you left town so fast? That part is not clear to me."

"You get a feel for these things."

"I don't see how you could get a feel for all the circumstances."

"I should never have tied up with Leon. People like that can do nothing but drag you down. He didn't know the first thing about meeting the public and he was never dressed properly. They'll bury that son of a bitch in his zipper jacket."

"How did you know, for instance, that Leon had cleaned out the bank account?"

"I always tried to help Leon and you see the thanks I got. I hired him to drive for me right after his rat died. He was with Murrell Brothers Shows at that time, exhibiting a fifty-pound rat from the sewers of Paris, France. Of course it didn't really weigh fifty pounds and it wasn't your true rat and it wasn't from Paris, France, either. It was some kind of animal from South America. Anyway, the thing died and I hired Leon to drive for me. I was selling birthstone rings and vibrating jowl straps from door to door and he would let me out at one end of the block and wait on me at the other end. He could handle that all right. That was just about his speed. I made a serious mistake when I promoted Leon to a higher level of responsibility."

I pressed the doctor with searching questions about the Houston blowout but I couldn't get any straight answers and so I gave it up.

SMOKE OVER THE PRAIRIE

CONRAD RICHTER

Smoke Over the Prairie

It is ground into dust now like Mobeetie and Tascosa, swallowed up by the grass and desert along with split ox-shoes, shaggy buffalo trails, and the crude cap-and-ball rifle. And how can I say it so that you who were not there may see it as I did, rolling, surging, fermenting under the brazen territorial sun, that vanished rude empire of which my father was a baron, a land as feudal as old England, larger than the British Isles, with lords and freemen, savages and peons, most of them on horseback, all here in America a little more than half a century ago, and yet in another world and another age that was just then—although we didn't know it—drawing to a violent close?

I remember, as a small boy, climbing up our roof ladder in the shadowy blot after sunset and telling myself that five days' journey west across the territory the sun was still shining on flocks of my father's hundred thousand sheep. And I can remember the cavelike darkness of some early-morning waking between blankets tossed over tanned buffalo hides on my huge bed and thinking that a thousand miles east on one of my father's mule or bull trains the sun was already shining.

And today I would give a great deal just to glimpse that same sun warming the walls of my father's house, known from Fort Dodge to the Old Pueblo as Gant's Mansion, a squat palace of adobe standing on the San Blas plain, and to see again its wide hall trooping with a grave procession of princely territorial governors and hook-nosed judges, of Indian agents like blue-eyed foxes, of brass-buttoned army officers, Federal officials, Mexican dons and *ricos,* and the hungry, grunting chiefs of the Utes, the Apaches and the Navajos.

But even then a cloud no bigger than your hand was beginning to cast a shadow over those adobe walls that stood thick enough to entomb horses. The smoke of the native cedar is blue and fragrant and melts into the air. This cloud on the eastern horizon was a smoke tamed by man, black, foreign, smelling of the pit, and had never hung over this wild land before.

I knew it was important that day my mother called to me in the hall. She sat massively in her armchair in her rooms, not a stout woman, but wrapped, even in summer, in shawls and overskirts, her eyes dark and bright like a bird's, in a quilted face which even then looked incredibly older than it was. All week I had been conscious of the clamp of her lip and the faint white spots, like touches of alkali, in my sister Juliana's cheeks.

"Go and ask your papa if he can spare the time from his business to talk to me," she said bitterly. "And you come with him."

I knew then that my father had not greeted her, although he had been back several hours from ten days among his sheep in the Canyon Bonito country. I had seen his dust-covered buggy pull up to the store, both horses lathered to the mane, as always when my father held the lines. I found him gone from the store, and I looked for him in his wholesale warehouses sprawling nearby, a kind of Ali Baba caves in barred windows, dim and odorous and heaped with inciting boxes, fat hogsheads, bulging bales, mountains of plump sacks, grain-bins, piles of hides to the roof, monstrous sacks of unwashed wool, and poisonous-looking copper ingots.

He wasn't there, and I went in turn to the clanging blacksmith shop, to the stables, where his late-driven horses stood in a kind of stupor, and to the wheelwright shop, choked with felloes and rims, blocks and shavings and the dismembered bodies of wagons that knew every ford and pitch hole on the Santa Fe trail.

Only one place remained where he might be, and I reproached myself that I hadn't gone there before—what we called the mansion office, a bare sweep of room with an adobe floor and little furniture except a battered desk whose drawers no one dared to touch. The place was empty, but a guttural of voices drifted from the bedroom beyond.

"Come in!" my father's voice called at my rap.

I lifted the iron latch and for an uncomfortable moment stood in the doorway.

A fire of *piñon* logs blazed in the bedroom fireplace, and on the floor with his back to it sat Guero, the Mescalero Apache chief, huge and greasy, with the eyes, nose and talons of an eagle, his red blanket thrown back from his shoulders, and bared in his rawhide belt a long American trade knife and the forbidden revolver.

And coolly talking to him from where he stood in a white bowl on the floor, washing himself from a second bowl on the marble top of the washstand, unclothed, unarmed, and unconcerned, stood my father, a powerful naked figure, not tall, but Herculean, in a black beard that twisted and stood out from his chin and cheeks like fine wire. And I noticed that the same stubborn, black, invincible growth curled from his chest and the hard cylinders of his legs.

So far, he had not even glanced at the open door, and now he looked up with some impatience.

"Come in, come in!" he barked, and I stepped hastily into the room, dimly realizing that he had not known who was knocking, that it might have been one of the Mexican women servants with, perhaps, the governor and his lady behind her, but that my father did not care. His unforgettable eyes fixed themselves upon me. "You know Chief Guero," he commanded sternly. "Go up, shake hands and ask him in Spanish about his family."

When my father had pulled on clean linen and fresh black broadcloth, he summed up his long talk to Guero: "Tell your people this: Tell them there is no danger from the railroad. It will bring no white people here to take away your rights. It makes big promises. It talks big words. Today it boasts. Tomorrow it is forgotten."

He left Guero sitting on the earthen floor of the office, bent voraciously over a huge bowl of steaming mutton stew.

"Now," he said to me in the hall, "you say your mother wants to see me?" For a moment or two as he stood there he reminded me of the male blackbirds I had often seen in the tules, drawing in their brilliant scarlet shoulder-straps and soberly ruffling their feathers until their strut and sheen had vanished and they looked subdued and brown. Then I accompanied him in silence to my mother's door. He knocked and, without waiting for an answer, formally entered.

"Nettie!" He bowed gravely, and in that single word still in my ear I can detect greeting, irony, dignity, indulgence and uncomfortable expectation of what was to come.

My mother made no answer except the further clamp of her lip and the faint, unaccustomed rose in her cheeks. She motioned me to come and sit beside her, which I did, painfully conscious that it was an ignoble role I was to play, like the favorite child in *Ten Nights in a Barroom*, by whom the regeneration of the father was to be made.

My mother's quarters, which she seldom left, seemed perpetually compressed with a stale and heavy air, the musty scent of Eastern carpets, stuffed chests and wardrobes, soaps, medicines and mothballs, all very distasteful to a boy. But today I felt that the sluggish air had been charged with sharp and potent currents. And when I looked at the golden-brown shawl which hung like a vestment about my mother's shoulders, there was almost the play of lightning upon it.

"Must I speak of it?" my mother began bitterly. "I should think you'd confess it yourself with shame!"

No step was audible outside the door, but the latch lifted and drew our eyes. Slowly the door opened. It was Juliana. I can see her today, framed in that massive doorway with the light like a nimbus behind her, quiet, grave-faced, a girlish figure in her full skirts and snug bodice, both of them dove-colored, and over the latter the gold chain and heart-shaped locket in which I knew she carried the picture of her father.

"John is here. Can't I stay?" she asked, and closed the door. With the hushed step of a young woman late to church, she crossed the room to a chair, and the appeal in her eyes as for a moment she glanced up at my father might almost have been at God.

My mother's eyes burned with maternal satisfaction at Juliana's presence.

"People are saying," she went on scathingly to my father, "that Mr. Rutherford has disappeared like other enemies of the high-handed interests in this territory."

I fancied I saw a hidden stain through the beard on my father's cheeks, and my mind traveled with a sort of horror to Vance Rutherford, tall, fine-looking, and gentlemanly, whom Julian had met at the Coddoms' in Captian. Up until the last ten days he had kept driving to the mansion in a livery rig to pay her attentions, and I had wondered what had become of his narrow-brim hat and the invariable desert marigold in his buttonhole.

"People say many things, Nettie, many things," my father said.

"Is he dead?" my mother demanded in a blunt voice, and I saw the locket hang motionless for a moment on Juliana's breast.

"No-o," my father said blandly. "Not that I know of." And the locket resumed its silent rise and fall.

"Then you warned him to leave the territory?" my mother accused.

"I may have"—my father lifted a square hand—"seen that he heard certain discreet things."

"You had nothing against him, Frank Gant, except that he's chief engineer for the railroad!" my mother challenged hotly. "Where can you find another young man in such a high position? Do you want your daughter to marry a cowboy or a buffalo hunter who rides and kills and gambles and soaks himself in the whiskey you sell like coffee and sugar over your counters?"

My father prudently said nothing. The color gathered in my mother's face.

"You're prejudiced against the railroad! I say, thank God for the railroad. It's the finest thing that could happen to this lawless land. It will bring schools and churches."

"They're not building it to bring schools and churches," my father reminded mildly. "They're building it to make it pay. They want to lay down eight hundred miles west and south in the territory. It's to cost eighteen thousand dollars a mile or more. That's fourteen million dollars." He ran his hand over his unruly black beard. "Fourteen million dollars when we already have trails that cost nothing and freighters who've built up their trains to more than five thousand steers and mules."

"Steers and mules!" My mother's eyes were blazing. "Have steers and mules ever civilized this country? How many shooting scrapes does the Capitan *Enterprise* print every week? Murders, they should be called—cold-blooded murders! And that doesn't count the lynchings and men who disappear and the women and children scalped by your friends the Apaches! Is it any wonder that good people refuse to come to this barbarous country?"

My father looked very humble.

"Aren't you confusing it, Nettie, with farming country like Kansas?" he asked. "That's a new country. This is old. White people have been here for hundreds of years, but they never got very far with farming. I've heard you say yourself it's only a desert. But this young promoter, Rutherford"—I saw Juliana's eyelashes quiver—"wants to spend fourteen million dollars to give the desert a railroad. He tells our towns to go in debt with bonds and buy railroad stock with the money. He tells them the railroad will someday be one of the biggest in the country."

I saw that my mother was staggered despite herself by the unanswerable facts and figures. She leaned forward appealingly.

"When one of your Mexican herders' relatives gets into trouble, Frank, you always feel sorry and help him out. Can't you feel sorry for an American who isn't much more than a boy, who works for the railroad company and believes what the higher officials tell him?"

"No," my father said slowly, and it was the first hardness I had heard in his voice since he had entered the room. I saw that he had straightened. "I have sympathy, Nettie, for a man who knows he is gambling and loses, and for a man who knows he may get hung for stealing a horse and steals it. But I have none for anyone who throws away other people's hard-earned money, who's gullible enough to swallow a wild dream like a fourteen-million-dollar railroad on the desert." He looked straight at my mother and went on, drawing in his bearded lips with great force: "Such a waster will never become a member of my house—not while I'm alive!"

There were streaks of chalk in my mother's cheeks, but what is hard to forget is Juliana. Quiet, the locket still moving gently on her dove-colored bodice, she sat on her chair, and her face was no paler than when she had come in. But the eyes that stared at my father were the eyes of a dead person. I was aware of my mother laying her ringed fingers, as if for divine strength, on the gilded covers of the thick family Bible that lay on the table beside her.

"God will punish you, Frank Gant!" she said.

Now that he had taken his position, my father had become his old self again, firm, robust, Atlantean, almost like a Nubian lion in his black beard and broadcloth, standing there with such living power that I felt that words, shafts, bullets and even the hand of God must glance off from him.

"Perhaps Julie feels badly now," he went on confidently, "but she'll get over it till I get back. My early clip's started to move east, and I'm leaving for St. Louis in the morning to sell it."

The plains had deepened in grass to my pony's knees before my father returned. He always remembered me from the St. Louis shops, with something not easily obtainable in his store—a boy's light rifle or silver spurs. Usually his gifts for Juliana were slighter—a sterling napkin-ring engraved with her name, a golden-leather album with the photographs of President and Mrs. Hayes in front, and once a mahogany lap secretary. I know that secretly he was very fond of her, but she was only a girl, an heir who would never carry on his name or smoke heavy cigars while making contracts with Kansas City jobbers or colonels of the quartermaster's department, or drive a buggy over a region half as large as New England, overseeing the lambing of a vast number of ewes and sleeping among the herders in all kinds of spring weather.

But no one could predict my father. When, hale, lusty, and radiating vitality, he left the mansion for the store, after greeting us on his return far ahead of his mule train, Trinidad brought in two canvas valises from the boot of a new buggy.

There were, I remember, taffetas and alpacas for my mother, but most of it, I glimpsed at once, was for Juliana. My mother held them up to her, one after the other, but all I can recall are a blue velvet riding-dress with an extraordinarily long skirt and a black, lathlike sheath dress, a style none of us had ever seen before, and in which, my mother promptly declared, no self-respecting girl would show her figure or could walk across the room if she did.

When I ran to the store with my new, silver-mounted bridle that was on the bottom of the second valise, my father glanced at me sharply.

"What did Juliana say?" he questioned. "Did she try on the dresses?"

I felt a faint chill up my spine, but one look at his eyes convinced me that I must tell the truth. No one today has eyes like his, blue-green in his black beard, leaping at times with a gusto that would stop at nothing, burning again with a deadly green flame and as quickly freezing to blue ice.

"I don't reckon she was feeling good, papa," I stammered. "She just went to her room and didn't say anything."

Al Sleeper, the head clerk, turned quickly to rearrange the wooden boot-boxes that stood in a pile on the floor, and the faces of the listening men stiffened as if someone had suddenly brushed them all with varnish. But my father's face did not change, neither then nor day after day when I saw him look up with a steeled expression to see what Juliana was wearing, only to find her monotonously, almost disrespectfully, in the dove-colored gray.

Something had happened to Juliana. There was a spring in a *cañada* of the San Blas plain that the Mexicans called El Olvidado. The grass was never so green as there, with a fringe of tules and red-winged blackbirds and the living water welling up cool and clear. My pony and I had often drunk there. But the last year something strange had come to the place. The tules were still there and the red-winged blackbirds, and the grass still looked green, but there was no water to drink.

It was like that with Juliana. She had the same clear skin and straight white path running back along the center of her smoothly parted, dark hair, and the heart-shaped locket still stirred to her breathing, but something clear and living had vanished. Her custom-made sidesaddle gathered gritty plains dust in the harness room, and her cream-colored buckskin mare grew wild on the range. Most of the time she spent quietly in her room, and when I came in, she would be sitting on the edge of her bed, a two-months-old copy of the New York *Ledger* or *Saturday Night* in her fingers, but her eyes would be gazing over the top of the pages and out of the deep window to the plain that already, in August, was a gray, imprisoning sea.

People in the territory were not different from people anywhere else, and I knew they were talking. Whenever Juliana was called into my mother's rooms to greet visitors, I saw them exchange guarded glances. And when she crossed to the store to match yarn for my mother's tireless bone needles, seeing almost no one, walking with open eyes like one asleep, customers watched her furtively, and Mexican women murmured sympathetically *"Pobrecita"* after she had gone. My father never murmured in his life, and his full-charged, indomitable figure remained as always, but more than once when my mother was not looking, I watched him glance characteristically at Juliana. And although his bearded face remained adamant, I fancied I could see a kind of Spartan pain afterward in his eyes.

Looking back now, I can understand perfectly, and everything falls into its place like the letters of the alphabet. But I was only a boy on my pony that day in Capitan when lawyer Henry Coddom asked me to come into his house. In the parlor a man was pacing up and down and, even in that dim room so soon after the bright sunlight, I saw at once that it was Vance Rutherford, tall, perhaps a little older, his cheekbones faintly haggard, a fresh desert marigold as always in the buttonhole of his high Eastern coat, and the familiar faraway look in his eyes which to me had never seemed to belong to the long fighting lines of his face.

I stiffened at the sight of him, but Vance Rutherford bowed in his impersonal, gentlemanly manner.

"Good morning, Johnnie," he said gravely, and asked me to sit down on the black horsehair sofa, where, for a time, like a pair of grown men, we spoke formally on trivial subjects, none of which touched the railroad or my family.

"Johnnie," he said quietly after a little, "will you take a letter to your sister and not let anyone else see it?"

He did not try to urge me. I thought of Juliana walking with mute eyes around the mansion, and I told myself that I didn't like to be the one to keep a letter from her.

"I don't care," I said, meaning I would do it, and he brought it out, and without either of us saying another word, I slipped it into a pocket.

The letter burned like a live coal all the way back on the saddle to Gant's, and I felt relieved that my father was in the Merino Valley and that I did not have to smuggle the letter past him like an Indian stalking out of the store with one of our butcher knives under his blanket. All afternoon I watched the men shovel the new crop of barley and corn into the dusty warehouse bins, and when I put my saddle and bridle away in the harness room in the last golden, stabbing rays of the sun, I found, with surprise, that Juliana's sidesaddle was missing. She did not come to the table for supper, and when I heard the long, doleful bugle of a prairie wolf after nightfall, I went to my mother.

"It's all right, John," she said, and I think she knew about the letter then. "Someone will see Juliana home or she'll stay all night at the Hudspeths'."

It was during the heavy hours of the night that I was awakened by the feel of a kiss on my cheek. I twisted my head on the bolster, and there was Juliana with a lighted candlestick in her hand. She didn't say a word, just stood there looking down at me, and there was in her face a shining something I had never seen before. It wasn't altogether real—the late hour, her illuminated figure against the blackness of the huge room, the strange luminosity in her eyes, and her appearance in the stunning blue velvet riding-dress my father had brought her. I had the singular impression that it was a dream, but when I reached out to see if I could touch her, she squeezed my fingers and I found her hand substantial and throbbing with warmth.

I thought it strange that she was not at breakfast, and when I looked into her room, the smoothness of the bright, quilted counterpane told me that her bed had not been slept in. Lupita and Piedad, two of the Mexican servants, professed to know nothing about it, but I knew, by the impassive restraint in which they moved away, that a feeling of excitement pervaded the house. And as I passed my mother's open door, I saw her wiping her eyes.

That afternoon my father drove home in time for supper. His beard was roan from the trail, and his eyes glinted through it like pieces of turquoise in the dust. As a rule, my mother took her meals in her rooms, where she ate in lone state from a massive silver tray covered with hammered dots. And I felt the keen import tonight when her full taffeta skirts came rustling to the dining room.

I think my father sensed it too. Twice I saw him glance deliberately at the empty chair standing with such silent power at the table. And before he spoke, his bearded lips tightened.

"Where's Juliana?" he asked, and the brown face of Lupita, the table girl, grew thin with emotion. But my mother's eyes burned with a triumphant light across the table.

"She's gone!" she told him, as if she had waited long for this moment. "She was married to Vance Rutherford at the Coddoms' last evening. They're halfway to Kansas by now."

I did not dare look at my father. Sitting there with my dark antelope steak smoking on the plate before me, I suddenly knew why Juliana had come in during the night to kiss me. And for a long, vivid moment I could see her in her blue velvet and Vance Rutherford with a fresh desert marigold in his buttonhole sitting close together in the bridal coach as they swept northeast across the territory, followed by a golden whirlwind of earthy cloud. And now, hours after they had left, it was as if I could still see their dust lying over the plain in the calm October sunlight like a long, motionless finger pointing out to my father the direction they had gone.

Every second I expected to hear him push back his chair and call for Trinidad to hitch Prince and Custer, his fastest buggy team. When at last I looked up, he had regained his indomitable control. But his face was like the faint grayness of winter snow through the heavy growth of black spruce on lone, powerful Mount Jeddo.

He did not speak during the rest of the supper. Lupita tiptoed around the table. The meal lasted interminably. For all of my father's lack of hunger, he did not allow himself to eat a mouthful less than customary. When he rose to go to the store, which always stayed open till ten o'clock, he must have been aware that every clerk and customer would by this time probably know. His beard and shoulders up, the deep smoldering fire in his eyes warning everyone he met, he walked steadily across the trail in the dusk.

Juliana wrote to my mother, letters filled with bright pictures of her new life. She and Vance lived in a beautiful brick house with a marble doorstep in Kansas City. She had bought a stunning maroon cheviot suit with pearl buttons and a bonnet with plumes to match. Every Sunday morning she and Vance attended church, and already at weekday breakfast she knew the day's news of the world. Her letters closed: "Give my dearest love to papa and Johnnie. Your affectionate daughter, Juliana." But if my mother ever ventured to give it, I never heard her.

All winter I did not mention her name to my father and never heard him speak it. I doubted if he ever would. When, sometimes, I would see him walking silently and rigidly about the place, it was as if he were trying by sheer force of will to erase her ghostlike presence from our hall and rooms, from the aisles of the store, and even from the territory. By the following spring it almost seemed as if she might never have been there. But once my mother read aloud from the *Enterprise* that Mr. and Mrs. Henry Coddom had been to Kansas City, and when she came to the words "they called on Mrs. Vance Rutherford, the former Juliana Gant," something wrenched open in my mind and Juliana was back in the mansion with us as real as she had ever been in the flesh.

It was only in this way she came that windy day in April when the dust was flying in yellow sheets across the plain. A private coach had stopped to buy grain for the horses at our feed corral. Someone walked into the mansion courtyard, and old Piedad came hurrying back through the hall with a kind of consternation on her wrinkled face. Rather curiously, I went to the door and for a moment had the feeling that Juliana had come. It was Vance Rutherford, a little heavier and more mature, his face solid and squarer, with a reddish mustache and a marigold as always in his buttonhole.

I stood uncomfortably in the doorway, not knowing quite what to do or say, but Piedad had gone on to my mother's rooms, and now my mother came with loud sibilations of taffeta skirts, seized both of Vance Rutherford's hands in hers, kissed him as if he were my brother, and poured out a dozen questions about Juliana.

"Juliana's fine," he said. "She wanted to come along, but I'm on business." His face sobered. "I've got to see Mr. Gant in the store and then hurry back, but I promised to see you first, so I could tell her how you all looked."

At the mention of my father, the bright, birdlike glint came into my mother's eyes. I saw that she itched to know the cause of his visit, but he did not offer to tell her, and when he left for the store, she feverishly insisted that I go along, as if my companionship might in some mysterious brotherly manner ingratiate him into my father's good graces.

It was the last place in the world that I wanted to be at the moment, and I kicked grimly at every bone and horn I met in the dust to the wide store steps. Through the open door I could see my father standing in a circle of respectfully listening men, his back and clasped hands to the cold, fat-bellied, unblackened stove. Then I stepped discreetly aside to let Vance Rutherford enter first.

It could not have been possible for more than a few of our customers to know Vance Rutherford by sight; yet when he stepped past the pile of carriage blankets at the door, something was in the air of the big store room that wasn't there before. Ike Roehl, halfway up a stepladder, soundlessly dropped an armful of ladies' zephyrs to the counter. Over by the sugar barrels, a clerk and customer stopped talking. In the silence that followed I could hear the windows rattling and the fine sand sifting across the small panes. And suspended on their nails along the ceiling, the rows of wooden buckets kept swinging silently in the draft.

"Could I see you a few minutes in your office, Mr. Gant?" Vance Rutherford asked.

I expected to see rushing into my father's face that volcanic violence from which I had often watched men shrink. Instead, he seemed to be seized by some strange perversity. Not long before, he had come in from overseeing the loading of fleeces on one of his eastbound wagon trains. The rolling brim of his hat was gray with dust. Wisps of wool clung to his broadcloth and buttons. And now he stood with his chin half-sunken on his chest and his eyes half-closed, as if warding off someone he intensely disliked, with a kind of ponderous lethargy.

"Anything you have to say, you can say it here," he rumbled.

Vance Rutherford stood very straight, but I saw him bite his lip.

"I wanted to talk to you in private, sir," he flushed, "so you'd be free to act as you thought best in the matter." He waited a few moments. "If you force me to make it public property, I'll do it." He waited again, and when my father made neither movement nor further expression, his face grew longer and harder, and I saw that it had not lost any of its fighting lines. "The railroad is coming into the territory, sir!" he announced tensely. "We're starting to lay track across the line in May."

None of the listening men moved so much as a finger, but I could feel a wave of something electric sweep over the room. Only my father seemed immune from it. He still stood like a dozing buffalo bull, only partly aware of what might be going on around him.

"You're coming as far as Capitan?" he grunted.

"We'll have trains running into Capitan in a year," Vance Rutherford promised.

My father lifted his massive head, and I saw his deep smoldering eyes.

"You still have railroad stock for sale?"

"We have, Mr. Gant," the young man said simply. "It takes money to build a railroad."

"I understand," my father rumbled on, "that you figure on spending millions in the territory?"

"Millions!" Vance Rutherford agreed. "But it will all come back to us, once we're in operation." He leaned forward earnestly. "Mr. Gant, you've been a pioneer in this country. You've had to deal with savages and outlaws, but those days are nearly over. The territory is on the threshold of prosperity. A flood of people are coming with the railroad. Schools and churches will spring up everywhere. It's going to be an empire, the Southwestern empire, sir. I can see the railroad a few years from now hauling train after train of passengers and rich freight all the vast distance from the Mississippi to the Pacific!"

I was fascinated by his eloquence. There was something magically convincing in his voice and enthusiasm, and for the moment I could actually see a railroad train sweeping triumphantly across our San Blas plain, and the Indians and Mexicans fleeing from it in terror. And, looking into the staring eyes of grizzled old teamsters, I believed they could see it too.

Vance Rutherford seemed to feel his power. He went on appealingly: "Mr. Gant, you're one of the biggest freighters in the country. You know your business, and if you do, you must know that the day of mule and bull trains is past. You've seen what happened along the Santa Fe trail in Kansas. You know what will happen to the wagon business in this territory as soon as we have trains running into Capitan. Don't you agree, sir, that it's good business for a freighter to sell his wagons and mules while there's a demand and put his money into the railroad?"

I heard a sound like a deep mutter that could be no longer withheld, and before I looked I knew that my father had thrown up his massive head and was standing there, rude and immovable, his shaggy beard throwing off defiance, and green fire like the dog star in his eyes.

"No!" he bellowed, and I heard the tinware on the shelves murmur his decree after him. "My only interest in your stock, young man, was to find out whether I could trust you and your fourteen-million-dollar-railroad officials to horse feed when they came through!"

I saw Al Sleeper open his mouth in a soundless laugh and a rancher from the Tres Ritos bring one hand down silently on his denim thigh. The spell of the railroad was irreparably broken. Customers and loafers nudged one another, and

Vance Rutherford looked as if he had been struck across the face. His temples twitched, but he stood his ground.

"I think, Mr. Gant," he said, with a great effort at dignity, "if the railroad ever asks it, your feed corral would be justified in extending credit."

I expected him to go, but for a long moment the two men continued to face each other—both iron-willed and unyielding; one, young in years, gentlemanly, with a flower in his buttonhole; the other, older, powerful, with streaks of wool and dust on his clothing; one of the new age, one of the old. Then the younger man turned silently and went out.

News of the coming of the railroad spread like a gold strike through the territory. Stories reached the store by stage and wagon train, by buckboard and carriage. The railroad was awarding contracts for grading, ties, bridge timbers and telegraph poles. The railroad contractors were buying herds of horses and mules. The railroad was blasting tunnels through the San Dimas Mountains. The railroad was crossing the mountains on the old wagon trail. All summer and fall the railroad expected to lay from one to two miles of track a day.

By Christmas the byword among the teamsters returning from the iron rails was: "Look out for the locomotive!" They reported the sleepy old Mexican village of La Luz booming since the railroad had arrived. The Capitan *Enterprise* announced with pride that Baldwin's was building a new, huge, eighty-ton locomotive for use in the territory and that it would be "in charge of men fully competent to handle the monster." And it added that Vance Rutherford, engineer for the railroad, had promised lawyer Henry Coddom that he was pushing construction with every resource at his command and that trains would be running into Capitan by the Fourth of July.

In the very next issue of the *Enterprise*, Capitan stores advertised in tall type that no new merchandise would come from the East until it arrived more cheaply and safely by steam train. My mother had always abhorred the trail, its clouds of dust, the shouts and curses of its drivers, the crack of whips and report of linchpins, and the snail-like drag of long files of chained steers. Ever since I could remember, she had shut it out with heavy brown hangings. But now she began to draw them back and sit at her knitting where she could see, at last, traffic slowly but steadily fading like late afternoon on the old trail. It seemed to give her a satisfaction as if the railroad were just over the rise, ruthlessly pushing the creaking freight wagons out of the way.

I knew that every vanished wagon sheet and silent wheel was a secret growing cancer in the heart of my father. He never alluded to it, but when I rode along in his buggy to Capitan, I could see the steely glitter in his eyes at sight of the copper ingots, which his trains formerly freighted to Kansas, piling up in great mounds at the proposed site of the new depot. And his eyes looked straight ahead when we passed teams unloading wool and hides into adobe warehouses that had sprung up like molehills where Henry Coddom had sold the railroad a tract of land for the new Capitan town site and which, already, people were calling Newtown.

There was acutally no more railroad to be seen in Capitan than out on the sand hills, but every day now rigs began passing our store on their way to Capitan to trade. Cowboys nightly celebrated the railroad by shooting up the town. There was talk of the *Enterprise* becoming a daily after the telegraph had arrived. I saw where Strome Brothers had torn down their old wooden hitching-rack and set up individual posts with citified snap chains. And the *Enterprise* boasted that there wasn't a vacant house in the town.

Up to this time I had never seen a railroad in my young life, and it seemed that our store and trail were being blighted by some mysterious and invisible weapon in Vance Rutherford's hand. This morning I noticed my father throw up his head to gaze at the northeast. When I looked, there it hung like a black dust cloud over the green of the prairie, the railroad at last. And as my father stared at the smoke funneling up persistently on the distant horizon, I saw the same wild defiance come into his bearded face as had that day at his sheep camp along the Rio Cedro when we had watched a Comanche or Kiowa smoke signal from the hills.

Every morning after this the smoke was there, and I came to think of it as the powerful black breath of Vance Rutherford, moving steadily, silently, inexorably southwest toward Capitan. Now it passed the red mesa, and now for a few days it changed rugged Mount Jeddo into an active volcano. And one day when it had reached some miles abreast of us, I could not resist galloping my pony secretly across the plain to a grassy swell from which I could see a whole bank being sliced away like cake. The prairie there seemed to boil with men and teams, with wagons, plows and drags. The air was filled with the flash of moving picks and shovels and the ring of iron hammers. And creeping back and forward in the background, hissing, sometimes outshrieking any mountain lion, glided one of Vance Rutherford's tamed iron monsters.

I was only a boy, but I could tell, as I rode thoughtfully homeward, that in this thing my mother called civilization there was no quarter, no compromise, no pity. It was not like your grazing pony that, after tiring you for an hour, would let you catch it, or like a wagon train that welcomed you with a blanket, food and the red warmth of a campfire. This was something of another kidney, of another and newer age.

After that initial challenging scrutiny, I never saw my father acknowledge the black smoke's presence. When he entered the store, the subject changed. Only once I heard him refer again to the railroad. A passenger on the halted stage boasted that a Mississippi-Pacific train had done twenty-five miles an hour crossing the plains. My father turned with heavy deliberation and stared him into confusion.

"Sir, I can do as much with one of my Kentucky buggy teams!" he scorned. "And if the trail is uphill, I have gold to wager that I can soundly whip your train!"

But some hours after the stage had gone, I saw him silent and solitary behind our warehouse, pacing measuredly around what none of us had ever seen before—a corral of his stilled freight wagons. Mute, deserted, and depressing they stood there, an unforgettable reminder of what had been. And late that evening when my mother sent me to take the St. Louis paper back to his office, I don't think he knew I was there, for I heard from his bedroom deep incredible sounds, like a man praying, which instantly riveted me to the floor. I couldn't understand a word he said, but the shock of hearing my strong father give way like that in secret shook me to my foundations.

Next morning at breakfast he was staunch and powerful as always, and I told myself that I must have been mistaken. And that afternoon I felt sure of it. I was counting twenty-, ten- and five-dollar gold pieces, silver dollars, halves and quarters—there was nothing smaller—on his battered desk in the mansion office when through the window I saw lawyer Henry Coddom climb determinedly out of his phaeton in the courtyard. The two men had not met since Juliana had been married in the Coddom parlor, and now, with Henry Coddom appointed attorney for the railroad in the territory, I could feel the clouds gather and thicken. When Piedad brought the visitor to the office door, he asked to speak with my father in private, and I was sent away.

Twenty minutes later Henry Coddom came out like a cuffed schoolboy, hat in his hand, his face crimson. And when my father stepped into the hall to order me back to my counting, there were still pitchforks in his eyes and I had never seen him more absolute and unconquerable. Then he became aware of my mother standing in the doorway to her rooms, color in her quilted cheeks and a newspaper in her hand.

"Nettie"—he inclined his head.

"Frank!" she begged him. "You didn't throw away your invitation?"

"Invitation?" His uncompromising eyes bored her.

"It's in the *Enterprise!*" my mother went on feverishly. "They're running the first train into Capitan the Fourth of July. The whole territory's going to celebrate. They expect crowds from every county. The governor and judges and politicos and all the big men of the territory will get on the train at La Luz and ride into Capitan. The governor of Kansas and his wife will be on the train and a Kansas band. They've telegraphed an invitation to President Hayes."

Granite had come into my father's face.

"I got no invitation," he answered harshly. "Henry Coddom came to tell me the railroad wants to build to California." His eyes blazed. "They want eighty miles of my land. They want to build through the Canyon Bonito. They want to blacken my grass, plow trains through my sheep, dump squatters along the Bonito all the way from Big Flat to Gant's Valley."

I am not sure that my mother heard him.

"Frank," she went on desperately, "it's to be the biggest thing that ever happened in the territory. The railroad's giving a banquet at the Wooton House. There'll be dancing till morning. And all the railroad officials and their wives will be there!"

It was almost as if my mother had mentioned Vance Rutherford and Juliana by name. With a titanic effort to control himself, my father turned without a word into the mansion office. And all the time my fingers kept building up fat piles of white and yellow coins, I could feel the raw emotion working in him. And from the next issue of the *Enterprise* we found that the railroad company was daring to drag him soon, like some petty thief or cattle rustler, into court in Bonito County, half of whose vast spaces he owned, to show why eighty miles of his choicest river pastureland should not be condemned for the railroad right-of-way.

For days afterward he remained around home, silent and implacable, waiting for the case to be called. And when I saw the dull fire leaping in his eyes, I knew he was forging the bolts of lightning he would let loose in that small adobe courtroom at Bonito. Of course Mr. Stryker, his lawyer, would be with him, but it was my father who would dominate the court.

"No judge in this territory," Al Sleeper declared, "can look Frank Gant in the eye and turn over his land to Henry Coddom and a Kansas railroad."

For weeks my father waited while the railroad pushed its mailed arm into Capitan, while June grew closer to July, and Juliana's cream-colored mare had a second colt that Juliana had never seen. And all the time I could see in my mother's eyes the hope that the case had not yet been called in Judge Tatum's court at Bonito, because he and Vance Rutherford expected to come to my father privately and settle the differences out of court in time to get him to the celebration. I knew that if anybody could reason with my father it was Judge Tatum, whom I had often seen slouched in the mansion office, an extraordinarily long figure with a face like a sorrel horse, his long legs up on the battered desk, a thick tumbler and a jug of my father's whiskey beside him, and my father laughing indulgently through his beard at what the judge was saying.

Then all hope of my father going to the celebration faded from my mother's eyes. One of his old herders, Gil Jaramillo, arrived in the mansion courtyard on a spent horse. Tall and cadaverous, his eyes rolling with the mad light of so many men who spend their lives with the sheep, he called out, "*Amo!*" with excitement as soon as he was at the door. And when my father had come into the hall, he stammered out in Spanish that the Cross V's, whose cattle ranch adjoined my father's Rio Cedro pastures, were warring on his sheep, driving some of them into the river, scattering the rest to be preyed upon by coyotes and wolves, and badly beating up the *caporal* and herders.

I expected to see the anger flame on my father's face. Instead it grew calmer than for weeks, as if news of violence and bloodshed was almost a welcome relief from this petty waiting for a summons to court. Within the hour he drove off for the Rio Cedro, sitting in his buggy like a king, Trinidad brown and solid beside him, and a change of horses galloping through the dust behind. And long after he had gone I could see him in my mind, whipping his team across a region half as wide as France, the goats leaping with flying beards from in front of the horses, the cedar branches whipping the buggy from both sides of the narrow trail, himself staying the night in some humble *placita* and, if there was a bed in the village, sleeping in it, and finally matching his strength against his enemies, who had always been putty in his hands.

I was glad he had gone that evening when the deputy from Bonito County arrived apologetically with the summons. But the gray glance of Al Sleeper held a queer light, and under his mustache, jutting out from his face like the waterfall of a roily mountain stream, his mouth looked forbidding. He spoke to my mother and early next morning sent the summons with a Mexican rider after my father, but I knew it was like a desert finch trying to catch an eagle.

The mansion seemed like a convent with my father gone. Our native villagers kept asking if we were not to ride with the governor on the bunting-trimmed train. I told them we didn't like crowds, that we had plenty of bunting in the mansion and that we intended to wait until there was room in Capitan to breathe. They nodded solemnly, polite Mexicans that they were, but they knew as well as I why we weren't going.

And now from morning till night the migration toward Capitan began passing our door—American ranchers and miners on the saddle, in buggy and buckboard; officers' families from Fort Gates in army ambulances with the side curtains rolled up for air; but mostly natives who had never seen the iron horse; Mexican families in heavy wagons, in a few private carriages, and on endless saddles; Ute Indians decked with bright ribbons, their bony ponies packed for trade; and aloof Navajos in red calicoes and blue velvets and clinking silver.

By noon of the Fourth all had passed. The last trip the stage would ever make by our door took place about one, the westbound coach crowded with passengers. It threw off our leather bag of mail, but failed to stop. And after it had gone and the trail lay quiet again, I suddenly realized that it looked different from what I had ever seen it, old, tired, abandoned, almost like the ruins of an ancient *camino* winding desolately over the plain.

About two o'clock I glimpsed a distant smudge of dust to the northeast, a smudge that swirled rapidly nearer, and finally I could make out our bay team plunging wearily toward home, my father driving and Trinidad still beside him, but only one horse galloping behind. My father swerved the foaming, bulging-eyed team into the mansion courtyard. As I slipped back into the hall, he said something to Trinidad, who at once drove away. Then I saw through my mother's doorway that she had stiffened in her chair and bent her face defensively over her knitting.

My father scarcely tossed a glance at me as he came in, haggard and grim, his hat, beard and broadcloth layered with dust. He halted in the center of the hall, from where his eyes could flash turbulently into my mother's room.

"Was Stryker here to see me?"

My mother's rigid needles kept moving.

"Yesterday, Frank," she answered.

"Well?" he breathed heavily.

"Judge Tatum appointed commissioners to condemn the land." My mother's lips were tight bands. "He told Mr. Stryker that no individual could stand in the way of progress and the railroad."

My father hadn't moved. My mother tried to leave the subject: "Did you settle the trouble with the Cross V's?"

"There was," my father answered harshly, "no trouble to settle."

"What do you mean?" For the first time she looked up at him.

"I mean," my father said, and now that he had started, the words poured out in a wild torrent, "that progress isn't above using the tricks of a blackleg gambler!" The green lightning had leaped from his eyes and at each successive sentence the bolt seemed to hurl itself again, as I had often watched it in a distant cloud, traversing over and over the same forked path. "There wasn't any sheep war. Nobody had beaten a herder. I didn't find a ewe touched. Somebody paid Gil Jaramillo to come here. They bribed him to lie to me. They had me drive hundreds of miles in a buggy and kill one of my best horses to keep me away from Judge Tatum's court!" Then he turned and went into his office.

I thought I could hear him moving about in his bedroom. There was a purr of wheels in the courtyard, and through the pane at the side of the door I saw Trinidad drive up in the red-wheeled buggy without a top.

My father came out almost immediately. He had changed his clothes, but the dust still clung to his beard and eyebrows. In his hand was the black-snake whip with which he had once whipped a herder for the arch crime of deserting his sheep, and I saw that the lash was still caked with dried particles of red.

"Frank!" my mother cried. She had run to her doorway. "Where are you going?"

He paid her utterly no attention. I don't think he knew she was there.

"Frank!" she screamed after him. "Whoever bribed Gil Jaramillo, it wasn't Vance Rutherford or the railroad! They wouldn't stoop to a thing like that!"

He went on out of the door. Never had I seen my mother move so rapidly. Her full skirts seemed to whisper in terror as they glided over the floor. Her hands seized my shoulder.

"Get him to take you with him!" she begged me. "He never does those violent things when you're along!" She pushed me out of the doorway and I saw the sun glinting on the sleek flanks of the dancing Kentucky team.

I ran to the right side, where the springs had already deeply settled.

"I want to go along, papa!" I shouted at him.

He looked down at me.

"You're sure you want to go along?" he asked, and at his mad eyes a chill ran down my spine, but I nodded. He told the impassive Trinidad to step out, and I climbed in beside him. Prince and Custer were crazy to be off. They had not been driven for days. One hand of my father pulled them back, rearing.

"Easy, boys," he said through his teeth and beard. "We'll have plenty time when we get there."

Crouching on the cushion, I told myself I couldn't see how trouble could happen on a day like this. The sky was a blue bowl and I could smell the freshness of last night's shower in the bunch grass all around us. Horned larks flushed in front of the horses. A road runner clowned at us, his crest and long tail rising and falling comically. But I did not laugh. Ahead, like a bed of mushrooms sprung up on the prairie, I could see the buildings of Capitan.

Halfway across the prairie something ran shining through the grass—the twin iron bands of the railroad. From here to Capitan they had built straight as an arrow, close beside the trail, as if to ridicule the earthy ruts, crude windings and arroyo dips of the sprawling old overland route. Here the railroad cut insolently over the trail, and the light buggy pitched on the rough planks of the crossing, but my father gave no sign that the railroad was there—not even when a wailing cry drifted over the prairie behind us and I knew without turning my head that the horizon must be stormy with smoke.

Within a mile or two the rails only a few yards from the trail were crackling. Our Kentucky buggy horses had grown uneasy and were trying to throw frightened looks over their shoulders, but my father held their heads with an iron hand. Twisting in my seat, I could see the afternoon sun sparkling on something that moved behind us, pursuing us, not galloping up and down like a buffalo, but gliding through the grass like a snake. The bulging smokestack was as high as the neck of a camel, the boiler as big as the belly of a horse, and below it a cowcatcher, long and pointed like Judge Tatum's nose, ran on its own pony wheels. A man rode in the cab that was as high off the ground as a buggy, and behind him streamed the coaches of the territory's celebration train.

I could hear a brass band in the cars now. It was playing "Dixie." Everything on the train was gaiety as it pulled beside us. Red, white and blue bunting fluttered from headlight, smokestack and whistle. The bell rang triumphantly. The small pony wheels spun. The black-and-gold driving shafts shot backward and forward. Faces pressed at the small, square windows, and on the open platforms of the short, boxlike coaches a few male passengers stood holding to iron railings and brake wheels. But for all the attention my father gave it, the train might not have been there.

So far the railroad and train had been slightly downhill. Now the train reached the foot of the steady prairie grade up to Capitan. The engine began to puff valiantly, and a cloud of cinders came flying back into our faces. Suddenly I realized that, although my father still sat like a bearded statue beside me, his thewlike fingers had let out some slack on the lines, and the long-denied horses were leaping.

I told myself it couldn't be a race, because my father wasn't racing. He just sat there deaf and unapproachable, but now I know that of all the matches between horseflesh and the iron horse that were to follow on the same rude course, this was the most intense and deadly in earnest. Heads began to appear out of the open car windows. Passengers waved, jeered and challenged. But the train no longer was moving faster than the buggy.

Suddenly something inside of me seemed to stand still. Peering round my father, I had caught a glimpse of a face at a car window. It was more of a lady's face than I had remembered, but the eyes under the nodding plumes were unchanged. They were fixed on my father with a look that I shall never forget, almost the look they had given him that day she had tiptoed into my mother's room two years before, a straining look of appeal that might almost have been at God. Only a matter of thirty or forty feet separated her from my father, but it might as well have been the width of Kansas. He did not turn. The horses raced on, and when I looked again, all I could see in the glass was the blurred reflection of prairie sky, and the face of Juliana had gone.

I had to keep bracing myself on the rocking cushion. The train beside us rode smoothly enough, almost contemptuously, over its new roadbed, but the buggy plunged from rut to pitch hole, and yet, window by window and now coach by coach, the buggy was gaining. Directly ahead I could make out a dense frieze of men's hats and ladies' parasols around the new depot. Nearer, on both sides of the railroad, the green plain blossomed with visiting tents and camp wagons. And now the trail just in front of us began to teem with American, Mexican and Indian spectators, who fell back whooping and shouting as we tore by.

I can still see Prince and Custer running, their heads outstretched, their manes wildly flinging, and at every jump the fine muscles on their hips appearing and disappearing like so many fingered hands. With both horses bent into shying half arcs, we breasted the laboring engine, passed it, left its bright flutter of bunting definitely behind us. And I told myself exultantly that my father had whipped the celebration train, humbled the railroad in front of half the territory. Then I saw ahead where the trail swerved sharply, and remembered that we had another crossing in store.

There was no necessity for my father to take it. He might have turned off the trail on the unfenced prairie. But my father never turned off the trail for anything, God or the devil, cruelty or mercy; so long as it lay squarely in his path, he knew no other justice. Leaning far to the side for the curve, he snatched the whip from its socket and the buggy reeled on two wheels for the crossing.

Through the din of the train I could hear the band playing magnificently. It sounded like "Columbia the Gem of the Ocean." High above it shrieked the voice of the engine whistling down brakes for the station. It seemed far enough away when it started, grew steadily louder, louder, till the sound seemed to split my ear. I saw my father drop the reins and felt him swing me up in his arms. There was a sound like chair legs crashing, and the blurred earth, engine, and the white faces of the engineer and frontier crowd turned over like the markings on a grindstone.

It wasn't exactly a pain in my back. I felt benumbed, as if an arrow pinned me down. My eyes seemed to be ground shut with dust and sand, and when I forced them open, I could see nothing but the dude hats of men who had come from the train and the gaily trimmed bonnets of the ladies all swimming around me in a kind of leisurely whirlwind.

Only one of the bonnets looked familiar. It was very near, fashioned with drooping plumes, and I knew that somewhere I had seen it before.

A portly man in a long coat with a velvet collar thrust a flask to my lips. I sputtered and strangled, but when I could breathe again, I felt better.

"Where's my father?" I asked them.

They all just stood there looking at me. I twisted my head and saw Vance Rutherford. He was close to me, a flower in his buttonhole, comforting Juliana, who was bitterly crying. When I closed my eyes I could still see my father sitting in the buggy beside me, aloof, powerful, absolute, his black beard turned stubbornly in the wind, the reins in his thewlike fingers. All these men from the train looked white and soft in comparison. They couldn't, I told myself, whip the bloody back of a herder who had broken the trust to his sheep. I wanted my father. One bark from his bearded lips, and most of this crowd would scurry like prairie dogs.

"Where'd he go?" I cried, and struggled to sit up. Vance Rutherford and the portly man helped me. The crowd fell back slightly. All I could see between tailored trousers and gaily flounced dresses were the iron bands of the railroad running triumphantly westward and glinting like mottled silver in the sun.

LESLIE SILKO

Lullaby

The sun had gone down but the snow in the wind gave off its own light. It came in thick tufts like new wool—washed before the weaver spins it. Ayah reached out for it like her own babies had, and she smiled when she remembered how she had laughed at them. She was an old woman now, and her life had become memories. She sat down with her back against the wide cottonwood tree, feeling the rough bark on her back bones; she faced east and listened to the wind and snow sing a high-pitched Yeibechei song. Out of the wind she felt warmer, and she could watch the wide fluffy snow fill in her tracks, steadily, until the direction she had come from was gone. By the light of the snow she could see the dark outline of the big arroyo a few feet away. She was sitting on the edge of Cebolleta Creek, where in the springtime the thin cows would graze on grass already chewed flat to the ground. In the wide deep creek bed where only a trickle of water flowed in the summer, the skinny cows would wander, looking for new grass along winding paths splashed with manure.

Ayah pulled the old army blanket over her head like a shawl. Jimmie's blanket—the one he had sent to her. That was a long time ago and the green wool was faded, and it was unraveling on the edges. She did not want to think about Jimmie. So she thought about the weaving and the way her mother had done it. On the tall wooden loom set into the sand under a tamarack tree for shade. She could see it

302

clearly. She had been only a little girl when her grandma gave her the wooden combs to pull the twigs and burrs from the raw, freshly washed wool. And while she combed the wool, her grandma sat beside her, spinning a silvery strand of yarn around the smooth cedar spindle. Her mother worked at the loom with yarns dyed bright yellow and red and gold. She watched them dye the yarn in boiling black pots full of beeweed petals, juniper berries, and sage. The blankets her mother made were soft and woven so tight that rain rolled off them like birds' feathers. Ayah remembered sleeping warm on cold windy nights, wrapped in her mother's blankets on the hogan's sandy floor.

The snow drifted now, with the northwest wind hurling it in gusts. It drifted up around her black overshoes—old ones with little metal buckles. She smiled at the snow which was trying to cover her little by little. She could remember when they had no black rubber overshoes; only the high buckskin leggings that they wrapped over their elk-hide moccasins. If the snow was dry or frozen, a person could walk all day and not get wet, and in the evenings the beams of the ceiling would hang with lengths of pale buckskin leggings, drying out slowly.

She felt peaceful remembering. She didn't feel cold anymore. Jimmie's blanket seemed warmer than it had ever been. And she could remember the morning he was born. She could remember whispering to her mother who was sleeping on the other side of the hogan, to tell her it was time now. She did not want to wake the others. The second time she called to her, her mother stood up and pulled on her shoes; she knew. They walked to the old stone hogan together. Ayah walking a step behind her mother. She waited alone, learning the rhythms of the pains while her mother went to call the old woman to help them. The morning was already warm even before dawn and Ayah smelled the bee flowers blooming and the young willow growing at the springs. She could remember that so clearly, but his birth merged into the births of the other children and to her it became all the same birth. They named him for the summer morning and in English they called him Jimmie.

It wasn't like Jimmie died. He just never came back, and one day a dark blue sedan with white writing on its doors pulled up in front of the boxcar shack where the rancher let the Indians live. A man in a khaki uniform trimmed in gold gave them a yellow piece of paper and told them that Jimmie was dead. He said the army would try to get the body back and then it would be shipped to them; but it wasn't likely because the helicopter had burned after it crashed. All of this was told to Chato because he could understand English. She stood inside the doorway holding the baby while Chato listened. Chato spoke English like a white man and he spoke Spanish too. He was taller than the white man and he stood straighter too. Chato didn't explain why: he just told the military man they could keep the body if they found it. The white man looked bewildered; he nodded his head and he left. Then Chato looked at her and shook his head. "Goddamn," he said in English, and then he told her "Jimmie isn't coming home anymore," and when he spoke, he used the words to speak of the dead. She didn't cry then, but she hurt inside with anger. And she mourned him as the years passed, when a horse fell with Chato and broke his leg, and the white rancher told them he wouldn't pay Chato until he could work again. She mourned Jimmie because he would have worked for his father then; he would have saddled the big bay horse and ridden the fence lines each day, with wire cutters and heavy gloves, fixing the breaks in the barbed wire and putting the stray cattle back inside again.

She mourned him after the white doctors came to take Danny and Ella away. She was at the shack alone that day when they came. It was back in the days before they hired Navajo women to go with them as interpreters. She recognized one of the doctors. She had seen him at the children's clinic at Cañoncito about a month ago. They were wearing khaki uniforms and they waved papers at her and a black ball-point pen, trying to make her understand their English words. She was frightened by the way they looked at the children, like the lizard watches the fly. Danny was swinging on the tire swing in the elm tree behind the rancher's house, and Ella was toddling around the front door, dragging the broomstick horse Chato made for her. Ayah could see they wanted her to sign the papers, and Chato had taught her to sign her name. It was something she was proud of. She only wanted them to go, and to take their eyes away from her children.

She took the pen from the man without looking at his face and she signed the papers in three different places he pointed to. She stared at the ground by their feet and waited for them to leave. But they stood there and began to point and gesture at the children. Danny stopped swinging. Ayah could see his face. She moved suddenly and grabbed Ella into her arms; the child squirmed, trying to get back to her toys. Ayah ran with the baby toward Danny; she screamed for him to run and then she grabbed him around his chest and carried him too. She ran south into the foothills of juniper trees and black lava rock. Behind her she heard the doctors running, but they had been taken by surprise, and as the hills became steeper and the cholla cactus were thicker, they stopped. When she reached the top of the hill, she stopped too to listen in case they were circling around her. But in a few minutes she heard a car engine start and they drove away. The children had been too surprised to cry while she ran with them. Danny was shaking and Ella's little fingers were gripping Ayah's blouse.

She stayed up in the hills for the rest of the day, sitting on a black lava boulder in the sunshine where she could see for miles all around her. The sky was light blue and cloudless, and it was warm for late April. The sun warmth relaxed her and took the fear and anger away. She lay back on the rock and watched the sky. It seemed to her that she could walk into the sky, stepping through clouds endlessly. Danny played with little pebbles and stones, pretending they were birds, eggs and then little rabbits. Ella sat at her feet and dropped fistfuls of dirt into the breeze, watching the dust and particles of sand intently. Ayah watched a hawk soar high above them, dark wings gliding; hunting or only watching, she did not know. The hawk was patient and he circled all afternoon before he disappeared around the high volcanic peak the Mexicans call Guadalupe.

Late in the afternoon, Ayah looked down at the gray boxcar shack with the paint all peeled from the wood; the stovepipe on the roof was rusted and crooked. The fire she had built that morning in the oil-drum stove had burned out. Ella was asleep in her lap now and Danny sat close to her, complaining that he was hungry; he asked when they would go to the house. "We will stay up here until your father comes," she told him, "because those white men were chasing us." The boy remembered then and he nodded at her silently.

If Jimmie had been there he could have read those papers and explained to her what they said. Ayah would have known, then, never to sign them. The doctors came back the next day and they brought a BIA policeman with them. They told Chato they had her signature and that was all they needed. Except for the kids. She listened to Chato sullenly; she hated him when he told her it was the old woman who died in the winter, spitting blood; it was her old grandma who had given the children this disease. "They don't spit blood," she said coldly. "The whites lie." She held Ella and Danny close to her, ready to run to the hills again. "I want a medicine man first," she said to Chato, not looking at him. He shook his head. "It's too late now. The policeman is with them. You signed the paper." His voice was gentle.

It was worse than if they had died; to lose the children and to know that somewhere, in a place called Colorado, in a place full of sick and dying strangers, her children were without her. There had been babies that died soon after they were born, and one that died before he could walk. She had carried them herself, up to the boulders and great pieces of the cliff that long ago crashed down from Long Mesa; she laid them in the crevices of sandstone and buried them in fine brown sand with round quartz pebbles that washed down from the hills in the rain. She had endured it because they had been with her. But she could not bear this pain. She did not sleep for a long time after they took her children. She stayed on the hill where they had fled the first time, and she slept rolled up in the blanket Jimmie had sent her. She carried the pain in her belly and it was fed by everything she saw; the blue sky of their last day together and the dust and pebbles they played with; the swing in the elm tree and broomstick horse chocked life from her. The pain filled her stomach and there was no room for food or for her lungs to fill with air. The air and the food would have been theirs.

She hated Chato, not because he let the policeman and doctors put the screaming children in the government car, but because he had taught her to sign her name. Because it was like the old ones always told her about learning their language or any of their ways; it endangered you. She slept alone on the hill until the middle of November when the first snows came. Then she made a bed for herself where the children had slept. She did not lay down beside Chato again until many years later, when he was sick and shivering and only her body could keep him warm. The illness came after the white rancher told Chato he was too old to work for him any more, and Chato and his old woman should be out of the shack by the next afternoon because the rancher had hired new people to work there. That had satisfied her. To see how the white man repaid Chato's years of loyalty and work. All of Chato's fine-sounding English talk didn't change things.

II

It snowed steadily and the luminous light from the snow gradually diminished into the darkness. Somewhere in Cebolleta a dog barked and other village dogs joined with it. Ayah looked in the direction she had come, from the bar where Chato was buying the wine. Sometimes he told her to go on ahead and wait; and then he never came. And when she finally went back looking for him, she would find him passed out at the bottom of the wooden steps to Azzie's Bar. All the wine would be gone and most of the money too, from the pale blue check that came to them once a month in a government envelope. It was then that she would look at his face and his hands, scarred by ropes and the barbed wire of all those years, and she would think "this man is a stranger;" for 40 years she had smiled at him and cooked his food, but he remained a stranger. She stood up again, with the snow almost to her knees, and she walked back to find Chato.

It was hard to walk in the deep snow and she felt the air burn in her lungs. She stopped a short distance from the bar to rest and readjust the blanket. But this time he wasn't waiting for her on the bottom step with his old Stetson hat pulled down and his shoulders hunched up in his long wool overcoat.

She was careful not to slip on the wooden steps. When she pushed the door open, warm air and cigarette smoke hit her face. She looked around slowly and deliberately, in every corner, in every dark place that the old man might find to sleep. The bar-owner didn't like Indians in there, especially Navajos, but he let Chato come in because he could talk Spanish like he was one of them. The men at the bar stared at her, and the bartender saw that she left the door open wide. Snowflakes were flying inside like moths and melting into a puddle on the oiled wood floor. He motioned at her to close the door, but she did not see him. She held herself straight and walked across the room slowly, searching the room with every step. The snow in her hair melted and she could feel it on her forehead. At the far corner of the room, she saw red flames at the mica window of the old stove door; she looked behind the stove just to make sure. The bar got quiet except for the Spanish polka music playing on the jukebox. She stood by the stove and shook the snow from her blanket and held it near the stove to dry. The wet wool smell reminded her of new-born goats in early March, brought inside to warm near the fire. She felt calm.

In past years they would have told her to get out. But her hair was white now and her face was wrinkled. They looked at her like she was a spider crawling slowly across the room. They were afraid; she could feel the fear. She looked at their faces steadily. They reminded her of the first time the white people brought her children back to her that winter. Danny had been shy and hid behind the thin white woman who brought them. And the baby had not known her until Ayah took her into her arms, and then Ella had nuzzled close to her as she had when she was nursing. The blonde woman was nervous and kept looking at a dainty gold watch on her wrist. She sat on the bench near the small window and watched the dark snow clouds gather around the mountains; she was worrying about the unpaved road. She was frightened by what she saw inside too; the strips of venison drying on a rope across the ceiling and the children jabbering excitedly in a language she did not know. So they stayed for only a few hours. Ayah watched the government car disappear down the road and she knew they were already being weaned from these lava hills and from this sky. The last time they came was in early June, and Ella stared at her the way the men in the bar were now staring. Ayah did not try to pick her up; she smiled at her instead and spoke cheerfully to Danny. When he tried to answer her, he could not seem to remember and he spoke English words with the Navajo. But he gave her a scrap of paper that he had found somewhere and carried in his pocket; it was folded in half, and he shyly looked up at her and said it was a bird. She asked Chato if they were home for good this time. He spoke to the white woman and she shook her head. "How much longer," he asked, and she said she didn't know; but Chato saw how she stared at the boxcar shack. Ayah turned away then. She did not say good-bye.

III

She felt satisfied that the men in the bar feared her. Maybe it was her face and the way she held her mouth with teeth clenched tight, like there was nothing anyone could do to her now. She walked north down the road, searching for the old man. She did this because she had the blanket, and there would be no place for him except with her and the blanket in the old adobe barn near the arroyo. They always slept there when they came to Cebolleta. If the money and the wine were gone, she would be relieved because then they could go home again; back to the old hogan with a dirt roof and rock walls where she herself had been born. And the next day the old man could go back to the few sheep they still had, to follow along behind them, guiding them into dry sandy arroyos where sparse grass grew. She knew he did not like walking behind old ewes when for so many years he rode big quarter horses and worked with cattle. But she wasn't sorry for him; he should have known all along what would happen.

There had not been enough rain for their garden in five years; and that was when Chato finally hitched a ride into the town and brought back brown boxes of rice and sugar and big tin cans of welfare peaches. After that, at the first of the month they went to Cebolleta to ask the postmaster for the check; and then Chato would go to the bar and cash it. They did this as they planted the garden every May, not because anything would survive the summer dust, but because it was time to do this. And the journey passed the days that smelled silent and dry like the caves above the canyon with yellow painted buffaloes on their walls.

IV

He was walking along the pavement when she found him. He did not stop or turn around when he heard her behind him. She walked beside him and she noticed how slowly he moved now. He smelled strong of woodsmoke and urine. Lately he had been forgetting. Sometimes he called her by his sister's name and she had been gone for a long time. Once she had found him wandering on the road to the white man's ranch, and she asked him why he was going that way; he laughed at her and said "You know they can't run that ranch without me," and he walked on determined, limping on the leg that had been crushed many years before. Now he looked at her curiously, as if for the first time, but he kept shuffling along, moving slowly along the side of the highway. His gray hair had grown long and spread out on the shoulders of the long overcoat. He wore the old felt hat pulled down over his ears. His boots were worn out at the toes and he had stuffed pieces of an old red shirt in the holes. The rags made his feet look like little animals up to their ears in snow. She laughed at his feet; the snow muffled the sound of her laugh. He stopped and looked at her again. The wind had quit blowing and the snow was falling straight down; the southeast sky was beginning to clear and Ayah could see a star.

"Let's rest awhile," she said to him. They walked away from the road and up the slope to the giant boulders that had tumbled down from the red sandrock mesa throughout the centuries of rainstorms and earth tremors. In a place where the boulders shut out the wind, they sat down with their backs against the rock. She offered half of the blanket to him and they sat wrapped together.

The storm passed swiftly. The clouds moved east. They were massive and full, crowding together across the sky. She watched them with the feeling of horses—steely blue-gray horses startled across the sky. The powerful haunches pushed into the distances and the tail hairs streamed white mist behind them. The sky cleared. Ayah saw that there was nothing between her and the stars. The light was crystalline. There was no shimmer, no distortion through earth haze. She breathed the clarity of the night sky; she smelled the purity of the half moon and the stars. He was lying on his side with his knees pulled up near his belly for warmth. His eyes were closed now, and in the light from the stars and the moon, he looked young again.

She could see it descend out of the night sky; an icy stillness from the edge of the thin moon. She recognized the freezing. It came gradually, sinking snowflake by snowflake until the crust was heavy and deep. It had the strength of the stars in Orion, and its journey was endless. Ayah knew that with the wine he would sleep. He would not feel it. She tucked the blanket around him, remembering how it was when Ella had been with her; and she felt the rush so big inside her heart for the babies. And she sang the only song she knew to sing for babies. She could not remember if she had

ever sung it to her children, but she knew that her grandmother had sung it and her mother had sung it:

> *The earth is your mother,*
>   *she holds you.*
> *The sky is your father,*
>   *he protects you.*
> *sleep,*
> *sleep,*
> *Rainbow is your sister,*
>   *she loves you.*
> *The winds are your brothers,*
>   *they sing to you.*
> *sleep,*
> *sleep,*
> *We are together always*
> *We are together always*
> *There never was a time*
> *when this*
> *was not so.*

C. W. SMITH

The Plantation Club

Curtis "Stoogie" Goodman stepped off the bus in our town with an alto sax and a suitcase of uniform remnants from a band which had collapsed in El Paso. Like our Chicano-migrants-turned-residents and redneck roustabouts, he stopped to recoup the means to move on and never made it. Mornings he washed dishes at the Winslow Café. Three nights a week he played at The Plantation, a nightclub in our small black ghetto.

Windowless but for the portholes head-high along the front, the club had the air of a steamboat long since dry-docked and crumbling. A plantation scene embellished the expanse of stucco above the portholes—a cotton patch with an Aunt Jemima at its border, a veranda where a colonel with a cigar chatted with a brace of belles whose parasols formed pastel nimbuses behind their curls. The street in front of the club was washboard sand littered with shards of glass—here black whores meandered along the shoulders. We Junior classmen cruised this block with only a driver visible and three or four others huddled on the floorboards.

"Hey, wheah you goin' boy?"

"Lookin' for some poontang!"

"You lookin' right at it!"

"How much?"

"They's different kinds!"

"I like it hot and greasy, Mama!"

312

"Lawd! You don't look that rich!"

Then we'd all spring upright, cackle yah-yah-yah, and leave a wash of sand spray to flap her skirt as we sped away, victors again, but over what we never knew. Cute, huh? After they started calling us "Cig-uh-RET Pee-tuhs" we didn't harass them as much.

Maybe that's why we didn't hear Stoogie until the summer before our Senior year in 1957 when Terry and I decided a little banter could liven up the night. With two of us the game was limited to an exchange that stalemated when we had to put up or shut up, but it beat going into orbit around the Sonic Dog, and we had already spent an hour on the main drag looking for that mythical nymphomaniac we dreamed would pull up in her Caddy convertible and bare her tits.

Drifting slowly by The Plantation, we heard an alto rise into melancholy flight on the opening bars of "Round Midnight." Confused, I thought I was hearing a record, but even that would have been a marvel: my gods—"The Bird," John Coltrane, Sonny Stitt, Sonny Rollins, Stan Getz, Cannonball Adderly—were so obscure in my town that to ask for an album by one at the music store was like asking for the latest from The Outer Mongolian Preschool Rhythm Band and Chorus in Concert. We had stumbled onto jazz via "Moonglow with Martin" on WWL in New Orleans, and we had spent countless nights since riding in our parents' cars listening to music such as we had never dreamed existed broadcast from some twelve hundred miles away by crow-fly and a century or so by cultural disposition to our remote corner of New Mexico. Barely a decade out of its boom, our overgrown crossroad had a ragged, honky-tonk energy, but it was cowboy country, and we had begun to feel misplaced in it, practitioners of an alien religion.

Terry stopped the car. We heard the opening phrase repeated with a minor variation in the fifth bar, the sound not exactly angry but anguished; midnight was a dark sponge soaking up every man's hope and illusion. Maybe that's too heavy, but we were stunned.

"You boys lookin' for somethin'?"

"No thanks," Terry said. He hooked a thumb toward the club. "Say, who's playing in there?"

"Buncha niggers, I'd say," the woman cracked over her shoulder as she strolled off.

Buncha niggers. We parked across the street and listened to that alto do its tricks on "C-Jam Blues" (a flimsy excuse to take a dozen choruses), "How High the Moon," "A-Train," "Blackbird," and three boogie-shuffle blues each in a different key. Now and then a black face poked its way into our vision, but we made no offers, asked no questions, and sat for an hour astonished that such a sound existed so far from either coast.

A long silence, then four men came out a side door at the rear of the building. Guessing them to be the group, we decided to brave asking if we could listen inside. As we walked toward the club, we got nervous. Our town was relatively peaceful; our schools had integrated soon after the Brown decision without much flap save a plethora of hysterical sermons delivered on the eve of the Apocalypse by our good Baptist brethren, but this wasn't our turf. The uncharted territory around the building hid conspirators whose razors flashed at the corners of my eyes. But—hell!—wasn't I safe? Hadn't I once shocked my Tennessee relatives by shaking hands with a waiter at their country club? Justice always saw that the pure-hearted were protected and that bigots got their due. . . .

We came up to the men at the door. In the dimness they were only vague shapes, but soon features emerged which I'd come to know well over the next year: R.B., the huge, affable drummer who worked days loading blocks of ice onto waiting trucks and who had been a Golden Gloves heavyweight champ; Candy, the piano man, a small Mescalero-Apache with a cataract on his left eye; Scratchmo, the eldest, with a thicket of wiry gray hair around his face, who spat tobacco into a coffee can perched atop the amplifier of his guitar, who always wore a red woolen shirt (hence the name) under faded denim overalls, and who displayed a perpetual half-smirk so ambivalent that even a year later I hadn't learned to decipher it; and Stoogie, a caramel-colored man whose baggy eyelids drooped as though he was forever on the verge of sleep—and who now lounged against the building with one sole flat against the wall, his cigarette an orange arc as he raised it to his lips.

"Hey, you guys are really good!" Terry declared. "We've been out in the car digging your jazz!"

Scratchmo turned and spat a gob of Beechnut juice onto

the sand behind him. "Hear that, Stoogie? These boys been digging our jazz."

Stoogie didn't straighten from his slump; only a flicker of his drooping eyelids suggested he was conscious of us.

"It's in the air," he muttered. He pushed away from the wall and headed back inside the building, followed by Candy and Scratchmo. R.B. hung back.

"Ya'll not old enough to drink, are you?"

"No sir," I mumbled.

"Haw!" He ducked his head toward the door and winked. "Anybody ask, you say you're with R.B., hear?"

Grateful, we scurried in behind him. The interior of the club smelled of beer and stale smoke; the crowd filled the intermission lull with loud talk and laughter. Trying not to lollygag, we aped the pose of jaded nightlife connoisseurs as we threaded our way through the occupied tables. Sitting just before the bandstand with our backs to the dance floor, we watched Stoogie ease down into a metal folding chair and pull his alto out of its open case. It was silver; I knew it had to be a Strad of saxes—a jazz counterpart to Jascha Heifetz would need a "fine" instrument—but soon I found out it was a crappy axe, one of the worst. The soft metal keys were always bending, which kept the pads from seating properly on their holes, and it was so out of tune with itself that Stoogie had to adjust each note with his ear and embouchure as he played. It was his tenth horn in as many years—he was broke so often that hocking them was his only resort; he could never keep one very long, though his metal Otto Link mouthpiece had been carried from one to the next.

Sagging in his chair like a sack of grain, Stoogie swung the sax on the pivot of his thumb with the Otto Link homing on his mouth; he waited, then at the last millisecond he parted his lips, snapped the mouthpiece in his jaws, and clamped his lips around it, a gesture faintly reminiscent of the end of conflict between a cobra and a mongoose. As he descended into "Summertime," a reedy edge serrated the contours of his voice, and he cut into the melody as if easing a knife into the jugular of a drowsy hog. The "high cotton" and "easy livin'" in the lyrics would seem to call for waltz-time on a banjo, but the melody contains more than a whiff of danger and despair, and Stoogie's first chorus ripped that disparity completely apart—his "summertime" was a stoop where junkies nodded, an alley where dark promises were kept.

Mouth agape, I gawked while phrases blossomed from the bell of his horn; but he might have been asleep, he was so still except for his hands. We sat five feet away, feeling faint huffs of breath from the horn, the strain of melody and improvised line as tangible as a string of sausages in the air before us. He began to sweat and his cheeks bellowed as he finished his fourth chorus and began working seriously to sign his name across the face of the tune. The dancers were warming up too, waving and whooping "Yaah!" as though his solo was the last-lap turn in an evangelical sermon. Had I looked around, I might have recognized them as the minor actors in the dramas played out by the oil-rich whites in town—janitors, maids, junkmen, yard boys, shine boys, dishwashers, and short order cooks—but I was too dazed to notice.

On the fifth chorus the line began to rise, and the tinge of bitterness which had colored his voice turned lighter as he explored the changes. Stoogie had, to backtrack on a metaphor, worked his way up from those fetid stoops, through the tenement and onto the roof, where he could lie on his back to watch winking lights of planes glide by like comets, silent, the engines lost in the muffled thrum from the street below, and beyond those arcing pinpoints a haze of stars appeared dimly through a scrim of reflected city light. Escape. For the moment.

When he was through, Scratchmo broke into laughter. "That's all right, man! All *right!*"

Stoogie acknowledged all the clapping and whistles from the audience with a nod but gave no sign he was pleased with himself.

"Man, I gotta get on the elevator," he said to Scratchmo. He got up, slowly, trudged off the stand and out the side door. The trio went into "Rock Me, Baby, All Night Long," with Scratchmo doing a passable imitation of Big Joe Williams.

After the gig, the quartet went separate ways, but before the club closed we bought R.B. a beer and pumped him for information. Stoogie had grown up on Chicago's South Side, dropped out of the eighth grade to make a temporary flight from the ghetto with a rhythm-and-blues band, married at eighteen, lost his wife to a pimp and gave up their child for adoption, took up with another woman who O.D.'d on heroin, spent a hitch in the navy, then drifted along the California coast playing in clubs and working menial day-jobs; he hit the bigtime briefly as a sideman with Billy Eckstine's band, but in New York he was swamped by squalor and bad luck—busted, he served a two-year sentence for possession of marijuana. Man! I thought. Stoogie's really paid some dues! Terry and I were unscathed by divorce, disfigurement, or poverty; our mothers made sure we got fresh vegetables and clean underwear, and our fathers had taught us how to shake hands and use hammers, pull triggers and paddle canoes. Our greatest living enemy was neither want nor oppression but the rampant rashes of acne which came with the chocolate orgies we indulged in and which we tried to banish with soaps and creams and a half-hour spent harvesting the night's crop at the mirror before dashing off to school feeling like living exhibitions of open, running sores. My greatest sorrow to date was having lost my first love to another at age fifteen.

Sooner or later I'd be in luck and some tragedy would really scar me. In the meantime, I'd have to settle for working on technique. We showed up at The Plantation every weekend night, and after a while we talked the group into letting us bring our horns. We would scrunch down against the back wall of the bandstand and try to hit the vein with the needle as the quarter roared away, creating a very soft but discordant clarinet-and-trumpet duet under them which must have sounded like an untuned radio to anyone out front. Now and then Stoogie'd lean back in his chair and say, "Go watch Candy's hand," and we'd tiptoe across to peer over Candy's shoulder as his left hand graphed out the changes to the tune. Or he'd say, "Harmony!" telling us to play a series of whole notes with the changes. It never occurred to me then, but this suggestion often came before one of his solos, so not only would our harmony give him support, it also kept him from having to contend with a lot of gobbling going on behind his back. Sometimes during Scratchmo's or Candy's solos, he'd lean over and play a simple riff and nod his head to get us to pick up that line, then he'd break into another parallel to it and nod again for one of us to imitate the second, so that when he soloed, he'd have a rocking good chorus of two lines behind him.

But I hated clarinet. I'd begun on it in the fifth grade, used it during my brief Dixieland phase, and had endured the agonies of marching and concert band with it, but I'd resolved six months before meeting Stoogie that I had to have a sax, the axe my heroes played. My parents had agreed to provide a matching grant. I had saved my wages from working after school and on Saturdays delivering pianos, earning a well-deserved reputation as a cheapskate date, and once in a while Terry and I had played dances in schools around the area. The horn had been on order for a month after I had been going to the club, and I had driven the owner of the store nuts asking about it daily.

.When it came, my alto was a brilliant gold hookah asleep in a red velvet pouf. A gen-yew-ine Selmer Mark VI, axe of the gods—*Downbeat* said so! With it I'd wail my way into Birdland with Kenton or Maynard or Art Blakey; I'd be on Ed Sullivan wailing away with my own Big Band and the girl who'd left me would eat her goddamn heart out! Move over, Sonny Rollins! Bite the dust, John Coltrane! A new star had risen!

When I fingered the keys, a soft *poomp* said they seated perfectly on their holes, the pristine leather pads the color of sand. The horn smelled of polish and oil and cork grease, and I gave it a good going over with beady eyes not so much to inspect it but to lay claim on it. I found a deep scratch in the lacquer under the low C key which wouldn't disappear when I rubbed it, so I decided to ignore it.

I was dying to show it off. But driving alone to the club—Terry had the flu—I began feeling as uneasy as I had felt excited. The worst player in town had a Selmer Mark VI, the best player had a Brand X nickel-plated monster. I kept assuring myself that I had worked like hell to scrape up half the cost and tried to forget that my parents had coughed up the other $200.

Looking it over, Stoogie didn't seem to begrudge my owning it. He advised exchanging the "legitimate" mouthpiece which had come with the horn for something like his Otto Link, which he slipped from his horn and secured onto the bit of mine after I had invited him to try it out. When he blew a few scales, I heard the Stoogie-sound with a new perimeter—rounder, more solid, its circumference laced with a fretwork of brass.

"Wow!" He shook his head. "Been a long time, man!" He blew a few more licks, pleased at how his phrases took to the air without much drag. "It's sure easy." He played to low Bb and above high F for notes I didn't know existed on the saxophone. "Man," he breathed, "this is a nice axe."

"Go ahead and play it," I offered quickly when he started to hand it back.

When the first set began, his solos contained new dimensions, but I was too lost in my skull to study them. He was playing MY horn, and MY horn sounded fantastic! Great music was being made on my horn and that gave me hope, as though his improvised lines would stick to the lining of the horn to be unpeeled by my breath. As they played on, I felt that after Stoogie had sort of primed the horn like a handpump on a waterwell, all I had to do was stick it in my mouth, take a breath, and—zoom—out would come phrases as rich, juicy, and evocative as Stoogie's! (No matter that in my bedroom I had gotten nothing but squawks, even though the fingering was similar to my clarinet's.) I got itchy to try it out.

But Stoogie wasn't in a hurry to turn it over. One tune led to another; a half-hour went by, then an hour—Stoogie's enjoyment spread to the others, and they began playing into break-time with no desire at all to quit.

What if he couldn't stop playing it? Refused to? On the dance floor, Friday night's drunks were whooping and hollering, and I looked too long at them—wow! I was the only white person there! Although a veil was actually descending over the scene, I could have sworn one was lifting, one composed of my delusion that we were all asshole buddies of the blue note. The hoisted veil revealed all these . . . niggers rocking and jumping, and one named Curtis Goodman was going to steal my goddamned brand-new Selmer Mark VI! I just knew that when they finished the set and I asked for the horn, he'd give me a dumb, droopy-eyed look and say, *Huh? You shoah talkin' some trash, white boy!* I'd treat it like a joke and say, Aw shit, Stoogie! Come on, man, let me try it out! *Hey Scratchmo! Who the fuck's this white boy callin' me Stoogie and jivin' about my axe, huh?* And Scratchmo would guffaw, slap his knee, then turn his sinister gaze to within an inch of my face and say, *Hey, boy! You'd best scat before I cut you three ways—wide, deep and quite frequently!* God! How could I prove the horn was mine? That scratch under the C key?

Miserable, I missed what was probably Stoogie's finest work in years, to judge by how everyone carried on when they broke after the set.

"Whew! That's a fine, fine horn," Stoogie said when he

handed it to me. "You better learn how to blow it." Humbled, I accepted the compliment to the horn and the proverbial boot from teacher to student with a nod. But when I took the horn and slipped the hook of the neckstrap through the holding hole, the horn hung from my neck like a gaudy brass albratross, so heavy I could hardly stand.

I begged off and slunk away. Driving home, I could feel my ears burning. How could I ever do justice to this horn that lay on the backseat of my parents' Ford like hot loot from a burglary? Only by practice could I earn the right to play it. And in return for those unofficial lessons I had taken for granted from Stoogie, I'd . . . save him. It wasn't fair that this black Paganini had to wash dishes at the Winslow Café. I'd talk the city fathers into making him an Honorary Mayor or an Artist in Residence! I'd find him a good gig where nobody would be allowed to request "San Antonio Rose" or "Anniversary Waltz." I'd get all the young musicians in town to chip in to buy him a Mark VI; I'd find a way to get the group on record. . . .

Every morning thereafter my horn reached my mouth when my feet hit the floor, much to my family's dismay. I bought an Otto Link. I got to school early enough to have a half-hour warmup before band, then I'd sneak away from study hall to the bandroom and remain there during lunch hour. I took the horn to work after school so that between deliveries I could play in the stockroom. After work, I'd play before supper, then until bedtime I blew scales, riffs I had learned from Stoogie, arpeggios from my Universal-Prescott book, improvisation exercises with my Music Minus One records, hot licks from my *Jimmy Dorsey One Hundred Hot Licks* book until, with a pair of chops hanging on my mouth like the limp fingers of rubber gloves, I'd put the horn up for the day.

At last I got to solo. A Saturday night and, as they used to say, the joint was jumping. The band had condescended to do "The Hucklebuck," and the air was charged with lascivious electricity as people bucked their huckles. R.B. started hammering out a stripper's beat with cymbal and bass drum crashes on 2 and 4; Stoogie, just returned from taking the elevator, was grinning so hard he could only play greasy honks. He looked back at us and jerked his head toward the mike: Get on up here, one of you!

Heart thudding, my hands suddenly slick and my armpits

spewing out a deluge, I stumbled toward the mike while the quartet vamped changes. My brain whirled to map out my melodic strategy, trying to recall the notes in those three simple chords—going about soloing like building a gun rack from a plan in *Popular Mechanics*. I reached the mike, stuck the mouthpiece between my quivering jaws, blew an A in the upper register and held it. Somebody on the dance floor said, "Yeah!" Though I'm sure now it was in reply to something like "Ain't he awful?" which mercifully, I hadn't heard, I dreamed that my A was really turning them on; I thanked my lucky stars for finding it and hung onto it, pausing only for breath. Along about bar eleven, I saw that I couldn't get away with taking another chorus with that A—it was weird, if not monotonous, and Scratchmo would jibe me all night about my two-chorus whole note. Something stunning in contrast was called for, a Yin to the first chorus's Yang, and the solution came in a flash—if I played enough notes, I was bound to get some right ones in; people would hear those and pick out their own melodic line from the heap of assorted phrases I would toss onto the air like articles on a clearance table in a bargain basement. And if I played fast enough, the clinkers would pass undetected.

It's a blessing no one was cruel enough to have taped that second chorus; I believe I played through the entire Universal-Prescott book in those twelve bars. I left enough "melodies" tangled in the air that an academy of musicologists could have devoted a lifetime to unballing them and still couldn't see through the skein of noise above the bandstand. But I had lost my musical cherry; I could survive that stretch of sound-time, and though I was terrible, I knew I couldn't get worse.

We had come to know the players in a western swing band at a local honky tonk and found that they too were jazz buffs, though their axes wouldn't have suggested it. Gradually I was getting a picture—musicians were poor outcasts given to fits of insanity; they had vices ranging from perversions to narcotics to alcohol; they were—in a word—outlaws. We tried to develop the Outlaw Outlook as a means of shedding our old skins. We began to imagine that The Plantation was our club and that we were inconspicuous there, though how we thought two white children in sunglasses and berets could have gone unnoticed among two hundred blacks is a testament to our innocence. At school, Terry and I went about laden with props—cigarette holders a la Dizzy Gillespie, *Downbeat* tucked under our arms. We jived along in a slouch, eyelids drooping, talking hiptalk, feeling more and more alienated from our classmates' concern for ball games and proms. We gave each other skin, we snapped our fingers and sang complicated scat riffs in those syllables the uninitiated find so strange. We quickly became insufferable, and that only ossified our belief that we were cool. I took to calling everyone, even my mother, "man." These were years when moustaches adorned only the upper lips of black pimps, Mexican revolutionaries, Italian barbers, and jazz musicians, and we were the only two persons in our school to sport them, save for Glenneta Price. Mine was probably no thicker or darker than hers and occasionally I had to sneak my mother's eyeliner to give those fine brown hairs a blacking. Terry was also working on a goatee, seven or eight hairs about two inches long which stuck out from his chin and curled into springs.

Part of the myth of Jazz Star required that we be out of our skulls as much as possible, so during the spring months we drank a good deal more than we really wanted to. We downed innumerable cases of beer and fifths of bourbon before settling down to the wine of the people, Thunderbird. Once when Woody Herman played a one-nighter in town, Terry and I each drank a quart of Listerine—definitely not recommended!—and wound up spraying the restroom with medicinal-smelling puke. How were we going to play jazz without paying any dues?

Inevitably we got more curious about Stoogie's dope. We saw it as a must for every Jazz Star's prop locker. Besides washing dishes and playing at The Plantation to keep his household—a Chicana and her four children—together, Stoogie also watered greens at the golf course on weeknights. He was growing his own stuff in a nearby pasture and was looking forward to a bountiful harvest come the fall. He worked out of a shed on a far boundary of the grounds, and sometimes we'd go out there, perch on fertilizer sacks, and listen to "Moonglow" on a portable radio while he made his rounds changing sprinklers. Stoogie had never offered us any of his homegrown. But neither had he forbidden it, so once when he was out on the course we smoked a joint. When he found us collapsed on the floor, giggling, he said, "You just best be sure when you walkin' on clouds you don't trip over the

Man." Point made—we sobered some and ended up at the Sonic Dog ordering triple-decker banana splits, tripping on the lights, and smothering the sillies with sleeves pressed against our mouths. Just your ordinary goofy high-school high.

We had few delusions about the effect of cannabis on our playing; we had heard Stoogie play stoned and the only difference I could tell was that he preferred ballads because they gave him time to think, and occasionally we'd heard him unable to quit grinning. Naturally, we had to try it, and we badgered Stoogie into letting us take the elevator with him at the club. While my notes felt good when they entered the warm, furry hollows of my ears, I lost track of the count, the meter, the changes, and the number of choruses. The distinct possibility was that I sounded very, very bad, which Scratchmo confirmed when I finished a solo and asked him how many choruses I had played—thinking about three—and he snorted, "How many fleas on a coon dog's ass?"

But it did wonders for our self-esteem. We became walking Hip Happenings:

A beatnik is standing on a streetcorner when all at once there's a terrific crash as a bus and a truck collide. In the aftermath, people are lying in the street wailing and moaning. A little old lady runs up to the beatnik: "You've got to do something, young man!" Beatnik, snapping his fingers: "I am, man—I'm humming the changes."

Not one of our peers understood that the beatnik was stoned. By August, as we got ready to attend the Berkeley School of Music, we had become unspeakably With It. One night Terry and I got stoned at his crib while we were digging some sides, and when I had to split, the mirror showed me two swollen orbs with a reddish wash against a yellow background. I'd walked over there and I'd have to walk home. Very cleverly, I decided to carry an empty beer can. As I floated home, I smirked—six months prior to this I would've been peeing my pants to think that the Man would catch me with illegal booze, and now here I was—practically a junkie no less!—using it as a decoy. Too much! Buoyant with self-discovery, I bopped along, humming the changes.

The crash came one night later. Caught red-handed

(green-handed?) by two white patrolmen outside the back door of the club after the gig, Stoogie and I and Terry were whisked to the station and separated for questioning before we could gather our wits.

"That colored boy sell you those two sticks of marijuana?"

"No sir!"

Sgt. Cheney was seated behind the Chief's desk. He peeled off the wrapper on a Snicker and bit into it.

"How'd they come to be in your shirt pocket?"

"Nobody sold them to me, I swear!"

The Snicker disappeared like a square turd returning to its point of origin.

"Thadwuddenwhhusss."

"Sir?"

He crushed the wrapper into a ball and pleased himself by scoring in the trash can.

"That wasn't what I asked."

My noncommunication games were having a short shelf life. Though Sgt. Cheney had proved himself to be a boor over the previous twenty minutes, he knew a nonanswer when he heard one. But the primary rule of antiaircraft gunnery is to keep throwing flak until you hit.

"Well, sir, we'd never tried any and we were just curious about it, you know, so we only smoked a little bit and decided we didn't want any more of it, and I really didn't like it much to tell the truth, and I don't think I'd ever do it again." As I squirmed in the hard wooden chair, the beret wadded in my hip pocket pressed into my left ham. The instant we had been busted, I had slipped my sunglasses into my shirt pocket; I had lost my cigarette holder in the patrol car, and, props gone, I could feel an older self rising to the surface—the youth whose classmates had elected him City Manager for a Day; the Boy Scout of some distinction; the son of decent, tax-paying citizens and church members; the promising debater and the best civics student Miss Hall ever had. I kept blinking—man, this couldn't be happening! We had meant harm to none, our destinies as Jazz Stars had already been mapped out and the supplies laid by—it would be grossly injust to have all that interrupted for such a stupid reason as having two joints in my shirt pocket. But Sgt. Cheney's glare was very real, and I had visions of my brilliant career being cut short, my parents disgraced, my teachers despairing, and my unfaithful girl friend secretly exultant that she'd managed to avoid being tied down to a convict.

"Something wrong with your hearing, son?"

"No, sir."

"Then where'd you get the stuff?"

"Found it."

"Aw-huh." He nodded. "Where?"

"Uh . . . it was on the parking lot, you know, out at the Sonic Dog."

"Were you by yourself?"

Haw! I thought. No witnesses, no contradictions.

"Yes, sir."

He smiled. "Maybe they had little tags that said, 'Smoke Me, I'm a Marijuana Cigarette'?"

"Uh . . ." Did that require an answer? "No, sir."

"Then how'd you know what they were?"

"They just looked . . . funny, you know. Not like regular cigarettes. And they smelled like mari . . . smelled weird, you know? So we just guessed."

"We?"

I flushed. "I mean after I'd already showed it to them."

"Uh-huh. And I reckon you gave some to that colored boy because he wanted to try a little too."

I nodded.

Sgt. Cheney sighed, rose and paced about the room, then eased a haunch onto the desk. He gave me a benign and fatherly look. "Now, I can tell you aren't a dope addict. I can see how a couple kids out for a lark decided out of curiosity to try the stuff, you see? Maybe you didn't know you can get hooked and start craving the stuff."

I wagged my head to encourage this line of thought. Innocence was my best guise and my spotless record the evidence to give it credibility. He had already asked my name and address and whether I had been in trouble before, to which I had given truthful answers, and it looked as though the end might be in sight. I covered my mouth with my hand as though to massage the muscles in my cheeks and let my insides go lax. Apparently Sgt. Cheney was going to give me Monster Drug Lecture #17 and let me off with a warning, and I prepared to tune him out. The Chief appeared annually in an all-school assembly to peddle the same propaganda, though with what I'd have to admit was a dramatic flair—he'd hold a heap of grass in his open palm and say, "I want anybody who wants some of this to come right down here and I'll give it to them for nothing." Then he'd pull his pistol from his holster. "But he might as well take *this* too because he'll be needing something to put him out of his misery!"

"So you smoked a little marijuana—is that any reason to spend a lot of your young life in jail?" Sgt. Cheney was saying. "I know you don't think so. We ain't out to wreck any lives here. Boys will be boys, we know that."

My head was bobbing madly in agreement: Yessir, two tadpoles curious as coons, that's us, sir, no kidding!

"And you say you found it?"

"Yessir."

"At the Sonic Dog."

I nodded.

"Then why's that other boy say you got it in Juarez?"

Had Terry said that? What did Stoogie say? The accused's right to one phone call popped to mind, but not only would my parents learn where I was, it was a definite sign of non-cooperation, and I still hoped I'd be able to talk my way out of the station.

"Well, I didn't. He was just guessing."

"He said ya'll both got it there."

All I could do was shrug to suggest that life was full of peculiar circumstances that defied credulity.

He eased his haunch off the desk. "Son, you're starting to piss me off!" He pulled a key chain from his pocket and jangled the keys as he moved behind the desk. They made a steady *clink* like a stack of coins passed through the fingers. My mouth was dry; I swallowed with difficulty. Were those keys to the cells? I shivered. He wasn't buying my story.

"You come in here and start talking like a straight shooter, then you bullshit me when I'm trying my best to appreciate your situation—you think I'm dumb?"

"No, sir."

"I don't have to give you the benefit of the doubt. I can lock you up and charge you with possession right now, you understand? It don't make a damn if it fell out of the sky, you got it! For all I know, you been peddling the stuff— maybe you gave it to them, maybe you sold it!"

"Oh no, sir!"

"I don't have any use at all for a slimy creep that'd get other people hooked just to line his pockets! We can put you up for twenty years for dealing in it—you want that?"

"I swear I wasn't doing that!"

"How about finding it—you swear to that too?"

I hesitated. "Yes," I said finally, with less conviction.

He threw up his hands in exasperation. "Well, if you don't beat all!" He strode to the door and grabbed the knob. "You're not even trying to help me! I got the dope and I'm going to put somebody in jail for it! I'd sooner have it be the pusher you got it from, but if I can't find him, you're the next best thing, you see?"

I did. With an icy clarity. Every crime had to have a criminal. It kept the books neat. Naïvely, I had assumed that everybody would get off if I could convince Sgt. Cheney of our innocent intentions, but the full implications of my choice grew terribly apparent as I sat looking up at him while he waited for me to make up my mind, hand on the doorknob. It was hard for me to believe there wasn't an alternative to telling the truth. His glare of contempt chilled my spine; I couldn't meet his gaze.

"Well come on, son! You still claim you found it?" he huffed. "You gonna sit there and tell me a white kid supplied a nigger musician with dope he'd never seen before?"

He kept staring at me. My jaw dropped a bit and my teeth parted as though I were about to speak, but what I'd say even I didn't know. My chin trembled; I shut my jaws and swallowed hard. I shivered again and let it stand as a shrug.

"Lord love a duck!" he spat and opened the door. "Bud?" he yelled down the hall. There was a distinct "Yah?" then Cheney roared, "Come get this silly sumbitch out of my sight, will you? Lock him up!"

He left the door ajar and strode back to the desk, refusing to look at me. He yanked the top drawer open and tossed a pad and pencil into it, then straightened out the objects on the desktop: everything was final. Wait! God! What'd they want to know? That Terry and I had asked Stoogie for a few joints to tide us over for the long drive to Boston in a couple of days? That Stoogie had given it to us? But those facts were no more the truth than Marilyn Monroe's circulatory system was a sex symbol—they'd believe that Stoogie had passed out free samples to get us hooked. Stoogie was a poverty-stricken black musician who'd paid heavy dues and who could play alto in a way that could make your heart sing! He wasn't a dope peddler! Was he? How could I be sure enough that I'd gamble twenty years of my life on it?

Bud's footsteps had grown to monstrous explosions in the hallway. When it came time to sign on the bottom line, how could I lie? Wasn't that perjury? Didn't lies always get caught in the courtroom, even ones told with good intentions? And wouldn't I just be piling trouble on trouble to keep on lying? I started shaking violently. I didn't want to go to jail! God! All my dreams . . . Bud's shadow fell across me when he walked through the door, and I blurted out that I hadn't found the stuff.

Later, I waited on one of the wooden benches outside the doors to the Magistrate Courtroom. My father wasn't thrilled to be awakened in the middle of the night to be told his son had been experimenting with narcotics and was at the police station where he could be released to his custody without charges filed. I dreaded the ride home. But I was more relieved than anything else, and I could take his anger as easy payment for my guilt. I'd told them not only the facts, which they were happy to hear, but also the truth, which they weren't concerned about. They didn't care that I had *asked* Stoogie for the stuff, that he hadn't offered it. I kept insisting that we were *all* innocent in the sense that Stoogie and I and Terry were three musicians, friends, fellow craftsmen sharing a pursuit, engaged in making jazz, and there was nothing sinister in our smoking the joints any more than if "Bud" shared a beer with Sgt. Cheney in his living room. They agreed that I was at least naïve, if not innocent.

I hadn't told them about Stoogie's stash at the golf course, narrowing my confession to what happened earlier in the night. I didn't know that Terry had told the same story more or less; I didn't know that Stoogie had clammed up, that in time they'd run a check and discover his first offense jail term. I only knew I was off the hook; even if I had to come back for a hearing or a trial, I wouldn't go to jail—my age, my parents, and my white skin had spared me that. With our horns, our high-school diplomas, and our tuition fees, Terry and I could proceed as planned to become players of and at jazz, props and accouterments intact, while Stoogie would serve another sentence, this one longer than the first: he'd be stripped of everything he needed to play except the only thing they couldn't take from him, the thing they'd unintentionally given him—the suffering, the soul, the reason for the blues.

The beret in my pocket pressed like a fist into the cheek of my ass. I pulled it out and absently brushed out the wrinkles in the black felt and was about to put it on my head when my arms failed me and I dropped it to the bench. Directly across the hall the varnished courtroom doors gave off a dull gleam. My eyes were drawn to the ceiling light, then to the figure in bronze relief it illuminated just above the doorway: it was the same image my eyes had idly skimmed day after day on the textbook cover of the civics course I had shown such promise in—Lady Justice in her robe, her arm extended to hold her scales, the platform leveled, weighing nothing, and for the first time I could see that she was blindfolded.

ALLEN WIER

Things About To Disappear

After nine months of sickness, slipping away from us a little more every day, my daddy died. Finally the cancer got an artery, it burst, and he went out in a rush. We buried him out on a windy, limestone hill beneath a twisted live oak. It was a time of leaving, the tail end of a sad summer. He was gone, and I was going, leaving Texas again.

Driving east, the air through the car windows felt like the outdoor side of a window air conditioner, and you could smell the wet air, sticky, East Texas hot. I had already left one landscape behind. In the few hours I'd been driving, the white caliche dirt had turned red, rugged hills had smoothed out, gotten more civilized, more used looking, brown grass had gone green, and every mile the trees got straighter and taller.

I had been through Buffalo, Tucker, Palestine, Ironton, Jacksonville. I had crossed the Trinity River way south of Trinidad where I used to cross, used to pass the pink motel all alone at the end of the narrow, old bridge and the fertilizer plant nearly hidden in live oaks on the other side of the river. Once I told a friend the Trinidad fertilizer plant was really a secret laboratory where strange beings from another world were collecting and processing human blood for their dying race. The aliens had taken human form and lived in the pink motel, the tall, futuristic looking water towers were really full of blood, the boxcars on the railroad siding brought bodies in, the brown smoke was from burning flesh.

My friend and I made a secret pact, if one of us ever needed the other all we had to do was send a note: Trinidad Aliens, Midnight, December 12. We would never forget. Now I don't even have an address to send the note to. And they've widened the highway at Trinidad, torn down the scary, wonderful, old bridge, and cut out most of the live oaks that used to make the fertilizer plant a secret alien laboratory.

After the Trinity I crossed the Neches, not enough water in the Neches to make one good tear. I left it behind, dry, waiting for water, forever for all I knew. I had two rivers left, two rivers more I knew, the little Angelina, the Sabine.

The sun was in the west, in the mirror. Sundown behind me and darkness coming ahead of me. Lights on in New York, dinner dishes done in Washington, drive-in movies dancing on in small towns all over Virginia, if you could see that far ahead. As the road rose and fell in the piney hills I held and lost this last summer sun. Leavetaking. I was playing it to the hilt. The tires were whining up and down the hills like a pedal steel guitar and all the old, sad songs about leaving were running like an old, slow record in my head, and I was holding the names of places sweet in my mouth, shaping them with my lips, feeling their flavor like hard candy on my tongue. Melodies of names, names like Dripping Springs, Round Mountain, Marble Falls, Spicewood, Calf Creek, Air. Names that seemed to echo when I thought them, San Saba, Cherry Spring, Mountain Home, Morris Ranch, Stonewall, Blanco. And the name of the man who had left me, the man I was leaving behind, his name I couldn't speak. And the name that rhymed with *breath* and was forever.

Now there were warning signs, and all down one side of the highway were bright orange tags on tall pine trees, tags the color of sunset, and then no trees at all, just a wide, red gash and the dark fingers of stubborn stumps and silent, orange earthmovers parked in the mud.

I topped a hill and a slow, black car appeared in front of me, weaving, back and forth, shoulder to shoulder, covering the whole road. I couldn't see through the glare of the last crack of sun caught on the rear window and flashing as the car careened back and forth in front of me. I honked my horn and flashed my lights, but the car meandered on like the dry riverbed of the Neches. Then, sudden as a dream, the car jerked left, shot off the shoulder and went through a sawhorse barricade where new lanes were being built over a ditch. Broken boards jerked up over me like puppets yanked up off a stage, and the car shot out onto a new, white slab over the ditch and up into the air like one of the spaceships I had imagined the aliens landed at Trinidad. And it stopped there, in the air, nose up. And that second caught and held for me like the car held in air, and I saw all these things: a bird gliding just before it dives; a kite the second its string breaks; a falling leaf; a thrown stick; a fish jumping and caught in the sun; a balsa wood plane at the end of a dip or turn; a man shot out of a circus cannon; a pole vaulter, high jumper, hurdler, lips puckered, muscles tensed, eyes closed, suspended over a bar; wooden rocker runners tipped almost vertical; the crest of a wave curling like a horn back into itself; a last breath held, maybe forever. Then the car rolled slowly over and fell gracelessly across the ditch, hitting the soft mud with an ugly sound, someone breaking wind; a boil lanced; nose blown; phlegm spat. The windshield popped out whole and shot like a clipped fingernail across the ditch. And I seemed caught there, dead still on the road.

Should I go down to the car, upside down in the ditch, surely flattened, surely full of death. Was there anything I could do down there. Should I keep going to the nearest telephone, call help, an ambulance, wrecker, cutting torches. Then, with help on its way, then go back to pull the bodies out. By the time I realized I had made the decision, I was a mile down the road, the black car invisible behind me.

A white frame house sat among pecan trees off to my right. Furiously I skidded up under the trees, nuts popping beneath my tires, emergency brake locking, sticks and nuts and porch boards snapping and cracking and creaking beneath my feet and the noise but not the feeling of the screened door beneath my first knocking. The screen was hooked, the door behind it open. I smelled the rust of the screen wire as I pressed my face against the door, imagined the red mesh, net, crosses, cross hairs printed on my skin. I looked in and yelled through my cupped hands. Inside a tall, silver, electric fan silently turned back and forth like the face of a robot. On a couch a woman with white hair in a white slip lay. I shouted for her to get up, to open the door. I banged, I pulled at the screen until one screw came out of the handle and it turned sideways in my hand. Inside, in a doorway to another room, I saw two, big, bare feet sticking out into the air. I yelled at them, "Come here, this is an emergency, get up." I drew back my fist, held a second like the car in the air, was going to punch a hole in the screen and unlatch the door, when it swung open against my chest toppling me back a step. An old, old man stood there, dark wool pants, white undershirt, a long, pink face and empty blue eyes. The face of a rabbit, long, white, rabbit feet on the bare floor. I hurried past him, thinking for a second there would be no phone. Then I saw it, black on a white doiley on the dresser, and started dialing 0 and talking at the same time, to the old, old rabbit man, to the body on the couch in the front room, to the nasal voice in the telephone.

"Who will pay for the call, sir?"

"I'll pay, I'll pay for the call." I yelled my home telephone number, cursed, yelled, "Emergency, emergency."

Again, I was caught, suspended in the moment, feeling the distance, the air in the receiver, in my ear, the feel and sound of a seashell. I saw all these things: A blue and white telephone book for Troup, Price, Laneville, New Summerfield, Gallatin, and Reklaw; the maple headboard and the bed which had a white chenille spread with the long shape of a body on it; a pink and white ceramic cat on the dresser by the telephone; two snapshots in the edge of the dresser mirror, one of a tall man and a tall woman in front of a fig tree, one of a younger tall man holding a string of fish out before his chest, holding the string with both hands so that it curved across his chest imitating the grin held across his face, the fish catching the light in the photograph like long, sharp teeth; a calendar stuck with two red thumbtacks into the light blue wall, a bright autumn picture above the days of the week, two brown spotted bird dogs holding a point forever.

The operator wanted to know if I wanted the state police in Jacksonville or Henderson. For a second I couldn't remember where I was. Had I passed New Summerfield? Had I crossed the Angelina River? No, I hadn't passed the river. Then, the police in Jacksonville wanted to know where I was. I gave them the highway number and started to hang up, when I heard the tiny voice in the telephone, irritated, saying, "Yes, but east or west of Jacksonville?"

"East," I said, I was sure of that.

"How far east?"

"Not far," I said, "not far. Just drive east, we're the only wreck on this stretch of the highway."

The old man was standing in the doorway. He hadn't spoken a word, just stared without comprehension. Skin hung in folds under his arms. I tried to explain again, I left some money to pay for the screen handle, to pay for the call if the phone company charged him. I left, the woman still on the couch unmoving, the fan still moving right to left like a beacon across the room. There were no curtains for it to ripple as it passed back and forth, only the steady turning to prove it was on at all, that and the way you could see blue wall through the spinning blades.

By the time I got back to the accident there were several cars stopped, people standing around. I parked and hurried down the incline, slipping in the mud. One wheel of the wrecked car was still spinning, the exposed underside of the car tilted toward me, a little girl was keeping the wheel going, prodding it with a piece of the broken sawhorse. The windshield was stuck up like a monolith in the mud, still intact. All around sticking up out of the grass or lying in the mud were parts of the wreckage: a headlight, roadmap, thermos, hubcap, pieces of clothing, a suitcase, a woman's purse. A small boy sat on the grass holding his head, blood all down his arm. A man in a brown suit, the cuffs of his pants splashed with mud and a long grass stain down the front of his white shirt like a wide green tie, was walking around and around the overturned car. The car was thrown across the ditch like a bridge, so that the roof stuck down into the ditch instead of being flattened, and every few seconds the man would bend down and look up into the car, making little clucking noises in his throat. One of the rear tires had a big hole in it, the other three tires were bald as the man in overalls who kept sticking his fist into the hole in the rear tire and saying, "They's damn lucky they wadn't killed; they's damn lucky they wadn't killed."

A man in a straw hat was squatted down by the car, and I went down to him. "I saw it happen and went on to call an ambulance," I told him. "Is the little boy hurt bad?"

"There's a woman pinned in there," he said. "I sent a car back to Jacksonville for an ambulance, should've been here by now. Maybe we ought to pull her out?"

"If she's got internal injuries we shouldn't move her, and there's no way of knowing," I said.

Then a man came down yelling, "What happened here? Let me through, what happened?" The man in the straw hat told him there was a woman pinned inside the car. "I've got the hearse up there," the newcomer said. "I drive for the funeral home in Palestine. We can get her in there and I'll drive her to the hospital." He got down against the front fender and started pushing. The man in the straw hat was pushing by the door and the bald-headed man took his fist out of the blown tire and started helping. I stood back, afraid to get in the way, hoping they didn't do more harm than good. Then the bald-headed man disappeared into the car.

It was dark now. Fireflies blinked farther down the ditch near the woods. Someone had pulled a pickup over and aimed the lights down onto the wreck, and dust danced in the beams of the headlights. They were pulling a woman out of the car, out through the space where the windshield had been. I went over to the man in the brown suit, her husband, I guessed. He was trying to pick up the strewn clothes from the suitcase that had been thrown from the car.

"Can I help you?" I asked.

"I got to get Lizabeth's dress folded up."

I tried to get him to sit down, but he kept talking about Lizabeth's dress. A woman came over and said he was probably in shock, but he'd be okay after a while. I asked her about the little boy, and she said he was okay, just a cut on the forehead and scared silly. I told her about seeing the accident happen and that I'd called an ambulance. "They're never there when you need them, are they?" she said.

I felt silly standing there, watching with the circle of onlookers, others who had stopped, boys in Levi's, men in business suits, overalls, women in dresses, shorts, a girl in a bright pink, two-piece bathing suit that caught the light from the pickup and glowed like teeth and fingernails in a bar with black lights. She was talking to three boys who were sharing their beers with her. I went back up the slope to see if I could help the man from the funeral home who had some people lifting an empty coffin from the hearse. They set it across a couple of remaining sawhorses and he lifted the satin-covered foam pad out of the bottom. As they disappeared down the slope carrying the coffin pad like a stretcher, I saw the moon coming up deep red on the far side of the highway, and from an opened car door I heard the tinny sound of an Oklahoma radio station's call letters and then guitar and fiddle as someone sang about love lost for all time.

The woman came, headfirst, out from inside the wrecked

car. Her face was white and puffy, her hair blue-black against the satin pad. She moaned, over and over, a monotone. Moaned and moaned, the whole time they carried her up the hill to the highway, moaned and moaned, as they put her into the hearse, moaned until the heavy rear door of the hearse clunked shut and blocked out the sound. The man in the brown suit wouldn't leave the car and Lizabeth's dress, so the man in the straw hat picked the little boy up and put him in the front of the hearse with the driver. He was crying and screaming, "Mommie," and "Daddy, Daddy," when the big, dark hearse, chrome shining in the headlights of the pickup, swung round and disappeared down the dark highway. The ambulance and the police still had not come.

People began to leave. The moon was higher, turning ivory, moonlight getting brighter as headlights went out and cars drove away. Finally only a couple talking with the man down by his wrecked car remained, and I was alone on the shoulder of the highway. Moonlight had moved onto the trunk of a tall cottonwood tree, the bark soft and lovely, splotches of soft browns and whites like the soft hide of a pinto pony, a delicate birthmark, it reminded me of the old man's rabbit face, and I wondered if the woman had moved from the couch, if the fan still turned regularly back and forth, if the old, old man had laid back down into the shape of himself on the white bedspread beneath the snapshot of his young self grinning down with long, pointed fish teeth.

And I remembered my daddy, in the last week of his last brave month. Remembered the evening I walked into the bedroom where he lay lost in the big double bed, disappearing before our very eyes, his arm going up like a chicken wing plucked and washed for frying, his skinny elbow over his eye, tears running down his sharp, bony cheek, "Don't see me this way, son, please don't," his face gone, only bones left, huge white eyes, nose, teeth, a medieval woodcut of Death. I remembered holding his long, thin fingers, how cool and dry they were, how soft, how much love I felt through those thin pads of his fingers, felt them twitch and tremble with pain and sadness, saw him smile at me, his lips unnaturally wide and pink in his disappearing face. The double windows in which the sickness had made him see men from outer space, aliens from another world who would stand outside his windows or come through the wall and stand around his bed watching him, those same windows growing dark, the soft gray color of slate when he called me in. He would ask me to look and tell him what I saw. Didn't I see that spaceship in the backyard? When I asked him if they were after him he said he didn't know, they just stood, watching. They were all young men with short hair and dark pants and white shirts and dark ties and they stood, arms folded across their chests, around his bed, watching him. He could make them disappear with his flashlight. I remember that last evening we talked, the stone gray squares of the windows, the soft light of an early evening in late summer that smoothed the angles of his protruding bones, softened the ravages of the cancer that was eating him even as we looked at each other, the soft, dim light giving him back, for a moment, his strong arms and full, joyful face, and he said, "You know, son, while I'm lying here the past sort of floats by like a good old movie, and I thought I'd reach out and grab some of it and give it to you." I remember suffering because I couldn't make him whole again, because I didn't have some magic thing to say to him, and he went on, "For instance, when I was a kid," here he stretched out his arm toward the window where I heard for the first time all summer the cicadas in the live oak, "we used to call them—what are those?"

"Cicadas?" I said.

"Yeah, that's right. We used to call them *Crickadees*." and he spelled it for me. And he told me that since I like words he thought I might like a word like *Crickadees*. And I tore off a piece of paper from the telephone pad by his bed and wrote it down and folded it up and put it in my wallet where it still is, *Crickadees*, smelling like leather and sweat.

I walked down to the man in the brown suit and the couple who had stayed to wait with him for the police, feeling my wallet tight against my hip, and asked if he wanted my name and address. "As a witness, or something?" I asked. He said he didn't guess he needed it, and the woman with him thanked me but said they lived nearby and could explain to the police.

So I got back into my car and drove on into the darker east, past the white frame house where perhaps two old people would imagine they dreamed about a frightened young man who came and tried to wake them, past two state police cars, lights flashing, headed west, where I had come from. Wondering about the wreck, about the man and the little boy and whether the woman was badly hurt, I drove on, across the lovely little Angelina River, through New Summerfield, away from the people who had given me my past and into whatever life I could find in the dark distances ahead, listening for Crickadees and loving so many things that were about to disappear.

Contributors

Edward Abbey (1927–)

Edward Abbey was born in Home, Pennsylvania. He was educated at the University of New Mexico, receiving his B.A. in 1951 and his M.A. in 1956. His special interest in the Southwest led him to spend many years working as a park ranger and fire lookout for the National Park Service. His work includes *Jonathan Tracy* (1956); *The Brave Cowboy* (1958); *Fire on the Mountain* (1962); *Desert Solitaire*, a personal history (1968); *Black Sun* (1971); *The Monkey Wrench Gang* (1975); *The Journey Home* (1977); and *Abbey's Road: Take the Other* (1979).

Rudolfo Anaya (1937–)

Rudolfo Anaya was born in Patura, New Mexico. He received his B.A. and M.A. degrees from the University of New Mexico. A resident of Albuquerque, he has taught in its public schools and at the University of Albuquerque. He received the Premio Quinto Sol literary award for his first novel, *Bless Me, Ultima* (1972). His other works are *Heart of Aztlan* (1976) and *Cuentos: Tales from the Hispanic Southwest* (1979).

Donald Barthelme (1931–)

Donald Barthelme was born in Philadelphia, Pennsylvania but grew up in Houston, Texas. He is primarliy a short story writer but is equally at home with novels and children's fiction. His stories appear regularly in *The New Yorker. Come Back, Dr. Caligari*, his first collection of short stories, was published in 1964. Subsequent works are *Snow White* (1967); *Unspeakable Practices, Unnatural Acts* (1968); *City Life* (1970); *The Slightly Irregular Fire Engine or the Hithering Thithering Djinn* a children's book, which received the National Book Award for children's literature (1971); *Sadness* (1972); *Guilty Pleasures* (1974); *The Dead Father* (1975); and *Amateurs* (1977).

William Brammer (1930?–1978)

William Brammer spent his career as a political press aide. His most prominent position was as press aide to Lyndon B. Johnson when Johnson served as senator from Texas. *The Gay Place* (1961), which reflects the political atmosphere Brammer experienced, won the Houghton-Mifflin Literary Award Fellowship. William Brammer died in 1978 in Austin, Texas.

Jerome Charyn (1937–   )

Jerome Charyn was born in New York City and received his B.A. degree from Columbia University. In recent years he has spent a considerable amount of time in Texas. He is the author of fourteen novels, most recently *The Seventh Babe* and *The Catfish Man*.

William Eastlake (1917–   )

William Eastlake is a longtime resident of Arizona. He has achieved prominence both as a novelist and as a short story writer. Many of his stories have been anthologized, and several have been selected for publication in *Prize Stories: The O. Henry Awards* and *Best American Short Stories*. His works include *Go in Beauty* (1956), *The Bronc People* (1958), *Portrait of an Artist with Twenty-Six Horses* (1963), *Castle Keep* (1965), *The Bamboo Bed* (1970), *Dancers in the Scalp House* (1975), and *The Long Naked Descent into Boston* (1978).

Ralph Ellison (1914–   )

One of America's most distinguished writers, Ralph Ellison was born in Oklahoma City, Oklahoma. His first, and only, published novel, *Invisible Man* (1952), received immediate acclaim and won the National Book Award for fiction. Ralph Ellison has held many academic posts and since 1970 has been Albert Schweitzer Professor in the Humanities at New York University. In 1969 he was awarded this nation's highest civilian honor, the Medal of Freedom. For the past fifteen years he has been working on a second novel, portions of which have appeared in literary periodicals.

Harvey Fergusson (1890–1971)

Harvey Fergusson was born in Albuquerque, New Mexico. In a literary career spanning almost thirty years, he wrote fifteen works of fiction and nonfiction about the Southwest. Five of his books capture the essential New Mexico: the novels *Wolf Song* (1927), *Grant of Kingdom* (1950), *The Conquest of Don Pedro* (1954), and the nonfictional *Rio Grande* (1933) and *Home in the West* (1945).

William Goyen (1915–   )

William Goyen was born in Trinity, Texas. He was educated at Rice University, where he received his B.A. in 1932 and his M.A. in 1939. His work ranges from novels to short stories and plays. His first novel, *House of Breath*, was published in 1950. Subsequent works are *Ghost and Flesh* (1952), *In a Farther Country* (1955), *The Faces of Blood Kindred* (1960), *The Fair Sister* (1963), *The Collected Stories* (1972), *Come, the Restorer* (1974), and *While You Were Away* (1978).

John Graves (1920–   )

A native Texan, John Graves was born in Fort Worth and now resides in the town of Glen Rose. He received his B.A. from Rice University in 1942 and his M.A. from Columbia University in 1948. He has been a contributor to magazines since 1947, and his stories have been selected for *Prize Stories: The O. Henry Awards* (1955 and 1962) and for *Best American Short Stories* (1960). His first book, *Goodbye to a River* (1960), won the Collins Award of the Texas Institute of Letters. His other works include *The Last Running* (1974) and *Hard Scrabble* (1974).

Robert Henson (1921–   )

Robert Henson is a native of Oklahoma. He teaches at Upsala College in New Jersey. His stories have twice appeared in *Prize Stories: The O. Henry Awards*.

Dorothy M. Johnson (1905–   )

Dorothy Johnson grew up in Whitefish, Montana. She has been a book and magazine editor in New York and a journalism teacher at the University of Montana. She has published sixteen books including three which have been turned into western movies, *A Man Called Horse, The Man Who Shot Liberty Valance,* and *The Hanging Tree.*

Louis L'Amour (1908–   )

Louis L'Amour is one of the best-selling authors of all time. He was born in Jamestown, North Dakota. He has been a longshoreman, lumberjack, elephant handler, hay shocker, fruit picker, and an officer on tank destroyers during World War II. Thirty-one of his westerns have been turned into movies. He has published more than fifty books.

Tim McCarthy (1940–   )

Tim McCarthy grew up in Vermont and now lives in a small Christian community in New Mexico. He attended Columbia University, Goddard College, and the University of New Hampshire. His stories have appeared in literary periodicals, including *Colorado Quarterly* and *Carolina Quarterly*.

Larry McMurtry (1936–)
Larry McMurtry was born in Wichita Falls, Texas. He received
his B.A. in 1958 from North Texas State College and his M.A. in
1960 from Rice University. Two of his novels have been translated into films: *Horseman, Pass By*, which was published in 1961
and made into the film *Hud*, and *The Last Picture Show*, which
was published in 1966. His other novels are *Leaving Cheyenne*
(1963), *All My Friends Are Going To Be Strangers* (1972),
Terms of Endearment (1975), and *Somebody's Darling* (1978).

Durango Mendoza (1946–)
Durango Mendoza grew up in Oklahoma. He is half Indian
(Creek) and half Mexican. He attended the University of Mis-
souri where his fiction won first prize in the 1966 Mahan Fiction
Contest.

N. Scott Momaday (1934–)
N. Scott Momaday was born in Lawton, Oklahoma, and is a
member of the Kiowa tribe. He received his B.A. from the University of New Mexico in 1958 and his M.A. (1960) and Ph.D.
(1963) from Stanford University. He is a poet, novelist and short
story writer whose interest in American Indian art, history and
culture are reflected in his writing. His first book, *House of Dawn*
(1968), received the Pulitzer Prize for fiction. His other works
are *The Way to Rainy Mountain* (1969), *Angle of Geese and
Other Poems* (1974), *The Gourd Dancer* (1976), and *The
Names* (1976).

John Nichols (1940–)
John Nichols was born in Berkeley, California. He received his
B.A. in 1963 from Hamilton College and now lives in New York.
He has worked as a blues singer in a Greenwich Village café, as
a firefighter in the Chicuahua Mountains of Arizona, and as a
short-order cook. His first novel, *The Sterile Cuckoo* (1965), was
made into a film.

Carolyn Osborn (1934–)
Carolyn Osborn was born in Nashville, Tennessee, and emigrated
to Texas in 1946. She now lives in Austin. Her first book, *A
Horse of Another Color*, was published in 1977. Primarily a short
story writer, she is a frequent contributor to literary magazines,
such as *The Texas Quarterly, Paris Review, Antioch Review, New
Orleans Review*, and *Ascent*. "My Brother Is a Cowboy" originally appeared in *The Roanoke Review*.

Opal Lee Popkes (1920–   )

Opal Lee Popkes, a member of the Choctaw tribe, was born in New Mexico and now lives in Columbia, Missouri. She is the author of eleven unpublished novels. This short story originally appeared in the anthology *The Man To Send Rain Clouds* (1974).

Charles Portis (1933–   )

Charles Portis was born in El Dorado, Arkansas, and now resides in Little Rock. He is best known for his novel *True Grit* (1968), which was made into a film the following year. His first published novel was *Norwood* (1966), and his latest is *Dog of the South* (1979).

Conrad Richter (1890–1968)

Conrad Richter was born in Pine Grove, Pennsylvania, but moved west in 1928 to gather material for his fictions about early American life. A novelist and short story writer, he is best known for his trilogy of American pioneer life—the novels *The Trees*, *The Fields*, and *The Town*. He received the Pulitzer Prize in 1951 for *The Town* and the National Book Award in 1961 for *The Waters of Kronos*.

Leslie Silko (1948–   )

Leslie Silko was born in Albuquerque, New Mexico, and grew up on the Laguna Pueblo Reservation, where she still lives and writes. She graduated from the University of New Mexico and went to law school before deciding to devote all her time to writing. She has published a book of poetry, *Laguna Woman* (1974), and a novel, *Ceremony* (1977). Her short stories and poems have been anthologized in *The Man To Send Rain Clouds* (1974), *Carriers of the Dream Wheel* (1975), *Voices of the Rainbow* (1975), *Yardbird Reader 5* (1976), and *The Remembered Earth* (1978). In 1974 she received the Award for Poetry from the *Chicago Review*. "Lullaby" was selected for *Best American Short Stories* of 1975.

C. W. Smith (1940–   )

C. W. Smith was born in Corpus Christi, Texas. He received his B.A. in 1964 from North Texas State University and his M.A. in 1966 from Northern Illinois University. A frequent contributor of short stories to magazines, he is also a novelist. His first novel, *Thin Men of Haddam* (1974), received the Jesse H. Jones Award from the Texas Institute of Letters. *Country Music*, his second novel, was published in 1975.

Allen Wier (1946–   )

Allen Wier was born in San Antonio, Texas. He now lives in
Hollins, Virginia, where he teaches at Hollins College. A novelist
and short story writer, he won a creative writing fellowship from
the National Endowment for the Arts in 1974. He has contributed
stories to a number of literary magazines, including *Southern Review, Carolina Quarterly*, and *Georgia Review*. His first collection
of stories, *Things About To Disappear*, was published in 1978.
Blanco, his first novel, was published in the same year.

ABOUT THE EDITOR

MAX APPLE lives in Houston, Texas, and teaches at Rice University. His first book, THE ORANGING OF AMERICA, was selected as the best book of fiction of 1976 by the Texas Institute of Letters. He is also the author of ZIP (1978), of numerous stories and essays, and of two screenplays.

START A COLLECTION

With Bantam's fiction anthologies, you can begin almost anywhere. Choose from science fiction, classic litera-by both new and established writers in America and ture, modern short stories, mythology, and more—all around the world.